COMMUNITY PRACTICE AND URBAN YOUTH

Community Practice and Urban Youth is for graduate level students in fields that offer youth studies and community practice courses. Practitioners in these fields will find the book particularly useful in furthering the integration of social justice as a conceptual and philosophical foundation. The book focuses on service-learning and civic engagement in immigrant-rights, food, and environmental justice movements and offers an innovative approach for courses.

Melvin Delgado is Professor of Social Work at Boston University where he is the Co-Director of the Center on Addictions Research and Services. He is the author of over 20 books.

Young people almost always play instrumental roles in social justice movements, and Melvin Delgado—easily among our most renowned scholars of youth and community—here makes yet another exceptional contribution to our understanding of the field, drawing upon empirical evidence in three contemporary movements in society.

**Dr Barry Checkoway, School of Social Work,
University of Michigan**

Using examples of civic engagement with diverse youth, Dr Melvin Delgado provides an innovative paradigm for environmentally focused social justice strategies aimed at promoting the engagement of urban youth in social activism and service learning.

**Dr Edgar Colon, Southern Connecticut
State University**

COMMUNITY PRACTICE AND URBAN YOUTH

Social Justice Service-Learning and Civic Engagement

Melvin Delgado

NEW YORK AND LONDON

First published 2016
by Routledge
711 Third Avenue, New York, NY 10017

and by Routledge
2 Park Square, Milton Park, Abingdon, Oxon, OX14 4RN

Routledge is an imprint of the Taylor & Francis Group, an informa business

Library of Congress Cataloging-in-Publication Data
A catalog record for this book has been requested

ISBN: 978-1-138-92595-3 (hbk)
ISBN: 978-1-138-92598-4 (pbk)
ISBN: 978-1-315-68348-5 (ebk)

Typeset in Bembo
by Apex CoVantage, LLC

This book is dedicated to Denise, Barbara, and Laura.

CONTENTS

PREFACE

All social intervention-focused books seek to influence readers, and this book is certainly no exception. Conventional social interventions are predicated upon a set of assumptions and values, which sometimes are implicit, and embrace a social paradigm to guide how an intervention unfolds. A re-shifting of paradigms is generally not a common goal in most books because in many instances books seek to assist practitioners in carrying out their duties rather than have them challenge the status quo.

This book introduces readers to the importance of experiential learning through two popular (as evidenced by the number of books and scholarly articles) approaches: service-learning and civic engagement. However, this book purposefully seeks to challenge the status quo and introduces a particular focus on service-learning and civic engagement among urban youth.

Any book focused on urban youth must refrain from embracing a paradigm based upon deficit or charity values and principles. Such a perspective emphasizes what is missing or wrong with youth and fails to take into account their social-ecological circumstances and the strengths that they possess. Their ability to socially navigate their way through life's difficult terrain must never be overlooked or minimized by practitioners, policy makers, and academics.

This book eschews a negative view of youth by stressing the importance of a "critical" stance on service-learning and civic engagement, and focusing on three social justice issues that are highly intertwined. A critical or social justice stance necessitates that practitioners and academics view urban youth within the context that profoundly shapes their lives and surroundings. When this context is detrimental to their well-being, interventions must alter these circumstances and facilitate youth empowerment and leadership development in the process.

Social issues associated with immigrant rights, food, and environmental justice provide examples of how social forces impede youth, and the communities they live in, from maximizing their potential. Fortunately, a number of scholars and practitioners have embraced this stance; this book draws upon their contributions and, more importantly, the contributions of urban youth themselves, since they are the ultimate beneficiaries of social justice service-learning and civic engagement. This book seeks to bridge social justice, youth organizing, and service-learning/civic engagement by highlighting key concepts and approaches that can make these two popular forms of experiential learning and intervention relevant for urban youth.

ACKNOWLEDGMENTS

Thank you to Cate Johnston. I would also like to thank the reviewers for their valuable feedback.

Marie Weil, University of North Carolina, Chapel Hill
Suzanne Pritzker, University of Houston, Central
Kelly Patterson, State University of New York at Buffalo
Kyuper College
CSU, Northridge
Southern Adventist University
University of Connecticut

SECTION 1
Setting the Context

1

OVERVIEW

Introduction

The twenty-first century ushered in a period of great excitement resulting from social justice campaigns—and even, in some cases, revolutions—to rectify acts of social injustice, with youth playing instrumental roles, although this was not new in the United States nor in other countries (Aronowitz, 2013; Shragge, 2013). Social activism is boundless in what it can accomplish and only limited by adults' lack of imagination in seeing youth as contributing members of society. Youth activism potential can reach from localized to national transformation efforts (Flanagan, Syvertsen & Wray-Lake, 2007; Piotrowski, 2014).

The potential of social activism involving educators and helping professionals has raised questions about how youth community practice fosters the advance of social justice as an integral part of practice, including social activism involving and led by youth (Delgado & Staples, 2007; Hardina, 2013; Staples, 2012). A variety of well-recognized avenues are open to educators and community practitioners, such as service-learning and civic engagement, to facilitate youth activism.

One example with substantial potential is youth work/critical pedagogies/youth studies. The potential role of youth-focused practice is well laid out in the following quote (Lavie-Ajayi & Krumer-Nevo, 2013, p. 1698): "Critical youth work is based on a dual focus, on individual psychosocial development on the one hand, and collective critical consciousness and the promotion of social justice on the other. . . . The model is comprised of a three dimensions: the streets as a physical and political place, the use of counter narrative, and the role the youth workers take as social capital agents."

Contextualizing place, space, and age together makes youth social activism a viable form of community practice in a wide variety of community settings (McLaughlin et al., 2009). United Farm Workers campaigns, for example, were an excellent training ground for young activists (Shaw, 2008), illustrating how this campaign served as a training ground for youth who eventually assumed adult activist roles.

Batsleer (2013) applies a feminist paradigm (Girls Work Movement), the ending of oppression based upon gender, to practice with girls and women in community settings, showing how participants-recipients benefit from engagement and preparing them for important roles in future change efforts. Initiatives providing youth with opportunities to engage with adults must assume a prominent role in community practice (Delgado & Staples, 2007).

Critical youth studies provide a conceptualization, language, and home to encourage youth use of critical thinking (praxis) and to create positive change in their lives. The introduction of participatory action research brings an added dimension to practice and critical youth studies (Quijada Cerecer, Cahill & Bradley, 2013). Youth activism, in essence, is a fertile subject for youth to study and undertake (Rogers, Morrell & Enyedy, 2007) and for community practitioners to embrace.

Youth as researchers, in turn, bring a missing dimension to this field, offering great promise for transformation and new knowledge and insights that can be applied to social activism (Reiter, 2014; Watson & Marciano, 2015). Mockler and Groundwater-Smith (2015) issue a call for using a "mosaic" approach towards research that taps multiple sources of "evidence" based on maximum participation, providing "a more complete" picture of a social phenomenon. Youth asking the questions they deem important is an essential core in development of this mosaic of evidence (Aldana, 2015; Richards-Schuster, 2015).

Community practice has evolved over the past several decades and expanded its reach into new and highly exciting and challenging arenas involving youth, particularly those in urban centers. This embrace of innovation has increased the reach of practice and reinforced an ethos of pushing the boundaries of what constitutes community social justice practice.

The quest for social justice is not relegated to democracies and can be found in totalitarian states where social justice movements of any kind are often labeled as revolutions (Abdelrahman, 2013; Pearce, Freelon & Kendzior, 2014). This quest is not restricted to any particular demographic group, with some groups facing multiple jeopardies or what is referred to as *intersectionality*, with low-income/low-wealth urban youth of color being an example. Global activism has also seen the intersectionality of youth and women highlighting a potentially powerful coalition of two disenfranchised groups, as in the case in Sudan (Hale & Kadoda, 2014).

This rather lengthy introductory chapter provides a roadmap for how social activism and three specific social movements will be addressed, and what community practitioners can do to foster youth activism and social justice through service-learning and civic engagement. Youth social activism is a critical ingredient in any healthy democracy, although adults may see these movements as misguided and tearing at a nation's social fabric (Lund & Carr, 2008; Yoder Clark, 2009).

Nevertheless, these social change efforts would not be needed if injustices did not exist and mechanisms to redress them were not broken. Youths' civic involvement early in their lives wields important influence in creating bonding (social capital) with the broader community (Duke et al., 2009). Social activism, in addition, can create new political realities (Blow, 2014, p. A25): "One of the people's greatest strengths in a democracy is the flexing of potential muscle and the exercising of political power, through ballots and boot leather." Democracy, however, is learned and socially constructed, and mechanisms must be in place to facilitate and enhance this learning (Saltmarsh, 2005).

Book Goals

The following five goals will be addressed in this book:

1. Provide a theoretical foundation and critique upon which to better appreciate the use of social justice service-learning and civic engagement for immigrant rights, food, and environment, and the key rewards and challenges each movement faces.
2. Provide readers with case vignettes on how youth are leading or significantly participating and contributing to using critical service-learning and social justice civic engagement in three movements, with a focus on urban centers and low-income/low-wealth youth of color.
3. Provide a conceptual framework and foundation from which to examine service-learning and civic engagement initiatives focused on youth activism in social change and social movements.
4. Raise a series of rewards, challenges, and possible strategies for increasing youth decision-making and leadership in service-learning and civic engagement using community practice involving immigrant-rights, environmental, and food justice campaigns.
5. Examine the potential of civic engagement and service-learning as vehicles for community practitioners to provide youth with opportunities to engage in social activism and become active citizens. Although educators, too, are playing important roles in these areas, the focus will be on community practitioners because space is too limited to cover both educators and community practitioners.

Significance of Social Activism

Social activism must be viewed within a democratic context. What constitutes "democracy"? Democracy is much more than electoral participation, and this perspective is much too narrow (Boulianne & Brailey, 2014). Unfortunately, democracy, in similar fashion to political capital, is too often thought of as voting in national and local elections, a narrow and sterile manifestation. Voting, however, takes place in many different settings, such as schools, community-based organizations, and houses of worship, and this activity is rarely referred to as democracy or political capital.

Democracy is also about free speech and protest of unjust laws and social conditions that push the marginalized to the brink of society and undermine their future prospects and dreams in the process. Some readers will argue that democracy and social protest are integrally related, with social protest being a highly visible indicator of the health of a democracy (Porta, 2013; Preiss & Brunner, 2013; Zimpelman & Stoddard, 2013). Polletta (2012) describes democracy as "ambiguous and radical." Theiss-Morse and Hibbing (2005), in turn, argue that to be good citizens democracy must be understood as "messy, inefficient, and conflict-ridden."

Levinson (2010, p. 2) poses the question of what constitutes a "good" citizen, raising additional questions as to who is asking and answering the questions, with implications for how social activism is viewed:

> What are the components of citizenship, and what does it mean to be a good citizen? These questions necessarily must be answered prior to any discussion about the aims or content of civic education. Can you be a good citizen if you don't vote? What if you vote, but are uninformed about most of the issues and candidates, or vote solely on the basis of a single issue? How important is it to be law-abiding? Is being economically self-sufficient a hallmark (or even a precondition) of good citizenship? Is never being a burden on others enough to make one a good citizen? How should we judge the act of protesting injustice via civil disobedience against the act of sacrificing oneself on the battlefield for the good of country?

Social protest is democracy at its best even though it can create tension and reactionary feelings. Good citizens are those individuals who are not afraid to act on their conscience for the greater good.

Ardizzone (2007, p. 39) poses questions that, when answered, set the foundation for youth social activism: "What makes learning to action? Why does social responsibility serve as an impetus for activism? What 'clicks' for these young people and how does their conscientization come about?" The normalizing of social protest, similar to other oppositional resistance tactics, can be a marker of a 'healthy' democracy rather than a disintegrating society. Living in a democracy does not mean that youth do not experience a heightened sense of surveillance due to mistrust on the part of adults and authorities, resulting in development of a "strong sense of betrayal by adults" (Annamma, 2014; Fine et al., 2003; Gutierrez, 2014; Ruck et al., 2008).

Weiss (2011, p. 595) calls for greater understanding and research on how youth cope with increased surveillance in their lives:

> The tragedies of Columbine and September 11th led public schools to step up surveillance practices in urban schools—producing an environment with less freedom and more control. While students are aware of the seeming powerlessness they face at the hands of security guards and surveillance technologies, they are also engaged in developing new ways to cope with, negotiate, and respond to these practices and injustices. Everyday surveillance is matched by everyday resistance. Not passively succumbing to the programs of surveillance in their schools and communities, students are navigating and responding in surprising, sometimes radical, ways. In an era of punitive public policies and school reforms, when urban teenagers are already perceived as threatening and misbehaving and labeled as deviant and criminals, research in search of resistance needs to seek out hidden transcripts and public protest.

Increased surveillance is in response to major events that have made the nation feel less safe, yet they are often based on profiles that signal out youth and other groups.

All segments of society must be free to engage in public dissent and not have it be relegated to the exclusive domain of one age group. Giroux (2014, p. 1) argues that democracy in the United States is in a state of crisis if viewed from a youth perspective:

> This is especially true for young people. While a great deal has been written about the budget busting costs of the invasion of Iraq and the passing of new anti-terrorist laws in the name of "homeland security" that make it easier to undermine those basic civil liberties that protect individuals against invasive and potentially repressive government actions, there is a thunderous silence on the part of many critics and academics regarding the ongoing insecurity and injustice suffered by young people in this country. As a result, the state is increasingly resorting to repression and punitive social policies at home and abroad.

Giroux raises a distressing flag about the undermining of civil liberties in the name of national security. Unfortunately, certain groups in society pay a higher price than others.

Boggs and Kurashige (2012, p. xiii) make a poignant statement about democracy and social change that is applicable to central themes in this book: "In times of crisis you either deepen democracy, or you go to the other extreme and become totalitarian."

Social activism can be a form of civic engagement and a way for free speech to be manifested; all demographic segments of society have this right. Civic engagement is a critical element of democracy and must be fostered among youth to ensure that democracy continues to flourish now and in the future as they assume adult status (Flanagan & Levine, 2010). Service-learning, too, can help youths to become more connected to their communities. Civic engagement and service-learning, however, must not be narrowly conceptualized to exclude social protest.

Costanza-Chock (2012, p. 5) offers a counter-narrative to prevailing adult sentiments about social activism and grounds youth social protest within a democratic frame, casting youth participation as healthy for a nation: "Youth are often dismissed for a lack of civic engagement, or attacked for being disruptive. Yet disruption of oppressive laws, norms, and practices is a crucial aspect of all liberatory movements: think of the struggle to end slavery, or to gain suffrage for women." The lessons and competencies youth activists obtain bring immediate and future rewards and translate into creating future engaged and contributing adult members (Lund, 2010), who, in turn, will hopefully encourage their own children to assume prominent roles in enhancing democracy.

United States urban marginalized youth certainly have not suffered from a lack of scholarly or public attention (Stolberg, 2015). Unfortunately, this attention has invariably been negative, causing the failure of educational and human service programs to meet their most pressing needs (Spencer & Spencer, 2014). They suffer from counterproductive views that have been compounded by racism and classism (Miller & Garran, 2008). These youth have been written off by society and considered surplus populations. Giroux (2012), a leading theoretician on the relationship between democracy and youth, calls them "disposable youth" (Macrine, 2011; Robbins, 2012).

I consider this topic of great significance and have devoted a considerable amount of time and energy over the past fifteen years researching and writing on urban youth and community practice. The evolution of community practice can be compared to an expanding universe with endless potential contributions to youth-led and youth-involved practice, and no more so than when it is social justice driven.

Youth and Social Justice Campaigns and Movements

Some social justice movements have been relatively quiet and peaceful—the "consumer" and "green" movements, for example—although this conclusion is certainly open to debate. Others have been loud and disruptive, resulting in police arrests and extensive media coverage, as in the case of the "Occupy Movement" in 2011–2012, for example (Gaby & Caren, 2012; Hayduk, 2012). As a result, there are many different sources and strategies for community organizing and social protest (Pyles, 2013; Schutz & Sandy, 2011). This abundance of conceptualizations makes this topic complex to grasp from a theoretical or practice perspective, making understanding of youth and social activism that more challenging to comprehend against this backdrop.

Unfortunately, regardless of the intensity of the movement or degree to which it is disruptive, this country's youth contributions have been invisible or minimized by adults who often are credited for leading these movements, covering them for the media, and authoring history (Gordon, 2010). This oversight limits our historical and current-day comprehension of how youth have shaped activism in the United States.

Some critics of youth social movements and activism believe that there are numerous opportunities presently in society to engage youth in "non-law breaking" and "constructive" pursuits without having them resorting to disruptive civil disobedience. They can pursue volunteering opportunities developed by adults as "constructive" alternatives, for example (Youniss & Levine, 2009). Others argue that youth have very limited access to engage in "meaningful" activities and decisions in their lives (Kirshner & Geil, 2010), and being included in social justice efforts by adults as equal partners in the cause is both desirable and viable.

The importance of social activism and how it gets manifested in democratic social movements and encouraged by community practitioners is well understood as a barometer of how well a society tolerates public dissent (Delgado & Staples, 2007; Meyer, 2009). It gives voice to social justice issues for those who have been wronged by those in power, and it is often in direct response to efforts to marginalize a group of people and forcefully quell their dissent. Practitioners, as a result, can find avenues for furthering youth social causes in ways that support their quest for justice (Nissen, 2011).

A society that addresses social dissent through use of police and military responses is a society that cannot address the concerns of injustices through reason and the law, as in the case of Michael Brown, Ferguson, Missouri; Eric Garner, New York City; and Freddie Gray, Baltimore. The deaths of these three African American young men, as well as others, served as rallying cries for racial justice demonstrations across the nation. Thus, social activism must be considered a key ingredient of healthy democratic societies. Community practitioners are in a propitious position to aid youth in seeking social justice and also in serving as role models for adults in the community (Tilton, 2010).

The early part of the twenty-first century ushered in a host of challenges for this and other nations and, in some cases, has shaken the very foundations of societies because of social injustices related to socio-economic class, race, and ethnicity (Leontidou, 2010). The bringing together of these injustices increases the importance of protest because it strikes at the heart of structural factors in a society.

Torres (2007) posits that post-modernity and globalization, as evidenced by declining economies and increasing dislocation of highly marginalized groups, has eroded political participation among those who are devalued. Gonzales

(2013) argues that contrary to conventional wisdom, increased Latino electoral participation alone will not result in empowerment and social justice for Latinos, for example. Instead, Latino youth activists and allies hold great promise for achieving social justice by engaging in social protest, which is a form of political participation.

This nation's economic recession that started in 2008 (Second Great Depression) and the perceived indifference to its effects offer an example of Torres' argument. Rachieff (2008, p. 1) addresses immigrant rights within a global perspective: "Today's critical labor struggles revolve around immigrants' rights, while today's struggles over immigrants' rights are grounded in workplace and labor organizing. Global, national and local histories have woven these issues tightly together." This erosion of rights has been accompanied by a rise in social activism, tapping the voices of the disenfranchised. Social activism does frighten nations by challenging sacred beliefs and raising concerns about how protests can translate into movements that can dramatically change or overthrow a government.

Youth played leadership roles during the "Arab Spring," although the popular media neglected this key point (Ezbawy, 2012; Lim, 2012; Ottaway & Hmazawy, 2011; Shehata, 2008; Staeheli & Nagel, 2013). Abdelrahman (2013) observes that Egyptian youth witnessed their transformation from "protestors," "demonstrators and strikers," "members of loosely structured networks" to the status of "revolutionaries." This identity was imposed by adults, undermining youth altruistic and social justice purposes for engaging in protest.

There is no generation in this country that did not witness a major social movement that was not predicated on social and human rights, resulting in demonstrations, boycotts, marches, and massive arrests. Many of these movements coincided with each other, influencing each other in the process, and drawing upon similar activists. However, popular media reporting gives the impression that there was no relationship between these movements and they existed in isolation from each other. A spatial justice perspective would highlight how they overlapped within communities because they overlapped in everyday lived experiences.

Most baby boomers and older adults remember the Civil Rights Movement of the 1950s and 1960s, considered the most significant social movement in the United States, and the cadre of activists it created (Bloom, 2001; Blumberg, 2009; Rury & Hill, 2013). This period witnessed new ways of thinking about social injustice in this country and the role of social protests in highlighting these injustices. There were other social movements that followed the Civil Rights Movement, frequently drawing upon the same cadre of activists (Foley, 2013). The following are five major social movements that most Americans are familiar with:

(1) The Anti-Vietnam War Movement of the 1960s and early 1970s was largely responsible for the United States withdrawing from that war (Dunham, 1998; Heineman, 1994; Huey, 2012).

(2) The Gray Panther Movement of the 1970s and 1980s, which sought to shift the thinking in this country as to what it means to grow old, leading to significant laws related to age discrimination (Powell, Williamson & Branco, 1996; Sanjek, 2009).

(3) The Women's Rights Movement of the 1970s led to efforts to introduce a constitutional amendment, and the liberation of women and this society's view of women changed dramatically in the process, even though the amendment never passed (Evans, 2001; Ryan, 2013).

(4) The Gay and Lesbian Liberation Movement, symbolized by the 1969 New York City's Stonewall Inn revolt (Cruikshank, 1992; D'Emilio, 2009), changed the life experiences of many. The successful quest for marriage equality, for example, could not have been possible without Stonewall and the social protests that followed.

(5) The People with Disabilities Movement during the 1980s brought with it an increased consciousness of how those with disabilities have been overlooked and marginalized, resulting in landmark legislation, such as the Americans with Disabilities Act of 1990 (Campbell & Oliver, 2013; McNeese, 2013; Switzer, 2003).

These movements touch upon five of the more prominent social issues of the 1960s to 2000 era of American history (Jones & O'Donnell, 2012). These social movements consisted of numerous other social campaigns that contributed to or were eventually subsumed by the broader social movement. It is best to think of social movements as consisting of many smaller social change campaigns that get categorized into an overarching movement, with each element playing an influential role in shaping its conceptualization and implementation.

When combined, movement significance is increased exponentially. Lopez (2008, p. 1), in commenting on Chicanos and the immigrant-rights movement, makes this very point:

> The United States in the twenty-first century continues to struggle with the issue of immigration. The anti-immigrant sentiment of the U.S. government and its citizens led to the formation, activism, and outcry of the twenty-first century Immigrants' Rights Movement. The demands of this movement have overlapped those of other social movements that started in the 1940s, such as the Civil Rights Movement, the Chicano Movement, and the Farm Worker Movement. Each of these movements, while approaching from different directions, addresses the ongoing violations and subsequent demands of the immigrant community.

[Handwritten margin note: Social Movements building and drawing off each other]

Grounding current social protest and movements within an historical context helps us develop an understanding of how historical social forces served as a foundation for current day events.

[Handwritten note at bottom: New generation needed to push for further reformation and social justice. Getting out of comfort zone]

Ling and Monteith (2014) address this very point in their book *Gender in the Civil Rights Movement* along with the intersectionality of gender and race identity within this social justice movement. Although the Civil Rights Movement focused on racial justice, it set the foundation from which to explore other social injustices (Castillo, 2014; Cohen, 2014; Eskridge Jr. & Eskridge, 2013; Navarro, 2014). Berger (2014), for example, highlights the multiplicity of perspectives on social justice organizing by focusing on African Americans'/Blacks' prison activism during the Civil Rights Era.

Social movements rarely have a very clear and specific change target that they address. The Vietnam Anti-War Movement is an exception since it specifically had the end of the war as the explicit goal. The Civil Rights Movement, in turn, had broader goals, ranging from removing barriers to voting, to ensure that African Americans and other groups of color had equal access to all the rights and privileges that Whites had. The three social movements covered in this book are broad in scope, with each of these movements consisting of multiple social justice goals. Some of these goals have more applicability in certain communities, with contextualization ensuring that socio-ecological factors are taken into account in any analysis and intervention design.

The start of this millennium has ushered in a number of social justice movements that have much to credit the earlier movements identified in the previous paragraph, and have provided a new generation with an opportunity to exercise democratic principles and engage in social justice-inspired social change goals. On the surface, these movements appear not to share much in common, but upon closer analysis they share many similarities, particularly for youth.

Loader, Vromen, and Xenos (2014, p. 143) echo this conclusion:

> The accusations that young people are politically apathetic and somehow failing in their duty to participate in many democratic societies worldwide have been refuted by a growing number of academics in recent years . . . Undoubtedly many young citizens have indeed become disenchanted with mainstream political parties and with those who claim to speak on their behalf. But this should not be misinterpreted as a lack of interest on the part of youth with the political issues that influence their everyday lived experience and their normative concerns for the planet and its inhabitants. As the recent waves of protest demonstrations by young people in all their different forms and contexts testify, the suggestion that the next generation of citizens is any less politically engaged than previous ones seems at least premature.

Youth eschewing conventional politics does not translate into a disengaged and alienated group. In fact, it can certainly be argued that youth are as engaged as any previous generation when engagement is viewed broadly rather than narrowly.

Youth historically played important roles in social justice campaigns and movements in this country, but have been overlooked or misrepresented by scholars and the popular press (Delgado & Staples, 2012; Harris, Wyn & Younes, 2010; Hart & Gullan, 2010; Willis, 2013). This lack of attention has painted a distorted picture of this group as one that is disengaged or apathetic politically and only interested in their own hedonistic pleasures (Harris, Wyn & Younes, 2010; McLaughlin et al., 2009).

This prevailing opinion has been advanced by adults, not youth, and has been further compounded by sentiments that this generation is not equipped to assume future roles as adults, with the exception of the youth development field (Lewis-Charp, Yum & Soukamneuth, 2006). Youth development is encompassing and evolving, making significant contributions to an adult corrective view of youth (Ramey & Rose-Krasnor, 2012; Walker, Gambone & Walker, 2011). In essence, the future of this country is in trouble as this generation ages out of being youth to become adults.

The immense popularity of the immigrant-rights, environmental, and food justice movements over the past decade has thrust these movements into the public limelight and inspired numerous communities across the country to undertake social justice organizing, opening up possibilities for youth to participate and assume leadership positions in these efforts (Hawken, 2007; Pellow, 2004; Rhodes, 2005; Schlosberg, 2007; Sze, 2007; Wittman, Desmarais & Wiebe, 2010).

These movements are not limited to this nation and can be seen worldwide. Rarely will a week go by that popular media will not have a story related to immigrant-rights, food, or environmental injustice. These movements, among others, have embraced social justice goals to help guide their activism, particularly within this nation's major urban centers (Delgado, 2013; Hess, 2009; McIntyre-Mills, 2003; Wolch, Wilson & Fehrenbach, 2005). Although it can be argued that no sector of society has escaped the consequences of the injustices these movements address, urban centers—and people of color in particular— have managed to assume the brunt of these actions. Youth must be expected to play significant roles in shaping and leading these campaigns, although they can have allies helping them.

Youth Oppositional Resistance

Youth oppositional resistance has emerged as a perspective for understanding a variety of youth acts that adults typically view as "acting out" or "unruly" behavior. A reframing of these acts as oppositional resistance introduces a critical political lens and language to understand their reasons for these acts and grounds them within the broader operative reality they face on a daily basis. This section uplifts several acts to illustrate the richness of this perspective.

Resistance can conjure up visual images of World War II and talk about covert resistance fighters undermining German occupation of their homelands by engaging in heroic acts. Adults have no difficulty comprehending this form of resistance and may even applaud it. It was violent and quite graphic, and there was no doubt about the social injustices that led to these actions. This form of resistance, although quite visible and heroic, is not the only form that it can take. Other forms of resistance are more prosaic and transpire during a non-war period, and are overlooked or mislabeled as acts of vandalism, particularly when youth are associated with these acts. Non-violent resistance can be viewed as a form of resilience and heroism when addressing social injustice (Ardizzone, 2007).

It is not a stretch of the imagination to view youth confronting dominant authorities as resistance (Cammorota, 2008; Chaskin, 2009; Gonzalez, 2008; Negron-Gonzalez, 2009). Immigrant youth, for example, risked hostile political environments and arrests to offer counter-narratives and oppositional resistance through engagement in social protests (Negrón-Gonzales, 2013). Oppositional resistance can be challenging from a definitional point-of-view, however (Daniels et al., 2010, p. 31): "Resistance can be problematized because of the challenges with defining it, locating it and categorizing it. It is not a simple concept, and we found as we delved into the term further, we developed a myriad of perspectives of its interpretation."

Costanza-Chock (2012, p. 1) captures the alarming state of youth affairs in the United States and why activism is a natural extension of their state of being: "Young people are often key actors in powerful social movements that transform the course of human history. Indeed, youth have been deeply important to every progressive social movement, including the United States Civil Rights movement, the transnational LGBTQ movement, successive waves of feminism, environmentalism and environmental justice, the labor, antiwar, and immigrant-rights movements, and more. In each of these cases, young people took part in many ways, including through the appropriation of the "new media" tools of their time, which they used to create, circulate, and amplify movement voices and stories. Yet today, youth are often framed in the mass media as, at best, apathetic, disengaged, and removed from civic action. At worst, youth (in the U.S., particularly youth of color) are subject to growing repression: increased surveillance, heightened policing, stop and-frisk policies on the streets, overbroad gang injunctions, and spiraling rates of juvenile incarceration."

Youth have played and continue to play active and meaningful roles in oppositional resistance through social protest in the United States and throughout the world. Some youth because of their marginalized status, are called upon to play an even greater role, in seeking social justice for themselves and their respective communities.

Disengagement from conventional political participation (electoral politics) is often a theme put forth by adults in authority but that does not mean that youth are politically disengaged as represented through the relevance of social activism (Hart & Gullan, 2010). Ito et al. (2015) argue that the rise of participatory politics engenders innovative ways for youth to achieve voice and influence public spheres through "connected civics." Youth build relationships and competencies through cultural production, participatory politics, and connected learning, countering adult prevailing views of disengaged youth. However, oppositional actions can often be misinterpreted by adults.

Youth oppositional behavior entails transforming personal problems into public problems, and the joining of forces with others facing similar oppression, as a constructive way of seeking validation and redress. One youth organizer (Carbajal) illustrates this by bringing together personal, social issues, and problems (Weiss, 2003, p. 26): "'Adults don't understand that, for youth, dealing with personal issues and making social change have to go hand in hand. Youth will fail if they don't have the kind of emotional support we spend so much time giving them,' he explains. 'They won't make it to the next campaign, if they don't feel like this is a place where they're comfortable, where they have friends, and where they can talk to us about their lives.'"

Oppositional resistance is an act of bravery to be celebrated rather than labeled as a problem. How youth activists are viewed by adults will go a long way towards framing their actions as democracy in action or oppositional resistance, and our scholarly understanding and reactions to these acts (Dimitriadis, 2011). Youth engagement in unhealthy acts and anti-educational stances, too, can be viewed from a resistance perspective, broadening the concept of resistance beyond a narrow social-ecological confine (Bottrell, 2009; Factor, Kawachi & Williams, 2011; Kamete, 2013; McLaren, 2003).

Akom, Cammarota, and Ginwright (2008, p. 2) tie critical youth studies, resilience, and resistance together, proposing that these concepts be enhanced through formal and informal arenas, using social protest as viable and effective way of transforming them into action:

> The importance of critical youth studies as a field of academic inquiry is that it goes beyond traditional pathological approaches to assert that young people have the ability to analyze their social context, to collectively engage in critical research, and resist repressive state and ideological institutions. However, another step is needed to further distance critical youth studies from essentialized perspectives by acknowledging that resistance can be attained through formal processes in "real" settings, through multi-generational collectives, and sometimes among youth alone. The belief that youth need new kinds of spaces where resistance and resiliency can be validated and developed through formal (and informal) processes, pedagogical structures, and youth cultural practices, is gaining currency in the field of critical youth studies and is vital towards creating a movement of social justice and equity.

Critical youth studies provide academics and practitioners the place and space for dialogues and theory building to advance a youth rights agenda and bringing youth as participants into this academic arena.

There are countless forms of oppositional resistance and not all can be considered productive from an individual and societal perspective. As a result, oppositional resistance benefits from categorization to increase our understanding of how opposition gets manifested by youth activists and facilitate determining the level of success of these acts. Solorzano and Delgado Bernal (2001) propose a four-type categorization to meet this need: (1) reactionary behavior; (2) self-defeating resistance; (3) confirmed resistance; and (4) transformative resistance. The first two are associated with negative consequences while the latter two bring political awareness and constructive behavior based on social justice.

There are many different types and targets of resistance with schools being a prime target of youth oppositional acts and behaviors, which should not be surprising since youth spend a major portion of their lives in schools and are not in positions of power within these institutions (Fine et al., 2008; Raby, 2005; Tuck & Yang, 2013). Resistance, in turn, can transpire in highly public acts such as riots (Hart & Gullan, 2010) and other, less obvious ways—through boycotts, for example (Ruglis, 2011; Tavener-Smith, 2014). Gangs, too, can be considered counter-hegemonic forms of individual and collective resistance (Brotherton, 2008). Hip-hop music gives voice to urban youth resistance (Brant & Tyson, 2014; Clay, 2012; Evans, 2014; Lamotte, 2014; Morrell & Duncan-Andrade, 2002); slang and coded language on race, too, is a form of resistance (Roberts, Bell & Murphy, 2008). Slam poetry, as in the case of Arizona's regressive legislation, provided youth with a vehicle for making calls for social action (Fields et al., 2014). Among adults, these forms of lyrics, music, and poetry are often considered offensive and disrespectful of adult authority (Kientz, 2013).

Youth oppositional consciousness is empowering with critical literacy being a major element enhancing their analytical abilities and shaping their degree of involvement and type of activism that holds the greatest relevance for them (Kwon, 2008; Lewis, 2013). Pearrow (2008) discusses how undervalued youth can achieve empowerment through civic engagement that is focused on social justice and social change and guided through the use of critical social theory. The greater the personal experience with and political consciousness of oppression that youth have, the higher the likelihood of participation in a social justice activism (Torres, 2007).

Youth do derive social and psychological benefits through engagement in resistance acts while serving the greater good (Nolan, 2011). This is particularly the case if their parents have a history of involvement in social causes. It is important to note, however, that youths' lived experiences are not limited to their age group but can, and often do, include the experiences of their adult family members and neighbors, as in the case of immigrant rights and Dreamers.

The importance of family in shaping urban youth subjective well-being is not surprising (Morgan et al., 2009), and it is not a conceptual stretch to see why social justice activism can also reach out to the injustices faced by family members. Altruism is alive and well among youth and they are rarely credited for caring.

Immigrant-rights, food, and environmental justice movements have served as mechanisms for channeling the concerns of adults into creating a society that is safe and healthy for this and future generations. The social injustices these three movements address can be found in many of this nation's cities existing side by side. However, many adult leaders have relegated youth to secondary status in recognition, level of participation, and decision-making in these efforts. Even when recognized by adults, these young activists are sometimes condescendingly referred to as "junior activists," or "activists-in-training," ignoring their talents and marginalizing their contributions, adding insult to injury.

The reader may react with total amazement concerning youth oppositional resistance as manifested through social protest. Social justice scholarly literature, with exceptions, has largely eschewed the contributions of youth as social activists (Ginwright & Cammarota, 2009). Three notable books stand out for their contributions to our understanding. Dearling and Armstrong's book, titled *Youth Action and the Environment* almost fifteen years ago (1997), outlined multiple ways youth can play significant roles in social movements. Franklin's (2014b) book, *After the Rebellion: Black Youth, Social Movement Activism and the Post-Civil Rights Generation*, specifically focused on one youth group of color. Finally, Fletcher and Vavros' (2006) book, *The Guide to Social Change by and with Youth*, provided invaluable guidance for advancing youth activism. This scholarly error of omission or commission follows traditional practices involving youth and other social change efforts in the Civil Rights and Anti-Vietnam War movements, which have either totally ignored the role youth played, or minimized it, in the nation's history (Gordon, 2010).

History is always written by adults with all of the foibles of viewing and interpreting events from this age vantage point. This inherent age bias limits how major national and international social events get addressed in the professional literature and who is highlighted for attention, misrepresented, or even ignored, as in the case of youth (McLaughlin et al., 2009; Taft, 2010). A similar argument can be made of men writing the history of feminist thought and women's search for social justice (Bhattacharjya et al., 2013). Women are experts of their own lives, as are youth.

Youth resistance during the Nazi regime has escaped serious scholarly attention and typifies how historical accounts overlook youth actions (Horn, 1973). The White Rose, The Eidelweiss Pirates, The Swing Youth, and the Helmut Hubener are four youth activist groups that actively resisted the Nazis. Unfortunately, the forty years since Horn's contributions has not shed much historical light on the role youth played. Rectifying historical neglect of their voices and acts is increasingly arduous because of the aging and eventual death of youth activists as they enter older adulthood.

Gordon (2007, p. 632) arrives at a similar conclusion from a sociological perspective:

> Although there has been an impressive surge in adolescent political organizing, scant sociological attention has been paid to studying the structures, strategies, and political action frames of these youth movements. This sociological inattention to adolescent political activism dovetails with a larger silence in the literatures on the social construction of youth, generational conflict, and age inequality: namely the ways in which ageism is understood, maintained, or contested by young people themselves, "on the ground," in everyday interaction.

Historians are not the only culprits of neglecting youth activism. Other academic disciplines, too, can be faulted.

Scholars have done a tremendous disservice by providing a distorted portrait of who has actively and significantly participated in key social movements in this nation's history, as addressed in Chapter 2. Scholarly efforts redressing this injustice are desperately needed, particularly those actively seeking the voices and interpretations of marginalized youth. The importance of youth having a history that they can call their own and draw upon cannot be overestimated. The emergence of the concept of "public history," or the history of everyday life outside of the classroom, refocuses this academic discipline's potential contribution to illuminating how oppression is manifested among the marginalized (Dichtl & Sacco, 2014). This movement has tremendous potential for youth shaping how their narrative and history is portrayed and shared across generations.

Franklin (2015) stresses that social activism would be a focal point in Black political historiography in the past century only if historians were to give this subject the attention it deserves. Aparicio's (2008) analysis of this critical point has profound consequences for how adults view—and, more importantly, how youth view—their contributions to this country's development. Creation of a documented narrative as well as pictorial history that can be retrieved by future generations helps to underscore the importance of viewing oppression from an historical perspective in order to understand and appreciate its present form (Delgado, 2015a).

Aparicio (2008, p. 361) goes on to stress the importance of the past (history) being a prologue for the present and future, and why youth of color benefit from a new interpretation of history:

> Black and Brown youth activists in the United States are creating new forms of politics and establishing new communities and networks; some of the most creative anti-racist projects are those in which youth activists use the Black radical past. Their work is not simply an exercise in acquiring

historical facts, but of creating new understandings of histories and of the relationships between Black and Brown activists over time and space. For many Black and Brown Afro-diasporic youth, re-imagining and resurrecting the Black radical past is an essential aspect of contemporary organizing. As such, their attempts to build coalitions are based in a sense of a shared past, a common network of "fictive kin."

Putting forth a new interpretation and recording of history means much more than adding an historical footnote. It means that interpretation can serve as a foundation from which to view the current day within a long and distinguished historical context.

The emergence of youth as a "proletarian class," with youth and adults engaging in a class struggle, offers a new, although contentious, lens through which to understand youth social activism (Côté, 2014 Giroux, 2014). Age-related distributive justice brings a lens to discussions that highlight how youth with particular backgrounds fall into a distinct social class (Irwin, 2013).

King's (2011) book *Stolen Childhood: Slave Youth in Nineteenth-Century America* makes an important contribution to our understanding that not all youth have the luxury of engaging in "youthful pursuits" and there is a long history to take into account in order to fully understand present-day events. In this case, the legacy of slavery hangs over urban African American youth. Although slavery was abolished well over a century ago, segregation and its consequences are alive and well in present-day America and cries for social justice efforts (Cohen, 2010). The Black Lives Matter movement has a long historical origin in this country that can be traced back to slavery, although its focus, understandably so, is on the present-day tragedies.

Nolan (2014) argues for a nuanced understanding of youth participation in what is referred to as "youth spaces," with immediate implications for urban youth of color, and the need of an epistemological approach to youth praxis that "embraces the messiness and inequalities of lived experience." There is a call for a broader epistemology to obtain a spatially nuanced and temporally evolving knowledge base of how the environment (space and place) shapes youth activism (Case & Hunter, 2012; Farthing, 2010; Teelucksingh & Masuda, 2014). Youth must play an active role in the decolonization of knowledge as a prerequisite for social action (Banales, 2012), and having them play an active role in research is a step in that direction (Delgado, 2006).

Thompson, Russell, and Simmons (2014), although studying employed and out-of-school youth in England, report on youth feelings of alienation, isolation, and lack of control over their lives that can be applied to the United States. Dire socio-ecological circumstances have not stopped youth from engaging in resistance behavior and social protest. These activist youth have sought to gain control over their lives by engaging others in collective action and providing a counter-narrative to prevailing adult views. Stereotypes distort reality, and academics and practitioners must guard against negative and positive youth stereotypes if a realistic view of youth is to guide social interventions (Sukarieh & Tannock, 2011).

Dohrn (2005, p. xiiii) captures the imagination, drive, and commitment of youth and how it translates into social activism and eventual outcome: "In my lifetime, young people have changed the world. From Little Rick to Greensboro, from Selma to Soweto, in Tien An Mien and Seattle, it was the young who dared to act in the face of the overwhelming certainty that nothing could be done. It was their direct action that educated, opened doors and minds, shattered the taken-for-granted. It will happen again. It's happening now." Youth are a community asset that cannot be ignored by adults and practitioners, and oppositional resistance is a public service in a democratic society.

Thomson (2009, p. 813) addresses the multi-faceted dimensions related to the concept of "voice" and applicability to participatory democracy: "The concept of voice spans literal, metaphorically and political terrains. In its literal sense, voice represents the speech and perspective of the speaker; metaphorically, voice spans inflection, tone, accent, style and the qualities and feelings conveyed by the speaker's words; and politically, a construct of voice attests to the right of speaking and becoming represented." Ensuring youth remain voiceless and silencing their dissent robs them of their agency (Applebaum, 2014). Their voices invariably have been further ignored by scholars, and this has seriously compromised the understanding of their contributions and potential to shape their social environment and challenge social injustices.

Drawing on first-hand experience of youth activists provides a scholarly and practice perspective that captures their voices and experiences in defining their "space" and "role" in social movements such as immigrant rights, environmental issues, and food justice. Other forms of youth activism, of course, have occurred. For example, youth organizing for educational reform has shown great promise (Conner & Zaino, 2014; Conner, Zaino & Scarola, 2013; Mitra, Frick & Crawford, 2011; Rogers, Mediratta & Shah, 2012; Warren & Mapp, 2011). The same can be said concerning urban youth of color organizing for juvenile/criminal justice (Hollingsworth, 2012; Kwon, 2006). These efforts can be conceptualized as a form of civic engagement.

Quijada (2008) draws on firsthand youth civic engagement experience, using immigrant rights and civil rights as case examples. Gordon and Taft (2011) bring a different but equally valuable perspective by arguing that scholars have emphasized studying how adults influence youth but essentially refrained from better understanding how youth socialize each other for political engagement. Taken one step further, how youth influence adults also has been totally absent from scholarly attention. There is no wonder as to why adult scholars and practitioners have a skewed understanding of youth, and why the topic of youth oppositional behavior may be alien to many readers.

The use of a socio-spatial analysis shows how everyday life shapes political collective action (Aguiree & Lio, 2008; Martin & Miller, 2003), which in turn shape collective identity. Urban youth identities are very complex and they develop "hyphenated selves," which can be viewed as a constructive, adaptive, and thoughtful narrative of self that responds to shifting social and political contexts and oppression in lived experiences (Banales, 2012; Katsiaficas et al., 2011). The political socialization process can be quite diverse, as well as the dynamics in the lives of children of newcomers, for example, with family and peers playing significant roles in this process (Solís, Fernández & Alcalá, 2013).

Futch (2013) arrived at similar conclusions concerning the importance of collective identity: "Findings suggest that collaboratively and purposefully crafting a collective identity provides youth programs with a useful way to cultivate meaningful results of participation for current members as well as provide an underlying identity framework that past participants can build on in new social arenas as emerging adults." A collective response through identity politics and social activism is a natural occurrence and influences collective identity (Franklin, 2014a).

Martinez (2014) argues that the undocumented youth movement has deliberately sought to push the boundaries of social inclusion without excluding other marginalized groups, such as adults, transgender populations, or other groups that have historically been criminalized and faced oppression in their lives. Burridge (2010) notes that this movement did not transpire within "pre-established frameworks and organizations" but sought new boundaries pertaining to citizenship, human rights, social and economic mobility. Youth activists can serve as role models for adult activists, assume leadership in their respective communities, and create new realities for adults to engage in with youth.

Bloemraad and Trost (2008) make the case for the importance of youth participation in political organizing, as evidenced in the 2006 Immigrant Rights protests. They advocate for a "model of bidirectional political socialization" in immigrant families, in which youth and parents influence each other to participate. This broadening of the socialization process helps explain the wide range of participants in the mass immigrant-rights demonstrations of 2006 and why youth played a pivotal role.

Pearce and Larson (2006) concluded based upon their study of youth engagement in a youth development program that youth go through a distinct engagement process that starts with developing a personal connection to a program's mission and progresses to making a commitment by engaging in program activities, with both peers and adults wielding influence in supporting their participation. An engagement stages perspective helps engender a youth-adult collaborative conceptualization of social protest.

Youth activist voices have not been tapped in this regard. Berger, Boudin, and Farrow's (2005) book titled *Letters from Young Activists* introduces this generation to a cadre of activists by capturing their voices on social causes in their unfiltered form and illustrating their motivations for engaging in what we call youth oppositional resistance. Kirshner's (2009) ethnographic research of youth organizers studied the role of the individual and the broader public and the importance of "power in numbers" in helping youth find their civic identity and voice. Ares (2010, p. 6), in turn, discusses how adult concepts of marginalized youth translate into youth counteracting a deficit identity: "This marginalization frequently results from the assumptions of deviance and the demonstration that can occur in adults' construction of deviance and the demonization that can occur in adults' construction of youth."

The identity that youth embrace through engagement in oppositional behavior is important for them and their community, with identity being shaped by perceptions of self within a socio-cultural context (Lee, 2010). Some may refer to themselves as "social advocates" rather than "social activists" even though the scholarly literature differentiates between these two labels (Ameen, 2012). Either of these identities is affirming, empowering, and brings social efficacy, casting youth as activists rather than victims, which is a counter-narrative to the labels adults place on youth who engage in oppositional resistance.

The role of adult-dominated media has further perpetuated society's negative views of youth, such as their inability to make socially informed choices (Checkoway (2005, p. 16): "Indeed, news media too often portray young people as perpetrators of crime, drug takers, school dropouts, or other problems of society . . . Professional practitioners adopt this view of young people and seek to 'save,' 'protect,' and 'defend' them." This narrow view of youth competencies and concerns has relegated them to a subservient role to adults, and this is reflected in all facets of media coverage (Janes et al., 2014).

Youth involvement and potential contribution to social movements, such as immigrant rights, environmental issues, and food justice, for example, is a natural extension of this viewpoint. Muhlke's (2008) *New York Times* article titled "Food Fighters" provides a moving, and highly detailed, set of food activist portraits that show how youth activism translated into adult activism and why opportunities to engage in food justice activities benefited them and their communities, which typifies the role youth activists can, and do, play in a variety of social justice movements while young and later when entering adulthood.

Lee (2009) analyzes the role that the Young Lords, a New York City Puerto Rican social activist group consisting of youth and young adults played in the late 1960s regarding food and environmental justice concerns, and how many of these participants went on to assume activist leadership roles as adults regarding social justice in this community. That time period proved fertile in the creation of future urban-focused activist leaders.

Social science views of youth resistance and oppositional culture are not without flaws. Debies-Carl, (2013, p. 110) addresses three specific shortcomings: "(1) the tendency to group all youth phenomena under a monolithic conceptual umbrella; (2) a preoccupation on the part of researchers with style and the consumption of goods; and (3) the assumed lack of rational behavior found in subcultures and an accompanying inability on the part of subcultures to achieve real goals or effect social change."

Each of these criticisms is open to further debate. This debate is welcomed and essential if we as youth community practitioners are going to make service-learning and civic engagement viable in social justice inspired campaigns and projects, and we are to understand the potential of youth oppositional resistance to transform communities and society.

Overview of Social Justice Movements and Social Activism

Social movements historically have enjoyed a long and distinguished attraction for scholars from a variety of disciplines, resulting in a wide range of theories and conclusions pertaining to their origins and outcomes (Giroux, 2011; Porta & Diani, 2006; Langman, 2005; Taft, 2010). The purpose of this section is not to attempt to duplicate what has been said by far more learned scholars than I. The goal is to provide an overview with the intent of grounding the reader in why social justice movements hold so much promise for increasing our understanding of youth activism and how they draw upon democratic principles and can be considered a "legitimate" form of service-learning and civic engagement.

Social movements and social activism are not synonymous. Social movements do not have to arise from social injustices, either, and can be spontaneous or carefully planned. Goodwin and Jasper (2009a, p. 3) provide a short, but very good, definition of social movements: "Social movements are conscious, concerted, and sustained efforts by ordinary people to change some aspect of their society by using extra-instrumental means." We could add the importance of a social justice and human rights perspective to this definition, to capture the spirit of this book and interject the significance of oppression and activism, with implications for helping professions such as social work, for example (Reichert, 2013).

Tracing the origins of any social protest movement is arduous at best (Weldon, 2011). However, the origin of the field of youth activism has a long, broad, and distinguished history in the United States, with many scholars tracing its beginnings to the youth rights movement of the 1930s and the Great Depression. Some, however, would go back to the American Revolution to trace the role of youth in seeking social justice (Nash, 2006). There is little dispute concerning its rapid evolution within the past decade, and the role that its embrace of social justice has played in shaping this intervention in the latter part of the twentieth and early part of the twenty-first centuries.

Youth activism's evolution has largely been fueled by its focus on democratic participation (civic engagement), social justice principles, informational technology, and themes related to a social and community-change agenda, along a variety of other important spheres in youths' lives (Checkoway, 2003; Delgado & Zhou, 2008; Evans & Prilleltensjy, 2007). School activism serves as such an example (Cammorota, 2008; Gordon, 2010; Stovall, 2005). Incidentally, the dramatic presence of social media this past decade has helped fuel this popularity.

Youth activism on immigrant rights, environment, and food also represents the latest manifestation of this popularity in social movements (Brodkin, 2009). These and other social movements have spurred youth to engage in civic activities that can be considered civic engagement, casting them as social change agents, resulting in new identities as "activists" (Makhoul, Alameddine & Afifi, 2012). Flanagan (2009, p. 295) provides a counter-narrative to prevailing and highly popular conceptions that have youth absent from involvement in social movements:

> Youth may be less likely than their elders to engage in conventional politics. But they are more likely to act on their beliefs in unconventional ways through public demonstrations, acts of civil disobedience, or even more disruptive forms of political action. Social movements' literature has regularly documented the inverse relationship between age and the choice of militant strategies that may pose personal risks. Often, this has resulted in public and media derision and dismissal both of the message and of the youth. However, youths' impatience and penchant for militant action has invigorated organizations and political movements. In the struggle against apartheid in South Africa, it was the militancy of youth that rejuvenated the African National Congress. Likewise, the willingness of the Student Nonviolent Coordinating Committee (SNCC) to get arrested for acts of civil disobedience against segregation revitalized more mainstream Civil Rights organizations in the United States.

Youth's propensity to engage in public acts of protest (oppositional resistance) and willingness to accept the consequences of civil obedience is admirable. Youth absence from major social movements would have been deeply felt.

Youth as "bona fide" social activists has slowly started to get attention in a small sector of the scholarly literature (Brodkin, 2009; Cammarota, 2011; Delgado & Staples, 2007; Ginwright & Cammarota, 2007; Ginwright, Noguera & Cammarota, 2006; Gordon, 2010; Peterson, Dolan & Hanft, 2010; Ross, 2010; Schusler et al., 2009; Sherrod et al., 2005; Vasquez et al., 2007). This attention is an important move forward because it advances our understanding of youth activism by bringing together scholars, adult practitioners, and youth activists and by giving voice to youth as they want to be heard and seen.

The increasing amount of scholarship in this area is promising for major theoretical and practice advances (Maddison & Scalmer, 2006). Ginwright and James (2002, p. 27) highlight the promise of this involvement: "Young people are joining together to demand a voice in the decisions that affect their lives. In the process, they are transforming policies and making institutions more accountable." A youth "right to engage in research" and shape the questions they consider important to answer brings a rights perspective to this activity (Evans, Fox & Fine, 2010, p. 97): "The capacity to do research, in this broad sense, is also tied to what I have recently called 'the capacity to aspire' . . . the social and cultural capacity to plan, hope, desire and achieve socially valuable goals."

An increased youth role in research introduces a missing nuance to our understanding of youth and social activism (Liebenberg & Theron, 2015). The questions they pose and the process used searching for answers shapes theory but equally, if not more importantly, shapes how urban-focused social justice activism gets researched and implemented.

Intergenerational (adult-youth) social justice campaign partnerships open up a rich area of practice, study, and scholarship (Brodkin, 2009) and increase the relevance of service-learning as a method because adults control the vast majority of the settings where this can transpire, particularly schools. Intergenerational efforts reflect better the composition of communities (Karasik & Wallingford, 2007; Kimbler & Ehman, 2014).

The research question of "so what" in social movements can be viewed from a variety of perspectives, including membership composition, level of participation, extent of news coverage, connectivity (social network) and sustainability of the movement, changes resulting from actions, cadre of leadership that emerged, and degree to which one movement influences another, for example (Goodwin & Jasper, 2009b). Fine (2012) asks provocative but critical questions regarding the calls for "evidence" that have applicability in the case of youth social activism: Why now? Whose evidence counts? What kinds of evidence are being privileged? What are we not seeing? These questions are quite profound if taken seriously because they strike at the heart of what constitutes knowledge.

It is necessary to think of social activism's impact beyond changing a particular law or social condition. It also changes participants, their peers, families, and neighborhoods. Just as importantly, current social movements influence tomorrow's social movement, as yesterday's movements influenced those of today. Measures of "success" must be multifaceted, nuanced, and longitudinal to capture the breadth and depth of a social movement and the relevant voices rather than silencing them.

Social movement tactics, which can be perceived as tearing at a social fabric, such as marches, sit-ins, boycotts, and demonstrations, for example, create visual images that can be awe-inspiring as well as frightening for a nation. Representational scholarship captures how social movements are "framed" in the media (McCurdy, 2012). These events get covered by the media, which shapes the narratives supporting these images, influencing public opinion—usually negatively—through framing protest as lawlessness and those protesting as criminals (Boyle, McLeod & Armstrong, 2012; Smith et al., 2001).

The invisibility of youth and women in this coverage undermines their contributions in social protests and leads to a much-distorted portrait of who is an activist or even has the right to be called one. Media bias can unfold by focusing on high-profile adults (generally male) to the exclusion of other leaders with different demographic profiles and statuses (Boykoff, 2013; Malinick, Tindall & Diani, 2013; Rohlinger et al., 2012).

The increasing globalization of social movements, in part fostered by advances in information communication, has added important dimensions to the understanding of these campaigns (Hamdy & Gomaa, 2012; Mare, 2013). Advocates for broadening analysis argue that social movements have global implications beyond the United States and must be analyzed accordingly. This does not mean that the local scene can be ignored because that is where these social issues are experienced on a daily basis, fueling the quest for social justice.

Youth activism is first, and foremost, focused on local rather than on national issues (Hart & Gullan, 2010; Pearce & Larson, 2006). Social movements have often been portrayed as national in scope; this coverage ignores their local grounding, history, and context and often highlights major events while ignoring the countless micro-aggressions that fed into a major national effort at achieving social justice (Hasday, 2014; Ling & Monteith, 2014).

Morris (2014) addresses the importance of low-visibility social protests, which, as a result of the lack of leadership star power, location, and lack of access to high-powered media, fly under the radar from national visibility. Nevertheless, these social protests feed social justice efforts in significant ways, particularly in the early phases, although these contributions go unrecognized. Various demographic groups such as youth fall into a low-visibility category. A national perspective fails to recognize how leadership is formed at the local level and instead uplifts major figures that are the faces of these movements. These adult leaders invariably tend to be male, adults, White, non-Latino, and highly formally educated. These are the profiles that can be expected in "leaders."

It is the central premise of this book that social movements in the United States owe a great deal to youth, and that the general adult public, practitioners, and scholars have not appreciated the important role youth have played in this socio-political process of engagement. Once we attempt to understand youth participation and leadership in social movements, we will then be in a position to support their exercise of democratic principles and embrace oppositional resistance. Society also benefits from the discovery of youth as a vital and contributing part of its social fabric.

Helping professions are paying increased attention to food and environmental causes of injustices. The emergence of eco-psychology as a branch of psychology captures the importance of promoting pro-environmental behavior, providing a window for understanding how youth develop attitudes and behaviors that seek to undo food and environmental crises in their lives and communities (Cintron-Moscoso, 2010; Hinds & Sparks, 2009). Social work, too, has started to pay closer attention to the interrelationships among food, environment, and social justice (Delgado, 2013; Gray, Coates & Hetherington (2012).

Service-Learning Versus Civic Engagement

The reader may rightly be puzzled by a book that attempts to cover two fields of practice that appear as one and the same, but just happen to be called by different terms. Are these two names for separate sides of the same coin? One side of the coin is usually associated with institutions of learning and the emphasis is on the learner (service-learning); the other side emphasizes service to community (civic engagement). Obviously, learning and service do transpire on both sides of the coin (Barry, 2014). However, the emphasis is different.

Complicating our understanding of civic engagement is that it is often closely associated with service-learning. The reader may ask why these two approaches towards urban youth are conceptualized as separate entities and appeal to different audiences. Civic engagement has a strong learning dimension to it, too. The distinction between civic engagement and service-learning may appear as thin to the casual reader. However, the differences are sufficiently important to warrant separate chapters.

There are similarities between these two concepts, and the distinction between the two may be perceived as much to-do about nothing and the product of academics with too much time on their hands. These distinctions blur when the prefix of critical or social justice is interjected. The distinctions, nevertheless, are significant, and the reader should have a rationale as to why they are dealt with as two youth approaches. This author, as noted, prefers to think of these two terms as being sides of a coin. One side is service-learning and the other is civic engagement. The coin is about youth, learning, and social justice service to the community.

Civic engagement is founded upon principles of partnership and sharing of power (Jacoby, 2003). Non-critical justice service-learning does not address power imbalances, and the emphasis is learner-focused, with adults being teachers and youth being students, a conventional role for both parties. Designing service-learning projects *with*, as opposed to *for*, the community, introduces youth to relationships based upon mutual trust and respect, increasing the likelihood of social justice values guiding a project and a shift in power (Jacoby, 2015).

Jacoby (2015, pp. 2–3) draws a distinction between service-learning and civic engagement:

> The terms and concepts of service-learning and civic engagement are often confounded. Civic engagement is the broader term and can be defined as acting upon a heightened sense of responsibility to one's communities through both political and non-political means . . . It is often described as active citizenship or democratic participation. Civic engagement thus comprises a wider range of activities than has traditionally been associated with service-learning, such as enacting ways to alter public policy, ranging from petitioning to protest and engaging at various levels in the political process.

Both service-learning and civic engagement can entail learning and service. Service-learning, for example, can be referred to as *community-based service-learning* to further confuse the reader.

It is also confusing to find terms such as *community engagement* in the literature, possibly giving the impression that this term is interchangeable with *civic engagement*. These two terms have different meanings. The former refers to a planned and coordinated effort to create opportunities for students or residents to engage in a project that can significantly alter a social situation. Community engagement refers to a philosophy and efforts, which do not have to be systematically planned or coordinated, of schools and community-based organizations to get various types and levels of participation or to collaborate with institutions to improve quality of life (Fitzgerald & Primavera, 2013).

Service-learning has been heavily influenced by educators and educational settings; civic engagement, in turn, is associated with community practitioners and community-based organizations, with learning not having been a central goal, although it is important. Service-learning and civic engagement have benefited from scholarship, and that is to be expected and encouraged. However, for the purposes of this book, they are treated as different but closely related. Their distinction blurs considerably when discussing critical or social justice service-learning and civic engagement because of the interjection of the importance of addressing social injustices and the set of values associated with justice.

Flanagan (2009, p. 294) brings a political analysis and corresponding social action to a discussion on youth civic engagement that also has applicability to service-learning when founded on social justice principles:

> These projects harness young people's frustrations and direct their anger toward social change, often targeting basic needs for textbooks and transportation or tolerance in schools and communities. Political skills are gained as youth gather information and critically analyze issues, including the political/power dynamics that underlie them, and ultimately learn how to speak on behalf of their group. Through such venues, they interpret the meaning of citizenship and understand their role as agents of change. An institutional setting is one context in which political views and identities take shape.

Social justice goals bring with them opportunities for development of knowledge and skill-sets that can shape many aspects of identity, including political.

Prentice (2007) warns against service-learning and civic engagement programs that are led by ideologues who push their social action agenda onto students without having student voices and decision-making shape these efforts. Richards-Schuster and Dobbie (2011, p. 234), in turn, advocate for the use of youth civic spaces for understanding how ecological factors foster or impinge on civic participation: "Youth civic spaces are environments in which youth participation in civic action is fostered—the pathways, structures, and vehicles that provide opportunities for young people to engage in critical discussion, dialogue, and action. The concept of youth civic space includes the formal and informal places in which youth civic engagement can occur and how the lived experience of those places contributes to young people's development as civic actors."

The blurring of the lines between civic engagement and service-learning is not arduous to accomplish. An embrace of similar values, adult roles, and social activism as a major activity of engagement and learning can almost make civic engagement and service-learning seem interchangeable. Yet, sponsoring organizations will generally be different, as will the vocabulary used to describe goals and activities.

Roberts (2008) discusses the role of experiential education and differentiates among three important dimensions common to both service-learning and civic engagement: (1) experience as interaction; (2) embodied experience; and (3) experience as praxis. Social-justice–directed service-learning and civic engagement encompass all three, but the immediacy and importance of praxis stands out.

The Promise of Community Practice

A community practice definition grounds youth practice of social-justice–focused change efforts. Banks and Butcher (2013, p. 7) define community practice as "work (paid or unpaid) that stimulates, supports or engages with 'active communities.' This covers a broad range of types of activity carried out for many different purposes by various types of people—from community-based initiatives by volunteers and activists with a view to providing their own services or challenging a policy, to community consultation exercises by service providers to gain the views of local residents/service users/other stakeholders about how to make improvements in services."

One of the goals of community practice identified by the authors is the "radical change in the distribution of power and resources." This goal fits well with youth social justice action and oppositional resistance. Further, the definition by Banks and Butcher is sufficiently broad to encompass local/regional/national differences, highlighting the challenges of any effort to "standardize" this practice without taking into account local context. Most importantly, this definition encompasses paid and unpaid practice and a range of practices that can fall under a community practice umbrella, including research (Stoecker, 2013).

Effective youth community practice requires an understanding of how context shapes community definition and values and how best to tap youth capacities in developing interventions (Henderson & Thomas, 2013). This process is facilitated when academics and professionals embrace residents as experts of their own lives. Context grounds youth understanding of social events impacting their lives and the options that they have to exercise agency (Richards-Schuster et al., 2013). Agency, however, can be applied to creating injustice and depriving individuals of their social rights (Opotow, 2011) and determines how youth define civic activity (Morimoto, 2013).

Youth community practice involving social justice campaigns and movements represents a rich area of study and practice with a long history in the United States (Burkemper et al., 2013; Delgado & Staples, 2007). The teaching of U.S. Labor history, for example, can be an attractive and highly engaging way of teaching urban youth about social change through social protest of work conditions. This must be done in a highly engaging manner, stressing youth participation and how workers of color played influential roles (Nelson, 2013), necessitating a re-examination of history to find their voices and actions in these struggles. The interrelationship between life history and identity can be effective for teaching history and social justice, and for youth understanding how their identity has evolved and been shaped by socio-cultural forces beyond ethnicity and race (Francis & Le Roux, 2012).

Azzopardi (2013) traces youth activism history as a social phenomenon to the mid- to late nineteenth century, when youth formed labor strikes in response to poor working conditions. Mary Harris "Mother" Jones organized the first massive youth protest in the United States, when child miners marched (100,000 in number) from the coal mines of Pennsylvania to the U.S. Capitol, with youth newspaper carriers soon following in their protest.

Community practice social justice change efforts conjure up a multitude of visions, public opinions, and theories, which is to be expected because of their significance within communities. This nation is certainly not at a loss for finding social justice–related concerns, particularly when discussing youth, and those who are highly marginalized stand out. The United States is a role model for the world in this regard (Bloom, 2001; Mumm, 1997).

Our understanding of youth social activism, particularly in major urban areas and involving youth of color, has increased, and this bodes well for future scholarship and practice (Clay, 2012; Kennelly, 2008, 2009). This cannot be said of community practice with youth to increase their agency (confidence and competencies) and advance social justice issues. This can only occur when youth voices are actively sought, translated into action, and captured for future generations (Cammarota, 2014; Mansfield, 2013; Richardson & Reynolds, 2012; Sarkissian & Bunjamin-Mau, 2012).

How youth make sense of pedagogy, literacy, and agency cannot be interpreted for them; their voices on these topics must be tapped and shared (Chang, 2013, 2015; Vincent et al., 2013). This does not mean that adults cannot play a meaningful role in the process. The scholarly literature on children/youth has suffered from a serious neglect of viewing agency from their political perspective (Bosco, 2010; Wyness, Harrison & Buchanan, 2004).

The influence of a development perspective on childhood has shaped historical opinions about this developmental phase. However, the emergence of a sociological perspective has offered great promise in expanding our understanding of children's agency (Moran-Ellis, Bandt & Sünker, 2014; Qvortrup, 2014). Pauliina Kallio and Häkli (2011) advance the notion that youth must be viewed as competent political agents whose entire existence is influenced by politics, and they have their own knowledge base, positions, and roles. Simply put, children's agency must not be overlooked (Graham & Fitzgerald, 2010; Lee & Motzkau, 2011), particularly as we discuss service-learning and civic engagement from a social justice vantage point.

Urban community practice can advance youth activism based on participatory principles (Fisher & Corciullo, 2011; Hammock, 2011). Community practice is recognized worldwide, although definitions vary by local circumstances and cultural influences on what constitutes practice and how social justice gets conceptualized (Boehm & Cnaan, 2012; Kegler, Rigler & Honeycutt, 2010; Trickett et al., 2011), particularly when discussing social action (Christens & Dolan, 2011; Christens & Speer, 2011).

Further, community practice has tremendous potential for furthering the social justice causes by and for youth, providing adult practitioners with ample opportunities to act as allies in these social causes. Youth activism provides an avenue through use of service-learning and civic engagement to achieve the goals of social justice often central to community practice, and enhancing youth competencies in the process (Yoder Clark, 2009).

The scholarly rewards and challenges of community practice are only matched by those of practitioners (Weil, 2012). The reach of community practice has resulted in an embrace of the importance of context and social justice-related causes (Ife, 2012; Reisch, 2012, 2014; Reisch, Ife & Weil, 2012). Context, in this instance, refers to geography (e.g., urban), demographics (e.g., age group), issues (e.g., police brutality), and target of changes (e.g., schools), to highlight some of the most significant aspects (Dar, 2014).

Although the concept of "community" can apply in urban, suburban, ex-urban and rural areas, it is undeniable that the urban context has shaped the conceptualization of community practice in this and other countries (Banks et al., 2013; Brueggemann, 2013; Delgado, 2011; Gamble & Weil, 2010). The spatial and demographic configuration, particularly density and diversity, is significantly different in urban settings—enough to warrant its own consideration in how community practice gets conceptualized (Delgado, 1999, 2000; Popple, 2012; Santiago, Soska & Gutierrez, 2014).

The role and importance of several key values, such as empowerment, indigenous leadership development, cultural competence/cultural humility, participatory democracy, assets- first, indigenous knowledge, and social justice, help guide community practitioners through the turbulent seas that are inherent in this form of practice, particularly when undertaken within a context that systematically targets and perpetrates injustices, as is often the case with urban youth (Delgado, in press).

Community practice is first and foremost about interventions within a community context (Chanan & Miller, 2013; Rothman, 2007; Shapiro et al., 2013), with an accompanying research agenda that is founded upon a set of values and principles (Ennis & West, 2013; MacNair, 2014). This statement may appear simple, but it is far from being so because practice and community are neither static nor do they have widely accepted boundaries (Orton, 2013; Scott, 2014), necessitating having organizations and professional education supporting these efforts (Butcher, 2013; Cheezum, 2012; Garcia et al., 2010; Thomas, O'Connor & Netting, 2011).

Ohmer and Korr's (2006) literature review on the effectiveness of community practice found few quantitative studies, which does not surprise this author because of the importance of contextual grounding in this type of work, and the difficulty of using quantitative studies for identifying influential nuances in shaping community practice.

My goal in writing about youth community practice is to expand the boundaries of what academics and practitioners conceptualize this practice to entail. Integrating an embrace of oppositional resistance as manifested through social action is a step in this quest. Pushing boundaries brings with it the joy and excitement of opening up new spheres of influence by making practice relevant and welcoming in marginalized communities (Chung & Probert, 2011).

The "pushing of the envelope" is undertaken with a deep appreciation of the consequences of expanding interventions into unchartered territory, not to mention the ethical challenges that will be encountered (Delgado, in press; Hugman & Bartolomei, 2013). For community practice to increase its influence, we must "go big or go home" because social justice is just too important to go "small."

Community practice must explore new arenas and perspectives to remain relevant, be a welcoming home to innovation, and reach new groups (Delgado & Humm-Delgado, 2013; Gutierrez, Gant & Richards-Schuster, 2014). Community practice involving urban youth and social activism is a natural evolution of our search for social justice because of how practice is predicated upon active and purposeful community engagement (Banks & Butcher, 2013). Youth programs that actively focus on social activism can serve to promote youth development values of shared goals, purposes, and self-determination (Jones et al., 2013).

The following two examples illustrate how practice can be community-of-color specific. Carlton-Laney and Burwell's (2014) *African American Community Practice Models: Historical and Contemporary Responses* examines how racial context (culture and place)—in this case, African American—shapes how community practices become conceptualized and implemented. Delgado's (2007) *Social Work Practice with Latinos: Use of a Cultural Assets Paradigm* addresses community practice with Latinos through the embrace of an assets perspective to counter prevailing deficit theories, practice, and narratives. These books view community practice as a means of addressing racial justice within these two communities and expand our understanding of what is possible as scholars and practitioners.

The field of community practice, with social work being one profession assuming a prominent position, is in a propitious position to make important contributions to youth and social justice campaigns and movements, and further move the field of youth oppositional resistance forward. Youth and social justice, of course, can be embraced by a wide range of academic disciplines and helping professions, and it is not the "exclusive" domain of community practice, which itself transcends a variety of academic disciplines and professions.

Community practice encompasses a broad arena of practice that can involve volunteers and professionals focused on working with communities stressing community capacity/development principles. Community practice has found a receptive audience in a wide variety of helping professions (Banks et al., 2013; Delgado, 2000; Hardcastle, Powers & Wenocur, 2011; Soifer et al., 2014; Weil, 2012, 2014).

This form of community practice is predicated upon a set of values that embrace empowerment (Cammarota, 2014; Nygreen, Kwon & Sanchez, 2006), social justice (Adams, 2008; Jacobson & Rugeley, 2007), participatory democracy (Checkoway & Gutierrez, 2006; Delgado, 2015a; Ghai & Vivian, 2014), civic engagement (Delgado, in press; Hart, 2013), cultural humility/competency (Endres & Gould, 2009; Gallardo, 2013; Racher & Annis, 2007), community leadership development (Eva & Sendjaya, 2013; Redmond & Dolan, P. (2014), and an emphasis on indigenous knowledge/popular education (Erstad, 2012; Litvina & Omelchenko, 2013) as salient values in guiding how community-focused interventions are conceptualized and implemented.

Youth community practice is only limited by our imagination and willingness to consider partnerships with youth to address a wide variety of arenas. Youth can play active and significant roles in engendering community economic development (Brodhead & Hood, 2006; Igietseme, 2014), community planning/economic development (Brennan, Barnett & Lesmeister, 2007; Derr et al., 2013; Perri, 2007), community policing (Miller, Hess & Orthmann, 2013), community research (Delgado, 2006), assisting highly vulnerable groups (Holtgrave et al., 2014), and public art (Cannuscio et al., 2012), for example, if provided with opportunities to do so.

However, community practice and social activism arguably offers the greatest potential for collaboration between adults and youth in a quest to achieve social justice. The potential of this relationship is further heightened when a geographic setting—in this case, urban—is introduced to help spatially frame how social justice gets conceptualized, researched, and addressed in practice (Brenner, Marcuse & Mayer, 2011; Fainstein, 2010; Fincher & Iveson, 2012; Soja, 2009).

Community organizations can play an influential role in helping urban youth of color clarify their expectations and opportunities for engaging in social activism, opening up opportunities for intergenerational efforts (Ginwright, 2007). Adults can foster youth social change campaigns and movements. However, this is only possible if adults are able to shift traditional views and roles for youth and be willing to assume positions as adult allies, as well as being able to embrace oppositional resistance as a political act.

Community-Based Organizations

Community organizations can act as bridges between youth and social protests and help the broader community understand oppositional resistance. All community-based organizations are in a position to engage and support youth because their spatial position makes them geographically accessible (Walter, 2009; Willis & Stoecker, 2013). These organizations take on even greater promise in cases where major institutions have failed youth (Minkler, 2012). They represent a rare safe port in the storm.

It is necessary to discuss the role and importance of community-based organizations, including faith-based organizations. Jackson-Elmoore, Hula, and Reese (2011) argue that faith-based organizations have a significant role to play in shaping civil society, and addressing social justice issues plays a significant part in shaping social change agendas. These organizations devote considerable time, energy, and financial resources to youth programming and can collaborate with other organizations in coalitions, service delivery, and social action agendas (Pipes & Ebaugh, 2002; Watts & Flanagan, 2007).

Faith-based organizations are part of the community landscape in addressing social injustice through a variety of approaches from policy advocacy to social action (Flores, 2012; Goddard & Myers, 2013; Mosley, 2013; Swarts, 2011). One study, for example, found a significant relationship between religious attendance and social change volunteering, a natural extension of an embrace of social justice values (Guo et al., 2013).

Hondagneu-Sotelo's book (2008) *God's Heart Has No Borders: How Religious Activists Are Working for Immigrant Rights* chronicles the important role that a religious community played in moving an immigrant-rights social justice agenda forward. Faith-based institutions, as a result, can be expected to continue to play influential roles in this area. Youth ministries, as noted later on in this book, can sponsor social justice learning and engagement initiatives.

Youth-serving organizations, in particular, have the obligation to positively help transform youth in ways that youth wish to be transformed (Blyth, 2006; Miller, Kobes & Forney, 2008; Purcell & Beck, 2010; Shiller, 2013), and arguably none more so than those that provide youth advocacy or foster youth activism (Forman, 2013; Kwon, 2008; Scott et al., 2006) or focus on recreation (Pryor & Outley, 2014), for example.

Youth-focused, community-based organizations fill an important void in the lives of marginalized youth because schools, the one institution where they spend a major portion of their lives, are often toxic to their identity and social being (Ardizzone, 2007). Adults exercising their leadership within these programs goes a long way towards having youth needs met and creating "socially just" spaces (Perkins et al., 2007; Suyemoto, Day & Schwartz, 2014; Hill, 2014; Walker, 2011).

This transformation can only occur if these organizations encourage breaking out of conventional views of engaging in youth-adult interaction that seriously undermine youth autonomy and social agency, resulting in further exploitation of youth under the guise of empowerment (O'Donoghue & Strobel, 2007; Quane & Rankin, 2006; Westheimer, 2011). One youth organization found that organizing agencies fostered increased civic activism and identity development when compared to other types of youth organizations (Gambone et al., 2006).

Empowerment represents a critical dimension in engaging youth (Cammarota, 2014; Morrel-Samuels et al., 2015), and this concept must be expanded to include interpersonal relationships (Christens, 2012, p. 114):

> Psychological empowerment has been theorized as a construct with emotional, behavioral and cognitive components. Yet, many studies have stressed that empowerment processes are contingent on interpersonal relationships. Moreover, theory suggests that power is developed and exercised through relationships . . . [and] makes the case that expanding our conceptions of psychological empowerment through the addition of a relational component can enhance our understanding of psychological empowerment and the effectiveness of empowerment-oriented community practice.

Empowerment is multifaceted and its potential can only be reached through an understanding of how a relationship based on mutual trust and respect shapes a transformative experience.

Anderson and Sandmann (2009, p. 1) see adults playing critical roles in fostering youth empowerment in youth serving organizations:

> Throughout the United States, there are countless organizations designed to develop the leadership of young people. These organizations aim to equip young people with the skills and abilities for making decisions and carrying out organizational responsibilities. Such leadership development is a result of sharing leadership and empowering young people to take the reins of the organization. However, in many cases we find adults sharing meaningless roles and responsibilities . . . It is important for us as practitioners to reflect on our organizations and our leadership practices that lead to or inhibit youth engagement.

There is no lack of community-based organizations serving youth. However, how many provide youth with an opportunity to exercise power in determining their goals and activities is a different conversation.

These organizations must do outreach to newcomer youth, which is a group that can be easily overlooked because of their documented status, and incorporate them into significant roles (DeFilippis & Faust, 2014). How well youth organizations engage LGBTQ youth, too, should not be overlooked because of the limited options they have in seeking affirming organizations willing to engage in social justice causes with them and on their behalf (Gastic & Johnson, 2009; Niblet, 2015), particularly when taking into account the role of intersectionality in critical analysis (Daley et al., 2008; Thinking, 2015).

Research based on a Belgium study found that youth membership in organizations increases the chances of engagement in social protest (Somma, 2010). Quintelier (2008, p. 355) addressed the type of organization that fosters the greatest amount of political participation as a result of civic engagement:

> Young people who are members of several organizations are more active in politics, while spending a greater amount of time in one organization does not increase level of political participation. Cultural, deliberative and help organizations are more successful than expressive, religious–ethnic and youth groups in fostering political engagement. Finally, organizations that allow young people to take up a leadership role, or to organize activities, encourage participation in political activities.

No one organization can possibly meet all youth needs, and there must be an openness to have youth participating in multiple organizations.

Socially connected youth, as opposed to those who are isolated or alienated, are more likely to be a part of a community's social fabric and willing to help others, making service-learning and civic engagement attractive to them. To accomplish this goal, youth must feel that they are respected and their voices sought in decision-making and acted upon by adults (Mitra, Serrierem & Kirshner, 2013). The methods used to achieve this aim must not muffle youth concerns, even though they may make adults uncomfortable through their exercise of free speech and the vocabulary they wish to use (Arnot & Swartz, 2012; Morsillo & Prilleltensky, 2007).

It is important to emphasize that there is a dramatic difference between the concepts of participation and inclusion, which are often used interchangeably. Quick and Feldman (2011) discuss the importance of distinguishing between participation and inclusion, with inclusion resulting in efforts at engaging in meaningful decision-making, valuing multiple ways of knowing, and sustaining temporal openness. Inclusion facilitates addressing social multiple issues. Voice, however, does not necessarily equate to actions, although voice is obviously an essential element for engagement in decision-making.

The same distinction must be made concerning "community-run" and "community-based" organizations. These two concepts, too, are often used interchangeably. In the former, decision-making is a shared process; in the latter, voices may be sought but not necessarily acted upon (Orsini, 2010). The label *community-based* may give the illusion of shared political power, but in all likelihood it means that the organization just happens to be geographically based in the community.

Taft and Gordon (2013) critically examine how adults may unintentionally undermine youth activist efforts at achieving social justice by creating mechanisms such as youth councils, a very common approach towards getting youth input and to direct or restrict their voices and actions into activities acceptable to adults: "Youth activists put forth a theory of democracy that emphasizes authority and impact, not just voice; they understand democracy as representing collective concerns and perceive youth councils as elitist and nonrepresentative; and they emphasize the value of controversy and contentious politics while expressing anxiety that youth councils can function as modes of social control that tame and channel youth dissent, rather than opportunities to foster youth political power."

Community-based organizations are the stewards of democracy at the local level and must witness and experience the brunt of youth social protest, too. Democracy, too, applies to organizations that have emerged to support social activism and care must be undertaken in these institutions to ensure that all voices have a place to be heard and taken into account in the decision-making process (DeFilippis, Fisher & Shragge, 2010; Hensby, Sibthorpe & Driver, 2012). Participation, not unexpectedly, has been found to increase youth voice, ownership, and outcomes (Barnett & Brennan, 2006; Mitra, 2006; Ohmer, 2007).

Guion-Utsler (2013) studied how students develop social justice allies in dealing with issues of oppression in critical social-learning and civic engagement—based at a university but applicable to any setting—and found five significant factors that support this goal: (1) self-understanding; (2) reflexivity; (3) recognizing the validity of multiple perspectives; (4) engaging with diversity; and (5) accepting personal responsibility for changing unjust systems. These factors are not surprising when youth engagement is grounded within values that emphasize social justice and agency.

Good intentions on the part of community practitioners and adults in leadership positions are not enough when engaging youth (Wearing, 2011). Further, youth are not monolithic and no one individual can represent the sentiments of all youth in a community because "youth" is a broad category that must consider a myriad of factors. Democracy, after all, has majority rule but must show consideration to the minority.

It is fitting to end this section with a quote from Barnett and Brennan (2006), who offer recommendations for how community-based organizations can help youth integrate into the everyday workings and decision-making of organizations:

> Consider new ways to involve youth and allow them to provide input in decision-making, problem solving and action-taking activities within local organizations, non-profits, volunteer groups, youth programs and non-governmental organization. This may include putting youth on advisory

boards, giving them voting privileges, and serving on committees. This step reflects the significance of local networks and may require more active collaboration with youth than before in order to engage them in ways that will open doors for them to contribute. As youth engage in more sustained positive relationships with adults, other youth, and community organizations, they will learn that they are valued citizens of their communities.

These recommendations are feasible but require a paradigm shift, which is rarely easy to achieve; however, when it occurs, it brings forth excitement and prodigious rewards.

Conceptualizing youth as assets brings the potential to positively transform communities and society; viewing youth as threats has the potential to achieve the opposite, including expanding correctional budgets (Harries, 2012; Song, 2014; Williams et al., 2014; Watson et al., 2015; Wilson, 2012). The importance of trust in social exchanges reinforces the potential for profound transformation (Marschall & Stolle, 2004).

Book Outline

This book consists of two major sections consisting of nine chapters and an epilogue: Section 1, "Setting the Context," which consists of five chapters, sets a conceptual context and provides a series of definitions, historical background, and key practice rewards and challenges. There has been an explosion of scholarly and practice interest in youth social activism; this section will highlight some of the latest and most significant developments in this field, setting the stage for examination of three specific youth social justice movements in the United States and the use of service-learning and civic engagement, although efforts in other countries will be included to show the worldwide appeal of youth social activism.

Section 2, "Reflections From the Field," consists of four chapters and an epilogue and addresses three (immigrant-rights, environmental, and food justice) social movements, drawing important lessons for practitioners and academics using youth civic engagement and service-learning. A series of brief case illustrations tie theory and community practice, making connections to improve practice and move the field forward. Brief case illustrations (versus lengthy, in-depth cases) allow for a wide variety of examples to be used to highlight the broad possibilities for critical/social justice service-learning and civic engagement initiatives.

Conclusion

This chapter expands the world of youth social activism and youth community practice involving service-learning and civic engagement with a focus on the United States, in addition to outlining how this book unfolds. Youth activism, including their role in social movements nationally, will continue to play a prominent role in this country, particularly as helping professions see value in fostering this form of protest. Service-learning and civic engagement is enjoying tremendous worldwide popularity and has the potential to use social justice-inspired values to transform the lives of marginalized youth and their communities.

This book bridges an existing literature gap on youth social activism, service-learning, and civic engagement, drawing important parallels among various types of youth social activism and grounding them within an urban context to increase understanding of the interrelationship between rights issues and their differences. Important questions will be raised on areas of confusion and tension for adult allies.

The importance of youth in these movements has generally been overlooked by scholars and the popular press, and, when addressed, it is often done from a very narrow focus. Youth have a place at the table of social activism, without limits to their influence, locally and globally. In other words, they have every right to set the table and determine the menu.

These movements were also selected because of their significant overlaps and appeal to urban youth of color. On the surface, these social issues appear to be distinct movements with minimal or no relationship to each other. Yet, they share much in common, with implications for youth engaging in age-specific and intergenerational social activism. Community practice must foster youth social activism, and service-learning and civic engagement represents vehicles for achieving social justice. Those embracing these concepts will embark on a journey with many twists and turns. There is no denying that our ultimate destination is both exciting and also imagined with some trepidation, but it is a journey that is worth taking and must be taken.

2
URBAN YOUTH AS A FOCUS

Introduction

A nation consists of many different demographic groups, with each representing a unique potential for contributions, experiences, needs, and views of life. In a democratic society, each of these segments share rights and privileges that allow them to assume a degree of safety and respect, along with opportunities to make contributions and dream about their futures. These dreams take on greater importance among those who have faced significant barriers in accessing the requisite resources to fulfill their aspirations and are cognizant of the struggles the previous generation faced, connecting past, present, and expected future (Yang & Alpermann, 2014).

The concept of hope, which can be expressed as dreams, extends far beyond career aspirations and material possessions and consists of many different and intangible elements, and it is important to recognize this (Aaltonen, 2013). Aspirations and expectations have also been substituted for youth hopes and dreams (Walsh, 2012; Yowell, 2002). Unfortunately, fears and nightmares are also a part of this discourse. Hopelessness is a dangerous and ever-present condition—one that must be addressed head-on in any form of community practice and scholarship.

Bishop and Willis (2014) conceptualize youth hope into four discrete but interrelated categories: (1) as a prime source of goals and happiness; (2) as enabling the pursuit of their goals; (3) as an asset to draw on when much else is lost; and (4) as a necessary and integral part of life. Youth also view hope as being closely associated with the availability of social support and positive social relationships to help achieve their goals (Larson & Tran, 2014). These relationships involve both peers and adults.

Denying rights undermines the fundamental premises a democratic society is founded upon: that all people are created equal. This ideal often serves as the foundation for the laws and policies governing a nation and development of a consciousness of fairness. When rights are violated, the aggrieved have legal and extralegal recourses, and engaging in social action is a viable approach for them to exercise. Fairness often resonates for youth in how they apply social justice to circumstances in their lives (Porfilio & Gorlewski, 2012). Unequal and "unfair" treatment resonates for youth.

Powers and Faden (2006, p. ix) set the stage for asking who should be the focus of attention and priority in the seeking of social justice in this country: "What makes any group of special interest within a theory of justice is contingent upon the totality of social arrangements that, in the aggregate, contribute to the combined adverse effect of various socially situated groups and ask the question: Under conditions in which various socially situated groups interact with one another under conditions of inequality, what inequalities matter the most?" Urban youth must be the focus of attention and priority in any quest for social justice, with service-learning and civic engagement offering practitioners accepted ways of using social justice values in shaping these approaches for reaching urban youth.

Social justice campaigns are not exempt from perpetuating injustices in the process of seeking justice. However, a social movement that systematically silences a major segment is at best misguided and not true to its central mission of eradicating unequal access, and the consequences resulting from society's ill treatment of those who are undocumented newcomers, the environment, and its food production, for example. Service-learning and civic engagement, too, can "miss the boat" and not embrace social justice goals, further marginalizing youth.

The undermining of social movement segments accentuates disempowerment and undercuts the moral high ground of these efforts (e.g., ethical, righteous, principled, virtuous) (Stewart et al., 2012). How can social protesters criticize a policy or institution when they themselves engage in discriminatory actions? The moral high ground of any justice effort is compromised when this occurs. Practitioners can rectify this exclusion through service-learning and civic engagement projects addressing social justice and youth empowerment.

Evans (2007, p. 693) specifically focuses on marginalized youth being disempowered by adults:

> Unfortunately, young people have no voice or influence in many of the contexts in which they find themselves. Furthermore, teenagers are often unequipped and under supported to participate fully and feel like they are making meaningful contributions to society. This is especially the case for young people who are disadvantaged or members of a minority groups. . . . [concluding] that they feel a stronger self-described sense of

community in contexts where they experience voice and resonance, some power and influence and adequate adult support and challenge.

These findings should not surprise adults with experiences in working with youth; they highlight the potential pitfalls of engaging youth without a clear embrace of their inclusion in decision-making.

This chapter provides a multi-faceted perspective on urban youth and why social activism has profound meaning in their lives and potential to achieve community transformation through service-learning and civic engagement. This grounding is essential in order to understand young people's past, current, and potential future contributions to social justice efforts.

Definition of Youth

This is a good juncture to ask the question of who are *youth* and how do they get categorized as falling into this group? The reader may at first glance wonder why this question needs to be addressed in this book; a definition of *youth* can probably be provided in a brief sentence. However, the definition is complex, with legal, social, psychological, political, cultural, and geographical (urban versus rural) considerations, and many a scholarly career exists because of the complexity of this definition (Furlong, 2009; Ho, Clarke & Dougherty (2015).

Definitions are contingent upon their social circumstances (Bucholtz, 2002), and who is asking and answering the question. A common way of defining *youth* is to focus on an age range or age cut-off, with voting age (18 years) being a popular cut-off. Others may argue that the cut-off should be 21 years because of the preponderance of legal statutes re-enforcing this age.

Any discussion of youth development and youth-led intervention brings into consideration critical socio-cultural factors influenced by national boundaries. In the United States, the youth-led field generally thinks of youth as being 13 to 18 or even 21 years of age. This definition differs considerably in other countries, particularly when addressing the outermost reaches, with youth being defined as up to the age of 29 years old, for example.

Such an age range has tremendous consequences for youth and social justice campaigns. *Youth* can also be thought of as a state of mind, which advertising agencies have been quick to recognize for marketing products. The question of at what age does youth cease to be "youth" is one that has implications for society and for youth participation in immigrant-rights, food, and environmental justice movements (Hine, 2000).

Youth is a distinctive demographic group but one with wide-ranging social connotations; historically, a member of it has often been viewed as an "adult in waiting," an "adult want-to-be," or a "miniature adult." The concept of "emerging adults" has received attention in an attempt to portray youth in a more positive image, but again the goal assumed is to become adults (Clevenger & Cadge,

2014). Efforts have imposed a form of adulthood level, creating an identity that, according to McAdams (2013), "selectively reconstructs the past and imagines the future in such a way as to provide life with purpose, meaning, and a sense of temporal coherence."

Such views place youth in secondary status to that of adults, with their definition always in relation to "adults." The social construction of "youth" or "adolescence" is predicated on critical notions and assumptions that are not fixed in stone. It is subject to interpretation and debate and must be contextualized to have significant meaning. Youth are not one-dimensional and can be considered as complex as adults (Lewis, 2011).

The youth development field has the goal of helping young people transition to adulthood as one of its primary goals (Delgado, 2002). There is little dispute in the field about the importance of civic engagement aiding this transition (Flanagan & Levine, 2010, p. 160): "The civic engagement of young adults—whether in the form of joining community groups, volunteering to help neighbors, or leading grassroots efforts to gain civil rights—is important to the health and performance of democracy. It is also important for personal growth and identity formation during the transition to adulthood."

We must strive to maintain focus on the importance of a "here and now" perspective on youth. Youth involvement and benefits derived from participation in social justice campaigns must emphasize present gains and rewards. True, future benefits should never be ignored. However, immediacy must "rule," so to speak. It would be unfair to think that adults are always willing to sacrifice immediate gains in search for future gains. Adults have had an extended history upon which to reflect and youth have not had that benefit.

Youth Deficit Perspective

Youth are a significant demographic segment in society and this takes on added meaning because of the symbolism and definition that most societies ascribe to this age group and the transition from youth to adult (Bomer et al., 2009; Tyyskä, 2014). Homeless or street children are a case in point because the vast majority of research on this group focuses on their deficits, problems, and needs. However, Bender and colleagues (2007), for example, found that an assets or strengths perspective revealed that these youth possess personal strengths, "street smarts," and an extensive knowledge of informal resources that assist them in navigating street life.

"Street smarts" is a concept that is underutilized for helping adults understand and appreciate how urban youth successfully socially navigate their hostile surroundings (Petrucka et al., 2014; Theron & Malindi, 2010). The knowledge and skills inherent in urban youth being street smart must not be dismissed by adults. Instead, we must endeavor to learn more about how these "smarts" get acquired and manifested in daily lived experience.

An adult view of youth depends upon where we sit in society. If we sit on Madison Avenue, they become an attractive marketing group that we seek to segment in an effort to meet a tremendous thirst for consumption of goods and services, which they are happy to oblige (Cahir & Werner, 2013; Kehily, 2014). If we sit in a position of teacher or mentor, they are our main constituency group, and we must prepare them to assume productive adult roles when they transition to this life stage. If we work in the entertainment music business, they are probably the most important buyer of our product, and we will sing their praises, no pun intended (Buckingham, 2014).

Finally, if we sit within the criminal justice system, we view them as clients and eventual prisoners with a host of drug-related addictions and violence-prone behavior, and when they are released, we need to protect the public and society from harm by them. There is no doubt that adults have a vested interest in youth, not to mention the hopes we have for our children.

Unfortunately, with rare exceptions, we associate youth with sex, drugs, rock and roll; gangs; babies having babies; poor impulse control; being very, if not totally, dependent upon adult guidance and education; and, in general, a group to be suspicious of, monitor, and control (Brake, 2013; Tilton, 2010, 2013; Waiton, 2013). In essence, it is a generation that society is straddled with or may consider "lost" (Corcoran, 2011), and one that may eventually threaten a democratic society's existence.

Costanza-Chock (2012, p. 5) provides a counter-narrative (oppositional behavior) to prevailing adult views of youth: "Youth are often dismissed for a lack of civic engagement, or attacked for being disruptive. Yet disruption of oppressive laws, norms, and practices is a crucial aspect of all liberatory movements: think of the struggle to end slavery, or to gain suffrage for women. We should recognize and respect young people as potentially powerful social movement actors, and allocate resources to support, amplify, and extend their impact." The conception of youth as possessing social agency counters the view of youth as inept.

The "radicalization" label has received increased saliency to describe a particular segment of youth (Corb & Grozelle, 2014; Keil, 2009). These images are both national and local in scope (Bernier, 2011), and they feed into racial and socio-economic class stereotypes and narratives involving low-income/low youth of color residing in highly segregated urban communities (McInerney & Smyth, 2014). This calls for a counter-narrative on the part of youth (Campbell, 2014; Rogers et al., 2014) and an explanation of why youth oppositional resistance has such saliency.

The subject of youth and social capital is one with a large social science following (Calvert, Emery & Kinsey, 2013; Holland, 2012; Stanton-Salazar, 2011; Suhonen, 2014). Bislet (2014, p. 847) provides an example of youth bonding and social capital, a concept that has great currency:

> Social capital is fast becoming a salient and exciting area of youth study. While debates about social capital during youth usually focus on its

presumed positive consequences, there is a current trend to label certain forms of networking, particularly bonding networks, as "perverse", "bad" or "dark". What is often referred to as the "down side" of social capital. Consequently, certain populations and increasingly young people who rely heavily on bonding networks to "get on" and "get ahead" in life are being labelled as social capital deficient at best or deviant at worst.

It is important that adults embrace the concept of social capital and modify it to reflect youth views as opposed to imposing our adult views of this concept and applying it to youth without the necessary modifications (Billett, 2012).

This negative identity, or what Goffman (2009) calls a "spoiled identity," however, can be labeled as deficit oriented and does not open up the possibility of viewing youth as contributing members of society (Sealey-Ruiz & Greene, 2011; Wheeler, 2014). Adults may even view youth wishing to remain in that stage indefinitely rather than face the harsh realities of being an adult (Mary, 2014), although urban youth of color may not have the luxury of exercising this so-called option (Ladson & Billings, 2011). We view them as adults-in-waiting at best rather than assets that can be enhanced and tapped in service to their communities and society (Hoffman-Kipp, 2008).

The pervasiveness of a deficit perspective and the immense influence it has in shaping adult attitudes, behaviors, and social policies towards youth cannot be underestimated, although some youth, fortunately, have not internalized this negative and disempowering narrative, as evidenced by their oppositional resistance to being controlled by adults (Camangian, 2013; Teruelle, 2011). This view is insidious and permeates how many adults in authority think and act in virtually all spheres of public policies.

Urban youth often represent sizable population groups and are both a source of crisis and hope for the future (Tilton, 2010). Unfortunately, the perception of a source of crisis prevails. However, when youth take an oppositional activist stance and identity, adults generally do not view their actions from a democratic participatory point of view, or even recognize their actions in some cases (Giroux, 2011), representing a travesty of justice.

As noted in the introductory chapter, youth are a nation's future and how we view, invest, and treat them in this life stage will have lifelong implications for the nation as they age out and enter adulthood. Youth as possessing strengths or assets is a counter-narrative to a deficit perspective (Masten, Liebkind & Hernandez, 2012; Urban, Lewin-Bizan & Lerner, 2009; Valois, 2014). Thus, an investment in youth results in an investment in the nation, with a future adult population better prepared to be a vital part of the nation's leadership and citizenry (Belfield & Levin, 2012; Chaaban & Cunningham, 2011).

A disinvestment in youth, which is often associated with neoliberal or neoconservative politics, in turn, results in a population age group ill-prepared to confront the challenges of the twenty-first century. In those cases with the most severe consequences, the result is a population group that requires significant resources focused on remedial or custodial care, against a backdrop of governmental budget cuts (Kennelly, 2011; Klodawsky, Aubry & Farrell, 2006; Vander Schee & Kline, 2013).

A youth deficit perspective views them as a financial detriment while an asset focus results in viewing money spent on them as an investment in human capital (Bridgeland & Milano, 2012; Walker & Saito, 2011). These dynamically different points of view wield influences on consequences and rights. An asset perspective stresses that youth have abilities that must be mobilized whenever possible. A deficit perspective translates into this age group being totally dependent upon adults.

It is critical that adults systematically challenge tacit assumptions pertaining to youth and no more so than when regarding marginalized urban youth (Amodeo & Collins, 2007; Weiner, 2006). A shift in paradigms from deficit to assets must result in policies and practice (Graham, 2011; Warren, Mira & Nikundiwe, 2008).

Historical Overview

A small number of scholars have devoted considerable attention to studying youth from an historical viewpoint and draw important lessons for how we, as adults and society, view youth today (Jones, 2009). An understanding of the role and importance of current day youth activism is best appreciated when present-day activities are grounded within an historical context (Costanza-Chock, 2012; Ellis-Williams, 2007; Musgrove, 2013).

A fair and accurate historical account and context, however, is difficult to uncover because of the biases that most historians have towards youth and their role in this nation's major social justice campaigns and movements, particularly youth groups who are undervalued. In addition, there is a desperate need to look at them from a multifaceted historical viewpoint in order to have a comprehensive picture. If they are invisible, overlooking them is quite natural for adults who shape and record knowledge. There is a need for a shift in paradigms to rectify these oversights.

Proehl's (2012, p. 171) comments on the role of children and youth in nation building address the potential role youth may have played historically: "Over the past decade, scholarship on the history of childhood has often examined the complex relationship between youth, nation-making, and historical change . . . [challenging] the widespread perception of children as passive agents in the development of American history, culture, and the modern nation-state. In addition to demonstrating how adult representations of children in literature, art, photography, media, and other cultural forms have instigated social change, they have also revealed how children, both living and represented, may function as historical actors."

The thought of children and youth as major historical actors rather than as passive subjects is certainly radical and worthy of even more scholarship.

The scholarship on this subject, as noted in the introductory chapter, is starting to reflect youths' important contributions to communities and society and fill in major historical gaps in the literature—which have compromised our understanding and appreciation of their contributions in the past—and set the stage for our increased appreciation of their present and potential future contributions. Youth capturing and recording their lived experiences, particularly their involvement in major social protest events, will help rectify their missing perspective, particularly at the local level (Delgado, 2015a). Teelucksingh and Masuda (2014), for example, advocate for the use of photo-elicited interviewing as a form of historical research that can provide a nuanced picture and interpretation of social events.

Youth social activism, as evidenced in China's Tiananmen Square, Native American Youth Movements, Anti-Apartheid Movements, Anti-Vietnam War Movement, Stonewall Rebellion, and Civil Rights Movement, for example, illustrates the scope of their interests and the intensity of their involvement in helping to shape the world around them on a national and international scale (Lewis, 2009; Juris & Pleyers, 2009), even though this age group is not highlighted in the academic and popular literature.

Costanza-Chock (2012, p. 1) echoes this important observation concerning the invisibility of youth in major social movement literature:

> Young people are often key actors in powerful social movements that transform the course of human history. Indeed, youth have been deeply important to every progressive social movement, including the United States Civil Rights movement, the transnational LGBTQ movement, successive waves of feminism, environmentalism and environmental justice, the labor, antiwar, and immigrant rights movements, and more. In each of these cases, young people took part in many ways, including through the appropriation of the "new media" tools of their time, which they used to create, circulate, and amplify movement voices and stories. Yet today, youth are often framed in the mass media as, at best, apathetic, disengaged, and removed from civic action.

Clearly, youth are a vital and very significant element in society and in the seeking of social change. Recognition of these contributions, however, has robbed society of an accurate accounting of their importance.

Efforts at seeking social justice have often resulted in socio-political repercussions that have comprised their education, health, and safety; further curtailed their rights; and even cost youth their lives. These consequences, however, did not curtail their drive and desire to demonstrate and seek social justice for themselves and others, demonstrating resolve and competencies that are often ignored by adults.

Social justice campaigns and movements often have intended and unintended consequences for those who play active roles in these change efforts.

Eills-Williams (2007, p. 107) characterizes the 1950s through 1970s as a golden era of social activism in the United States for African American youth: "There is a nostalgic, even romantic remembrance, of an era filled with youth led boycotts, sit-ins, walk outs and protests . . . The African American community celebrated youth activism in schools, churches and civic organizations. Youth were on the forefront, fighting for social justice."

Youth activism takes on great prominence in the case of African Americans because of a high percentage of youth in their population, the social conditions they face on a daily basis, and the limited outlets that they have to exercise their rights in a structured and peaceful manner. In essence, formal civic engagement options are severely limited in seeking social justice (Franklin, 2014b), necessitating the creation of innovative ways of engaging these and other marginalized youth in meaningful social justice pursuits. Porfilio and Gorlewski (2012), for example, advocate for using the arts as an innovative and attractive means for enhancing youth citizenship with a potential for achieving significant social change.

Social activism is a viable alternative to conventional civic engagement and social-learning activities, which, although of importance, may not have the cache and meaning that a social injustice-inspired effort would have that collectively brings youth into alliance with others facing similar circumstances and challenges. The power of the group creates collective learning, collective identity, memory, and social capital that can be harnessed for collective good (D'Ambrosi & Massoli, 2012).

The concept of the collective in a society that favors and glorifies individualism may be hard to fathom on the part of adults since "American Exceptionalism" is predicated on individualism. However, in many cultures represented by urban youth of color, collectivity has a power that is unmatched and cannot be ignored in order to understand youth social activism.

Demographics and Youth

There are few practitioners who welcome an opportunity to dwell deeply into demographic statistical profiles, trends, and charts. This reluctance does not take away from the need to do so. Demographics provide important insights as to the major reasons why this nation must focus on youth, particularly urban youth of color. Demographic profiles and trends assist a nation to appreciate the current and projected composition of its population, helping to determine its assets and needs. No demographic sector should be underestimated in its potential to contribute as well as receive from society.

Demographics have far-reaching policy implications. Nordås and Davenport (2013) put forth the position that large youth cohorts, which are sometimes referred to as "youth bulges," can make a nation more concerned or susceptible to anti-state political violence by youth. As a consequence, governments are aware of this potential threat and will enact policies and efforts to prevent youth from engaging in social activism that threatens those in positions of authority. This reaction can be thought of as a form of "moral panic" (Goode & Ben-Yehuda, 2010) because governments fear the potential of youth to create social instability (Cincotta, 2013). More specifically, males within these bulges are perceived to represent the greatest threat (Weber, 2013).

Youth bulges can have potential economic consequences because of the increased competition for employment, housing, and other resources in society (Hart & Gullan, 2010). This nation's baby boomers are a testament to how a bulge creates competition (Delgado, 2015b). Increased competition, in turn, can result in disillusionment, tension, and eventual conflict. Youth without unfulfilled dreams translates into youth with a lack of faith in society's institutions and its elected officials.

Cities play pivotal roles in social justice movements (Miller & Nicholls, 2013). In the case of youth of color, their concentration in the nation's cities has to be considered an asset in moving social justice issues forward on national agendas (Cauce et al., 2011). For example, it is estimated that one out of every seven urban-based adolescents and young adults (16–24 years of age) is unemployed in the United States (Burd-Sharps & Lewis, 2013).

Demographic on Cities: Youth of Color

Demographics must be grounded within a global context in order to appreciate the meaning of these numbers at a national level. This contextualization serves to heighten the importance of trends (U.S. Agency of International Development, 2014). In late 2011, it was estimated that the global population reached seven billion inhabitants, with half under the age of 30 and 1.7 billion aged 10–24 years. It is estimated that there are 1.1 billion youth ages 15 to 24 in the world, the largest number in human history, with a potential to achieve significant social change beyond their numbers.

According to the 2010 U.S. Census Bureau (2010b), there were 42.2 million in this age category in America. However, this age group is even more prevalent among African Americans with 6.4 million (6,398,000) (U.S. Census Bureau, 2010b), Asians (1.7 million, or 1,740,000) (U.S. Census Bureau, 2010a), and Latinos (7.9 million, or 7,914,000) (U.S. Census Bureau, 2010c). It is easy to see why youth of color, particularly those in urban centers, represent a vast and untapped source for involvement and leadership in social movements.

The browning and graying of the United States will have profound and unprecedented implications for the nation as a whole but particularly for its urban centers (Sundstrom, 2008). The convergence of these two trends creates two distinctive bulges. Baby boomers among older adults will create panic because of fears of how they will bankrupt the nation's Social Security and medical systems (Delgado, 2015b). The youth of color bulge will be addressed in Chapter 3.

Further, when youth are viewed from a geographical or spatial-analysis perspective, critical dimensions are highlighted on why certain social issues go beyond being viewed locally, and take on national, if not international, significance when examining social movements and social activism, for example. Globalization is a phenomenon not restricted to economics.

The concentration of social sequences, such as excessively high rates related to arrests, drug-related problems, school drop-out, health inequities, high under- and unemployment, and homelessness, for example, are often highly concentrated within distinct urban geographical boundaries. The "inner city" is one of the more popular names given to these geographical areas.

Youth-Adult Partnerships

The construct of youth-adult partnerships is considered vague. We need to rectify this shortcoming and make these relationships an important part of research and community practice with youth. Zeldin, Christens, and Powers (2013) propose that these relationships consist of four core elements (authentic decision making, natural mentors, reciprocity, and community connectedness). How each of these elements is addressed is influenced by context.

Youth-adult partnerships built upon a foundation of meaningful roles— although not to be equated with equality—and mutual respect, helps engender trust, a critical element in social justice endeavors (Arnold, Dolenc & Wells, 2008; Mitra, 2009). The role of trust and social capital are indispensable in the development of an understanding and fostering of youth social activism and other forms of civic engagement (Hart & Gullan, 2010; Zeldin, 2004).

Youth-adult partnerships/collaborations are often advocated as a key strategy in community building (Camino, 2000), although they are certainly not limited to this arena (Krauss et al., 2013). For example, youth resiliency has been found to increase in youth-adult partnerships (Ungar, 2013). The potential of youth-adult partnerships is increased when the adult partners are in their early twenties and not far removed from their adolescent years (Kirshner, 2007). They can serve as an important bridge between youth and much older adults.

The nature of these relationships, and how best to unfold them to maximize youth benefits, is a subject that is receiving increased scholarly and practice attention. Although the benefits of a successful collaboration between youth and adults are understood, it does not mean that challenges are not present. Zeldin and Leidheiser (2014, p. 6) note, for example, that there are a number of significant challenges to effectively implementing quality youth-adult partnerships (Y-AP): "There exists a broad array of theory and research identifying the cultural, institutional, and historical barriers to Y-AP in the United States. Our culture tends to separate persons of different ages thus minimizing the opportunity for youth voice and intergenerational collaboration."

Adults can play influential roles as youth allies (Nygreen, Kwon & Sanchez, 2006). Adult allies with past, or current, experiences in social justice campaigns can help reinforce and create a sense of purpose and empowerment in youth-led campaigns (Checkoway, 2011; Goodnough, 2014; Gordon, 2010; Travis Jr, & Maston, 2014). When youth engage with adults in partnerships where they feel they are respected and their voices heard and taken into account, they derive greater benefits from participation in organized activities (Serido, Borden & Perkins, 2011).

There are numerous challenges in youth-adult partnerships, with three standing out, emphasizing the importance of relationships and decision-making (Camino, 2005): (1) adults embracing the position that youth should do everything of importance; (2) a "hands-off" mentality that has adults essentially get out of the way and turn over power to youth; and (3) the focus on youth as the marked category. Effective youth-adult relationships require that adult staff receive requisite training and support (Zeldin & Leidheiser, 2014).

Zeldin, Camino and Mook (2005, p. 121) speak to youth-adult partnerships and the challenges in making these partnerships function and make a series of recommendations: "(1) gain clarity and consensus on the purpose of Y-AP, (2) mobilize and coordinate a diverse range of stakeholders, (3) create favorable narratives about Y-AP, (4) construct theories and stories of organizational change, (5) affirmatively address issues of power, and (6) institutionalize new roles for youth." They go on to note that although it is difficult to come by, time for reflective dialogue is essential. The quality of these interactions, and the need to build in ongoing evaluation to ensure that reflective dialogue occurs and is informed by the latest scholarship on the subject, are also crucial (Camino, 2005; Jones & Perkins, 2005; Waterman, 2014).

Anderson and Sandmann address collaboration and the role that empowerment can play in maximizing the benefits to be derived from this relationship (2009, p. 6):

> Viewing empowerment through the lens of youth-adult partnerships provides an opportunity to develop a model of empowering behaviors specific to this context. The inherent power and responsibilities of adults in the youth-adult partnership require the empowerment theories, which are based on business models, to be tailored for the youth-adult context. Based on the literature of empowerment and youth-adult partnerships as well as personal experience, we posit a five-construct model of empowering practices for youth-adult partnerships. For the youth-adult partnership context, we have defined empowering practices as actions taken by adults for the purpose of enabling youth to execute leadership in the organization.

Given the definition, the following five constructs were identified: 1) fostering self-efficacy, 2) setting a context for action, 3) structuring the task, 4) creating a sense of ownership, and 5) coaching for performance.

Youth need to dictate when and how adults participate in these social action campaigns. Delp, Brown, and Domenzain (2005) report on a pilot youth leadership program that stresses classroom and internships for youth (service-learning) and social action on workplace and community health issues, which places adults in positions as allies. The creation of places and spaces for youth to enhance their capacities in an affirming and empowering manner sets a requisite context for their leadership potential to emerge and be sustained (Blanchet-Cohen & Brunson, 2014).

Youth Activism and Gender as a Focal Point

A multifaceted view of youth activists is not possible without an understanding of how gender influences participation in social action and praxis, for example (Lindsey, 2015). There are numerous aspects to a social justice campaign and demographic factors, including the role of gender, and influences, can unfold throughout what is referred to as lived experiences (Irwin, Edwards & Tamburello, 2015; Yates, 2015); how these factors psychologically influence participant experiences and takeaways can vary (Christens & Speer, 2015).These "discourses" are not necessarily harmonious, and internal tensions and conflicts are a natural part of these efforts, with participant characteristics playing a role in how these tensions materialize (Pellow & Brehm, 2015).

Unfortunately, our view of how demographic characteristics influence participation in social protest is limited. For example, the role and influence of peers in political socialization of youth is under-researched and this should not come as any great surprise (Gordon & Taft, 2011). Hyde (2015) focuses on the experiences of women activists within social work and concludes that they have been virtually ignored in the scholarly literature, representing a serious gap in our comprehensive understanding of how gender influences social protest. Unfortunately, this gap is not restricted to social work.

Gordon (2008, p. 31) specifically addresses the role of gender in participation and visibility of youth as political actors within their communities, with profound implications for how political consciousness gets manifested in social protests: "Specifically, the gendered ways in which youth conceptualize and negotiate parental power influences whether or not, and in what ways, youth can emerge as visible agents of social change in their communities. For girl activists, there is more of a marked discontinuity between their political ideals and their political action because of their conflicts with parental power than for boys."

Youth Leadership in Social Activism

Adults may grow to accept youth in social activist roles, but taking it one step further and thinking of youth in leadership roles in social action campaigns and social movements may be too much to imagine or accept. However, youth as leaders in social change is a logical extension of youth as social activists (de los

Angeles Torres, 2013). Further, youth leadership must not be framed as a future goal since youth can be leaders in the here and now, too (Houwer, 2013).

Opportunities to exercise leadership are plentiful when youth are fulfilling key decision-making roles in social action campaigns that they are leading. For example, leadership competencies such as public speaking can be made available and supported in numerous ways (Salvio, 2013). The experience and skill-sets developed through leadership will carry over to other realms in the life of youth activists. Youth who are burdened with issues of class and race find that opportunities to exercise leadership are limited essentially to gangs when positive alternatives are not available (Venkatesh, 2008).

Richards-Schuster and Dobbie (2011, p. 234) discuss the role and importance of youth places and spaces where they can gather and undertake civic action:

> Youth civic spaces are environments in which youth participation in civic action is fostered—the pathways, structures, and vehicles that provide opportunities for young people to engage in critical discussion, dialogue, and action. The concept of youth civic space includes the formal and informal places in which youth civic engagement can occur and how they lived experience of those places contributes to young people's development as civic actors. It extends discussions regarding the physical locations of youth civic engagement to include the activities, perceptions, and interactions within them.

These spaces cultivate youth praxis and adults can play a role in this type of endeavor (Baldridge et al., 2011). Safe spaces encourage dialogue about oppression and ways of addressing it.

Furman (2012) advances a well-accepted conceptual argument concerning youth leadership being built upon praxis and a multifaceted vision of social justice (personal, interpersonal, communal, systemic, and ecological) and youth being able to reflect and engage in action. Praxis, as addressed in Chapter 3 and operationalized in Chapters 4 (service-learning) and 5 (civic engagement), necessitates engagement in "difficult" conversations (Toporek & Worthington, 2014), critical consciousness, and exercise of leadership competencies.

Critical consciousness can consist of four key elements (Cipolle, 2010, p. 7): "developing a deeper awareness of self; developing a deeper awareness and broader perspective of others; developing a deeper awareness and broader perspective of social issues; seeing one's potential to make change." These elements bring this concept to life in an affirming, empowering, and socially focused manner by fostering a social knowledge base and competencies with a social justice purpose.

Schusler and colleagues (2009, p. 119), in discussing youth development and environmental action, for example, note the need for youth developing competencies as well as achieving social change in the process of doing so: "Environmental action is a process of co-creating environmental and social change while building individuals' capabilities for further participation contributing to personal and community transformation." These goals are not mutually exclusive and will be a central theme in any serious discussion of youth social activism. In fact, the introduction of a youth development paradigm brings an important element into any discussion about how adults can play a role in youth social activism, with service-learning and civic engagement as possible mechanisms.

Akom, Cammarota, and Ginwright (2008) argue for a new paradigm (Critical Youth Studies) that takes into account the reality of being urban youth of color for a better understanding of their social circumstances and actions that result in addressing social justice-related concerns. This paradigm brings a social ecological frame to any analysis that increases our understanding and appreciation of what youth do about their plight.

This emerging perspective is strength, or asset-based, and stresses their competence to organize for self-protection and self-advocacy. In essence, these youth are resistant and can engage in resistance to oppressive forces as a constructive means of channeling their energies, and commitments to equal rights. Dissent can be considered an integral part of democracy and youth exercise their rights through social activism (Wayne, 2007). We can go so far as to argue that dissent is also essential for intellectual and social progress for any group (Gilchrist et al., 2010).

Focusing on youth assets, their rights to engage in collective social justice action, and the focus of their criticism, all comes together to form a philosophical and theoretical foundation for youth social change efforts in this country, although certainly not restricted to this country. Altering the social-political circumstances that oppress youth is logical and channeling their energy into social change activities is constructive.

Jarrett, Sullivan, and Watkins (2005), based on their study of programs offering youth leadership opportunities, found that youth develop relationships with adults in stages: (1) a stage of suspicion and distrust; (2) a stage of facilitated contact; and (3), a stage of meaningful connection. Youth access translates into instrumental (information and exposure to adult world) and experiential (emotional support and encouragement) resources that can be applied in other spheres of their lives. These resources are essential in preparing youth to assume activist leadership roles, with potential tensions and conflicts being part of this experience (Libby, Sedonaen & Bliss, 2006). How these differences are resolved is part of learning how to become a leader (Blanchet-Cohen & Bedeaux, 2014).

Youth and Immigrant-Rights, Environmental, and Food Justice Movements

Campaigns, by and for youth, known as youth-led or youth-driven, capture a perspective towards social activism that has a long history and deep philosophical, practice, and academic implications. Consumer-led or consumer-based interventions, too, capture important distinctions. The casual observer may not see any distinction between a campaign that involves a community and one that is led by a community. Leading social action versus being involved represent distinctive overarching constructs that incorporate different roles and degrees of empowerment as central tenets of an intervention, and ground these interventions within a justice foundation.

The Funders Collaborative on Youth Organizing (Torres-Fleming, Valdes & Pillai, 2011, p. 5) scan of youth organizing found a receptive field for integrating social justice issues:

> The work of youth organizing and community organizing is vastly multi-issue. Furthermore, youth organizers approach the issues they are working on in their campaigns intersectionally. The long-time school-to prison-pipeline campaigns illustrate this clearly—young people see the connection between the poor qualities of their local schools and the prisons being built next door. Youth organizers in the environmental justice movement are addressing such things as health disparities, climate change and food justice. As funders think about how best to support the field, it is important to understand that communities experiencing great inequities do not work on their issues in silos.

Life cannot be compartmentalized and neither are social action campaigns. True, funders like to support discrete projects because it makes it easier to see what they are buying. However, community issues are highly interrelated.

Brodkin's (2009) highly detailed documentation and analysis of an environmental campaign (opposition to construction of a power plant) in a Los Angeles Latino community, and how this action was largely supported by Latino high school students, highlights the role youth-involved and youth-led social justice campaigns can play in broader food and environmental justice movements; viewing these campaigns from a spatial perspective (community) facilitates this view and understanding.

Checkoway and Gutierrez (2006, p. 6) note that it is important for adults to create quality experiences for youth in situations where adults are leading the social change effort:

> Who has responsibility for facilitation of youth participation? Although participation initiatives may be youth-led, or intergenerational in their origins, we recognize that none of the ones described here is truly youth-led. However, we reiterate that the quality of participation is not contingent on this approach, and that it is as likely that quality youth participation might be adult-led or intergenerational as it is that youth leadership might not be participatory.

Thus, whether or not the social campaign is youth-led or has sizeable levels of youth participation, the quality of the experience must be center stage, and this has important implications for social-justice–focused service-learning and civic engagement efforts.

Although this book examines youth-involved and youth-led social activism, particular attention will be paid to youth-led immigrant-rights, food, and environmental justice efforts because of young people's unique contributions to these three social movements. Simply defined, youth-led immigrant-rights, environmental, and food justice movements are efforts to change behavior that systematically involve youth in key decision-making roles, with the outcomes of these campaigns benefiting them, their communities, and society (Zeldin, Camino & Calvert, 2007).

This "simple" definition is misleading and fraught with conceptual and methodological challenges because of the fluidity of how concepts get defined and operationalized in the field or in the "real world." Delgado and Staples (2007) highlight the tension that exists when it is essential to delay gratification (self-regulatory behavior) when conceptualizing and implementing social change interventions. Adults, too, encounter this challenge. Nevertheless, it takes on added importance with youth.

Lombardo, Zakus, and Skinner (2002), as well as Delgado and Zhou (2008), apply a social justice perspective towards health promotion and youth, introducing youth social action as a vehicle to connect locally, nationally, and internationally, in pursuit of health. Rights can be justified by any one or combination of these principles. Youth leadership and involvement in immigrant-rights, environmental, and food justice campaigns face challenges associated with a disenfranchised group because of how society distributes rights and privileges based upon age (Delgado, 2009).

Urban youth cannot be viewed without an appreciation of how social context influences their development and worldviews and what constitutes social injustice in their lives (Elliott et al., 2006). The urban context or terrains in which they function either facilitate or hinder their participation and development of their citizenship attitudes, skills, and identity (Clay, 2006; Driskell, Fox & Kudva, 2008; Suyemoto, Day & Schwartz, 2014; Walker, 2011).

Youth empowerment, too, must be viewed within this context (Jennings et al., 2006; Travis & Leech, 2014). Social justice campaigns require mechanisms to ensure inclusion and not further reinforce injustices. These and other social justice campaigns have the immediate goal of altering oppressive forces, but also must include goals of enhancing the capacities of those involved, and have them be an integral part of society. In essence, there are multiple agendas that must be sought and realized.

As noted in Figure 1, the field of youth-led social activism is built upon a set of key practice arenas and concepts that come together to make these campaigns distinct, but it also owes much to and shares much with other fields. Each of

FIGURE 1 Community Social work Practice With Youth on Immigrant Rights, Food, and Environmental Justice

these practice arenas and concepts individually wield tremendous influence and, when combined, they effectively shape activism that is powerful, innovative, and with direct benefits to youth, their families, community, and society (Checkoway & Gutierrez, 2006; Peterson, Dolan & Handft, 2010).

These campaigns, nevertheless, are not exclusively directed at youth, but also may encompass social justice-related issues that severely impact their families, neighbors, and communities where they live. In essence, these efforts are not "all about me," which is counter to adult prevailing views that youth are self-centered and egotistical, necessitating a socio-ecological perspective in order to understand fully the process and outcome of youth social activism.

Multiple "streams" flow together to form youth social activism and highlight the richness of the field, the need to take a multi-disciplinary perspective, and the importance of developing language and concepts that unite practitioners, academics, and youth. These streams also highlight the complex challenges, which are not unique to youth, in achieving the goal of unity in the search for human rights and social justice. The activist age inherently presents a set of challenges that are legal, moral, and social-political, making the understanding of this phenomenon that much more significant and difficult to achieve.

Youth-led immigrant-rights, environmental, and food justice campaigns encourage application of "unconventional criteria" for determining the most appropriate evaluation methods and avoiding discipline-bound methodologies. These innovative approaches lend themselves to use of video, art, music, theater, quilting, and other methods that are attractive to youth. Adult staff and evaluators, too, must be fluent and comfortable with these methods.

It is impossible to grasp the meaning of being a youth without a profound understanding of the social and economic justice themes of why a social change project is important to them. Much research and scholarly work remains to be done to ensure that youth-directed social activism has an influential future in this country (Velez et al., 2008), setting the stage for cross-national comparisons.

Krishner (2014, p. 49) draws attention to the foundation upon which youth activism is based and how youth are creating new identities that are affirming:

> Youth activism is a form of political engagement in which young people identify common interests, mobilize their peers, and work collectively to make their voices heard in the public square. Research on youth activism is interdisciplinary, emerging out of scholarship on youth development, civic engagement, cultural studies, and social movements. Youth activism is an important domain of research for two broad reasons. First, youth activists defy societal stereotypes about teenagers, such as that they are self-involved, impulsive, or unprepared for participation in mature community activities. Understanding youth's accomplishments in activism can challenge and expand conventional notions about adolescence as a developmental stage. Second, understanding youth activism as a developmental context is important, particularly for youth who feel marginalized from their schools or communities.

Rethinking youth and their knowledge base and skill-sets opens up a new world of thought about their capacities to be effective change agents.

Society can only thrive when it has invested resources in youth and has provided them with opportunities to realize their potential and dreams. Their ability to be contributing adults valuing and embracing social justice principles is based on their preparedness to contribute.

Conclusion

The demographic picture that was presented captures the numerical significance that urban youth of color present to the nation today and tomorrow. Further, concentration within the nation's major urban centers further increases their significance within these geographical settings, potentially bringing potential moral panic as society contends with the consequences of urbanized youth of color.

The youth-led immigrant-rights, environmental, and food justice movements are full of promise for altering the circumstances that marginalized youth find in this society, bringing rewards and challenges for youth, practitioners, and academics. Lessons learned and skills acquired will influence other aspects of their lives and communities (Conner, 2014). The next decade will witness important developments related to research and theory development, which will significantly alter perceptions of what is and what is not possible for youth. The evolution of the field will continue and much will be learned that influences youth and adult-inspired activism.

3

A SOCIAL JUSTICE AND RIGHTS PERSPECTIVE

Introduction

Social justice is a concept that knows no political boundaries or historical era, with liberals/progressives and conservatives/arch conservatives singing its praises (Burawoy, 2015; Schulz, 2007). The concept of social justice is not even restricted to humans, as evidenced by a movement to help ensure that animals are not abused (Matsuoka & Sorenson, 2014) or Mother Earth is considered, as addressed in Chapter 7 where the focus is on environmental justice. In fact, it is virtually impossible to find someone who openly proclaims a stance against social justice. Plato, too, has sung its praises: "The last of those qualities which make a state virtuous must be justice, if we only knew what that was" (Buchanan, 1977).

Nevertheless, the seeking of justice has resulted in countless numbers of deaths and untold suffering for those seeking to achieve it and those refusing to acknowledge injustices. In essence, social justice is in the eye of the beholder, with one person's justice being someone else's injustice. The difference between a terrorist and a freedom fighter can be which side of the gun one is facing. Yet, there is no denying the importance of the concept, regardless of where one stands on this equation, as evidenced by the strong emotions it elicits. Justice, simply put, is a rallying cry for collective action. The quest for justice, for example, resulted in the American Revolution, and this event led to countless other revolutions across the world; it has the power to bring radical transformation.

Social justice is a philosophical stance, goal, and process (Mitchell, (2013). Social justice campaigns and movements are an essential part of democracy and serve many important functions in this society, including providing an avenue and language for bringing together disparate groups in search of a common purpose. In the case of urban youth from different ethnic and racial backgrounds, age and similar life circumstances are a common denominator.

However, one important function that stands out is that it brings much-needed attention and publicity to particular forms of injustices. These forms of social injustices have either been overlooked or are not considered egregious enough to warrant dialogue or debate, and this has certainly been the case when discussing urban youth in the United States. These injustices, however, can be very public and take on extreme acts, as in the case of military dictatorships, for example (Bellino, 2014).

Nevertheless, the presence of a wide variety of social justice campaigns diverts attention from the overall picture or state of being in certain urban communities in the United States. Although there are core similarities between social justice campaigns and movements, there is no denying that particular injustices may stand out as salient because of how they impinge on youth lives and the lives of their loved ones (Ugor, 2014).

A youth perspective on these social issues adds a dimension often missing, although the potential of service-learning and civic engagement as a viable means of introducing their voices and actions is only now being realized in this arena. Age-related distributive justice, as already noted, brings a lens to discussions that highlight how youth with particular backgrounds fare in comparison to other demographic groups (Irwin, 2013).

Youth rights must be cast against a broader movement or constellation of human rights (Libal & Harding, 2015). Youth activism as manifested through protest and other forms of oppositional behavior is best understood through a social justice or human rights perspective, bringing forth a discussion of how daily lived experiences with oppression can get translated and turned into positive action for themselves, their families, communities, and society. This perspective is relevant when discussing youth from less privileged backgrounds (Futch, 2011; Morrell, 2008). One youth activist noted (Ginwright, 2003, pp. 10–11): "I learned that you might be a kid, but you still have rights. We can prove to the adults out there that we do have a voice and we want to stand up for what we believe in."

This discussion can be very erudite/philosophical or practical. The latter holds the greatest relevance for youth; academics prefer the former. However, there is little dispute that theory and concepts will wield critical influence on how this understanding and action unfolds. How the findings from these debates and discourses find their way into classrooms and the field will go a long way towards determining the relevance of the academy.

It is important to pause and acknowledge that there are many different versions and interpretations of human rights (Bajaj, 2011; Libal & Harding, 2015b). Fregoso (2014, p. 583), for example, proposes an alternative vision and definition of human rights that embraces collectivist politics of "social justice" by arguing that:

> a decolonial understanding of rights, beyond the conventional definition of human rights premised on a Western cosmology that foregrounds the

human as an autonomous individual/agent unyoked by the surrounding world; beyond a circular conception of rights as the individual possession of the human inhering in 'his' sovereign being; and beyond the provincial understanding of human and rights as inscribed in law and the state, and as universal and transcendental. I propose a shift in focus away from the liberal doctrine of human rights codified in law and the state, toward alternative, human rights contingencies, as modeled by the collectivist politics of social justice activists and creative practitioners.

A human rights perspective emphasizes points related to dignity and the legitimacy of social actions that seek to alter current thinking and resource allocations.

Engagement in social justice-focused campaigns is not an effort to channel "excess" or "youthful" energy or have it viewed as acting-out behavior; participation is best understood as an effort to right a serious wrong or grave unfairness, and not thought of as a passing phase. The "fearless" or "inflammatory" speech, depending upon one's political perspective, is integral to these campaigns and ensures that voices that were ignored in the past are no longer ignored in a democracy (Jack, 2004). Youth oppositional behavior, as addressed earlier, brings a language or vocabulary to label injustice from a youth viewpoint, and the actions emanate from analysis.

Participation and leadership, as the case may be, results in societal and individual changes or transformations, and seeking to achieve social justice goals is good for society and those who seek it. The benefits are multifaceted and significant for youth, the adults they engage in partnerships with, their families, and their communities, too.

Youth in these communities face incredible challenges in having their voices heard and respected, and having their basic needs met in a manner that preserves their dignity, self-respect, rights—and, in some instances, life, such as in avoiding being shot by the police. Socially navigating these forces takes a tremendous amount of energy and drive that could be better spent in other pursuits. Further, marginalized youth face incredible challenges in finding established mechanisms through which they can exercise democratic principles. Schools, where they spend the bulk of their day, are often an example of unresponsive and oppressively adult-run systems.

Development of an awareness of why these youth face these struggles becomes important in shaping a response that does not blame them for their socioeconomic circumstances and stigma (Gardner, 2011). Youth-led mental health campaigns, for example, can specifically address the stigma of adolescents with mental health issues in ways that are different from adult-led efforts (Bulanda et al., 2014). In essence, development of a collective identity represents a critical step in analyzing their predicament and what is needed to change their dire social and economic situations and those of their families and community.

Social justice activism in the United States in the early part of the twenty-first century has covered a range of topics, with youth playing active roles in shaping these social actions. As already noted, three social movements stand out and will be addressed in this book, bringing excitement and potential for significant youth involvement because of how they resonate in the lives of youth and those they care about.

These three social justice movements can find relevance in any geographical area and region of the country, with appeal to a wide spectrum of the population, regardless of their ages and backgrounds. However, when examined from an urban context, their importance only increases in significance for youth and their families, and serves as a foundation for important critical work on the part of youth that can transcend other spheres of social-justice–inspired work.

The preceding chapters have set the stage for the importance of a social justice and human rights lens for shaping urban youth collective responses to oppressive acts. Nevertheless, collective reflexivity, although not receiving the attention it deserves in the professional literature, is a powerful mechanism and draws upon our knowledge base regarding the role and importance of collective memory, learning, and identity (Rheingans & Hollands, 2013). The transformative power of the group is certainly significant.

A social justice/human rights perspective does not preclude development of an awareness of youth strengths and their community's assets. Youth gaining awareness of their abilities plays an influential role in shaping their potential roles and leadership within social justice campaigns, and brings a positive outlet for their strengths (Fox et al., 2010). These assets, incidentally, must play a prominent role in shaping service-learning and civic engagement activities, as noted in Chapter 4.

This chapter focuses on social justice and its many manifestations, how it evolves and shapes youth activists in their quest for social justice, and challenges for adults interested in supporting them in this journey. Social justice serves as a philosophical and theoretical foundation that unfolds according to the circumstances that individual groups encounter. Age is a key factor that offers a unique and often overlooked view of how social justice is conceptualized and acted upon in democratic societies. However, when rights are viewed within an age context, some age groups are more equal than others, with youth not being one of the privileged groups.

Social Justice

Social justice is a concept and philosophical stance that has universal qualities and must also be viewed through lenses that are highly contextualized to take into account socio-ecologically specific aspects. In the case of youth, it is age-specific, bringing an added dimension to discussions concerning intersectionality or multiple jeopardies (Johnson, 2011; Tarulli & Skott-Myhre, 2006). Urban youth of color bring elements of socio-economic-class, race/ethnicity, skin color, gendered identity, and documented status, to note but a few (Doetsch-Kidder, 2012).

The life experiences of the children of newcomers, for example, go far beyond a singular focus on ethnicity, and must take into account gender and generational power relations within their communities, including the role and influence of extra-familial influences, social contexts and structural constraints, and the role of youth as generators of social capital (Shah, 2007). In essence, their lives are quite complex and we do a disservice by reducing it to ethnicity; that is an important but not the singular factor in their lives (Delgado, Jones & Rohani, 2005).

Social justice goes beyond race/ethnicity, gender/sexual identity, or socio-economic class, and it can also involve beliefs intersecting to form an experience and worldview of oppression that is not simple in construction, but profound in shaping identity and future prospects (North, 2008). A rights perspective that is premised on the rights of youth to be nurtured, protected, respected, and meaningfully involved shapes youth-adult interactions and efforts targeting them (Head, 2011). Further, bringing a spatial justice perspective to this analysis facilitates addressing the interplay of these factors within a geographical area (space and place) and context.

Identity and social justice are closely associated and this is important to emphasize because social justice taps into values, and values are essential ingredients of social identity (Farnsworth, 2010). In many ways, we are what we believe in. Social justice civic engagement and service-learning require the commitment of the whole self to the endeavor. Authenticity is a concept that emerges on countless occasions during the process of dialogue and reflection (reflectivity), shaping identity and strengthening conviction about social change (Wilson & Schwier, 2009). An embrace of social justice values is an essential motivator for participating and benefiting from social justice service-learning and civic engagement, too (Schamber & Mahoney, 2008).

A social justice construct has found its way into most helping professions and the scholarship guiding social interventions (Hardcastle, Powers & Wenocur, 2011; Kumashiro, 2009). It has always held a prominent role in social activist campaigns, including those involving youth that have indigenous origins without adult community practitioner involvement, serving to unify professions embracing youth activist campaigns. One organizing principle involved in social justice campaigns is the importance of empowerment and ensuring participation and decision-making by those most affected by the issue of injustice (Travis & Ausbrooks, 2012; Travis & Leech, 2014).

Social justice can be defined as consisting of four essential and interrelated components (Clifford & Burke, 2009, pp. 123–124): "1. Fair distribution of goods and services to people based on equal opportunity. 2. Limitation of institutional discrimination and oppression. 3. All people are equally free to use opportunities without discrimination. 4. Equality as the end position, with goods and services shared fairly between individuals and groups."

Clifford and Burke's social justice components integrate different forms of social justice. The operationalization of a social justice construct provided by Clifford and Burke (2009) above illustrates a broad approach towards examining justice and injustice, and does not eliminate youth or tie youth status to that of their parents and other adults. It lends itself to examining how social justice activism can address these four elements and why use of fairness as a concept is one way of operationalizing youth social justice.

Allen (2014, p. 49), in addressing food and environmental justice, sees value in the introduction of a social justice perspective and its value to both and other movements coming together:

> As movements increase their focus on social justice, they can engage in critical reflection and dialogue to interrogate the nature of conditions of injustice and the causes behind these conditions. This would include examining how practices and discourses of racism, classism, and sexism—along with the ways they intersect—have shaped, reflect, and reproduce the food system. This process must privilege the participation, perspectives, and priorities of those who suffer from injustice. It can then best illuminate strategic definitions and pathways that can move toward transformation of a food system grounded in conditions of social justice.

Social activism without reflection and dialogue can be misguided and not maximize the potential of those involved—youth as well as adults.

Introduction of a spatial dimension to this construct facilitates the joining together of various social justice issues and movements, which on the surface may seem to have very little common but upon closer scrutiny share much in common. A focus on urban communities and the importance of social ecology provides a holistic perspective on how select social forces impinge on the lives of residents who share certain socio-demographic characteristics.

Spatial Justice

Social justice movements invariably focus on particular injustices and often fail to reach out to other movements in an effort to unite several different causes. Failure to reach out may be due to an inability to see connections or it may simply be that they do not wish to lose momentum with their own cause since initiating and sustaining a movement takes much more time, energy, and resources. This outcome is understandable because not all social injustices attract the same individuals, tap the same resources, or seek similar outcomes or redresses. Consequently, potential opportunities to unite several movements are not sought even though they embrace social justice goals.

Taking a spatial approach to social movements has the potential to achieve this goal (Chatterton, 2010; Rogaly, 2012). This viewpoint stresses how the place and space where people live is impacted by social forces providing concrete examples in how they get manifested in everyday lived experiences. In essence, a geographical unit of analysis serves to bring together all those who share a community through a common frame of reference, and facilitates development of an understanding of their shared predicament as well as their assets (Filbert & Flynn, 2010).

A spatial perspective is not limited to social justice and applies to other aspects, such as social and cultural factors (Frink et al., 2010, p. 69): "The social and cultural activities within any space are therefore important because they are not just interactions between individuals over time in a common location, but because the social and cultural practices in which they are consistently engaged become shared over time . . ." Space, however, is central to our understanding of spatial justice (McClay & McAllister, 2014). Thus, social justice becomes very concrete and shared experiences facilitate exchanges and understandings through the bringing together of other forms of social oppression, facilitating youth activist and their adult allies grasping the power of intersectionality in shaping discourse and analysis (Coe, 2014).

The inclusion of marginalized groups by society—and possibly also marginalized within urban communities of color—increases the importance of social activist campaigns and movements that can further unite communities rather than continue to perpetuate disenfranchisement, as in the case of youth. A focus on urban communities as a geographic entity brings a spatial justice perspective that unites various social movements (Dikec, 2001; Helfenbein & Huddleston, 2013; Mayer, 2012).

We can ask: Why does it make a difference to view youth and social change from a spatial and social justice perspective? Is this is an academic distinction without any real world consequences? Iveson (2011) argues that a spatial justice perspective can serve as a "common cause" or "glue that binds" together radical theorists and activists across their differences and diverse foci of their change efforts. A focus on the rights of the city, nationally and internationally, too, brings a spatial dimension and grounding to social justice (Mayer, 2013; Mitchell, 2003).

There are many benefits to the use of a spatial justice (Brown et al., 2007, p. 7):

> The idea of "spatial justice" can be a useful way to reframe cultural and political work so that both analyses and tools become more precise. The important work of defining new terminology, however, always carries with it the related danger of endless classification, obscuring the fact that language it does not solve problems and, indeed, that many people have been fighting for justice-in-space for a long time—especially indigenous peoples and people of color.

A spatial justice approach also facilitates comparing neighborhoods within communities and between different cities, too (Bowen et al., 1995), allowing a contextualization that would be impossible otherwise.

Adultism

The invisibility of youth in national justice movements can be explained by the use of an adultist perspective on their worth and contributions. *Adultism* is a term that is increasingly finding its way into the scholarly literature since Flasher (1978) discussed this concept over 25 years ago, and the concept has survived since then for very good reason. *Adultism* is differentiated from *ageism* because the latter can include both youth and older adults while adultism specifically focuses on youth (Haydon, 2012). It is impossible to discuss social justice and youth without introducing this concept (Adams, Bell & Griffin, 2007; Laursen, 2014; Stewart, 2012).

Anyone who has worked with or taught youth will find that this term will resonate in discussions with them on how their opinions do not matter, or "what gives adults the right" to do or say something (Delgado & Staples, 2007; Roach, 2009). Youth political organizing, particularly that related to schools, can be viewed as a contested response to adultism in a system that is youth-focused but does not value their inputs or seek to empower them (LeFrançois, 2014; Gordon, 2010; Shier et al., 2014). Arches (2012, 2013) brings together service-learning, youth development and social action, in this case university students and school youth, to address adultism by teachers.

Adultism has been defined by Checkoway (1996, p. 13) as "all of the behaviors and attitudes that flow from the assumption that adults are better than young people and are entitled to act upon young people in many ways without their agreements." Adults perceive themselves to be in the privileged position of knowing what is best for youth simply based upon having been a youth at some point in their lives and being in a position of power. This exalted position serves as a rationale for imposing adult will. Adults are either explicitly or implicitly superior to youth. The same argument has been made for substantiating slavery, sexism, and other forms of oppression.

Ceaser (2014, p. 167) discusses the pernicious and multifaceted consequences of adultism in educational settings and the insidious manner they get manifested: "Findings reveal that adultist expectations were placed on youth in conversations and in work demands. Adultism also intersected with other social locations such as race/gender/class and led youth to engage in resistance strategies against me, an adult they could control." Ceaser's observations are not limited to educational settings and have applicability to any setting where adults are in control, which covers quite a large landscape.

The immigrant-rights (Abrego, 2006; Gonzalez, 2008; Velez et al., 2008), environmental justice (Agerman, 2001; Pezzullo & Sandler, 2007), and food justice movements (Marcias, 2008; Vasquez et al., 2007) have had to reconcile disconnects between their central goals and social justice. The subjects of race and socio-economic class, for example, are an integral part of the immigrant-rights (Velez et al., 2008), environmental justice (Allen, Daro & Holland, 2007; Faber, 2007), and food justice (Feenstra, 2002; Slocum, 2006) dialogues. However, the subject of adultism or ageism towards youth, with rare exception, has not entered into these discourses, thereby limiting their reach into under-represented age groups, such as youth and older adults, for example.

Fostering an Embrace of Social Justice

Why is there a need to foster an embrace of social justice and have urban marginalized youth shaping this agenda? Fine and Ruglis (2009, p. 20) answer this question quite eloquently and paint a picture of oppression in the lives of urban youth of color and the dismal future that awaits them if we stand by and blame them for the social circumstances:

> As critical scholars of public education and mass incarceration, we witness in our daily work the soft coercive migration of youth of color, especially poor youth of color, out of sites of public education and into militarized and carceral corners of the public sphere. We watch as educators and youth try to negotiate conditions of systematic miseducation, criminalization, and the scientism of high-stakes testing. And we observe how ideologies about merit, deservingness, and blame drip feed into the soul, tagging some bodies as worthy and others as damaged. We write this essay to make visible this critical geography of youth development and dispossession.

The social consequences of youth being fed into adult-controlled systems that ensure oppression continues are well understood from a social, economic, and political vantage point.

Before specifically addressing three forms of social activism campaigns/social movements and the subject of activism, it is necessary to identify what key elements must be present for youth to engage in social protest. For the purposes of discussion, three elements will be highlighted: (1) development of social responsibility; (2) agency; and (3) praxis. These three elements are highly interrelated but will be treated separately for the purposes of facilitating discussion in this section.

1. Development of Social Responsibility

Social responsibility by youth represents a key element in social-justice–driven initiatives and enhances their knowledge and competencies (Wray Lake & Syvertsen, 2011, p. 11): "Social responsibility is a value orientation, rooted in democratic relationships with others and moral principles of care and justice, that motivates certain civic actions. Given its relevance for building stronger relationships and communities, the development of social responsibility within individuals should be a more concerted focus for developmental scholars and youth practitioners. During childhood and adolescence, the developmental roots of individuals' social responsibility lie in the growth of executive function, empathy and emotion regulation, and identity. Efforts to cultivate children and adolescents' social responsibility in the proximal settings of their everyday lives should emphasize modeling prosocial behaviors."

The fostering of social responsibility benefits all segments of society, beginning with the communities where youth reside and extending nationally and across borders.

2. Agency

The concept of agency has, and continues to be, applied in a variety of settings, populations, and social circumstances. Youth agency consists of numerous elements that, when they converge, result in a profound transformation in the lives of highly marginalized youth. Agency captures the innate capacity of individuals to function independently and to exercise options in their lives (Baker, 2011). These options are predicated upon the belief that meaningful social change is possible and that our actions can make a difference (Cipolle, 2010).

Agency is socially and culturally constructed (Meyer & Jepperson, 2000) and can have many different meanings and manifestations, including an evolutionary perspective grounding it within a time period, depending upon the academic or professional background of those using it, and the context it is being applied within (Beaumont, 2010; France & Roberts, 2014; Pasque & Harris, 2013).

There is a strong argument to be made that it is not possible for youth to seek and obtain rights without corresponding agency (Reynaert & Roose, 2014; Ugor, 2014). In fact, agency is closely associated with culture and identity, and this is indicative of its importance (Côté & Levine, 2014; Hemming & Madge, 2012). Compassion and agency, too, are closely interrelated (Quinn, 2014).

Social agency transforms youth into social actors, and critically informed research facilitates this transformation (Rodríguez & Brown, 2009; Mason & Hood, 2011). Agency, in turn, is not possible without praxis, as discussed in the next section.

Youth as active social agents provides a counter-narrative to prevailing disempowerment by adults (Daniels et al., 2010, p. 19): "We consider youth agency to be the voice of young people around the world and the energy youth bring to social, cultural, and educational change. As youth are active agents in and of themselves . . . we contend that the cultural and social practices resulting from youth agency are valuable resources for change."

Knowledge is power and an essential element of empowerment (Horn, 2014; Lee, 2013; Mosedale, 2014). An empowered individual is someone who possesses agency or the ability to define their own life choices and goals, engendering confidence (Joseph, 2012). Knowledge must have significance in the lives of youth for it to be owned and used by them in their daily lives and when undertaking extraordinary acts, as in the case of social activism (Billett, 2008).

Rhetoric stressing rescuing or saving low-income/low wealth youth of color, although well-intentioned, diminishes youth and their community's agency (Baldridge, 2014). Youth agency is increased when they have control and receive nondirective assistance when needed, allowing them to deliberate without conforming to adult expectations, but still having accessibility to adults under their own terms (Ares, 2010; Larson & Angus, 2011).

3. Praxis

Readers may be very familiar with the concept of praxis, particularly those with histories of involvement in doing anti-oppression practice and scholarship. Arriving at a consensus definition of praxis is challenging because this is a concept with wide appeal across academic disciplines and there is a plethora of definitions. A number of fields arguably stand out because of their contributions to our understanding: philosophy, sociology, political science, psychology, anthropology, arts/humanities, and education.

The following definition, although simple in composition, captures the essence of how the literature defines praxis (Cipolle, 2010, p. 157): "Critical reflection and action with the goal of social change for equity and justice." This definition encompasses several key perspectives that fall into five categories: (1) knowing/reflecting, sometimes referred to as insight (Lykes, 2013); (2) action/doing in context (Vaughan, 2014; White, 2007); (3) relationship/communication (Drake, Fergusson & Briggs, 2014; Moore, 2011; Ross, 2014); (4) intentionality and commitment (Erbstein, 2013); and (5) belonging to something bigger than oneself (Reynolds & Chun, 2013).

The whole is more important than the parts because each of these categories are integrally related to each other. In essence, praxis is about knowing, doing, and being in context (Gormally & Coburn, 2013). One dimension does not significantly mean without the others. Praxis is not an event or an episode in time but a journey over a period of time.

No two journeys are ever similar and therefore praxis defies standardization, making it arduous to make predictions about timeframes and outcomes. This may be hard to comprehend because we live in a society that is obsessed with time and seemingly in constant search for ways to shorten time frames and become more efficient. Praxis and social activism are integrally related and closely tied to critical literacy, without a time clock. In essence, there are no shortcuts.

Youth as Researchers of Social Justice

"Making sense" of situations is a popular way of framing the importance of research in raising consciousness and using vocabulary that is youth-friendly, as in the use of "fairness" as a way of framing social justice. Youth as researchers is not a new idea; it has been addressed by a variety of academics interested in empowerment and participatory democracy (Delgado, 2006; Fine, 2009; Rheingold, 2008).

Youth playing instrumental research roles focused on social justice issues brings them into a central and powerful role in determining the type of information they consider essential to shaping how social justice issues get conceptualized (Kaplan, 2008; Marshall & Rossman, 2010; Suzuki & Mayorga, 2014). Fifteen-year-old James Turner stated it quite eloquently in the following (Weiss, 2003, p. 1): "Nobody listens to youth, and nobody used to listen to me, but because we're organized and have a lot of research behind us, people listen."

Community-based participatory research (CBPR) has been identified as a promising approach towards youth involvement in social justice research (Cammarota, 2008; Rodríguez & Brown, 2009; Merves et al., 2015). The principles guiding CBPR stress empowerment, critical theory, participation, and social change resulting from the research (Ferrera et al., 2015; Hacker, 2013). Bringing together participatory research and participatory media, for example, encourages civic engagement (Rheingold, 2008; Watson & Marciano, 2015). Youth engaged in mapping vacant properties illustrates how their view of their environment can lead to social activism and advocacy (Teixeira, 2015).

Torre and Fine (2006) do an effective job of illustrating the importance of youth shaping the research questions and process in order to document how injustices have impacted their lives. Research that effectively links marginalized youths' lived experiences with history and policies grounds social actions addressing injustices. The emergence of critical research, in similar fashion to other prefixes used in this book, introduces social justice values, principles, and action into the research endeavor (Cahill, 2010; Morrell, 2004). A critical social research paradigm poses questions such as "For what purpose?" "With whom?" "If not now, when?" (Fine, 2006).

Creswell (2013) addressed these questions from four philosophical research assumptions: (1) ontological—what is the nature of reality? (2) axiological—how do values influence the research process? (3) methodological—what is the language and process of research? and (4) epistemological—what can be considered knowledge?

These philosophical assumptions are highly interrelated and shape the research experience for the researchers and their collaborators and, in this case, youth who are seeking to alter the social circumstances oppressing them (Delgado, 2015a; Berg, Coman & Schensul, 2009; Cammarota & Romero, 2009; Hattam et al., 2009). Prior (2013), in turn, identified five key questions that concretize

Crewell's philosophical assumptions: (1) What to know? (2) What is known? (3) What is knowing? (4) Who knows what? (5) How to know?

Youth and Social Activism: An Overview

The need for social change must first be experienced and recognized before an initiation of a campaign to change oppressive situations (Daniels et al., 2010). Quiroz-Martinez, Wu and Zimmermann (2005) argue that the late 1990s witnessed a dramatic shift in how youth organizing was conceptualized, resulting in youth viewing their struggles and unity through a lens focused on their age. Youth activism is certainly not restricted to the United States and can be found throughout the world (Frei, 2014).

Motivation to engage in social protest can be multifaceted. Invariably, youth motivation consists of permutations and combinations of reasons, such as personal experiences, peer role models, family influences, witnessing injustices, direct violence, and metaphysical angst, for example (Ardizzone, 2007). Not all reasons are of equal strength, yet there is no denying that marginalized youth are not at a loss for finding reasons to engage in social protest.

Ardizzone (2007, p. 84) sums up quite well the value of social activism in the lives of urban marginalized youth:

> Inner city youth activists have firsthand experience with structured violence. For many, the recognition of this structured violence is a major factor in their decisions to work for peace and justice, supporting Freire's notion that conscientization is an essential ingredient for radical social movements. Through their involvement youth activists see beyond themselves, nurture pro-social behavior, and work for the common good. Inner city youth activists witness injustice and rather than becoming hopeless and apathetic, or perpetrators of direct violence, choose to work for social change.

Social injustice is not an abstract concept for urban youth of color, with few unable to share a personal story of how their lives have been impacted by oppression.

Social activism is an attractive avenue for youth to direct their outrage about injustices in their lives. Adults assisting and joining forces in helping them direct their attention and energies in a purposeful and highly focused manner helps ensure that actions have a high likelihood of achieving a measure of success, although not without tensions and challenges. Further, these youth-adult partnerships help break down barriers that serve to keep different age groups apart from each other.

Lombardo, Zakus, and Skinner (2002, p. 363) make an important observation concerning today's youth and why the use of social activism to actively engage them has such meaning to them: "Today's youth are coming of age in a complex world impacted by global forces. However, they generally feel disenfranchised from socio-political processes . . . Youths may turn to social action to speak out and effect change in relation to issues touching their lives. The challenge is to find ways of engaging and empowering young people in community participation and social change." One of the most formidable challenges that must be surmounted is adults' dismissive attitudes towards youth and their rights as members of a democratic society.

There are a variety of ways of labeling or capturing this perspective. Gordon (2007), for example, stresses the importance of examining ageism, or adultism, from a multifaceted perspective that goes beyond an emphasis on the conventional view that has focused on macro-level forces and ideologies. The perspective of youth collective experience, politicized, along with responses to adultism, enhances our understanding of how they socially navigate adult power and its abuses, and the role social movements play in channeling their concerns and responses.

Scholars have developed principles upon which to appreciate the potential contributions of youth to social justice campaigns and movements. Ginwright and Cammarota (2006, pp. xvi–xix), for example, identified four key principles regarding youth activism that can serve as a foundation for youth leadership and involvement in immigrant-rights, environmental, and food justice movements: "(1) Young people should be conceptualized in relationship to specific economic, political, and social conditions; (2) the youth development process should be conceptualized as a collective response to the social marginalization of young people; (3) young people are agents of change, not simple subjects to change; and (4) young people have basic rights."

Ginwright and Cammarota's (2006) principles set a foundation from which youth can assume positions as citizens with rights and privileges, as well as possess the requisite wisdom and competencies to play meaningful roles in their lives and seek social justice for themselves, their families, and their communities. The concept of students as citizens also has emerged, highlighting their rights (Bergen & McLean, 2015). As youth exercise agency through social change efforts, the beneficiaries of these efforts go beyond youth activists and encompass their families, communities, and society.

Poncelet's (2014) youth research in the South Bronx, New York City, found that: "(1) raising youth participants' critical consciousness, encouraging their contributions to local knowledge production and exchange, and empowering their sense of civic efficacy are key to yielding transformative outcomes; (2) youth define their neighborhoods in terms of positive and supportive social bonds fostered in the struggle against spatial inequities; and (3) youth distinguish youth activism from activism in general, which they perceive to be what adults do, and conceptualize the former as the collective response by youth and their adult allies to community-based struggles."

Poncelet's key findings show why getting youth to take an active and substantive role in defining knowledge areas of importance in their lives, and their unique views on social activism, must be incorporated into any initiatives seeking to engage them, service-learning, civic engagement, or otherwise. Identifying and mobilizing neighborhood support systems or assets are essential elements in youth mobilization social justice causes.

Competencies youth gain from engaging in social change initiatives translate well into making them more competent adults with the skills and vision for a new United States as they transition into adulthood. The identity they assume as civic-minded citizens with a desire for social justice will also transpire in the process. If youth can be convinced that the predicaments they find themselves in are the result of their actions and backgrounds, and there is nothing that they can do but resign themselves to their reality, society effectively has them under control. However, if youth resist this narrative, they can exercise agency to alter their circumstances.

Conner (2012) focuses on what distinguishes youth organizers from their adult counterparts and notes five distinctions: (1) engaging in organizing is engaging in learning; (2) youth organizing seeks to foster youth development and effect social change; (3) although youth involvement in social change can transpire in a number of arenas, educational reform is one of the fastest growing forms of social justice in the field; (4) youth-led programs offer youth the greatest flexibility in determining their needs and shaping their campaigns; and (5) youth organizing offers great promise in reaching out to and engaging marginalized urban youth of color.

Christens & Dolan (2011) found that youth organizing can result in a range of community-level benefits, including new program implementation, policy change, and institution building. Further, these efforts create social capital through intergenerational and multicultural collaborations. Intergenerational social capital gains can be bridging rather than bonding because they capture how divides can be breached.

How can adults foster youth social activism? Conner (2012) made six recommendations: (1) Get students there and keep them involved; (2) Set the right tone; (3) Make everyone's knowledge count; (4) Allow young people to be catalyzed by issues that are important to them; (5) Flexibility in communication (embrace youth-friendly means); and (6) Multiple venues for action. These recommendations create a context and climate for welcoming and supporting youth activists.

Emotionality and Social Protest

Emotions and youth seem to go hand-in-hand. However, the close relationship between the two is rarely framed in a positive light. Yet, a show of emotions is a marker for indignation and outright anger at a social injustice. Thus, it is impossible to discuss social campaigns and movements in depth without drawing attention to the importance of the emotional connections or even anger (Jasper, 2014) associated with social protests, for participants as well as observers of demonstrations (Jasper, 2011; Van Stekelenburg & Klandermans, 2013), and the political consequences (Amenta et al., 2010). Participation in social protests impacts all senses, which contribute to the "ambience" or energy associated with public demonstrations; being part of a crowd brings an added dimension to how emotionality impacts others.

Opotow (2011) speaks to the role of social injustice in generating strong emotions: "Social injustice, motivated by emotions evoked by morally laden cognitions about right and wrong, can motivate individuals, groups, and nations to take action, including violence and war, in order to right perceived wrongs." These "strong" emotions help connect participants across demographic differences, including ages, and are a means of expression that goes beyond mere reliance on words, written or spoken.

These emotional connections can be seen across the lifecycle and among different demographic groups (Ellis, 2002; Goodwin, Jasper & Polletta, 2009; Flam & King, 2007). However, the emotional responses, or what is sometimes referred to as emotional energy, provide youth with a powerful motivator for energizing and connecting what appears to be, on the surface, disparate groups of youth in pursuit of a common social change agenda (Brown & Pickerill, 2009). The collective experience in seeking these changes results in collective learning and memory, further reinforcing how emotions shape life experiences and identities.

The Coming Together of Three Social Movements

The call for thinking of these food, environmental and immigrant-rights social injustices as having a common core is not new, preparing activists, youth as well as adults, to engage in these forms of social justice causes. A number of scholars have addressed the needs and processes of bringing these social justice issues together. Thinking of these social justice campaigns and movements as sharing enough commonalities that they can come under one roof provides organizations with tremendous flexibility in creating a cadre of youth activists with sufficient flexibility to engage in various social justice issues.

Gleeson (2008) discusses how organizing for immigrant labor rights brings newcomers into other spheres of social injustices. Wald (2011), in turn, posits that the food justice movement can emphasize workers' and immigrants' rights. Cheap labor in the food industry, along with unhealthy work and living situations, add a dimension to discussions of social justice and immigrants (Marcelli, Power & Spalding, 2001; Rohe, 2006; Siqueira et al., 2014; Sziarto & Leitner, 2010).

There is a call for coordinating social justice movements to increase the long-term impact of these "critical moments" (Becher, 2012). Bringing immigrant rights to the discussion of food and environmental justice represents the latest efforts at unifying these movements, which can be facilitated from a neighborhood (spatial) and youth viewpoint because, unlike their adult counterparts, youth do not have a vested interest in a single-issue and can see interconnectedness between injustices. Youth possess energy, a willingness to explore, and they are not encumbered with conventional thinking, possessing a deep belief that anything is possible. These qualities make them an ideal group to undertake social activism.

Schlosberg (2013) sees the value of broadening the sphere of discourse of environmental justice to include other forms of injustices, with immigrant-rights being one example. Expanding this discourse serves to ground marginalized people's life experiences in a "real" manner because it is rare for someone to be marginalized because of one characteristic or circumstance. Conceiving of 'environment' as where we live, work and play, for example, contextualizes this concept in an encompassing manner. Consequently, we can argue that immigrant-rights issues impinge on food, environmental, and other forms of injustices because of their vulnerable positions.

Immigrants often live in neighborhoods with severe environmental and food issues, and in all likelihood work in jobs that expose them to unhealthy food and negative environmental forces, with little recourse in seeking justice because of their document status (Brady, 2014). Their ability to obtain help is also compromised, making the consequences of their marginalized status that much harder on them and their families. Their social status makes them invisible and without the political power to influence elected officials.

Gottlieb and Fisher, (1996, p. 193), over twenty years ago, brought together food and environmental justice, seeing the parallels and potential of these two movements coming together to achieve significant social good: "Environmental justice and community food security represent parallel though largely separate movements whose linkage would help establish a new community development, environmental, and empowerment-based discourse. Environmental justice has been limited by its risk discrimination focus, even as environmental justice organizations have shifted to a broader social justice orientation, eclipsing their earlier environmental focus. Community food security advocacy, while offering a concrete example of linked agendas and constituencies, has yet to effectively outreach to environmental justice groups. Coalition building efforts, such as the Community Food Security Empowerment Act, present that opportunity."

Bringing together coalitions as a mechanism to increase overlap between social movements helps bridge existing gaps and barriers to increase the impact of youth and other activists at the community level.

The immigrant-rights, environmental, and food justice movements have much in common and lend themselves to examining youth engagement (service-learning and civic engagement) in social justice campaigns. Gottlieb (2009, p. 7) proposes an interesting way of conceptualizing both food and environmental justice to bridge these two movements:

> One crucial way to expand the reach and breadth of the environmental justice movement and environmental justice action and research agendas would be to extend the environmental justice slogan that the environment is "where we live, work, and play" to include "where, what, and how we eat." The linkages between an environmental justice and food justice approach can extend beyond traditional notions of environmental or food issues to address issues of health, globalization, worker rights and working conditions, disparities regarding access to environmental (or food) goods, land use and respect for the land, and, ultimately, how our production, transportation, distribution, and consumption systems are organized.

Gottlieb's conceptualization also can be applied to immigrant-rights social activism, serving as a bridge between various social protests at a community level. It can be argued that the separation of these movements fails to acknowledge that people live in communities (spatial) where this form of separation between these justice issues is artificial, including other forms of injustices not covered in this book (Sze & London, 2008). Youth are adept at seeing this disconnect. Each of these social movements, however, is worthy itself of the support it has received and the substantial bodies of scholarly work and media coverage of activities focused on it.

Having community-centered efforts bridging these three movements increases the relevance of social justice campaigns and highlights the impact of injustices in everyday life (Soler-i-Martí, 2014). Sze and London (2008) introduce the concept of praxis, and as discussed, a concept closely associated with social justice efforts, as a way of illustrating how social movements intersect, leading to more sophisticated spatial methodologies and critical social theory construction. Taking a spatial justice perspective through a focus on urban communities provides the necessary geographic-focused lens through which to understand why these three forms of social injustice have particular appeal to activists.

Youth Rights

The emergence of the "youth rights movement," or otherwise known as the "youth liberation movement," reflects the emergence of youth political consciousness and critical literacy with direct connections to social justice values and principles, and their marginalized standing in society worldwide (Bhabha, 2013; Canton, 2014; Moll & Renault, 2014; XIE & LIAO, 2011). A youth rights paradigm challenges conventional views of youth and their capabilities, resulting in potential conflicts involving adults in positions of authority (Stoecklin & Bonvin, 2014).

Youth rights can be viewed from two fundamental perspectives: (1) nurturance rights consist of a right to be safe, cared for, and legally protected; and

(2) self-determination, which usually entails political, self-expression, and participation rights (Ben-Arieh & Kosher, 2014). However, self-determination rights invariably get overlooked by adults. Self-determination is grounded within socio-political concerns and bound to generate disagreement and even tensions in how adults interpret this right.

A youth rights perspective on social movements highlights the fundamental importance of participatory democracy for a significant segment of society (Goodwin-De Faria & Marinos, 2012; Invernizzi & Williams, 2013; Percy-Smith & Thomas, 2010). A right to free speech is not the exclusive purview of adults. Highlighting youth rights introduces adult roles and responsibilities and the maintaining of a balance, which at times is subject to tensions inherent in any relationship (Jones, 2012).

This perspective takes on significance when youth are marginalized because of their age, sexual identity, intellectual and physical abilities, ethnicity/race, and economic standing (Shah, 2011, p. 2): "Youth organizing groups do so [nurture leadership and organizing skills], in part, by attending to the lived cultural and political experiences of young people, while also providing safe and inviting spaces for youth." Wearing (2011) argues for a rights perspective and inclusive practice enabling self-confidence, resilience, and capacities of youth to counter social exclusion and development of a counter-narrative.

In a report titled "Youth as Effective Citizens" written by the International Youth Foundation (Pittman, Ferber & Irby, 2000), an emphasis is placed on youth as a valuable constituency, stressing the importance of finding highly imaginative ways of creating engaging and empowering situations. Ginwright, Noguera, and Cammarota (2006) and other scholars argue that youth have been rendered as second-class citizens, severely limiting their participation in society, simply by their age rather than because of an act they have committed. Limiting their voices and participation translates into limiting their potential contributions (Mitra, Serrierem & Kirshner, 2013; Pittman, Martin & Williams, 2007; Smith 2010).

The emergence of civic engagement as a form of intervention provides a widely acknowledged avenue for youth to play an active role in their communities and society. However, civic engagement has been conceptualized rather narrowly to only include "acceptable" ways of participating, as determined by adults and the institutions they represent. Thus, youth can participate and contribute as long as they do so following adult guidelines, rules, and procedures. In essence, adults dictate what is acceptable and not acceptable. Chapter 4 addresses this point in much greater detail.

Although the 1989 United Nations Convention on the Rights of the Child popularized youth rights worldwide and served as an impetus for nations to re-examine conventional views of youth, their rights in the United States has a history that is far older (Keniston, 1962). Consequently, the question of what rights do youth possess in the United States is not a recent occurrence. Its historical context highlights the long struggle for social justice, making this topic more than just a "fad."

More specifically, the youth rights movement in the United States can be traced back to the 1930s, and it was greatly influenced by the efforts exercised by the American Youth Congress in 1936 (pp. 1–2):

> Today our lives are threatened by war, our liberties threatened by reactionary legislation, and our right to happiness remains illusory in a world of insecurity . . . We the Young People of America . . . announce our declaration—A Declaration of the Rights of American Youth. We declare that our generation is rightly entitled to a useful, creative, and happy life, the guarantees of which are: full educational opportunities, steady employment and adequate wages, security in time of need, civil rights, religious freedom, and peace. We have a right to life . . . We have a right to liberty . . . We have right to happiness . . . Therefore, we the young people of America, reaffirm our right to life, liberty, and the pursuit of happiness. With confidence we look forward to a better life, a larger liberty and freedom. To those ends we dedicate our lives, our intelligence and our unified strength.

The Youth Rights Movement set the stage for youth social activism, and the Great Depression served as the context of this historical moment (Reiman, 2010).

The American Youth Congress captures and successfully conveys the fundamental beliefs and principles associated with a social justice perspective that is youth-centered. Their declaration of rights highlights the desire and abilities of youth to assume a position and status in society that encourages them to exercise greater voice and decision-making powers in their lives. A generational lens highlights common experiences of an age group and exposes justice-related issues and concerns specific to their circumstances.

Cohen (1945, pp. 16–17), in a *New York Times Magazine* article written over seventy years ago and approximately ten years after the American Youth Congress declaration, identified ten youth rights by invoking the American Constitution, which builds upon those promulgated by the American Youth Congress, and does so in a vernacular that reaches out to a typical citizenship:

    I. The right to let childhood be forgotten;
    II. The right to a 'say' about his own life;
    III. The right to make mistakes, to find out for oneself;
    IV. The right to have rules explained, not imposed;
    V. The right to have fun and companions;
    VI. The right to question ideas;
    VII. The right to be at the romantic age;
    VIII. The right to a fair chance and opportunity;
    IX. The right to struggle toward his own philosophy of life; and
    X. The right to professional help whenever necessary.

Cohen's set of youth rights captures the operative reality of the challenges that youth face in our society, while maintaining the importance of youth hope and energy for altering their immediate social environment. Males (1996, 1999), like Cohen, is quick to point out the severe disadvantages youth face in this society. These disadvantages are compounded when youth are also further marginalized by their racial/ethnic background, sexual identity, abilities, and low socioeconomic backgrounds. These "multiple jeopardies" highlight barriers many youth face in becoming valuable contributing members of society.

Critical Literacy

Paulo Freire has shaped much of the thinking on critical literacy and praxis. When community practice embraces social justice as a guiding value or philosophy, which is the foundation upon which community practice must take towards marginalized youth if it is to undertake initiatives of relevance in their lives, then the role and importance of critical literacy becomes an obvious "tool" for adults engaging and working with youth (Duncan-Andrade, 2006; Marri & Walker, 2008; Street, 2014). Gruenewald (2008, p. 308) synthesizes "critical pedagogy" and "place-based education" and introduces the concept of "critical pedagogy of place," with an emphasis on the spatial aspects of social experience, in an effort to introduce a critical social analysis into thinking and discussion of the environment.

Pope (2014, p. 241), in turn, introduces the concept of "critical civic consciousness" in bridging the work of Giroux and Freire in an attempt to bring school and community-based worlds together:

> This conceptual article describes critical civic consciousness, a new theoretical framework suitable for engaging in research on school-based civic engagement opportunities when they occur. The framework incorporates elements of Giroux's critical citizenship and Freire's conscientização to critically examine existing descriptions of the civic opportunity gap in the United States. Critical civic consciousness offers a means of conceptualizing civic engagement opportunities that moves beyond the common sense correlation between in-school experiences and later "real-world" applications that permeates existing research on the topic.

Critical civic consciousness dialogue provides practitioners and academics with a tool or window to discuss many of the concepts related to rights and social justice covered in this book.

This dialogue is a two-sided exchange because adults, too, can enhance their critical literacy skills by learning from youth allies (Johnson, 2014; Luke, 2012). Learning is a lifelong undertaking and it is not restricted by age. In addition, the process of acquiring critical literacy skills is founded upon a relationship based upon mutual respect, compassion, and understanding (Daniels, 2012). Learning is a fundamental element before action can transpire, and continues once actions unfold. For learning to transpire, youth must first consciously be aware of their own oppression and how their respective groups have been oppressed historically (Ardizzone, 2007; Deardorff, 2015).

Engagement in what has been called "dialogues of resistance" is founded upon mutual trust and space to explore and reflect, representing an avenue through which praxis can occur (Grady, Marquez & Mclaren, 2012). There is a propensity in the literature, however, to examine praxis as an individual phenomenon or experience, even though it can and often does transpire within a group or collective.

Critical literacy consists of two key words. Shor (1999, p. 2) argues that "literacy is understood as social action through language use that develops us as agents inside a larger culture." Anderson and Irvine (1993, p. 82), in turn, provide a definition of critical literacy and tie it to the importance of social action: "critical literacy is understood as learning to read and write as part of the process of becoming conscious of one's experience as historically constructed within specific power relations."

The process of self-reflection and discovery are integral to critical literacy and so are taking a moral stand and taking action (Shor, 1999, 2012). It is also about adults being able to take the position that they are not infallible authorities (Aukerman, 2012). This is particularly challenging because of our adultist tendencies.

Rogers and Schaene's (2014) review of the literature uncovered four foundational areas of the critical literacy field that lend themselves for debate and critique, with theoretical and practical implications for youth social activism: (1) context; (2) reflexivity; (3) social action; and (4) a deconstructive–reconstructive stance toward inquiry. A social justice thread cuts across these four areas. Critical race theory is an example of how these threads inform racial justice (Abrams & Moio, 2009).

Bishop (2014) poses a series of questions on youth organizing that address critical literacy: How do urban youth organizers engage in critical literacy praxis as they become activists? How do urban youth organizers articulate a vision of themselves as activists? Critical literacy praxis focuses on structures, structural violence, and power systems, and translates this knowledge into cycles of action and reflection on the critical socio-political issues impacting on their lives. The scope of intersectionality unfolds in praxis, bringing various forms of oppression in individual lives and corresponding actions (Cho, Crenshaw & McCall, 2013; Cox, 2011).

Critical literacy offers an ideological framework that fosters the development of a knowledge base from which empowerment can occur and oppose oppressive forces in the institutions serving and educating them and society (Johnson, 2014; Hung, Lim & Jamaludin, 2014; Morrell, 2004, 2008), including how youth gender and gender identity shapes this discourse (Gordon, 2008; Russell et al., 2009; Taft, 2010; Williams, 2014). Critical literacy is not restricted to youth and has applicability to all oppressed groups regardless of their age.

Connor (2014, p. 447) examined learning outcomes and learning environment of 25 former youth organizers in a program that promoted social change:

> Results show that the learning outcomes and the features of the learning environment that the participants identify reflect key tenets of Freirean critical pedagogy. As young adults, the participants indicate that they continue to draw on the critical thinking, introspection, communication, and interpersonal skills they developed as youth organizers, and they highlight the value of relevant content, an open atmosphere for discussion and debate, and peer education in promoting such durable learning.

Connor's findings advance the need for an atmosphere where youth can be affirmed and be free to express themselves and learn based upon their individual needs.

Bishop (2014) addresses the role of critical literacy in shaping youth organizers, and his findings reinforce the central thrust of Connor's (2014) conclusions concerning the importance of social action: "Youth organizing programming . . . can offer a generative, safe space within community-based organizations from which to engage young people in critical reflection upon their social and political contexts, to collectively envision and take action for positive change. As a space not congested by external measures of formal education, organizing projects provide an informal youth development platform through which critical literacy learning is more fully realized . . . [and] call for further creation of such safe spaces for ethical, intersubjective, social justice youth activism."

Critical literacy can be conducive to youth engagement, as in the case of using media as a mechanism for altering public perceptions of marginalized youth (Athanases & de Oliveira, 2014; Goodman, 2003; Hauge, 2014; Nixon, 2014). Shiller (2013), in turn, addresses how adults and community-based organizations can create a cadre of urban youth through civic engagement.

All age groups are capable of using media when it is adjusted to take into account developmental stages and abilities (Montgomery, 2014; Tyner, 2014). Adult allies can enable youth to undertake research projects with social significance in their lives, explore written materials and documents of direct relevance to their surroundings, and develop visions of a more just society (Janks, 2014).

The use of satire and humor, through the use of political cartoons and geopolitics, for example, has been found to be effective in critical literacy efforts with youth (Hörschelmann & El Refaie, 2014). Use of photovoice as a mechanism to help youth explore their geographical surroundings (places) and attach political meanings to these spaces is another example of how critical literacy can be used to help urban youth (Burke, Greene & McKenna, 2014; Dakin et al., 2014; Pritzker, LaChapelle & Tatum, 2012). The reflexivity resulting from discourse sets the stage for social action (Delgado, 2015a; Suffla, Seedat & Bawa, 2015).

Development of group projects such as creation of video or photo exhibitions can add new competencies to go along with increased literacy (Chonody,

Martin & Welsh, 2014; Fortin et al., 2014; Friesem, 2014). Helping professions, too, can engage in using media skills, although unfortunately this potential has not been realized, as in the case of social work, for example (Johnston-Goodstar, Richards-Schuster & Sethi, 2014).

Kirshner (2007) addresses youth learning through activism and identified four distinctive qualities of learning environments in these undertakings: (1) collective problem solving; (2) youth–adult interaction; (3) exploration of alternative frames for identity; and (4) bridges to academic and civic institutions. Each of these qualities has an underlying theme of critical literacy as a conceptual glue and vehicle for assisting youth activists in grounding their newfound knowledge and competencies, which, in turn, will lead to social activism on their part.

Critical literacy can be obtained within and outside educational settings, providing adult allies with a vehicle to aid youth in acquiring requisite knowledge and eventual skill-sets that enhance their abilities to engage in social-justice–related work (Checkoway, 2013; Kellner & Share, 2005; Rogers et al., 2014). Youth literacies acquired outside of the classroom are significantly more important than the ones they acquire within the classroom, with far-reaching sociopolitical implications (Rogers et al., 2014). Outside the classroom, youth are not encumbered by institutional pressures to conform to adult expectations of what constitutes a "good citizen."

Informal learning environments facilitate the use of context (where "real life" is experienced) and the legitimacy of informal or indigenous knowledge as a means of grounding the meaning of this form of education. It is a lens through which individuals gain greater clarity in their everyday world, providing a vocabulary that gives meaning to new insights (Leonard & McLaren, 2002; Lewison, Flint & Van Sluys, 2002; Street, 2003).

The more everyday life is viewed as the context for the acquisition of critical literacy knowledge and skills, and their ability to question, the greater the meaning youth will ascribe to these lessons (Kim, 2013; Vasquez, 2014), and the higher the likelihood that social change can result (Lankshear & Knobel, 2011). Critiquing by its very nature is engaging of youth (McInerney, 2009). The importance of critical literacy is multifaceted for all parties engaged in discourse, and education and too important to be restricted to any one setting (Johnson & Vasudevan, 2012; Morrell, 2008).

The youth knowledge that ensues from critical literacies serves to benefit youth as well as the adults they are engaged with (Kincheloe, McLaren & Steinberg, 2011). Praxis, simply put, is emancipating/liberating (Fuller & Kitchin, 2004; Johansson & Lindhult, 2008; Mayo, 2004), and human flourishing is not possible without it (McCormack, & Titchen, 2006).

Coffey and Farrugia (2014, p. 461) address conceptual challenges in embracing the concept of agency and applying it to youth:

> Agency is a conceptual problem for youth studies. While the term is used in many analyses of young people's lives . . . the nature and conceptual

meaning of agency remain ambiguous: agency is a 'black box' which while fundamental to youth sociology remains unpacked. Ontological and epistemological confusion about the concept means that appeals to agency in contemporary youth sociology beg the very questions they claim to answer. Nevertheless, the concept has become central to the conceptual and political basis of youth research, coming to stand for practices that are "bounded" by structures and resist existing states of affairs. This limits the explanatory power of theoretical frameworks in youth studies, and does not serve the ethical commitments of a politically engaged discipline. Identifying conceptual and normative problems raised by the way agency is deployed, this paper argues that a conceptually powerful and politically engaged youth sociology must move beyond the problem of agency as it stands, and incorporates theoretical perspectives on youth subjectivities and social action that indicate possibilities for how this might take place.

Youth agency is certainly not without conceptual and methodological challenges, but it is worth the time and struggles inherent in solving these challenges. These challenges are not adults' to solve, but they can be solved in partnership with youth.

Agency has currency in youth studies because of how it brings together key elements related to social justice and social change (Lesko & Talburt, 2012). Any effort to accomplish such a noteworthy goal is bound to bring incredible challenges and tensions, and if successfully addressed, have significant impact on youth well-being, setting the stage for potential leadership as adults.

Conclusion

Social justice knows no boundaries and lends itself to creation of political and identity consciousness when integrated into experiential education, and this serves youth well in their quest to change their socio-economic environment and how adults behave towards them (Clay, 2006). A social justice perspective on food, environmental, and immigrant rights brings together what appears to be seemingly unrelated movements, increasing the potential of achieving meaningful changes in communities and society.

This chapter provided a foundation upon which to appreciate how social justice movements influence who participates in change efforts and why they do so, taking a youth point of view. Social justice campaigns and movements are obviously not restricted to the United States (Koffel, 2003). The following chapter provides community practitioners with a well-established mechanism through which to introduce or reinforce social justice values in shaping how service-learning gets conceptualized and implemented in youth social activism.

4

COMMUNITY PRACTICE AND SERVICE-LEARNING

Introduction

It is appropriate to start this chapter by posing the perennial question of how adults can best foster youth service to a community. More specifically, how can adults from all walks of life foster and enhance youth social activism and further the causes associated with social justice? We can stand by and observe or even marvel at youth engaging in protest. We can even go so far as to create learning situations within the organizations that we control to foster youth activism and the principles these campaigns and movements are founded upon. Tapping youth cultural assets further enhances their potential to address social justice issues within their communities (Borrero et al., 2012; Rodríguez & Oseguera, 2015).

Adult social activists, in addition to being youth allies, can also be role models for youth, particularly in cases where youth have multiple jeopardies and have had few opportunities to come across adults with interests in social justice and social activism, and who also have faced similar forms of oppression in their lives, with lesbian youth being such an example (Harris, 2013; Llera & Katsirebas, 2010; Sadowski, Chow & Scanlon, 2009). Multiple oppressions result in even more complex lives, increasing the importance of adults, as well as other youths in the lives of those with increased challenges.

Differentiating "education" from "schooling" opens up new ways of viewing how knowledge can be acquired and made more relevant for the learner, regardless of their age (Reis, Ng-A-Fook & Glithero, 2015). Service-learning is considered the most powerful and far-reaching educational reform movement in the United States (Sheffield, 2011), and any review of the professional literature will attest to this popularity (Reason & Hemer, 2014).

Service-learning, a form of experiential learning, is a goal, process, program, community development model, philosophy, and pedagogy (Butin, 2010;

Kielsmier, 2000) resulting in a myriad points of view. As a pedagogical tool, it brings together social and academic benefits, adding value to each and transforming each in the process, and no more so than when introducing social justice values and goals within a context that can help marginalized youth. Service-learning has also been referred to as "contextual learning."

Harkavy and Hartley (2010) trace the philosophical and historical roots of service-learning and how context shaped its evolution. The 1930s are often cited as a significant decade in the development of service-learning, with the publications of seminal books such as Hanna's (1937) *Youth Serves the Community* and Counts' (1932) *Does the School Build a New Social Order?* However, there is no disputing John Dewey's influence.

Eyler (2009) credits the theoretical roots of service-learning to John Dewey's *Democracy and Education* (1916), *How We Think* (1933), and *Experiences and Education* (1938), which are often cited as establishing a foundation for service-learning. Harkavy and Benson (1997), in a book written almost twenty years ago and still relevant today, identified four propositions that have roots in John Dewey's seminal service-learning work: (1) Reflective thought is a response to the challenges faced in daily lived experiences; (2) Learning is enhanced when the learner is active in a meaningful way in learning/service activities; (3) All learners have the potential to make significant contributions to their own learning; and (4) Knowledge for the sake of knowledge is not the purpose of engagement, but knowledge for the betterment of the community is the central goal.

John Dewey's influences have extended to civic engagement because of its emphasis on experiential learning (Coleman & Gotze, 2001; Fiorina, 1999; Hildreth, 2012). Deans (1999), however, ties Dewey's theories and Paulo Freire's critical pedagogical theories together to support social justice service-learning, bringing a more modern influence.

Service-learning has surged in popularity over the past four decades as an attractive concept and strategy for creating learning situations for youth that can translate into a wide range of positive individual outcomes, as well as the communities that are the beneficiaries of their service-focused efforts (Furco & Billig, 2002; Gibson et al., 2011; Tinkler et al., 2014). It is no mistake that service-learning has worldwide appeal and a bright future (Anitsal et al., 2014; Sachau et al., 2014).

Traditional service-learning approaches are increasingly being challenged when discussing groups facing serious social challenges in their lives. Kinloch, Nemeth, and Patterson (2014), for example, advocate for the reframing of conventional service-learning as active learning and participation experiences with urban youth through the application of critical literacy and an embrace of social justice concepts. Making service-learning relevant for urban youth is only possible through its grounding in their immediate social-economic-political circumstances, which is a theme that will resonate throughout this book; a plethora of scholars and practitioners support this stance.

There is nothing inherent in service-learning that makes it political or apolitical in how it is conceptualized. Service-learning can be apolitical, and unfortunately this approach has generally eschewed "radical" social justice causes and in the process concentrated on teaching academic subjects, with service taking on a secondary role, ignoring social issues in the process. Social justice projects may bring political pressure on institutions sponsoring these projects, making them unpopular. Apolitical projects, however, hold little appeal to marginalized urban youth.

When service-learning targets marginalized youth and communities, its benefits are greatly increased when goals are focused on social justice and youth play a significant role in dictating how the projects unfold (Scott, 2008). If service-learning is based upon interlocking elements of critical pedagogies, a counter-narrative emerges that subverts facets of formal education that alienate and oppress students with histories of being silenced and marginalized (Gillis & Mac Lellan, 2010; Hart, 2006).

Service-learning must be based on social justice values and goals (Gilbride-Brown, 2008; Griffin & Ouellett, 2007). It is important that the reader understand that there is no consensus in the field that social justice must have a prominent place or play any part in service-learning (Hartley, 2009).

Epiphanies experienced through service-learning have the potential to be transformative and last a lifetime (Bamber & Hankin, 2011; Meyers, 2009; Rendon, 2009). Ardizzone (2007, p. 22) touches on this point but arrives at a different conclusion: "While inner city youth activists have had critical or thought-provoking experiences, none of these experiences can be viewed as epiphanic—in that they were not 'life-altering' or instantaneous calls to action." Where these moments of clarity, epiphanies, or critical events can transpire can certainly be debated, but their significance cannot.

Bowen (2014) argues that service-learning that does not link social justice education to service-learning undermines the potential of this pedagogy, and a deficit or "charity" paradigm, which tends to be the norm, undermines the transformative potential of this learning approach. A "charity" perspective does not mean that youth do not benefit from the experience when compared to a social justice motivation, or that it does not make youth feel good about their service (Moely, Furco & Reed, 2008). Whether the recipients view the experience as welcoming, positive, or transformative must be taken into account in assessing the value of these services.

A charity paradigm can manifest itself with students preferring to engage in direct practice and the sponsoring organization more than willing to oblige (Bowen, 2014; Bringle et al., 2006; Cone, 2003). Cipolle (2010, p. ix), too, addresses a deficit or charity paradigm in service-learning:

It is difficult to get preservice teachers to see marginalized communities in the context of larger power struggles, and some White, preservice teachers see themselves as "saviors," maintaining a deficit view of the children they are tutoring. Students' essays often reflect minimal growth toward a criticized understanding of reality, and they have difficulty critically reflecting on both their personal biases and the structured causes of poverty at the same time.

Egger (2008) and Tilley-Lubbs (2009), too, address this point and arrive at a similar conclusion.

Having community residents assume "expert" roles helps to ensure a non-charity view of the service provided by youth and casts them into an unfamiliar role in the process (d'Arlach, Sánchez & Feuer, 2009). Further, it acknowledges that all communities possess assets that can be mobilized and partnered within service to communities (Delgado & Humm-Delgado, 2013).

Cipolle (2010) makes an important contribution on the significance of this form of relationship in her book titled *Service-Learning and Social Justice: Engaging Students in Social Change*. A call for "decolonizing" curriculum has occurred in response to this missed opportunity at addressing social justice, with implications for oppressed groups (Goodman et al., 2015).

This rather lengthy chapter introduction should ground the reader for what is to follow; the primary goal is to provide a conceptual introduction on social justice (critical) focused service-learning fostering urban youth activism in service to their community. Although service-learning enjoys wide popularity, major conceptual and philosophical schisms exist within this practice arena for undertaking community practice with urban youth (Mayhew & Fernández, 2007; Phillips, 2011).

Definition of Service-Learning

Defining community service-learning is arduous (Link et al., 2012). Service-learning has been in existence for a long period of time and this has resulted in numerous definitions describing this major educational-social intervention (Desmond, Stahl & Graham, 2011; Hale, 2008; Verjee, 2010). In 1990, there were 147 definitions of service-learning (Kendall, 1990), and one can only imagine how many more definitions have been added over the past 25 years. Remarkably, the vastness of the literature and definitions has not caused great confusion or controversy about this method, although this is not to say that major differences do not exist (Hart, Matsuba & Atkins, 2008).

Before addressing a definition of service-learning, we need to differentiate between service-learning and community service because they may simply be thought of as interchangeable. Youth community-service is not linked to curriculum or pedagogical goals, thereby placing learning in the hands of youth without the benefit of educational goals (Dymond, Renzaglia & Chun, 2008). Thus, when learning does transpire it is a secondary goal rather than as a specified or primary goal. This topic re-emerges in the next chapter on civic engagement.

Service-learning is dynamic and the differences in definition and implementation must be acknowledged because not all projects share the same goals and philosophical foundation, with differences related to skill-sets and reflexivity, civic values, critical citizenship, and emphasis on social justice activism, to note but a few key elements (Britt, 2012; Henry, 2011; Love, 2008). Introducing social justice into service-learning does not automatically translate into an acceptance of these principles, necessitating youth active engagement in a process of discourse and discovery (Boyle-Baise & Langford, 2004).

Bringle and Hatcher (2009, p. 38) capture the essential elements found in most definitions:

> Service learning is defined as a course-based, credit bearing educational experience in which students (a) participate in an organized service activity that meets identified community needs, and (b) reflect on the service activity in such a way as to gain further understanding of course content, a broader appreciation of the discipline, and an enhanced sense of personal values and civic responsibility.

Learning, partnerships, structured activity, mutually beneficial collaboration, and community are all essential elements or components of service-learning (Bringle, Clayton & Price, 2009; Frost et al., 2010).

The inclusion of social justice values in this definition explicitly shifts its political stance away from apolitical or neutral, making services provided non-charity based. "Doing with" is dramatically different in philosophy, foundation, tone, and motivation when compared to "doing for" (Verjee, 2010). "Doing for" is politically conservative and charity-based, with the outcomes being immediate or very limited in scope. Personal transformation will not be associated with a charity paradigm for the provider or recipient of the service.

Jones and Steinberg (2012) identify serious shortcomings on how service-learning can be conceptualized in a multitude of ways, making comparisons challenging at best, and compromising a comprehensive understanding of this learning approach, which is often its central goal:

> Research on service learning suffers from a lack of clarity in defining service learning as an independent variable. In practice, many community-based activities that carry the label service learning run the range of one-time service events as part of a course with little reflection and academic integration to service experiences of several hours per week during a semester with frequent and deep reflection.

There is always room for conceptual clarity in discussing social-justice–inspired service-learning (Cipolle, 2010).

Service-learning can be viewed from a variety of perspectives according to settings, goals, time period covered, and degree to which a project seeks to achieve social justice. This flexibility allows local circumstances, organizational missions, contexts, and goals to guide how projects get conceptualized and carried out in a wide variety of urban settings and with different age groups. However, there is no denying that the likelihood of schools playing critical roles as originators is quite high, although this method is not restricted to schools.

Benefits of Service-Learning

The field of service-learning has enjoyed tremendous popularity in the United States and other nations the past 20 years, opening up new possibilities for using this method to teach youth academic and non-academic subjects (Chupp & Joseph, 2010; Donaldson & Daughtery; 2011; Harre, 2007). Not surprisingly, the benefits of service-learning have played a significant role in moving this field forward.

Service-learning has extensive literature to draw upon, and it has resulted in a number of literature reviews. Celio, Durlak, and Dymnicki (2011), in a meta-analysis of the literature on service-learning benefits for students, found evidence of significant personal and academic benefits gained through participation. Warren's (2012) review of the literature, in turn, found positive influences on student learning outcomes irrespective of the way learning was conceptualized and measured.

Goethem and colleagues (2014), too, undertook a meta-analysis of the effects of community services on youth (adolescents) and found that community service resulted in academic, personal, social, and civic gains. However, findings reinforced the importance of reflection, an important aspect of praxis. Community service-learning without an opportunity to reflect resulted in negative benefits. In the case of urban youth of color, this reflection provides an opportunity for critical analysis, which leads to social action (Nieto & McDonough, 2011).

Service-learning is ideally suited as an intervention method to help address social issues of race and privilege in a manner that both increases youth awareness but also changes behaviors through acquisition of personal experiences and narratives (Espino Lee, 2011). It has been found to promote moral and social development (Ferrari & Chapman, 2014). Although the results have been mixed (Bernacki & Jaeger, 2008), they can be enhanced through service-learning.

Psycho-social (wisdom and values), too, can be enhanced through participation in service-learning (Bailey & Russell, 2008; Zins & Elias, 2007). In essence, character development must be an essential goal of service-learning (David, 2009). Learning about diversity and cultural humility, too, take on significance in service-learning projects (Bassey, 2010; Jay, 2008), particularly those that are social justice and urban focused.

Service-learning can also help youth develop an appreciation for how resistance to change can manifest itself in service-learning projects led by youth and the organizations sponsoring and receiving the service (Brabant & Braid, 2009;

Hart, Matsuba & Atkins, 2008; Simons et al., 2011; Thomson et al., 2008; Weil, 2011). Learning how to identify and address resistance necessitates having specific knowledge of how it can manifest itself, and few formal courses teach this knowledge. Thus, it has to be obtained on the job or in the "real world." Youth acquiring skill-sets that can be used to identify and overcome resistance can transfer them to other spheres of their lives.

The reach of service-leaning can be quite dramatic. Service-learning, for example, has also even been proposed as a way of stemming school dropouts/ increasing retention while concomitantly creating a cadre of youth who are not only academically qualified to continue on to college but possess a strong sense of civic responsibility (Bridgeland, DiIulio & Wulsin, 2008; Kinloch, 2014; Simonet, 2008). Increasing political and human capital among these youth can have a significant and wide-reaching influence within communities that historically have not had college graduates within their midst.

How service-learning gets structured and delivered has a bearing on who benefits. Mironesco (2014), for example, found that when service-learning is flexible in conceptualization and operationalization (online, hybrid, etc.), taking into account student needs and circumstances, non-traditional students benefit, increasing retention and learning because it takes into account their schedules and other time demands. Butin (2015, p. 5) posits that those "most wishing for the success of critical service-learning are those whose dreams are most fulfilled."

The climate in which service-learning transpires influences how students benefit from service-learning, which is an aspect of service-learning that rarely gets addressed in the literature (Levesque-Bristol, Knapp & Fisher, 2010, p. 208): "Results showed that when service-learning contributes to an enhancement of the positivity of the learning climate, then positive forms of motivation, civic skills, problem solving, and appreciation of diversity significantly increased over the course of the semester. Results also showed that type of involvement, amount of in-class discussion, and reflections are important factors contributing to the effectiveness of the service-learning environment." A welcoming and affirming organizational climate does not just happen. Organizational culture is shaped by leadership and an explicit embrace of values that must be clearly articulated to staff and to the external world.

When critical reflection is integrated into service-learning, it provides students with an opportunity to connect this form of experiential learning to personal troubles and social issues, engendering the strong possibility of transformation occurring as a result of their participation and investment of energy and time (Molee et al., 2010). When service-learning is combined with youth participation or activism it benefits their community and the broader society and helps youth learn and create a positive social and political identity for themselves (Harre, 2007; Torres-Harding & Meyers, 2013).

Taines (2012) found social activism to be viable for engaging students who felt alienated or not fully engaged within their school, making social activism particularly attractive for youth who also have limited social purposes and outlets for their frustrations and anger. Butin (2007), in turn, refers to this form of service-learning as "justice-learning" because of how learning is closely tied to social justice. The introduction of a justice focus goes far beyond semantics because of how this value base shapes all aspects of service-learning.

We learn especially well, and with great significance and profound meaning in our lives, when we are emotionally invested in meaningful learning (Berger, 2015). Experiential learning becomes even more attractive to youth who have not been able to find success and fulfillment through conventional academics. Experiential learning is an overarching construct that can incorporate community service, internships, civic engagement, and service-learning.

Memories gained through experiential learning, particularly when collectively experienced, can be lasting and quite significant. Service-learning, as well as civic engagement, can create meaningful learning when based upon a clear and comprehensive understanding of urban youth needs and aspirations.

Service-learning that is based in social justice is within the reach of all youth, regardless of their physical and intellectual abilities, bringing this method of learning and serving within the grasp of all youth, and showing potential to be a universal form of engagement and service (Carter, Swedeen & Moss, 2012; Carter et al., 2010; Cooper, Cripps & Reisman, 2013). Brill (1994), well over 20 years ago, addressed the educational and social values of involving youth with disabilities in service-learning projects that systematically take into account the nature of their disabilities.

Service-learning programs for youth with disabilities benefit them by providing opportunities and experiences that can facilitate their transition out of school as they age out (Law, 2002; Lorenzo et al., 2015; Walker, 2014). Social justice service-learning undertaken by youth with disabilities that results in activism is an arena open for innovative efforts. Real-life experiences, combined with necessary adult supports and the right circumstances, create experiences and memories that can be tapped in their transition away from school to careers. With proper supports, youth engaged in service-learning can develop insights and plans for post-secondary school life and roles as social activists.

Service-learning projects also can serve to give students without disabilities insights and learning about youth with disabilities, particularly social issues and discrimination (Lawler, Joseph & Narula, 2014; Santos, Ruppar & Jeans, 2011; Shaw & Roberson, 2009). In essence, the benefits can be experienced by both groups of youth (Mueller, 2014). Adults involved in these efforts, in turn, also can benefit by expanding their knowledge and experience base.

Finally, community benefits must not be lost in any discussion of service-learning (Kelshaw, Lazarus & Minier, 2009). Benefits can be instrumental or expressive, or both, and must be viewed short- and long-term to more accurately be assessed. It is also important to emphasize that any effort at assessing community benefits must take into account both formal and informal types and have the community play an active role in determining how assessment or evaluation will transpire.

Approaches and Elements of Service-Learning

Any discussion of the approaches we can take toward implementing a service-learning program must be done against a backdrop of the explicit and implicit goals guiding these initiatives. Ideally, for service-learning to achieve its lofty goals it must address the heart (passion), head (cognition), and hands (practical skills) of youth (Sipos, Battisti & Grimm, 2008). Assessing these three dimensions, although challenging, is essential in order to grasp how to approach establishing a service-learning program with a social justice base.

The hyphen in service-learning is there for a very good purpose and Eyler and Giles (1999, p. 4) state that "service-learning should include a balance between service to the community and academic learning and that the hyphen in the phrase symbolizes the central role of reflection in the process of learning through community experience." Service must never be an afterthought in service-learning, and it certainly will never be in the case of critical or social justice service-learning. Social justice service-learning, in turn, results in a lived experience for all parties, making for a longer lasting impact (Blundo, 2010).

Any discussion of theoretical approaches towards service-learning must avoid using a charity paradigm to guide efforts, as addressed earlier in this book, and this point is important enough to revisit in this chapter. Service-learning programs based on a charity paradigm look perfectly typical. Verjee (2010, p. 7) addresses the typical activities that can be associated with a charity paradigm:

> The charity paradigm of service-learning, therefore, promotes a view of citizenship that involves the transfer or reallocation of resources such as money, food, shelter, knowledge, labor, time, etc. to individuals or groups who have fewer resources. Food is donated, shelters constructed, urban community gardens built, re-cycling programs developed, and neighbourhood playgrounds are designed for children living in poverty. Students also tutor, paint buildings, serve in soup kitchens, build databases and other such things, and much of the research on service-learning is focused on the impact these experiences have on student grades, attitudes and sensitivities . . .

The reader may argue that there is a need for these activities that otherwise would not be offered. Avoiding the pitfalls of a charity paradigm will be a challenge because many in this movement may stress the importance of helping without the requisite socio-political grounding.

The power of service-learning must go beyond focusing on activities and embrace a theoretical and value base that has more profound implications beyond providing immediate assistance. There are a myriad of ways of bringing service-learning to life and this facilitates incorporating local context, goals, and budgets in shaping projects and their potential impact on both youth and the focus of their services within the communities. Progressive engagement in multiple service-learning experiences opens up the possibility of building upon prior gains as opposed to conceptualizing service-learning as a one-time event in their lives (Colby et al., 2009).

Service-learning has undoubtedly found a home being sponsored through schools and transpiring within communities. However, service-learning can also take place within schools (Wallace, 2013). Nevertheless, the undertaking of service-learning within communities, although increasing the need for planning, logistical, and political considerations, brings an element of excitement for students, particularly in the case of marginalized urban youth with few opportunities to both serve and impress adults within their communities.

Short-term service-learning, although advantageous from a scheduling and commitment perspective, has its share of challenges, such as staff capacity to train and supervise, limited options for project selection, timing and project management, and academic calendar restraints (Tryon et al., 2008). It is still possible to develop relationships and achieve concrete results in this time-intensive format, however.

The popularity of online courses, not surprisingly, has found its way into service-learning, bringing a new dimension to experiential learning (Guthrie & McCracken, 2010). Mironesco (2014) reports on the success of a hybrid service-learning course, opening up new possibilities. Apprenticeships, or internships, are another form of service-learning (Ainley & Rainbird, 2014). Internships covering an extended period of time, with requisite supervision, support and academics are popular ways of operationalizing service-learning among helping professions.

Finally, immersion represents one of the latest ways of conceptualizing service-learning, and this approach has particular appeal involving projects in foreign countries and even in efforts within the United States (Dick, Carter & Ingram, 2014; Koch Ross, Wqendell & Aleksandrova-Howell, 2014). The popularity of faith-based youth civic engagement short-term mission trips is but one example of these types of organizational efforts to aid communities (Beyerlein, Trinitapoli & Adler, 2011).

Living and serving in a community 24 hours per day over an extended period of time ranging from a few days to weeks or even months is not accessible but to those who are privileged. True, scholarships can be made available to enlist youth without the financial resources to sustain them during that period. However, urban youth from non-privileged backgrounds often have to find part-time work for those still in school in order to help their families financially, or they may have responsibilities for caring for siblings or parents with severe health needs or disabilities, for example.

In turning to political dimensions or foci of service-learning, conceptualizing enhancement of youth political competencies as a vital component of civic learning opens up a wider range of options for channeling this knowledge and inclinations into social activism. This takes on particular meaning when discussing marginalized urban low-income youth of color and their experiences with discrimination (Flanagan et al., 2009).

The definition of service-learning that was provided earlier in this chapter did not stress the importance of identifying and incorporating youth assets into activities and programming, and offering a counter-narrative argument for the use of service-learning. Fortunately, the past decade has witnessed an increased amount of scholarly and practice attention being paid to rethinking youth policies, including identifying and measuring youth assets (Bersaglio, Enns & Kepe, 2015; Delgado, 2006; Forman Jr, 2004; Woodman & Wyn, 2013). This paradigm is counter to the more conventional—and, unfortunately, highly popular—deficit perspective addressed earlier in this book and the charity paradigm discussed earlier in this section, although it is not without theoretical challenges (Adams et al., 2010).

The fostering of serving-learning among urban children and adolescents has been found to promote learning and well-being, while also giving back to communities, and the process results in concrete and lasting influence. Critical service-learning, in turn, gives license to adults to be transformed through their engagement experience (Frederick, Cave & Perencevich, 2010).

McKay (2010), too, concludes that critical service-learning, which builds upon critical literacy and praxis, achieved through youth activism can result in positive outcomes, such as promoting resilience and emotional learning. However, service-learning projects that are intended to prepare youth for engagement in electoral politics will need to address youth concerns that this form of participation may be viewed as ineffectual (Sylvester, 2010).

Electoral politics, even when narrowly defined, goes beyond voting and can also consist of helping to register new voters, making financial contributions, and volunteering in candidate election efforts, for example (McGarvey, 2005). Further, the undertaking of civic education as part of service-learning and civic engagement, too, can result in deeper and more nuanced understandings of citizenship, an increased development of a sense of efficacy as citizens, and an increased awareness of self (identity) in relation to others and their communities (Iverson & James, 2013).

Ollis (2011) examined learning within a youth activism context and concluded that a wide array of knowledge and skill sets are acquired while protesting, raising the importance of these experiences and the role service-learning can play within educational and community-based organizations. Although the options available to undertake service-learning are extensive, there is little debate that critical or social justice inspired service-learning has much to offer.

Community Practice and Service-Learning Approaches

Although much has been undertaken and written about service-learning, there certainly is always room for innovation and thinking outside the box (Deeley, 2010), particularly when service-learning is social-justice–based and involving urban marginalized youth. Stover and Bach (2012) show how using young adult literature as a call to social activism is a viable form of service-learning.

There is always the danger that service-learning only seeks to meet the needs of the initiating institution with only symbolic efforts at meeting community needs (Stoecker et al., 2010). Social justice inspired service-learning and community practice is one area that is ripe for innovation, such as that offered through social justice campaigns, and for helping to ensure that the community in service-learning does not become an afterthought.

The emphasis on service in service-learning means that youth, as in the case of this book, provide a service that is welcomed and meaningful to the communities where they reside. Learning, if thoughtfully supported and based upon a strong and clear value base, will ensue and all participants, youth as well as communities, benefit. In the case of social justice, an injustice is addressed (Miller, 2014).

The knowledge and skill-sets acquired through participation in service-learning and social activism must encompass a multi-faceted perspective, ideally with youth in the lead, in order to fully appreciate this learning and experience. Larson, Walker, and Pearce (2005) found in a study comparing youth-driven with adult-driven programs that youth made significant greater gains when they were in charge. These gains translated into youth having a high degree of ownership and empowerment and increases in the development of leadership and planning skills. These findings apply to youth and social activism, too.

For those of us in institutions of learning, we must make social justice as central theme in what we teach rather than relegate this important subject matter to a particular course, class, or week (McKenzie et al., 2008). No subject matter should eschew a social justice lens, with service-learning representing an attractive vehicle for achieving both educational and service goals (Hytten & Bettez, 2011).

Social justice material can be integrated into any number of academic subjects. It is important, however, to emphasize that social justice service-learning can also occur at the elementary school level (Wade, 2007). Maulucci (2012) and Coleman (2014) report on how to integrate social justice themes into science courses. Hoyt (2008), in turn, shows how ethical decision-making can be taught through service-learning. It can be integrated into the teaching of math (Bartell, 2013; Gutstein, 2003, 2012; Leonard et al., 2010). Ransom (2009) integrates social justice themes into a public speaking course, which is an essential competency for leadership development. Leydens and Lucena (2014), for example, advocate for the embrace of "humanitarian engineering" that embraces social justice values in guiding its application.

Academic subjects such as art (Bell & Desai, 2011; Tobey & Jellinghaus, 2012), photography (Bogre, 2012), economics (Ziegert & McGoldrick, 2008), science (Buxton, 2010; Cartwright, 2010), geography (Bednarz et al., 2008), accounting (Gallhofer & Haslam, 2004), English-language arts (Dover, 2013), composition (Finn, 2013), language arts (Epstein, 2010), children's literature (Forest, Kimmel & Garrison, 2013; Graff, 2013), engineering (Baillie, Pawley & Riley, 2012), and science (Lester et al., 2006), too, can serve to raise consciousness about social justice and direct students towards efforts at addressing social justice in their lives.

Service-learning involving social activism requires careful attention to how classroom and field learning will transpire and participants will be selected for the program (Cermak et al., 2011; Kajner et al., 2013). A number of approaches have been proposed, including those that challenge the status quo in society through the embrace of social justice (Dooley, 2007). Those embracing social justice and upsetting the status quo in their efforts to operationalize service-learning to address oppression, as noted earlier, must be prepared for political backlash (Hartley, 2009).

Pompa (2002, p. 68) explains her reservation: "Unless facilitated with great care and consciousness, 'service' can unwittingly become an exercise in patronization. In a society replete with hierarchical structures and patriarchal philosophies, service-learning's potential danger is for it to become the very thing it seeks to eschew." Robinson (2000) goes so far as to label forced voluntarism as a form of depoliticized practice or a "glorified welfare system." This perspective may seem "over the top," but it must be viewed against a social justice and oppression backdrop to appreciate this charity view of service.

Mitchell (2008, p. 62) stresses the need for social justice inspired learning-service: "Developing experiences with greater attention to equality and shared power between all participants in the service experience and challenging students to analyze the interplay of power, privilege, and oppression at the service placement and in their experience in that placement will ensure that a critical service-learning pedagogy questions and problematizes the status quo." There is a tremendous amount of responsibility that cannot be ignored when undertaking social justice or critical service-learning for all parties, adults as well as youth. It is not sufficient to raise consciousness on social oppression without a willingness to move a social change agenda forward, with each phase being carefully thought out and planned (Sheffield, 2015).

Hodson (2014, p. 67) advocates for implementation of a four-part curriculum that can be used to prepare social activists, with its final stage involving a hands-on experience:

> First, learning about the issues, that is, focusing on the science and technology aspects of important socioscientific issues (SSI), recognizing the social, cultural and economic contexts in which they are located, developing the nature of science knowledge that builds robust understanding of

contemporary scientific practice, and acquiring the media literacy necessary to access and read with critical understanding a wide variety of information sources. Second, learning to care about issues and the people impacted by them, including a focus on dealing with controversy, addressing values and developing concern for the views, needs and interests of others. Third, engaging and managing the powerful emotions often generated by SSI. Fourth, learning about sociopolitical action, taking action and evaluating action. For this key fourth element, the author advocates a 3-stage apprenticeship approach comprising modelling, guided practice and application.

Hodson's curriculum is but one example of how social justice service-learning can be conceptualized. Grounding in why social conditions exist and how youth can learn and act upon their learning is necessary, regardless of model used.

Not surprisingly, there is no one model or approach that captures the essence of this field. A variety of approaches towards service-learning reflect well on the flexibility of this way of thinking about education and its adaptability to a variety of settings and goals. Kirshner (2006), for example, advocates for the use of "youth-centered apprenticeships" in after-school and community-based organizations, as a way of having them learn about social activism, and providing a service in the process. Immersion service-learning, too, has been found to aid in social activism learning and action by providing a more "real-life" experience of what it means to be engaged in a substantial way (Koch et al., 2014).

Once a project is selected, adults can facilitate the learning process by providing readings, guest speakers, journals, and group feedback from the class. Historical re-enactments can be used to highlight key social justice issues that lend themselves to this format (Haverkos, 2015). Creation of documentaries or mobile stories (use of mobile phones) through youth writing and produced documentaries provide ways for youth to record and share their experiences and learning in service-learning projects with each other and the outside world, including communities (Charmaraman, 2013; Ranieri & Bruni, 2013).

Outside speakers can be invited into the organizations sponsoring service-learning projects to complete the feedback loops and increase transparency, an important element in fostering trust-based relationships between community-based organizations, and this includes schools and the communities that they serve. In essence, service-learning is open to creativity and innovation, allowing local circumstances to dictate how a project can unfold.

Community Practice and Service-Learning

As emphasized throughout this chapter, conventional or traditional forms of service-learning are quite different from critical or social justice service-learning (Mitchell, 2008, p. 50): "There is an emerging body of literature advocating a 'critical' approach to community service learning with an explicit social justice aim. A social change orientation, working to redistribute power, and developing authentic relationships are most often cited in the literature as points of departure from traditional service-learning." The differences are so stark that no one (youth, parent/legal guardian, practitioner, or academic) would be confused by how these two approaches unfold in the world of practice.

Service-learning can transpire in virtually any setting. However, it has found particular favor in education and academic settings and programs (Butin, 2005; Hirsch, 2011; Kinloch, 2012). Miller and Engel (2011) argue for an expansion of the public sphere in civil society, bringing forth implications for service-learning: "Civil society is situated, conversed, and created in myriad places, including civic groups, ethnic societies, and—particularly in poor urban neighborhoods—churches." It is possible to conceptualize schools as a hub, with numerous spokes emanating from the center representing service-learning projects that can be conducted in collaboration with a wide range of community settings.

Community settings that specifically reach out to youth and have reputations for addressing social justice issues, as addressed in the introductory chapter, have the greatest potential for making contributions to social action and youth. These types of settings enjoy positive reputations within communities, are accessible from a variety of perspectives (geographical, physical, psychological, cultural, and operational), increasing their attractiveness for service-learning projects. In addition, they can provide pathways for youth to engage in social activism and learning through focused discussions and activities (Maton, 2008). Social justice inspired service-learning, however, cannot be conceptualized and implemented without reliance on Freirian notions of problem-posing education, conscientization, and praxis (Smyth, Down & McInerney, 2014).

Le Grange (2007) counters the argument made in some circles that the theoretical foundations of community service-learning are weak. Nevertheless, not unexpectedly, program planning and corresponding theory are considered a neglected aspect of service-learning (Sandmann, Kiely & Grenier, 2009), opening up possibilities for practitioners making a substantial contribution to this field. Building a bridge between service to community and learning requires that this bridge be developed on both ends of the project and not from the school to the community, which is typical of service-learning initiatives (Kielsmeier, 2010). Communities, too, can engage in this process and meet schools mid-way through an equal partnership.

Community practitioners will not be at a loss in using service-learning in developing community-focused youth social activism projects, as evidenced by the wide popularity of this approach and the upsurge in scholarly literature on this subject matter. Practitioners can propose projects to schools and have them be community initiated. A number of factors have been found to foster youth activism and/or participation in civic activities.

Adult-ally ability to interweave youth development, community development, and social change enhances youth opportunities to engage in social action but with adult support (Christans & Dolan, 2011). Incidentally, this form of community development can be considered radical in some circles (Ledwith, 2011), and this support can transpire in a variety of obvious and less obvious ways depending upon the requests made by youth.

Harre (2007) has concluded that the extent of parental voluntarism becomes a key factor influencing youth participation in the civic life of their community, and it would be artificial to consider youth participation without understanding the role and support of their parents, a topic that, incidentally, does not get sufficient attention. Community organizations are in excellent positions to develop family-focused service-learning projects that can serve their needs, although this approach is counter to the individualistic approaches that are common in the field. Family social-justice–focused service-learning brings an exciting dimension that is open to innovative thinking and approaches.

Community practice and research go hand in hand. It is not surprising that scholars have made a number of recommendations for future research on youth service-learning, which incidentally also have implications for the conduct of community practice in this arena. Although the benefits of service-learning are well established, there is a call for experimental research to more firmly establish the worth and value of service-learning (Furco & Root, 2010), in addition to a call to have youth play prominent roles in conceptualizing and carrying out research involving their service and learning. Having established the need for further research, there certainly isn't a paucity of data or information on the benefits associated with service-learning.

Schusler and Krasny (2008) recommend that research focus on obtaining a nuanced understanding of youth experiences, guiding principles that have the greatest impact, educator practices, participant characteristics, educational setting, and finally, how service-learning impacts on adults, community, and culture. Viewing service-learning from a multifaceted perspective helps ensure a comprehensive understanding, which is much needed when focused on urban youth of color, although it is challenging from a research perspective.

The nature and challenge of creating effective service-learning partnerships must rest on a set of principles to guide all facets from conceptualization to planning, implementation, and evaluation. Tinkler and colleagues (2014, p. 209) propose a set of six guidelines for this form of intervention from a process and structural point-of-view: "1) Be attentive to the community partner's mission and vision, 2) Understand the human dimension of the community partner's work, 3) Be mindful of the community partner's resources, 4) Accept and share the responsibility for inefficiencies, 5) Consider the legacy of the partnership, and 6) Regard process as important."

Tinkler and colleagues and other scholars (Ambrose et al., 2010; Egger, 2008; Gonzalez, 2014; Jacoby, 2003; Mitchell, 2008) have stressed that a foundation based upon an awareness of trust, resources, and needs is essential in the crafting of interventions based upon collaborative partnerships. The initiation and development of service-learning partnerships can take one of three paths between the initiating institution and community-based organizations: (1) tentative engagement; (2) aligned engagement; and (3) committed engagement (Dorado & Giles, 2004). Trust levels and goals will dictate which of these three approaches is to be pursued and has the highest likelihood of success (Wolfe, 2013).

A major selling feature of school-based service-learning is that it emphasizes the learner. Unfortunately, it generally pays little or no attention to the community. Blouin and Perry (2009) address the research question of whom does service-learning really serve from a community-based organizational perspective on service-learning. The authors identified three major obstacles in implementing service-learning projects: (1) issues concerning student conduct; (2) poor congruity between course and organizational objectives; and (3) lack of effective and open communication between instructors and organizations. Deliberate planning and clear expectations will help minimize the likelihood of failure and the emergence of ethical conflicts and dilemmas.

Cruz and Giles (2000) issued a call for research focused on service-learning and communities. Unfortunately, progress has a long way to go before fundamental questions get answered on the process and outcomes of service-learning, particularly research that is community participatory or emancipatory action-based, and for service-learning to be worth the investment of time and tangible resources by community-based organizations (Bushouse, 2005; O'Shea, 2013).

Roehlkepartain (2009) argues that community-based organizations, in similar fashion to their educational counterparts, too, have much to gain by using service-learning in their programming. Organizational expectations of the benefits to be derived through participation in these ventures play an important role determining whether or not they wish to participate in these types of projects (McReynolds, 2014; Mike, Kelleher & Kaestner, 2014).

Practitioners can mobilize organizational resources to create practice communities that are local and can serve as facilitators for bringing together youth activists and their adult allies. This goal can be facilitated in cases where practitioners work in organizations with social change missions. Expertise and access are not to be minimized in youth projects with a social justice foundation.

Achievement of a critical consciousness is an on-going experience rather than episodic (Cipolle, 2010, p. 14):

> Once individuals develop a social-justice orientation to service, their task is to mature their critical consciousness. Information is needed to better understand the political and economic systems that perpetuate inequality and injustice. Service experiences are with advocacy, political, and/ or grassroots agencies committed to transformative action. Reflection

is centered on understanding how power and privileges operate to the advantage of the dominant class as to the exclusion of others.

Cipolle's charge provides an excellent rationale for practitioners assuming an influential role in helping to unite social activists within and across communities.

The role of social broker is facilitative rather than "expert"-driven because the journey towards critical consciousness is not one that is taken alone, and the journey is more important than the destination itself. Namely, critical consciousness is a goal that requires constant education, reflection, dialogue, and critical self-examination and is best done within a collective of others with similar goals and experiences.

Finally, the subject of evaluation, a different dimension to research, takes on significant importance, particularly if service-learning efforts are to be evaluated by how they have impacted the lives of community residents they have targeted. Evaluation of the service-learning experience must have significant participant involvement in making the determination of the learning that has transpired and the key questions that need answering (Bryant & Payne, 2013; Fletcher, 2012; Nabatchi et al., 2012). The research competencies and confidence youth acquire become part of their learning experience, and these, too, must be captured as part of evaluating their experiences.

Conclusion

The potential of service-learning for supporting and enhancing youth activism in the United States has only recently started to be explored, although service-learning has a long history. In similar fashion to any beginning, its transformation will be inevitable as more examples are found and the lessons learned shared with the world. The integration of social justice values and goals has introduced a new and exciting perspective to this form of youth engagement and social activism.

The benefits of service-learning are widely accepted for both youth and community. However, the potential of service-learning focused on social justice issues, such as food, environmental justice and immigrant rights, to engage youth and address urban community needs/issues, makes this method attractive for community practitioners, although it introduces challenges for community organizations sponsoring these initiatives.

5

COMMUNITY PRACTICE AND CIVIC ENGAGEMENT

Introduction

One of the primary goals of education in a democracy should be to prepare youth for assuming a meaningful role in society (Barrett & Zani, 2014; Roholt, Baizerman & Hildreth, 2014; Torres-Harding et al., 2014). Few democratic societies would take issue with the fundamental premises that this statement is founded upon because of the importance of a citizenry feeling and being an integral part of society.

Democracy, as it is often said, is not a spectator sport; it requires an engaged and well informed citizenry to thrive, with the spotlight falling on youth who will assume this mantle when they achieve adulthood, if viewed from an adult perspective (Musil, 2009). It can be argued that active and well informed youth are also necessary for democracy to thrive. For youth to be meaningfully engaged and informed citizens, they must be able to critically evaluate their lived experience (critical consciousness) and be able to engage in social action against societal inequities and injustices (Thomas et al., 2014).

The popularity of civic engagement, or civic participation, and the concerns and issues that it attempts to address in a democratic society, sets the stage for an engaged citizenry in this and other societies (Sherrod, Torne-Porta & Flanagan, 2010). High levels of social responsibility, an essential aspect of democratic societies, have been found to be positively associated with greater involvement in civic and political actions among urban adolescents (Armstrong, 2011).

Informing and tapping this sense of commitment and responsibility can be a strong motivator and opens the door for active youth citizenship, which can unfold in a myriad of ways to take into account their lived experiences and quest to achieve social justice (Birdwell, Scott & Horley, 2013; Simmons & Harding, 2011). Further, civic and political participation has taken on greater significance for a wide variety of reasons, including youth seeking admittance to higher educational institutions, placing youth who are not active at a distinctive disadvantage in highly competitive admission processes that favor those applicants from privileged backgrounds with extensive service and extracurricular activities (Snellman et al., 2015).

Golombek (2006) argues for a citizenship definition that emphasizes youth civic participation, rather than an age perspective, at which point they can be recognized officially as citizens. Finding ways of increasing meaningful engagement in a democratic process is an ever-constant search, with civic engagement offering great promise for achieving this goal and complementing service-learning as a strategy and method. Although learning is central for service-learning, civic engagement emphasizes service. Youth activism represents one way of engaging youth in civic engagement, particularly when focused at the local level (Torney-Purta & Barber, 2011).

Einfeld and Collins (2008), however, draw relationships between service-learning, social justice, multicultural competence, and civic engagement, and note that an increased awareness of social inequality does not necessarily translate into a corresponding commitment to engage in social justice action. Consequently, the bridge between increased awareness and social action is not clear-cut or automatic.

Civic engagement, which is sometimes referred to as "deliberative civic engagement" (Barrett, Wyman, & Coelho, 2012; Nabatchi et al., 2012) is often held up as an attractive and efficient way to help accomplish this noble goal, similar to how service-learning is considered in many educational circles. This method is meant to ensure that the social fabric of a democratic society remains strong by creating a caring and involved citizenry (Battistoni, 2013; Kahne, Chi & Middaugh, 2006).

Civic engagement projects cannot be mass produced because society is not homogeneous in composition. These efforts are best constructed when tailored to specific groups, helping to ensure that the goals and necessary resources are efficiently used, as well as the organizational characteristics of the institutions sponsoring this form of intervention are reinforced.

Civic engagement is not an age-specific intervention, thereby allowing age to be a sufficiently important demographic factor in determining how civic engagement projects get shaped and with specific attention to involvement of youth in decision-making roles (Adler & Goggin, 2005; Coleman & McCombs, 2007; McBride, 2006; Pasek et al., 2006). Just as importantly, civic engagement transpires within a social context, and this grounding provides a door for practitioners to plan and implement programs with the community as a focus, taking into consideration socio-economic, gender/sexual identity, cultural, and political factors (Lenzi et al., 2014; Levine, 2011).

The popularity of youth civic engagement over the past decade is based upon the amount of funding, research, and scholarship on the topic (Nenga & Taft,

2013; Metz, 2014), although its popularity varies across states and regions of the country (Kawashima-Ginsberg, Marcelo & Kirby, 2009), and among youth of differing demographic backgrounds. Popularity is based upon an understanding of the importance of social justice engagement (Thomas et al., 2014): "Today's youth will be facing challenges that will require more active civic engagement and activities that promote social justice. Both social justice orientation and civic engagement are related to personal factors, including individual and collective social identity."

Civic engagement can continue to expand in popularity by engaging previously unreached groups, such as urban youth of color (Bedolla, 2012), but it cannot take a cookie-cutter approach, reaching all youth in the same manner regardless of demographics and social circumstances. This approach towards service, too, must avoid a charity focus that further undervalues service recipients as being less worthy.

Civic engagement cannot be apolitical in how it is planned for marginalized youth, requiring integrating social justice goals into activities (Wells, 2014). The emergence of the concept of "critical civic engagement," in similar fashion to its "critical service-learning" counterpart, grounds civic engagement within a youth social justice context, acknowledging that "business as usual" is not the way to move forward in engaging these youth (Fox et al., 2010).

Civic engagement learning can transpire in a number of ways, such as tutoring, workshops, through supervision, internships, and independent studies, for example. The methods used can be tailored to take into account an individual's primary or preferred method of processing learning and the goals directing the project. Learning can be accomplished without losing sight of the service being provided.

Civic engagement, as already noted, must be contextualized to take into account local community circumstances and the backgrounds of participants, in similar fashion to service-learning, to have meaning and for it to be shaped in a manner that maximizes its appeal and potential contributions for both participants and communities. Motivation for engaging in civic engagement is closely tied to this grounding. Assessing motivation to engage in a social-justice–related service-learning experience is important (Omoto, 2014). Civic engagement, too, must take into account generational status and organizational factors of sponsoring institutions, particularly their mission and trust level and relationship with the community (Jennings & Stoker, 2004).

This chapter summarizes the literature on the subject matter, as well as identifying key concepts with direct applicability to youth social justice-related activities. Again, a specific focus will be on an urban and youth context in the hopes of illustrating how social justice is related to place and space, dictating how this value gets shaped and addressed by urban youth. Civic engagement focuses on community-based organizations and serves as an alternative to service-learning, which usually originates in school settings, although civic engagement can transpire in schools and service-learning can occur in community organizations.

Definition of Civic Engagement

There are explicit and implicit values embedded in a definition, and they wield prodigious influence on how a definition gets implemented in the day-to-day world, and eventually gets researched. Any definition of civic engagement is not restricted to youth but can also be applied to adults of all ages, too. Democratic societies must foster and rely upon civic engagement as an instrumental means of helping to ensure that its citizenry plays a vital part in the social fabric of the country, and not just when it comes to voting, which is much too narrow in perspective.

Armony (2004), however, raises provocative questions concerning the role and importance of civic engagement in a democracy, and calls for a much broader definition and conceptualization of civic engagement that is more inclusive of activities that normally do not fall within the conventional views of this type of approach. The inclusion of social activism is an example of how civic engagement can be conceptualized to be more inclusive of new activities.

Brabant and Braid (2009), however, specifically address the challenges in the defining of civic engagement and why each institution must develop one that is specific to their mission and circumstances: "For 'civic engagement' work to have meaningful and long-term impact upon students, partners, and postsecondary institutions, each institution must undertake the difficult work of defining civic engagement for itself such that the definition aligns with the institution's educational mission and local context . . . civic engagement is inherently political and that definitional dilemmas have arisen from the conflation of the terms service-learning and civic engagement."

It sure seems true that no two engagement projects are alike. Nevertheless, the charge of having each institution defining civic engagement based upon their own circumstances, although noble, is not very practical, particularly when these institutions seek external funding through grants, and this makes developing a comprehensive understanding of the field arduous, if not impossible. An understanding of nuances beyond core elements helps us understand how local circumstances influence how civic engagement gets conceived and operationalized.

Although both service-learning and civic engagement can teach youth about politics and social change, for example, the latter is first and foremost about civic knowledge and behavior, which can take many different shapes, and emphasizing learning, which can focus on civics, but does not have to. Both approaches, as already noted in the introductory chapter, share much in common and both can take a politically "neutral" stance towards social justice. An argument can be made that a "neutral" stance simply means that one favors the status quo and current power dynamics, which results in oppression.

There is no clear or consensus definition of civic engagement (Trudeau & Kruse, 2014), and this should not come as any surprise. The simplest definition is "social action for a public purpose in a local community" (Langseth & Plater, 2004, p. 10). Ehrlich's (2000, p. vi) definition of civic engagement, however, has withstood the test of time and is widely accepted, and it is sufficiently encompassing for use in this book, although not without its limitations for the purposes of this book: "Civic engagement means working to make a difference in the civic life of our communities and developing the combination of knowledge, skills, values, and motivation to make that difference. It means promoting the quality of life in a community, through both political and non-political processes." An explicit embrace of social justice values, principles, and goals is missing from Ehrlich's definition.

Reimers (2007) notes that efforts to create civic engagement through civic education must go beyond a simple emphasis on acquisition of knowledge concerning political institutions and governmental process, to include competencies in how to use this information to create a more just democratic society. Civic knowledge acquisition can occur within and outside of school and so can the focus of actions resulting from this knowledge. Knowledge without corresponding action is of very limited use when discussing social injustice (Ardizzone, 2007; Levine, 2007; Warren, Mira & Nikundiwe, 2008).

Otis' (2006) description of the Lexington Youth Leadership Academy shows how it is possible to empower youth, develop leaders, and have them meaningfully involved in community change projects. Provision of consultation, when requested, is also another way community-based organizations can advance a social justice agenda (Flores et al., 2014).

Organizations that focus on fostering civic engagement must embrace the belief that it is only through active and meaningful involvement of those experiencing problems and oppression that true sustainable civic engagement can occur (McGarvey, 2005). Community-based organizations have the social and moral responsibility to ensure that their resources are directed towards bettering the lives in multi-faceted ways, including not just meeting their expressive and instrumental needs but also addressing the social forces that undermine their potential (Checkoway, 2013; Goddard & Myers, 2013; McQuade, 2014).

Noguera and Cannella (2006) examined urban youth agency, resistance, and civic activism, and concluded that youth engaged in social action redefine traditional or conventional civic engagement, countering the prevailing one-dimensional view of youth as un-contributing and resistant members of society. Urban youth public commitment to social justice and its various manifestations can be viewed as a form of agency and critical consciousness (oppositional) rather than simple resistance (Collins et al., 2013).

A socially just definition of civic engagement must reflect a quest for social justice. Making a significant difference in the quality of life takes on different meanings if applied to a youth from a middle or upper-middle class existence versus one from a lower socio-economic class.

Benefits of Civic Engagement

The benefits of youth civic engagement are well recognized in practice and academic circles. Experiential (learning, psychological, and social) and instrumental (concrete) gains are associated with civic engagement. However, communities, too, benefit. Nevertheless, most of the professional literature highlights individual gains with community benefits and those who initiate or coordinate civic engagement projects being generally overlooked, in similar fashion to service-learning.

This shortcoming can and will prove troubling in moving this field ahead as the call for evidenced-based practice increasingly gets associated with civic engagement efforts. A narrow focus on what constitutes "evidence," however, will also prove troubling for the field (Archibald, 2015), putting pressure to narrowly define it in the interest of proving its effectiveness. Such a narrowing of approach is antithetical to the focus and goals of social justice.

Youth civic engagement has the greatest impact in affecting civic and educational outcomes in emerging adulthood (Chan, Ou & Reynolds, 2014). Youth involved in community civic engagement have the potential to expand their awareness and social responsibility for other community residents, encourage mutual obligations and collective capacities (Flanagan et al., 2015).

Civic engagement can promote moral behavior and help shape identity formation (Crocetti, Jahromi & Meeus, 2012; Jones et al., 2014). Adults, too, can benefit from civic engagement with youth. Shaw-Raudoy and McGregor (2013) put forth the concept of co-learning in youth-adult "emancipatory partnerships." Students can teach adults when the role of expert is not restricted according to age and position within a program and instead is based upon knowledge and insights (Rhoads, 2009).

Conner (2011, p. 923) found in a follow-up study of youth organizers that they experienced important personal gains as the result of their participation in social activism: "Although most respondents remain committed to the issues they came to care about as youth organizers, they express these commitments in various ways, including through traditional and nontraditional forms of civic engagement. They also credit a diverse set of programmatic factors with having influenced them. The findings introduce the various process and outcome factors that the participants find salient, raising implications for future longitudinal or survey research."

In a unique study of Latino civic engagement in three cities (Miami, Phoenix, and Chicago), Latino cultural citizenship was closely tied to place in shaping how it got manifested (Price et al., 2011), adding a new dimension to the benefits of civic action. This necessitates initiatives engaging Latinos in a manner that takes this into account: how conception of place shapes how they are engaged in local social activism.

It is impossible to discuss youth civic engagement without addressing the potential role of mentors. The role of mentor is multifaceted and usually encompasses sharing of knowledge and life experiences, facilitating, advising, observing; equally important, it includes being co-learners and beneficiaries of engaging in mentoring (Kafai et al., 2008). Mentoring is considered an effective method for engaging youth and creating youth-adult relationships that are sustainable (DuBois et al., 2011), although successful youth mentoring necessitates a team approach (Sue & Craig, 2014).

Unfortunately, when the concept of youth mentoring is discussed, it conjures images of a formalized relationship between mentor and mentee. However, youth have had significant relationships, with adults as well as peers, that have influenced them in profound ways and these relationships have been informal. In other words, the word "mentor" was never introduced in these relationships. How best youth can benefit from a mentoring relationship necessitates a careful assessment of the qualities and approaches that best meet their needs.

Youth development mentoring can be a major aspect of interventions premised on this paradigm's principles (Liang et al., 2013). Youth understand the value of mentoring, particularly when initiated by them (Schwartz et al., 2013; Spencer et al., 2013).

The concept of *high-resource adults* has emerged in the literature to describe adults who are in a position to assist youth in socially navigating institutions and the community (Sullivan & Larson, 2009). Connecting youth to high-resource adults though mentorship or other forms of relationships introduces the importance of strategic thinking and planning regarding youth and their relationships with adults and potential mentors.

Youth helping youth and peer education are not only viable but also effective ways of tapping youth assets (Sadowski, Chow & Scanlon, 2009; Suárez-Orozco, Pimentel & Martin, 2009; Wallace, 2013; de Vreede, Warner & Pitter, 2014; Vickery, 2014). Interestingly, the concept of *high-resource youth* does not appear in the literature. The same cannot be said about *high-risk*, however.

Approaches and Elements of Civic Engagement

Although there is a call for youth civic engagement initiatives, there still remains a high level of confusion, lack of clarity, and inconsistent operationalization of this approach for youth engagement (Amnå, 2012; Shaw et al., 2014). The introduction of "community" as a focus or context for civic engagement brings all of the challenges inherent in any effort to target or involve people where they live, school, play, worship, and work (Fernández & Langhout, 2014).

In similar fashion to service-learning covered in the previous chapter, many similar concepts can be found in civic engagement, particularly when it seeks to engage in social justice-related service. Sherrod (2006), for example, identified social justice, neighborhood, and community as critical elements in fostering and shaping civic engagement initiatives that seek to promote citizenship and social activism among urban youth. These concepts also can be found in shaping social justice service-learning.

There are a wide variety of ways of defining community, compounding development of a universal understanding since community can be geographical, ethnic/racial/cultural/socio-economic class (identity), psychological, or concentration of facilities, and any permutation and combination of these four definitions. There is a tendency to think of "community" in simplistic and homogenizing ways and, in the process, overlook its complexity. Further, youth definitions of what constitutes community must not be overlooked (Link et al., 2012).

A number of scholars advance a broader conception of civic engagement. Checkoway and Gutierrez (2006) argue for a broader interpretation of youth participation, or civic engagement, to include social protests and social planning, for example, with the latter embracing social justice inspired protests and movements. Even evaluation and research, too, can be participatory and predicated on social justice principles, increasing the connection with social protests (Bulanda et al., 2013; Checkoway & Richards-Schuster, 2004; Delgado, 2006).

Civic engagement can take a variety of forms. In similar fashion to its service-learning counterpart, it can vary according to its goals, its scope, and the number, frequency, or duration of activities (Boland, 2014; Checkoway, 2009). This adds to the confusion of what can be called civic engagement. Community-based service-learning (CBSL) is often used to describe service-learning, for example, making it arduous for the typical practitioner to differentiate this approach from countless others using the term *civic engagement* (Martin, 2014).

Mason (2012) speaks to youth civic engagement and young people living in marginalized urban areas, and the importance of both youth and community benefiting from this form of engagement. These youth, however, have generally not been responsive to organized civic engagement efforts and there has been a call for more research and scholarship on the barriers that have caused this gap in participation (Zagofsky, 2013).

Although in need of a nuanced approach, the popularity of civic engagement has still resulted in an extensive body of literature examining this method, including its benefits (Fitch, Steinke & Hudson, 2013). There have been a number of literature reviews on its benefits, facilitating our understanding of this method. Not unexpectedly, the focus of these reviews has been on youth and not the recipients of the engagement (service), which is the community.

Motivating youth to volunteer is recognized for the benefits that they derive, which are multi-faceted (Young, 2010). Encouraging civic engagement with a critical lens among children and adolescents can promote their well-being, and benefit communities and societies in the process through immediate and instrumental changes, as well as preparing current and future leaders (Fisher et al., 2012; Hart, Matsuba & Atkins, 2014).

Civic engagement represents a win-win for all parties when conducted in a meaningful and culturally affirming way, which means it has relevance for youth and their worldview and social circumstances and those who foster this form of engagement (Bee & Pachi, 2014; Eidson, Nickson & Hughes, 2014; Kim,

2014). Relevance cannot ignore social injustices, although politically unpopular for adults sponsoring projects seeking to achieve justice.

Civic engagement and intergenerational efforts are well recognized in the field of community practice, facilitating youth-adult initiatives (Holtgrave et al., 2014). A nuanced understanding of civic engagement is in order, particularly when this activity is contextually grounded (Read & Overfelt, 2014; Zaff et al., 2011), such as in an urban setting. This grounding must not make light of how oppression impacts the lives of all residents, the old as well as the young, and the role of political participation in their lives (Delgado, 2015a).

Ekman and Amnå (2012) make a civic engagement distinction between salient and latent forms of "political participation," which has important ramifications for youth activism. The salient form is conceptualized as consisting of electoral politics, in addition to social protest and "extra-parliamentary political action." The "latent" form is commonly labeled as "civic engagement" and "social involvement."

Barrett and Brunton-Smith (2014, p. 5), too, differentiate between political-focused civic engagement and participation, and present a definition that is greatly similar to that of Ekman and Amnå's: "engagement as having an interest in, paying attention to, or having knowledge, beliefs, opinions, attitudes, or feelings about either political or civic matters, whereas 'participation' is defined in terms of political and civic participatory behaviours."

Youth civic engagement can be undertaken in a myriad of community-based places and thus provide practitioners with ample ways of reaching particularly marginalized youth sub-groups (Mannino, Snyder & Omoto, 2011; Morimoto & Friedland, 2013). Houses of worship are often prime institutions where youth can volunteer (Kurien, 2013), and these institutions can also sponsor social-justice–inspired activism projects (Chapter & Mustapha, 2010; Swarts, 2011). Schools (Galston, 2007; Watts & Flanagan, 2007) and universities, too, are popular settings (Soska & Butterfield, 2013).

Civic engagement, in similar fashion to service-learning, can cover a wide range of activities from conventional to those that are highly innovative, such as civic journalism, through use of social media, blogging, and networking sites (Farnham et al., 2012), for example. Conventional approaches can have youth volunteering in ways that do not challenge social organizations or the social forces that actively oppress those from marginalized backgrounds. Volunteering is a notable pursuit but it rarely places youth in positions of authority.

Gaining greater knowledge of a wide range of youth opportunities to participate is needed to move the field forward and open up new arenas for social justice-based projects and meet specific needs of youth (Checkoway & Gutierrez, 2006; Percy-Smith & Thomas, 2010). Social-justice–inspired civic engagement can result in participation that is both individual changing and collectively driven (Dolan, 2012). Unfortunately, adults who view youth activism as "acting out" with very little merit devalue these efforts as misguided at best.

Collins, Neal, and Neal (2014) note the role and influence of collective efficacy, a resident perspective of united capacity to undertake coordinated and interdependent action on issues that affect their lives, as an aspect of civic engagement. This perspective introduces collective benefits rather than the conventional focus on individual benefits. Further, it ties well with collective memory and collective learning as reported in the literature, emphasizing the role and importance of groups (Gosine & Islam, 2014).

Christens and Kirshner (2011, p. 27) tie together youth organizing and youth development, and draw implications for increasing the attractiveness and viability of using this form civic engagement in community practice:

> Youth organizing combines elements of community organizing, with its emphasis on ordinary people working collectively to advance shared interests, and positive youth development, with its emphasis on asset-based approaches to working with young people. It is expanding from an innovative, but marginal approach to youth and community development into a more widely recognized model for practice among nonprofit organizations and foundations. Along the way, it has garnered attention from researchers interested in civic engagement, social movements, and resiliency.

Community organizing has gained in acceptance and in the process has become a viable option for community engagement projects for youth and adults.

Finally, community civic engagement can increase empathy and future intent for engaging in community action, increasing the potential benefits over a lifetime (Lakin & Mahoney, 2006). A lifecycle perspective on youth community-focused civic engagement makes investment in youth a wise investment for the future of a community and nation. Lost opportunities, in turn, make loss of investment in youth that much greater over a lifetime.

Operationalizing Civic Engagement

The popularity of civic engagement has not surprisingly engendered numerous ways or perspectives of viewing this subject, which can encompass settings, ages, race/ethnicity, and gender identity, for example. There is no one framework or way of classifying civic engagement that enjoys universal consensus. In addition, there are a wide variety of ways for how civic engagement can be structured to take into account project duration, funds, time commitments, and goals. Tailoring civic engagement projects to take into account local needs makes this approach appealing for use in community-based organizations.

Youth possessing confidence about their civic and political abilities positively influences their motivation and expectations (Manganelli, Lucidi & Alivernini, 2014). Motivation and ideology, in turn, play influential roles in school-based youth civic engagement and influence the nature and extent of activities they engage in (Mannino, Snyder & Omoto, 2011; Morimoto, 2010).

Youth possess altruism towards those in need but may do so without a strong ideological investment. However, youth with a strong activist orientation may have difficulty in connecting these sentiments with school-based efforts. Unless the school is exceptional and encouraging of social activism, these needs can only be met outside of these systems and in community organizations.

Civic engagement can have youth serving youth, for example, drawing upon different motivations for youth when compared to their adult counterparts (Haski-Leventhal et al., 2008, p. 834):

> Youth volunteering for at-risk youth can have an impact on the clients' willingness to receive help as well as the youth who volunteer . . . Findings show that youth volunteers have different motivations, benefits and costs than adult volunteers. Youth volunteers are more relationship oriented; adult volunteers are more service oriented; and the volunteer group plays several important roles in youth volunteering. The clients (at-risk youth) perceived the youth volunteers as helpful and described how volunteers their age changed their world view and empowered them to volunteer themselves. In addition, there are blurred boundaries between youth clients and volunteers.

Unfortunately, our understanding of youth engaging in civic initiatives targeting other youth has been limited because as adults our interests have focused on how adults can reach out to and serve youth.

Shah (2011) examined youth motivation from a different vantage point and found that youth involved in community organizing had increased motivation and aspirations when compared to youth who were not involved: "Eighty percent of students noted their grades improved and 60% reported that they took more challenging coursework due to their involvement in organizing. Eighty percent of youth reported plans to pursue a college education and close to half of the sample said they expected to obtain a graduate or professional degree beyond college."

Participation, or civic engagement, as manifested through social action provides youth with an avenue to channel their desires for social justice and social change (Checkoway & Aldana, 2013). Youth motivation can be fostered in the case of those youth in situations where civic engagement is an integral part of being in a program. Motivation is increased when they see that participation results in learning for the future, developing competence, and pursuing a salient social purpose (Dawes & Larson, 2011).

A motivational perspective on participation is in order and necessitates a multi-faceted view. It is most appropriate to start with youth. Understanding what motivates youth to participate in civic engagement leads to development of projects that can tap their specific motivations in structuring activities and maximizing their outcomes (Ballard, 2014). Understanding motivations helps to assess organizational reasons for engaging in service-learning projects (Stoecker, Tryon & Hilgendorf, 2009). Finally, motivation of service recipients, too, must be assessed, although that dimension is sorely lacking in the professional literature.

Voight and Torney-Purta (2013) put forth a three-part typology of youth civic engagement that offers guidance on the processes and contexts that shape youth participation, with implications for civic engagement and youth social activism: (1) development of a distinction between student volunteers and those who eschew doing so; (2). those who engage (social justice actors); and (3) those with strong civic attitudes but infrequent civic behaviors (social justice sympathizers).

Understanding that not all youth wish to engage in volunteering, and that the same can be said for adults, helps in outreach and the structuring (time and activities) of civic engagement to maximize limited resources and outcome. For example, exposure to community violence during adolescence has been found to influence youth reluctance to get involved in community service (Chen, Propp & Lee, 2014).

Further, youth may be reluctant to engage in community service in certain sections of a community with reputations for violence. Consequently, special efforts to counteract these experiences must be undertaken to acknowledge the influence of violence in their lives. Pairing youth up is one method of counteracting concerns and fears. Having program staff with a high visibility can also be effective. Providing community service in these areas can also serve the role of breaking down barriers that isolate youth from the rest of the community, which is a public service that generally goes unrecognized.

In turn, there are three primary ways of classifying socially critical youth voices (Smyth, Down & McInerney, 2014): (1) an inward perspective—a focus on immediate physical and lived surroundings; (2) and outward orientation—the consequences of social forces; and (3) an action or activist commitment—social organizing to resist oppressive forces. This framework helps contextualize lived experiences and channels these experiences into actions specifically directed at youth achieving social justice.

These voices can find a receptive and viable audience through carefully crafted civic engagement projects that have social meaning for them, their families, friends, and community. The use of critical literacy can enhance youth options to engage in civic engagement (Hope & Jagers, 2014). Not all youth, however, may be interested in civic engagement, and when they are, social activism may not be at the top of their list. Consequently, civic engagement initiatives must effectively screen and assess civic interests of youth to better maximize their contributions and needs.

Civic engagement, particularly when it is guided by social justice values and principles, offers tremendous potential for meaningful youth engagement in their quest to seek justice and give back to their communities. The multitude of approaches civic engagement can take brings sufficient flexibility in how to engage in this form of practice. Community practitioners, in turn, can foster social justice civic engagement as addressed in the following section.

Community Practice and Civic Engagement

We, as adults in positions of authority in academia and communities, must not define civic engagement along very narrow and apolitical ways, such as "volunteering," for example. Rarely will the use of the term *volunteering* conjure up images of social action, social justice, or even excitement. Instead, the term conjures up images of caring and helping in the most charitable manner. Exciting? I doubt it would elicit that response from youth responding to outreach efforts to get them to sign up for a project. Is this important? Yes, of course. However, community practice using civic engagement with marginalized youth would be hard pressed to engender wide enthusiasm on their part.

Watts and Flanagan (2007) argue that even though civic engagement has received wide recognition, its focus has been generally limited to maintaining current social and political institutions and processes rather than action for social justice. Thus, civic engagement can take a variety of forms, including social activism. Civic identity, too, is shaped by these and other oppressive experiences (Rubin, 2007). Marbley and Dawson (2008) make a similar argument by stressing the attractiveness of a social action agenda as a means of increasing African American youth community and civic engagement.

Kim and Sherman (2006) stress the importance of civic engagement with purpose and significance, rather than an activity to keep youth busy and out of trouble. Adults, too, want to have meaningful participation rather than viewing civic engagement as a way to pass the time or meet some work requirement, so this goal is not restricted to any age group. The principles civic engagement is founded upon strongly encourage participation that can benefit the community and those engaged in community service. In other words, it is a win–win for all parties.

Harris, Wyn, and Younes (2010, p. 9), based on an Australian study but with relevance to the United States, note the need to disentangle youth disinterest in conventional political systems from their interests in social and political issues in their lives:

> We argue that there is further complexity in the reshaping of participation in times of social change, especially for a broad "mainstream" of young people who are neither deeply apathetic about politics nor unconventionally engaged . . . suggests that many young people are disenchanted with political structures that are unresponsive to their needs and interests, but that they remain interested in social and political issues and continue to seek recognition from the political system. At the same time, their

participatory practices are not oriented towards spectacular antistate activism or cultural politics but take the form of informal, individualized and everyday activities.

Providing alternatives to conventional political participation expands the options of youth civic engagement to reach a broader youth audience.

Camino and Zeldin (2002) identified five pathways for youth civic engagement to unfold in a democratic society: (1) public policy/consultation; (2) community coalition involvement; (3) youth in organizational decision making; (4) youth organizing and activism; and (5) school-based service-learning. Three qualities, however, stand out and youth community practitioners can help shape the quality of youth experience: youth ownership, youth-adult partnership, and facilitative policies and structures.

Community organizations can systematically and strategically foster civic engagement through the use of four strategies (Shier, McDougle & Handy, 2014): (1) actively engaging volunteers and donors (planned and coordinated effort); (2) facilitating the bringing together of community members (fostering of social bonding); (3) fostering collaboration with organizations within and beyond the community; and (4) promoting community education and awareness campaigns. Hiring of practitioners with interests and competencies in youth civic engagement, particularly when founded upon social justice values, increases the likelihood of success and popularizing projects as viable options. Enthusiasm, after all, is contagious.

Civic engagement projects can be thought of as consisting of various types of food items that can be part of a menu, so to speak, and youth have options as to which item is attractive to them. Social action projects can be part of this menu with an understanding that not all youth may wish to engage in these types of projects, just like a food menu will have items that are attractive and unattractive.

Staff screening and hiring for commitment to this form of learning and service generally gets overlooked in the literature, which is strange considering the instrumental role they play in these programs (Dymond, Renzaglia & Chun, 2008; O'Meara, 2008; O'Meara & Niehaus, 2009). Developing protocols for selecting and evaluating staff are other contributions that community practice can make to the field. The supervision of staff, too, can benefit from a systematized approach that lends itself to community practitioner input (Daud & Carruthers, 2008).

Campbell and Erbstein (2012, p. 63) propose three implementation principles to guide meaningfully engaging youth in community change efforts, which have applicability to civic engagement: "(1) asking the right strategic questions in the right order; (2) creating organizational structures and processes that integrate youth and adults into joint decision making; and (3) marshaling boundary-spanning community leaders with diverse skills and extensive networks." Clearly, youth-adult partnerships are central in these principles and can be applied to youth social justice campaigns and movements, maximizing the power of these relationships (Zeldin, Christens & Powers, 2013).

Civic engagement can be implemented through acts engagement (voluntarism) and/or social protest (Zaff et al., 2010). A differentiation is in order when discussing civic engagement that is community organization-initiated and that which is school-initiated. The former generally emphasize product and specific outcomes; the latter emphasize individual educational and learning outcomes (Worrall, 2007). In addition, youth organized activities can be classified along four dimensions according to their: (1) breadth; (2) intensity; (3) duration/consistency; and (4) engagement (Bohnert, Fredricks & Randall, 2010). These dimensions bring rewards and challenges based upon the initiating organizational setting and these two classification approaches lend themselves for use in discussing youth civic engagement projects.

Again, it is important to pause and reemphasize that adults and their institutions, communities, as well as youth, can benefit from civic engagement and this form of intervention works best when all parties see themselves as benefiting, and this helps to ensure that a non-charity viewpoint dictates this form of intervention (Geller, Zuckerman & Seidel, 2014). Schusler and Krasny (2015, p. 363) see important parallels between scientific practice, education, and civic engagement: "Scientific practice and civic engagement share several characteristics, including questioning assumptions, understanding systems, considering alternative explanations, and debating critically within a community . . . environmental action involves a civic-science synergy because it concurrently engages youth in civic and scientific processes through which they can develop the critical dispositions and skills characteristic of both endeavors."

Youth activism, as found in Shah's (2011, p. 2) research on building transformative leadership, has viability as an activity for civic engagement: "Youth organizing groups represent uniquely supportive organizational settings that provide necessary and important opportunities for youth to become engaged in the civic and political life of their communities." The "climate" these organizations create to foster youth engagement and leadership becomes an organizational goal and part of their mission. This just simply does not happen by accident (Ginwright, 2010; Mitra, 2006).

The relationships that form between youth and individuals in authority will surely be tested in the course of carrying out civic engagement projects when focused on youth and urban communities of color (Baldridge, 2014). Potential tension areas, however, represent opportunities to develop skills that aid youth in social navigation throughout life. Youth are natural problem-solvers and are quite capable of undertaking action projects that come with all of the fortes and foibles associated with "live" community change projects, including responding to strong political forces (Fehrman & Schutz, 2011).

Evaluating youth civic engagement efforts necessitates using methods that can capture nuanced aspects and command of youth language, which will not come as any great surprise to those with experience in collaborating and working with youth (Andolina et al., 2002; Norvell & Gelmon, 2011). Language is very much a part of culture, and youth bring a distinct culture. Flexibility in roles and a willingness to negotiate roles to respond to local circumstances takes on greater relevance in efforts to determine the success of youth activism civic engagement (Epstein, 2013).

Watts and Flanagan (2007, p. 779) speak to the importance of conceptualizing youth activism as an option within civic engagement:

> Although there is certainly value in the current civic engagement litera-ture, much of it focuses on the maintenance of social and political institu-tions rather than on action for social justice. To promote a better balance, and one more relevant to the lives of youth of color and other marginal-ized young people, we offer a framework for empirical research on youth sociopolitical development. The focus is on the relationship between social analysis (including critical consciousness) and societal involvement that includes the full range of service and political work. Because youth is the focus, we also include a brief discussion of a distinctive challenge that adults face in doing just work with young people—namely, adultism.

Civic engagement can have prodigious potential for individual and commu-nity transformation when tailored to different groups, including youth.

Gordon and Taft (2011) approach the topic from a youth-centered perspective and examine how youth can influence other youth to engage in social activism and civic engagement: "teenage activists, who are largely left out of this litera-ture, represent a different process by which youth engage in politics . . . although the existing literature emphasizes the roles and responsibilities of adults in shap-ing young people's civic capacities, the roles that young people play in socializing each other for political engagement is underexplored." Youth civic engagement does not have to be restricted to any particular youth age group. However, youth engaging with other youth regardless of their ages still has particular social and political appeal.

Knowledge and skills obtained through civic engagement can be transforma-tive. For example, interventions seeking to enhance youth civic engagement played an influential role in helping Arab youth acquire the requisite skills to play a prominent role in the Arab Spring uprisings, illustrating the potential of civic engagement to result in significant transformation within a country (Stae-heli & Nagel, 2013). These acquired skill-sets can be used to accomplish other goals and tasks.

Any discussion of civic engagement must guard against the imposition of an adult conceptualization of what "engagement" means. Gordon and Taft (2011) critique the existing professional literature that has emphasized the roles and responsibilities of adults in shaping young people's civic capacities and advance the argument that this adult-centered approach has undermined our understanding of how youth socialize each other for political engagement. Developing a comprehensive understanding of youth activism is not possible until we give greater prominence to their contributions to other youth.

Conclusion

The potential and promise of youth civic engagement allows community practitioners a wide range of options to engage youth in pursuit of social goals while concomitantly enhancing their experiences, knowledge, and competencies in the process. Opening up the world of civic engagement options remains a goal for practitioners, introducing possibilities of engaging in social activism proving attractive for many urban marginalized youth, although not all can or should be expected to find this form of engagement attractive.

Civic engagement remains highly attractive as a means of undertaking community-based interventions, but it is still fraught with limitations, challenges, and socio-political considerations when applied to urban youth and social justice projects. These challenges are not insurmountable and are within the reach of practitioners in addressing urban social justice. Section 2 that follows provides theory and field-based examples of how social justice civic engagement and service-learning can be applied to urban youth life and circumstances.

SECTION 2

Reflections From the Field

6

YOUTH AND IMMIGRANT RIGHTS

Introduction

At first sight, the reader may wonder how immigrant rights can be closely tied to environmental and food justice. The latter two campaigns and movements may not be a far stretch, but on the surface the topic of immigrant rights seems totally unrelated. Food and the environment relate to surroundings and immigrant rights are squarely focused on people. Using spatial justice analysis brings the commonalities of these movements to the surface and makes them easier to understand and appreciate (Soja, 2009).

The interjection of youth and immigrant rights brings together an age group and a national issue that can be considered "explosive" and opens up possibilities for innovative ways of thinking about this social issue (Martinez, 2014). A social-ecological analysis of immigrant youth, particularly those in this country whose parents are undocumented, will uncover the stark reality that they and their parents are under siege and intense scrutiny (Nicholls, 2013a, 2013b). Fine and colleagues (2008) address the effects of educational policies on immigrant youth, particularly undocumented youth, their English language ability, and the limits placed on them after high school graduation as a result of their legal status.

These youth share all of the oppressions that their citizen counterparts face with the addition of their legal status (Gonzales, 2008, p. 221): "As undocumented residents, many of the young students are without full political rights, cannot naturalize, and cannot vote." Martinez (2005) strikes a theme raised earlier in this book about expanding what is meant by political/civic engagement and focuses on participation in "unconventional politics" by comparing Latinos and non-Latinos, finding that Latinos participate less. However, the influence of segmented assimilation may result in significant differences between Latino sub-groups in terms of conventional political participation. This argument can be useful in explaining barriers to political participation and why undocumented youth are not likely to participate in certain forms (Abrego, 2006). Youth trajectory in society is often closely linked to that of their parents, so they have a great stake in the immigrant-rights movement beyond filial concerns and responsibilities (Gonzales, 2008).

This chapter sets a context for a multi-dimensional view of youth in immigrant-rights social justice, a rationale for case selections, and presents case illustrations that highlight this intersection, with implications for service-learning, civic engagement, and community practice.

Undocumented, Unauthorized "Illegals": What is in a Label?

The topic of labeling is one that many professions must contend with, including social workers. The slogan "Label Jars and Not People" comes to mind in discussing the deleterious consequences of labeling. How an issue gets "labeled" is not just an academic exercise because the label is predicated upon values, dictates discourse, and in many cases sets in motion how a social condition needs to be addressed. Consequently, it is necessary to pause and examine this topic closely.

Immigration is considered one of the most significant phenomena of the twentieth and early twenty-first centuries, with profound impact on both newcomers, host countries, and countries of origin, further increasing the significance of globalization's impact on countries (Pachi & Barrett, 2014). There are very few social topics that can be raised about which everyone in the United States seems to have an opinion. The question of undocumented, unauthorized immigrants, or "illegals," unfortunately, is one of them (Semple, 2011).

The average person on the street may not have an opinion about the nation's deficit or what position our country should take towards involvement in a Middle Eastern nation's internal dispute. However, they will definitely have an opinion about how this nation should control its borders, and what we should do with those who are in this country without legal permission. A similar opinion can be extracted about English and whether or not it is the official language of the United States. Few people do not have strong feelings on this issue.

The term "illegal alien" is an example of conjuring up of images and identities of being less worthy at one extreme and less human at the other (Menjívar & Kanstroom, 2013) This highly politically charged topic has caused a highly political response in the form of the immigrant-rights movement (Lyons, 2008). The label used to describe individuals in this country who are non-citizens has profound psychological, cultural, economic, political, and social consequences. Anytime an "illegal" label is used as a prefix to describe someone, it is never good for their identity, their ethnic/racial group, and for the community they reside within.

Latinos, probably more than any other ethnic or racial newcomer group, symbolize the topic of undocumented ("illegal aliens") immigrants to the United

States and the struggles of maintaining their dignity and fight against oppression (Delgado & Staples, 2012; Ochoa & Ochoa, 2007; Velez et al., 2008). Aguirre, Jr. and Lio (2008), however, point out the unique struggles that Asian Americans and Pacific Islanders face and why they have partnered with other groups of color to address immigrant rights, affirmational action, and social justice.

Immigrant-Rights Challenges and Rewards

Bolivar and colleagues (2002) address the opportunities and challenges unique to social justice and organizing with immigrants, and also discuss some of the main challenges with using social activism as a means of redressing a social wrong. Social activism is never easy under ideal circumstances and that is why when it does occur, as in the case of immigrant rights, it takes on greater significance within and outside of their respective communities (Garcia, 2013).

These challenges can be quite significant but not insurmountable, as evidenced by the prevalence of this social movement (Bolivar et al., 2002): (1) fear of getting involved in social protest; (2) histories of activist killings and retribution in homelands with dictatorships; (3) coming together as Latinos may mean putting aside historical animosities between groups; (4) finding the right vocabulary that can bridge cultural differences since certain words do not necessarily translate between groups; (5) skepticism about achieving change; and (6) undocumented immigrants are often reluctant to take on prominent leadership positions for fear of being arrested and deported. Clearly, the wind is against their active engagement and leadership in public protest, yet they do engage and persist against prevailing sentiments and forces.

Although the challenges can be quite formidable, there are numerous opportunities for engagement (Bolivar et al., 2002): (1) the existence of extensive social networks within newcomer communities; (2) the potential role of the church as a key institution for supporting social change; (3) strength in numbers by living in Latino communities; (4) the belief that social injustices undermine families and communities, making seeking change salient and immediate; (5) mutual learning transpires through involvement in social causes; and (6) organizing is a family affair and lends itself to multigenerational change efforts, and in the case of youth, preparing them to assume future leadership positions in local organizations and communities (Apaliyah et al., 2012).

Youth activists have challenged governmental definitions of citizenship and belonging through first-person testimony and civil disobedience (oppositional resistance), disputing the premises used to substantiate deportations, for example (Carrasco & Seif, 2014). Immigrant-rights protests are particularly receptive to inter-generational partnerships.

Social movement intergenerational mobilization was evidenced in the 2006 immigrant-rights demonstrations (Bloemraad & Trost, 2008; Lyons, 2008). Hosang (2006) brings a different dimension to this discussion by describing engaging of youth in collaboration with adults, rather than having separate youth-led campaigns, arguing that most issues affect the entire community, and it does not make sense to separate by age, but youth often come to the forefront of organizing efforts in immigrant families due to language skills and because they "get it first" politically.

Immigrant Rights and Food/Environmental Justice

Zimmerman (2011, p. 17) concludes that the immigrant-rights movement has implications far beyond those who are undocumented:

> It is a movement whose claims to national belonging fundamentally challenge the basis of inclusion into the national community at a time when the rights of both citizens and non-citizens are exponentially narrowing. If a test of a society is how it treats its most vulnerable members, then immigrant youth's claims to citizenship have tremendous implications not only for the rights of immigrants, but for the quality and legitimacy of U.S. democracy for decades to come.

The role of social media was indispensable in helping these youth reach out and connect with other youth and adult allies (Zimmerman, 2012).

A review of the social justice work undertaken by the United Farm Workers Union during the 1960s and 1970s illustrates the strong interrelationship among immigrant rights, food, and environmental justice for Latinos in the United States, arguably the largest undocumented group in the country. Harrison (2008) ties together agriculture, farm labor, and environmental justice by showing the deleterious interrelationships among pesticides, farm workers, and consumers.

Spring 2006

The spring 2006 social demonstrations set a context from which to focus on specific concerns related to immigration status and rights. Spring 2006 will go down in the annals of United States history as the time when the immigrant-rights movement received the positive national attention it deserved and raised this form of social protest to an area worthy of considerable public and scholarly attention.

The 2006 protests set a national backdrop to immigrant youth and social protests, offering a variety of perspectives on how best to understand and capitalize on these acts. Fox and Bada (2009, p. 1) address the immigrant-rights social protests of 2006 from a civic engagement perspective, and these demonstrations are rarely conceptualized as a viable form of civic engagement:

> Immigrant rights mobilizations represent a watershed in the history of civic engagement in the U.S. Never before had so many foreign born

literally "come out" for the right to be included. Indeed, in many cities, never before had so many taken to the streets for any cause. Practitioners involved in the policy debate, scholars who measure immigrant political opinion, as well as migrant leaders themselves were all caught off guard. This raises questions about the social foundations of the marches—what kinds of social and civic practices, networks and organizations made them possible?

These highly visible and salient forms of social protest provide a window for increasing our understandings of how immigrant rights are conceptualized in communities across the country.

Over a period of several months, a series of demonstrations took place in approximately 140 cities and 39 states across the United States, such as Atlanta (Associated Press, 2006; Immigration Laws, 2006; Rockwell, 2006), Chicago (Immigration Laws, 2006; Johnson & Hing, 2007; Newman, 2006; Olemdo, 2007; Pallares & Flores-Gonzalez, 2010; Wang, 2006), Dallas (Zlolniski, 2008), Denver (Gonzalez, 2006; Immigration Laws, 2006; Newman, 2006), Houston (Radcliffe, 2006), Los Angeles (Associated Press, 2006; Immigration Laws, 2006; Johnson & Hing, 2007; Newman, 2006; Zlolniski, 2008), Milwaukee (Associated Press, 2006; Immigration Laws, 2006), New York (Immigration Laws, 2006), Phoenix (Associated Press, 2006; Immigration Laws, 2006), San Antonio (Clark, 2006), San Diego (Sanchez, 2006; Soto, 2006), San Francisco (Immigration Laws, 2006), San Jose (Bloemraad & Trost, 2008), Santa Ana (Gonzales, 2008), and Washington, DC (Immigration Laws, 2006).

Hundreds of thousands of immigrants and their allies came together in protest, and numerous activities followed these protests, furthering the importance of this social justice issue (Gonzales, 2008; Pulido, 2007). A review of the above list of cities is illustrative of how this social justice issue knows no geographical boundaries in this country, with major urban centers playing prominent roles in shaping the immigrant-rights narrative.

In one poignant protest display in New York on May 1, 2006, an estimated 12,000 people formed human chains across the city at exactly 12:16 pm to symbolize the December 16, 2005 passage in the House of Representatives of a controversial immigration reform bill that would have made undocumented immigrants felons, among other issues (Immigration Laws, 2006).

In another memorable display, more than 500,000 protesters gathered in downtown Los Angeles on March 25, 2006 in a peaceful rally that was larger than any in the memory of most Americans (Associated Press, 2006). Overall, it is widely agreed that "such mass demonstrations advocating for the rights of immigrants are unprecedented in American history" (Johnson & Hing, 2007, p. 98), bringing this social issue to the fore in this country.

The visual images of these demonstrations will probably still be vivid in the reader's mind because of their size and the amount of print and visual media devoted to them. Many saw these demonstrations as the start of a new Latino civil rights movement in this country and the most recent significant national effort at influencing the 2005 to 2006 109th Congressional House Representatives (H.R. 4437) in their efforts to criminalize the undocumented, and those who assist them, and separated families (Zlolniski, 2008).

This act introduced the language of national security protection and focused on antiterrorism, making it significantly different than previous efforts at immigration reform. If enacted and enforced, it would have resulted in the deportation of between 10 to 12 million undocumented residents, the majority of whom would have been Latino (Jones, 2006).

Media and Immigrant Rights

The role of media in the quest for immigrant rights, as already noted, plays an important, although disputed role in how this social justice issue is viewed. The news media, with exceptions, emphasized negative images but also included positive elements (Velez et al., 2008, p. 24):

> Given the barrage of images in print and on television of Latina/o youth being arrested, sprayed with mace, or confronting law enforcement during the spring of 2006, we expected a purely negative framing. Instead, we discovered that reporters combined some positive with mostly negative language to describe these youth. Conflicting portrayals within a news story often occurred within the same paragraph, or even within a sentence.

A shift in narrative, however, is never easy or completed within a short period of time.

Nevertheless, questions have been raised about how the 2006 immigrant-rights demonstrations influenced national public opinion on this social injustice issue. Branton and colleagues (2015) suggest that the protests influenced Latino immigration policy preferences, but the impact was not consistent across demographic groups and was shaped by generational status and the intensity of the protest level at the community level. Baker-Cristales (2009), in turn, examined the influence of media and the social construction of citizenship and how vocabulary and language were a central focus of the discussion.

It is important to note that any discussion of media would not be complete without touching upon the role of communications technology and the conveying of information/news. One Los Angeles reporter captured well the role of technology in the organizing of youth in the 2006 Los Angeles demonstrations (Gold, 2006; p. A1):

> It didn't take long before most of Garden Five High's roughly 2,200 students knew what was coming, without the knowledge or involvement of

teachers or parents . . . The bulletin crossed over an invisible but critical line between teens who were friends but attended different schools. Students began posting their telephone numbers, and soon dozens more pledges to participate were obtained through phone calls and instant text messages.

Social media and youth go together regardless of their documented status.

Regional or National Social Justice Issue?

As noted earlier in this chapter, the subject of immigrant rights is one that has received considerable media and political attention from elected officials and promises to continue to do so in the near future, particularly in the upcoming presidential election. Is this a regional or national issue? There is no region of the country that is not affected by newcomers, and particularly those who are undocumented, bringing a national frame of reference to the topic. In essence, this is not a "southern" or "New England" regional phenomenon. It is neither exclusively rural nor urban, although cities have high concentrations of newcomers and media outlets to publicize their social injustice situations.

Further, the subject of the undocumented can cross racial and ethnic lines, offering a potential to build bridges between different groups. For example, contrary to common opinion that has African Americans being indifferent or even hostile to those seeking immigrant rights, there is important support for this social justice movement (Lenoir, 2007; Zamora & Osuji, 2014). This is particularly important from a spatial perspective because of the high number of African Americans who live in urban areas of the country, often within the same geographical community as newcomers.

The Pew Hispanic Center's (Suro & Escobar, 2006, p. 1) findings on newcomer concerns reinforce the importance of an immigrant-rights social agenda:

> More than half (54%) of Latinos surveyed say they see an increase in discrimination as a result of the policy debate, and three-quarters (75%) say the debate will prompt many more Latinos to vote in November. Almost two-thirds (63%) think the pro-immigrant marches this year signal the beginning of a new and lasting social movement. And a majority (58%) now believes Hispanics are working together to achieve common goals—a marked increase from 2002, when 43% expressed confidence in Latino unity.

These social demonstrations created a sense of collectivity and hope that crossed numerous regional and state borders. Further, the meaning of citizenship was altered as the result of individual struggles to gain membership and reshaped what it meant to be a citizen in this country (Flores, 2003).

Newcomer Youth and Social Justice

Undocumented youth face far more oppressive forces and corresponding consequences than their counterparts with legal status/citizenship. There are those who would argue that all youth face oppressive forces in this society and age brings together youth from disparate backgrounds. However, undocumented youth of color bring additional sets of oppression that their counterparts or those who are White, non-Latino, and privileged, do not, and particularly in the case of those who reside in the nation's inner cities.

The consequences of undocumented status are multifaceted and illustrate why it is so important in their lives and communities. They, for example, face even greater risk and embarrassment over simple things such as buying a cell phone, getting a library card, renting a movie, not being able to work to cover educational costs, limited access to social services and healthcare, and an inability to obtain a driver's license, making transportation that much more arduous (Gonzales, 2008).

Those who are undocumented face many of the same challenges as their documented counterparts, plus additional legal barriers, up to their graduation from high school (Abrego, 2006): "Ironically, their social incorporation sensitizes them further to the contradiction that, despite their academic success, they are barred from the opportunity to integrate legally, educationally, and economically in US society"; the link between membership and rights (Flores, 2003); growing up in the US they have the same expectations and aspirations as documented/citizen youth, but their legal status separates them (Abrego, 2006; Gonzales, 2008); any social activism or speaking out is a risk of deportation (Gonzales, 2008). Having lower socio-economic status means they are less likely to be politically active in the conventional sense of the word (Gonzales, 2008).

Social-Political and Economic Consequences

As already noted, undocumented status directly affects future possibilities (education, jobs, etc.): the limits opportunities to mobilize around these issues (Abrego, 2006); the struggle to open doors that are closed to them based on lack of full citizenship/membership (Flores, 2003); the need to create a space where they feel comfortable and can express themselves often means making demands on society (Flores, 2003); in order to achieve their goals, there have to be legal changes to remove the barriers (Gonzales, 2008); immigrant-rights groups may be the only way available to do something for themselves and their families when education, jobs, etc., are limited by undocumented status (Gonzales, 2008); options are so limited that pushing back is sometimes the only choice they have (Gonzales, 2008); legal status blocks them from participating in more traditional political forms, so their turn to social activism/protest (oppositional resistance) represents a viable and natural option.

Education and Social Justice

Education is the one right they do have and learning leadership skills in school as well as connecting with role models and peers helps build skills to become activists (Gonzales, 2008; Martinez, 2005). Schools exist in every community and are therefore easily accessible.

Undocumented youth are entitled to a quality public education (Gonzales, 2008); in addition to difficulties of attending college, achievement after high school is limited due to their undocumented status, complicating job possibilities and career development (Abrego, 2006). Even if they do manage to go to college, job opportunities and careers are still very limited after graduation (Gonzales, 2008). The educational arena brings undocumented justice to an institution that is supposed to prepare youth for assuming productive roles within a democracy.

However, education, probably more than any other system, highlights the injustices undocumented youth face in this country and why this aspect of immigrant rights has found saliency among youth: Compromised or no access to public education K–12; no access to federal financial aid for college; classification as international students in college and thus paying more; reduced chances of post-secondary education; lower motivation to succeed, especially when youth watch older siblings/family members excel in high school and get stuck in low wage jobs because they can't afford college (Abrego, 2006). The list of barriers can go on, highlighting the barriers these youth face in achieving upward mobility in this society.

Finally, we need to acknowledge that the goals related to the Dream Act may not be embraced by all immigrant-rights activists. Aguirre Jr. and Simmers (2011), for example, consider the Dream Act as an excellent example of how neoliberal educational policies are channeling newcomer youth into "productive roles within a homogenous culture and corporate social order." This stance has not received very much attention in academic circles, but raises critical questions concerning one of the key goals associated with this social movement.

Civic Involvement

Corrunker (2012) compared the U.S. immigrant-rights movement with global counterparts and found strong parallels along three dimensions: (1) leadership of undocumented immigrants; (2) visibility; and (3) measures of "deservingness." In the United States, there is a paradox when discussing how newcomer youth may possess low levels of civic education and engagement but have a high sense of community obligation and play an active and significant role in social protest (Seif, 2011).

Velez and colleagues (2008) focused on Latino youth participation in the 2006 protests, and argued for a need to understand how to civically engage immigrant youth as a key part of citizenship. They used Latina/o Critical Race Theory as a framework for studying Latino youth activism and studied newspaper articles focusing on the 2006 protests, as well as examining youth roles and their media portrayals.

Newcomer youth have tremendous potential to contribute to their communities and newfound countries if this potential is recognized and fostered by adults (Masten, Liebkind & Hernandez, 2012). A deficit or charity paradigm will not help them achieve their potential; a re-shifting in paradigms to one based on assets and social justice will.

Youth Social Activism

Bacon (2007) examines the state of immigration reform and the labor and human rights issues associated with this movement, drawing parallels to the civil rights movement:

> Everywhere in this country immigrant communities are growing, defying the raids intended to terrorize them—organizing and speaking out. This movement is a powerful response to Congress' inability to pass a pro-immigrant reform bill. It can and will resist and stop the raids, but its potential power is far greater. Like the civil rights movement four decades ago, the political upsurge in immigrant communities makes a profound demand—not simply for visas, but for freedom and equality. It questions our values. Will local communities share political power with newcomers? Will workers be able to organize to turn low-paying labor into real jobs? Will children go to school knowing their teachers value their ability to speak two or three languages as a mark of their intelligence, not their inferiority?

A focus on national implications of immigrant-rights activism must not overlook their impact at the local level and the systems in place where they come into contact on a daily basis.

Gonzales (2008, p. 221) notes that immigrant-rights protest movements have generated important sociological questions, including what they mean for youth-led activism:

> In the aftermath of these large demonstrations, scholars, politicians, and pundits have tried to make sense of how they happened and what they mean for the future. Many asked if this was the beginning of a new civil rights movement, if it was a rebirth of the Chicano movement, and if these protests were a flash in the pan or part of a larger political agenda. While the first two questions are provocative, it is the final question that has perhaps the greatest relevance and importance to scholars, policy makers, and elected officials: would such participation translate into broader political participation by immigrant communities.

The power derived from participating in social demonstrations goes from the immediate satisfaction of being part of a collective effort and can also translate into engagement with local politics beyond that of voting in public elections.

Johnson and Hing (2007), however, see Latinos being a part of a broader, more ethnically and racially inclusive, civil rights movement. In the case of this book, will these movements result in greater political participation from immigrant youth, and for that matter, the adults in their community?

There is wide acknowledgement that newcomer youth have played a significant role in youth activism campaigns in the United States, and their participation and experiences can carry over to numerous other social issues beyond immigrant rights. The cadre of activists and lessons-learned can engage in other social justice issues, such as food and environmental justice, for example.

Gonzales (2008) argues that immigrant youth have played a significant role in the resurgence of youth political activity in the United States, and nowhere is this more prevalent than with the immigrant-rights social movement. Wayne (2007) echoes this point and addresses the central role youth played in immigrant-rights demonstrations in general, but particularly in San Francisco's demonstrations.

Wayne (2007, p. 5) also goes on to display the common perception that youth participation was spontaneous, without planning:

> Youth fast organizing has been mistaken for ephemeral and spontaneous activity, rather than the outcomes of international and continuous organizing. Technology has made its largest impact in this area: diffuse organizing is no longer the result of "diffusion," but rather of lightening speed communications. In this respect, spontaneity is an illusion generated by fast-technology, and can mask deeper structures of organized behaviors as well as explicit group identity.

Youth social protests have entailed having them involved as planners, and they have used social media as an effective mechanism to rally others and adult allies.

The reader, I am sure, has a clear understanding of why immigrant rights is considered such a crucial social justice issue in the United States, but no more so that in its centers of population known as cities. These geographical areas of the country facilitate large groups coming together to share their outrage, and these centers have maximized media exposure to capture and disseminate the stories and images across the country and the globe.

Benefits of Civic Engagement

Before examining the potential benefits of civic engagement for those who are undocumented, it is important to touch upon the role of acculturation. Stepick and Stepick (2002) examine immigrant youth civic engagement and the intersection between acculturation of youth and political participation, and they conclude that immigrant youth face a unique situation, focusing on multiple identities and asking what that means for civic engagement. They draw a connection between civic engagement and youth becoming more "Americanized."

McGarvey (2005) identifies a series of advantages for newcomers to engage in civic participation/engagement: (1) education and acquisition of skills; (2) building social capital through networks; (3) contributing to positive social change; and (4) becoming an active member of American society and helping reinvigorate democracy. McGarvey (2005), in turn, identified four foundation principles that should guide civic engagement efforts: (1) meaningful engagement of those most affected; (2) engagement commences where newcomers start (daily lives); (3) education informs all by stressing learning; and (4) relationships are important and should be across all segments of a community.

Seif (2010, p. 447) argues that immigrant youths' civic participation, or engagement, does occur but not in conventional ways:

> When scholars study immigrant youth civic engagement, they face special challenges that include the varied ways that these youth and their civic practices are defined and measured. Most researchers agree that we cannot use the experiences of adult citizens to define and forecast youth civic engagement . . . It is also problematic to use parental patterns to predict immigrant youth's civic engagement because the next generation is more acculturated to the United States.

The broadening of civic engagement to include activities that are not easily measurable is needed, although quite challenging from an evaluation point of view.

In fact, civic engagement has even been seen as a mechanism through which youth and adults can come together on issues of shared interest (Balsano, 2005). Aldana (2008, p. 97) argues for a broader conception of civic engagement for Latinos that goes beyond conventional electoral politics:

> There is also a trend for greater civic engagement by Latinos particularly at the local level, even among those ineligible to vote. This trend is especially important as the federal government devolves in this area, while states seize greater immigration powers. Latinos alone will not determine U.S. immigration policy, but all of these trends reveal that they are becoming an important voice in a much needed civil rights movement on behalf of immigrants in this country.

Civic engagement that fosters a social movement takes on great significance because of its long-term implications.

The context in which newcomers grew up in their homelands profoundly shapes them. Newcomers who have spent more time in a more participatory context in their countries of origin, and who are in closer contact with these societies, are more likely to get involved in civic associations at their new destination (Voicu & Rusu, 2012). Civic engagement is important in their lives and cultural motives play an instrumental role in this engagement (Jensen, 2008; Stepick, Stepick & Labissiere, 2008), and these civic associations understand the social justice they must play to be relevant in their respective communities.

Civic engagement is important in the lives of newcomer youth (Levine, 2008). The role of supportive relationships helps foster their continued engagement and achievements (Suárez-Orozco, Rhodes & Milburn, 2009). In a South Florida study of newcomer youth's civic engagement, it was found that it does not differ from that of natives. However, newcomer youth are more likely to engage in civic actions focused on helping their ethnic group, which unfortunately, gets overlooked by conventional measures of civic engagement because those measures are too narrow in scope (Jensen & Flanagan, 2008).

Community Practice/Service-Learning Approaches and Considerations

Youth participation in immigrant-rights social protest has been found to be transformative because of how youth consciousness is raised and their identities affirmed as active and full members of their community and this society (Getrich, 2008). They do not perceive themselves as "junior" members of society.

Service-learning focused on immigrant rights must embrace the goal of equality in society and social activism, grounding activities within a socio-political context taking into account social justice values and principles. It is impossible to address undocumented injustices without calling upon social justice. Immigrant rights is a social justice issue that will be salient for years to come, and these youth can be expected to play an influential role in how justice is served in both their roles as youth and eventual adulthood.

Integration of food and environmental justice issues can serve as a backdrop to assume a more prominent place in immigrant-rights social justice. Three case illustrations were selected. The first case focuses on health, conceptually grounding immigrant rights with food and environment. The second case emphasizes the use of an internship for social justice service-learning. Finally, the last case uses language-focused service-learning.

Case Selection Rationales

The three social justice service-learning case examples focused on in this section illustrate a variety of approaches and goals in applying this experiential method to immigrant rights. The first case uses health as a subject to introduce academic materials and opportunity to bring about social change. The second example shows how a state-wide organization provided an internship focused on social action campaigns. Finally, the last case shows the power of language and culture in shared learning between university students and community residents.

Case Illustrations

Gould, Mogford, and DeVoght (2010) discuss a secondary-school in-school example of social-justice–inspired service-learning involving academic subject matter, and show how youth are taught about social determinants of health (socio-ecological) and trained on using social action techniques to reduce health inequalities within their respective communities. Academic subjects allow a variety of instructional methods to be used that facilitate inviting guest speakers from the community, use of personal journals, and use of documentaries, in addition to more conventional methods associated with education.

The subject of health was one that youth could relate to for themselves, their families, and friends. Consequently, it brings immediacy and saliency to a social issue. Introducing health as a subject can also serve to unify a host of other social justice issues for youth and allows them to see relevance in the subject and a potential to address a variety of social injustices through a focus on one condition.

The next case example relies on internships as a way of implementing social justice service-learning goals. The Massachusetts Immigrant and Refugee Advocacy (MIRA) Coalition offers two youth organizing internships. MIRA is an advocacy statewide membership organization focused on newcomers (immigrants and refugees). Their website (http://www.miracoalition.org) explains: "MIRA advances this mission through education and training, leadership development, organizing, policy analysis and advocacy."

Interns work with the organizing team to engage MIRA member organizations and allies in campaigns and actions and carry out organizing strategies to enhance and create local structures that create and support immigrant leadership and advance a pro-immigrant agenda. The following is an intern responsibility description from the MIRA website:

> Assist with the development of campaign materials (blast e-mails, fliers, letters, endorsement forms, etc.); Work with the organizing, policy, and communications teams on New Americans Civic Participation during election season. Help with voter registration drives and voter registration data entry; Participate actively in the creation and outreach of public engagement events, trainings and workshops. Help to coordinate the membership process (new members, renewal of membership, etc.); other duties as assigned by supervisor.

Intern activities reflect a wide range of social-justice–focused goals, bringing flexibility to how service-learning can be operationalized to tap different student competencies and learning goals.

This final case illustration focuses on the use of language and culture as a basis for a service-learning project. d'Arlach, Sánchez, and Feuer (2009) report on a project that draws upon key social justice concepts, particularly Freire's theory of critical consciousness, to bridge school and community. The project was titled "Intercambio," or "Exchange." The project title symbolizes the potential of a project based upon sharing values and principles. The project was based at a community-based organization (Centro Romero). Meeting in the community provided residents with the comfort and safety of meeting in a setting that was considered safe. Intercambio covered an academic year (9 months) and involved having three-hour weekly meetings. The first half was devoted to discussions concerning social justice issues.

Intercambio focused on language and cultural service-learning projects and involved university students and nine community residents who were newcomers. This was unique because of its emphasis on making sure that it was not based on a charity paradigm, putting community residents in the position of teachers and experts by having them teach Spanish and share narratives that provided insights into the role and importance of their culture in helping them navigate their immigrant status (d'Arlach, Sánchez, and Feuer, 2009, p. 11):

> The first ingredient of community members' success in Intercambio is accepting the community has worthwhile knowledge to impart. When the spirit of reciprocity is central to the service-learning course, the community members feel encouraged to teach the knowledge they possess. Reciprocity is key because community members are often so powerless in our society's hierarchies (e.g., illiterate, poor, undocumented, limited access to resources) that it takes time for them to hear their own voice, to value their opinion, and to speak up.

Knowledge comes in many different forms and an ability to tap experiential or informal knowledge (newcomers) opens the door for an exchange with those possessing formal knowledge (university students).

The project's success was the result of interplay of three key elements: (1) reciprocal, long-term engagement; (2) time to reflect on current issues necessary; and (3) acceptance that reflection can be an arduous process. Humanizing newcomers by understanding their perspective is only possible when students set a grounded context from which to learn and serve.

Language acquisition has great promise for service-learning and for newcomers, particularly when grounded on open discussion of issues using a social justice framework. These discussions can easily incorporate issues related to where newcomers live, work, eat, and play, bringing the potential of food, environmental, and other forms of social injustices into discourses.

Community Practice/Civic Engagement
Case Illustration Considerations

Case Selection Rationale

Youth leadership opportunities are an important theme in social justice civic engagement. Leadership while people are young and the potential for adult leadership as they age out can benefit society. The two case examples (Boston and Chicago) are presented to show how this theme is recognized, acted upon, and takes different shapes in the field. Youth leadership cannot be neglected in carrying out critical civic engagement.

Case Illustrations

Social-justice–inspired civic engagement and immigrant-rights case illustrations are numerous. The Boston Chinatown Neighborhood Center's Youth Center provides youth with cultural enrichment and educational supports, such as ESL, homework tutoring, and college workshops/tours.

In addition, and most importantly from the vantage point of this book, they also engage in youth leadership development, as noted on their website (http://www.bcnc.net):

> We train youth to be leaders in their communities through a pipeline of training, practice, and ultimately youth-led project development. The first stage is YouthLead, a volunteer youth leadership program that trains 15–20 youth leaders over one year and incorporates videomaking, community-based field trips, and a chance to gain basic leadership skills. YouthLead part 2, is a second year of practicing the skills gained in the first year of YouthLead, mainly though organizing projects and events for the youth at the Youth Center. The highest level of leadership at the Youth Center is the Youth Advisory Group, a youth-led group of leaders who work on projects with the support of staff to improve the Youth Center and the community. We also partner with Charlestown High School (CHS) to provide the Chinese immigrant Student Leadership program for Chinese immigrant CHS students who have self-identified or been identified by teachers or peers as being interested in developing leadership skills.

Youth leaders, in turn, get involved in a wide variety of community issues related to immigrant rights and other issues social justice issues related to newcomer status.

The second case illustration, too, focuses on leadership development. The Illinois Coalition for Immigrant and Refugee Rights' Youth Civic Leadership Academy, based in Chicago, provides youth with competencies to mobilize their political capital to address social justice issues of the undocumented within their respective communities (Youth Civic Leadership Academy, 2015): "The Youth Civic Leadership Academy is committed to training tomorrow's leaders today. Trainings focus on immigrant civic engagement, community organizing skill, volunteerism and community building, and personal leadership development."

The Youth Civic Leadership Academy has five objectives: (1) Engage socio-economic disadvantaged youth in taking responsibility to help improve their circumstances; (2) Develop the knowledge, skills, and social capital required to effectively participate in local, city, and state government; (3) Enhance self-confidence, self-discipline, and self-esteem; (4) Improve student academic achievement; and (5) Engage youth with appropriate non-family role models and mentors of color, such as local, city, and state elected officials. The emphasis on youth engagement, leadership, and enhancing competencies through organizational support blends the key elements of social justice engagement, learning, and leadership, which facilitates urban youth of color meaningfully becoming a part of social justice campaigns.

Conclusion

The dynamics and visual imagery of mass social demonstrations epitomized by the 2006 immigrant-rights marches across the country have a powerful impact on making a social justice issue involving one group become a social justice issue for an entire nation. This chapter has laid out for the reader the saliency of youth immigrant rights as a social action campaign and movement, and one that promises to remain part of the national political landscape for decades to come. The case illustrations operationalized social justice, immigrant rights, and multiple social injustices, including food and environment.

The appeal and the issues associated with immigrant rights, when viewed from a spatial justice perspective, bring in other social justice issues—in this case, food and environmental justice. This makes immigrant rights a social justice issue with the potential to bridge many other forms of social justice when viewed at the community level. The following chapter on environmental justice will illustrate how this justice issue impinges on immigrant rights and food justice, as well as offering a multitude of social-justice–inspired service-learning and civic engagement projects.

7

YOUTH AND ENVIRONMENTAL JUSTICE

Introduction

The emergence of environmental justice as a social movement has great appeal to urban youth when it is conceptualized in a manner that highlights its impact on their immediate lives and those of their families and friends (Dias & Callahan, 2015; Irby, 2015). Youth, when presented with a wide number of ways of conceptualizing this social issue, can focus on the aspect with the greatest meaning and immediacy to them, as the case examples used in this chapter will illustrate. The reader may argue that food justice and, in the case of newcomer communities, immigrant rights would have greater saliency.

This, however, may not be the case (Quiroz-Martinez, Wu & Zimmerman, 2005, p. 2): "For decades, the environmental justice movement has been developing holistic solutions . . . how young people across the country are not only fighting the dynamics of environmental injustice, but organizing and leading the way to a new reality. They are working intergenerationally, innovating new approaches and honoring the work of their elders. They are making connections across issue areas and communities, and advancing a vision of a healthy movement that is sustainable for the long haul." Youth abilities to make connections and to have adult allies encouraging them make environmental justice attractive for service-learning and civic engagement projects.

Environmental social justice issues can be viewed narrowly, for example, with a specific and exclusive focus on toxic environmental concerns. However, environmental justice can also be viewed or grounded within a neighborhood context and from a broader socio-ecological-political perspective, tying in community, immigrant-rights, and food justices as three examples of social justice perspectives that are interconnected (Sasser, 2011).

One can easily include numerous other social justice issues under the rubric of environmental justice. Obesogenic environments, for example, limit youth opportunities to engage in physical exercise, compounding poor diets, and eventually leading to being overweight or obese (Boone-Heinonen & Gordon-Larsen, 2012; Gallo, Townshend & Lake, 2014).

The emerging popularity of environmental justice, however, is due largely to an increased attention and emphasis within schools and community-based organizations, as evidenced through service-learning and civic engagement projects and initiatives. Greater awareness of environmental justice, in turn, has created more opportunities for youth to find an aspect of this social injustice that attracts them.

Evolution of Environmental Justice

Increasing the relevance and immediacy of environmental justice by tying this issue to other justice issues of equal or greater prominence from a local point of view, such as food and immigrant rights, for example, casts a wider net in its appeal and potential impact on urban youth and their neighborhoods (Schusler et al., 2009; Zani & Barrett, 2012). Social justice issues do not exist in silos from each other. This perspective can present major conceptual and research issues for academics. However, from a resident perspective, it does not, as in the case of urban youth.

Working on one social issue impacts other social issues within the community, particularly when viewed from a spatial justice perspective. It changes how youth and other residents think about the challenges they face. Environmental justice can be framed in numerous ways to appeal to urban youth and their communities, particularly when taking a spatial justice lens in focusing the impact of the environment on their lived experience (Bencze et al., 2015).

Tracing the origins of any social movement such as environmental justice is bound to create differences of opinions (Agyeman, 2005; Cole & Foster, 2001; Taylor, 2011). Concerns about the environment have evolved over a period of several decades from initial worries about nature ("Earth Day"), endangered animals, population growth, and impacts on the atmosphere, to list but several salient aspects of this movement (Bond, 2004; Carruthers, 2008; Ehresman & Okereke, 2014; Reitan & Gibson, 2012; Sasser, 2014; Wilson, 2010).

The introduction of a social justice perspective, however, effectively translated environmental concerns to health and safety in the present world. Environmental hazards and amenities are not distributed evenly across society (Haluza-DeLay, 2013); consequently, "ecological health," for example, is closely tied to a socially just existence in a democratic society and provides an attractive "handle" for framing environmental justice in a way that can appeal to urban youth and their communities (Gardner, 2013).

Environmental justice's focus on "fair" and "meaningful" participation on the part of all groups in the development, implementation, and enforcement of environmental laws, regulations, and policies (Taylor et al., 2006), too, has evolved tremendously since its conception and presents an excellent lens through which structural factors affecting health (inequalities) can be assessed (Agyeman, 2005; Lee, 2002; Schlosberg, 2007). This broad and inclusive perspective provides social activists with multiple points of foci for their actions, helping to ensure the likelihood that no segment of a community is overlooked.

The term "environmental racism" eventually led to terms such as "environmental injustice," and "environmental inequity" (Faber, 1998; Lester, Allen & Hill, 2001; Rhodes, 2005). I contend that the emotionally charged nature of a "racism" label made it arduous to rally a broad cross-section of groups to focus on just race. Thus, the need emerged for a more encompassing and less emotionally charged term to bring disparate interests together. Two significant events stand out as playing instrumental roles in making environmental justice of relevance to communities of color.

In October 1991, the First National People of Color Environmental Leadership Council occurred in Washington, DC (Bullard & Lewis, 1996). This conference sought to capture the manifestation of environmental justice among communities of color and the successes achieved at bringing social change. In October 2002, a massive demonstration (The Second National People of Color Environmental Leadership Council) took place in Washington, DC, marking the largest and most culturally diverse gathering of environmental activists, including youth, in the nation's history, signifying the saliency of this issue for communities of color (Quiroz-Martinez, Wu & Zimmerman, 2005).

The term "environmental justice" has since replaced "inequity," and further broadened the movement's concern and reach beyond race. Morland, Diez Roux, and Wing (2006, p. 171) touch upon how this movement has expanded and continued to have closer ties with civil rights: "The environmental justice movement brought racial and economic discrimination in waste disposal, polluting industries, access to amenities, and the impacts of transportation planning to the public's attention." Environmental justice focuses on social and health inequities, and brings a social-economic class and racial lens to the discourse because of how certain segments of this society have disproportionately suffered as a result of the consequences from omission or commission of environmental policies (Saha, 2013).

Schlosberg (2013, p. 37) speaks to the evolution of environmental activism into spatial expansion and into exciting new realms, including how environment is conceptualized with implications for social justice campaigns: "More recently, there has been a spatial expansion of the use of the term, horizontally into a broader range of issues, vertically into examinations of the global nature of environmental injustices, and conceptually to the human relationship with the non-human world." This more encompassing definition of environmental justice facilitates the introduction of intersectionality and the cumulative impact this injustice has on youth and other residents with multiple jeopardies.

Environmental Justice and Urban Communities

Again, spatial analysis, with the unit of analysis being the geographical neighborhood or community (e.g. urban), facilitates an understanding of why environmental justice can have salient appeal for urban youth (Harvey, 2010; Marcus, Omoto & Winter, 2011; Soja, 2009). Environmental justice is at its apex in appeal when the issue is specific, immediate, and perceived as winnable by urban youth. More specifically, why is the environment of great concern to urban youth, who are facing many other social, economic, and political challenges in the present and in the future? Schools and community organizations can foster this interest by providing options for engaging in social action and helping to develop youth competencies in this area (Salvio, 2013; Schusler, 2013).

An understanding of why youth embrace environmental justice is essential in the recruitment and support of youth efforts with this social justice. One study of young environmental activities found that their main influences on their environmental action were multiple, with parents, experiences outdoors in childhood, friends, role models, teachers, and youth groups and formal youth gatherings influencing them (Arnold, Cohen & Warner, 2009; Schusler et al., 2009).

The United States' Great Recession had a disproportionate impact on youth (16–24 years), for example (Belfield & Levin, 2012; Bell & Blanchflower, 2011; Lundberg & Wuermli, 2012), and this this impact was extensive and multifaceted when viewed from environmental (places and spaces) and social-cultural perspectives when discussing youth in this nation's inner cities. Further, this economic dislocation also resulted in youth feeling socially disengaged and being distrustful of adults in positions of authority (Day, 2014; Zaff et al., 2014).

The introduction of critical pedagogy into environmental education, too, brings environmental justice within the domains of service-learning and civic engagement arenas, and introduces school and community organizational settings to each other, facilitating the introduction of environmental justice in social activism initiatives, and opening up other ways of conceptualizing environmental justice to make it more attractive to urban youth (Cole, 2007), including grounding it within academic subjects.

The reframing of how environmental issues and concerns got re-conceptualized to embrace social justice is widely credited for making this social movement salient in the lives of many who previously did not see it as relevant, and particularly those residing in marginalized neighborhoods (Taylor, 2000). This reframing has taken various manifestations reflecting evolutionary thinking to take into account lived experiences and contextual grounding.

Environmental education based on social justice values and principles makes this education relevant for marginalized youth and provides a knowledge foundation for activism resulting in "local ecosystem services and human and community well-being" (Andrzejewski, Baltodano & Symcox, 2009; Tidball &

Krasny, 2011). The topic of urban agriculture and social justice, too, has emerged and resulted in an understanding of how it can support or dismantle unjust structures and how forces can perpetuate an inequitable system, using a critical race theory lens (Reynolds, 2015, p. 240):

> Many studies have documented the benefits of urban agriculture, including increased food access, job creation, educational opportunities, and green space. A focus on its social benefits has fed an association of urban agriculture with social justice, yet there is a distinction between alleviating symptoms of injustice (such as disparate access to food or environmental amenities) and disrupting structures that underlie them. Despite its positive impacts, urban agriculture systems may reinforce inequities that practitioners and supporters aim to address.

Urban agriculture is not possible if the soil is polluted, leading to questions about what caused this to occur, why it has persisted, and why nothing has been done about it, which are all environmental justice issues.

Environment and Health

An environmental health frame, for example, can translate into environmental health justice, and when a spatial dimension is added, such as urban, this brings it to the local level and resident homes, increasing the saliency of urban environmental justice (Masuda, Poland & Baxter, 2010). Having a place for physical exercise, using sports such as skateboarding or basketball, for example, can be considered environmental justice issues by using spatial concepts to highlight lack of exercise/sporting spaces in low-income communities when compared to upper-middle class communities (Day, 2006; Vivoni, 2009). The addition of fears of crime compounds this injustice when police avoid patrolling areas designated for sporting activities or areas lack proper lighting for night-time play.

Sze's (2007) book titled *Noxious New York: The Racial Politics of Urban Health and Environmental Justice* analyzes how environmental health got manifested in four New York City neighborhoods in the late 1980s and 1990s, concretizing how environmental racism gets connected to environmental justice in predominantly communities of color. Searching for environmental hazards is not difficult in these communities, and youth can make the requisite connections in shaping activist responses that are salient at the local level.

Kudryavtsev, Krasny, and Stedman (2012) focus attention on the impact of environmental education on youth's sense of place in the Bronx, New York City. The summer period provides community-based organizations with an opportunity to conduct environmental justice educational programs (skill development and environmental monitoring). The benefits of environmental education can also encompass increased social capital goals (Krasny et al., 2015).

There are other examples of making environmental justice, such as researching the number of alcohol (liquor stores and bars) establishments in urban low-income communities of color (Romley et al., 2007, p. 48) and the conclusions will not come as any great surprise to the reader; they show why this framing of environmental justice has saliency: "Mismatches between alcohol demand and the supply of liquor stores within urban neighborhoods constitute an environmental injustice for minorities and lower-income persons, with potential adverse consequences for drinking behavior and other social ills." Social activism and alcohol policy issues in inner city communities have resulted in an effort to address this environmental health issue (Herd & Berman, 2014).

Access to nutritional foods and the absence of barriers and structures for physical activity are social justice issues that can be viewed from a variety of justice perspectives, including environment and health (Alkon, 2008; Cutts et al., 2009; Delgado, 2013). Lack of access to safe public swimming pools can be framed as environmental justice as in parks and playgrounds (Lewi & Nichols, 2014). Youth exposure to urban violence, too, has a long history as an environmental justice/ health issue (Selner-O'Hagan et al., 1998).

Agyeman and Evans (2003, p. 53), in turn, provide an example of how environmental justice and sustainable development overlap:

> Two concepts that provide new directions for public policy, environmental justice and sustainability, are both highly contested. Each has tremendous potential to effect long-lasting change. Despite the historically different origins of these two concepts and their attendant movements, there exists an area of theoretical compatibility between them. This conceptual overlap is a critical nexus for a broad social movement to create livable, sustainable communities for all people in the future.

Thus, bringing together environmental, food, and immigrant rights is not a far conceptual stretch but has clear and applicable practical manifestations and implications.

Although these justice issues all lend themselves to a spatial justice viewpoint, environmental justice, because of its emphasis on geography, stands out and particularly benefits from a spatial justice understanding (Stanley, 2009). Schusler and Krasny (2008) identify six guiding principles for youth environmental activism: (1) youth as contributors; (2) genuine participation; (3) deliberate action; (4) inquiry; (5) critical reflection; and (6) positive youth development. These principles highlight the role of authenticity and a focus on strengths, participation, and praxis in shaping youth conception of environmental justice.

There are a number of perspectives community practitioners can take to assess the saliency of environmental justice issues. Prince (2014, p. 697), for example, touches upon a rarely discussed aspect of the physical environment by addressing the role environment plays in shaping future conceptions of self: "Identity research indicates that the development of well-elaborated cognitions about one-self in the future, or one's possible selves, is consequential for youths' developmental trajectories, influencing a range of social, health, and educational outcomes. Although the theory of possible selves considers the role of social contexts in identity development, the potential influence of the physical environment is understudied. At the same time, a growing body of work spanning multiple disciplines points to the salience of place, or the meaningful physical environments of people's everyday lives, as an active contributor to self-identity. Bridging these two lines of inquiry . . . show[s] how place-based experiences, such as belonging, aversion, and entrapment, may be internalized and encoded into possible selves, thus producing emplaced future self-concept . . . visioning one's self in the future is inextricably bound with place; place is an active contributor both in the present development of future self-concept and in enabling young people to envision different future possible places. Implications for practice and future research include place-making interventions and conceptualizing place beyond 'neighborhood effects'."

A spatial justice perspective places environmental concerns within the grasp of youth and social activism (Anguelovski, 2013).

Expanding the options they have to conceptualize their most pressing concerns and offering opportunities for engaging in social change (Schwartz et al., 2015), such as, in the case of newcomers, where they live and exposure to hazardous air pollution (Hernandez, Collins & Grineski, 2015).

Walker (2012, p. ill) provides a broad assessment of how environmental justice can shape social activism through a series of questions:

> Environmental justice has increasingly become part of the language of environmental activism, political debate, academic research and policy making around the world. It raises questions about how the environment impacts on different people's lives. Does pollution follow the poor? Are some communities far more vulnerable to the impacts of flooding or climate change than others? Are the benefits of access to green space for all, or only for some? Do powerful voices dominate environmental decisions to the exclusion of others?

The theme of exclusion is powerful in Wilson's questions, and it has implications for how to engage youth.

Intersectionality and Environmental Justice

An intersectionality perspective brings together issues of social justice and poverty, feminism, and environmental justice in a cogent and conceptually coherent fashion (Dantley, Beachum & McCray, 2009; Di Chiro, 2008). Physical access for youth who have mobility disabilities brings to the fore how negotiating city streets can be challenging, particularly when these streets go unrepaired or do not have snow removal because their community is a low priority for governmental agencies (Kafer, 2013; Taylor & Józefowicz, 2012; Wasserman et al., 2013).

Environmental hazards have a disproportionate impact on residents with disabilities (Abbott & Porter, 2013). Youth in these neighborhoods, particularly those with multiple physical and intellectual challenges, face a future that will severely limit their opportunities to maximize their potential contributions to their families and community (Skrbis, Woodward, & Bean, 2014).

Terry (2009, p. 5) provides one example which illustrates intersectionality, environmental justice, and feminism:

> Both climate change itself and related policies are likely to have wide-ranging effects on gender relations, especially in developing countries. Poor women face many gender-specific barriers that limit their ability to cope with and adapt to a changing climate; these must be removed in the interests of both gender equity and adaptation efficiency. At the same time, gender analysis should be integral to the appraisal of public policies designed to reduce carbon emissions. To date, gender issues have hardly figured in international policy discourse, including the UN Framework Convention on Climate Change and its Kyoto Protocol. However, this may be changing thanks to feminist lobbying and the increasing involvement of gender specialists in this field.

[handwritten margin note: What specific gender barriers?]

A gendered analysis introduces a key demographic into discussions of environmental justice and highlights a much overlooked element.

Coalitions have been found to have viability when discussing environmental activism (Mix, 2011). They also provide an opportunity for different demographic groups to come together in a fashion that does not diminish or make invisible any particular group. Youth can participate without fear of becoming invisible and powerless in the process. An understanding of intersectionality broadens the possibility of coalitions being developed that deal with environmental justice from a variety of demographic perspectives (James & Iverson, 2014).

Youth Activism and Environmental Justice

The topic of environment and its importance knows no age limit. Adults of a particular age will remember the beginning of the Earth day celebrations of the early 1970s, and the attention that it brought to the importance of saving our environment, and in the process, saving the inhabitants of this planet. The introduction of socio-economics alters the dialogue from one that emphasizes the importance of saving the earth for future generations to one of quality of life, or even immediate life and death, as in the case of urban communities of color (Knaus, 2014).

Environmental justice, in similar fashion to immigrant rights and food justice, can encompass a wide terrain, from racial inequalities to access to parks without congestion to exposure to environmental pollutants (Peréa et al., 2014; Reyes, Páez & Morency, 2014; Rigolon & Flohr, 2014; Sister, Wolch & Wilson, 2010). Exposure to environmental pollutants has deleterious health consequences (Bullard, Johnson & Torres, 2011). Health outcomes are further compromised as the result of poor health services, resulting in significant health inequities.

Hawken (2007, p. 3) brings a social justice agenda to the environmental movement: "A Native American taught me that the division between ecology and human rights was an artificial one, that the environment and social justice movements addressed two sides of a single dilemma. The way we harm the earth affects all people, and how we treat one another is reflected in how we treat earth." Thus, it is not a social issue that can or should be defined within narrow parameters, although academics elect to do so to facilitate research and scholarship.

Community Practice/Service-Learning Case Illustrations

Case Selection Rationale

Preparing youth for being active and meaningful members of society necessitates that education prepare them for these roles as well as provide them with the skills to continue their learning. Addressing environmental justice in the classroom in a manner that helps them learn science and apply it to real-life situations, for example, can be accomplished within and outside of the academy (Britton & Tippins, 2015; Burek & Zeidler, 2015). Service-learning in community-based organizations opens up ways of bringing together this method and environmental justice, as well as other forms of injustices, as illustrated in the Miami Youth L.E.A.D. case. The REEP: Roxbury Environmental Empowerment Project (Boston) case illustration, in turn, reflects on how community-based organizations can work with schools to institute environmental justice service-learning projects.

Case Illustrations

Service-learning undertaken by community-based organizations has the potential to expand this method beyond school-based settings, as noted in the following case illustration based in Miami, Florida. Youth L.E.A.D. addresses environmental justice through a focus on access to healthy food.

Youth L.E.A.D. (Leading Environmental Activism through Democracy) seeks to educate and empower marginalized urban youth as activists through training and service-learning projects. This organization merges food and environmental justice in seeking social justice and focuses activism on urban food deserts where residents have low access to healthy food options and explores how environmental injustices limit the community's access.

Two social justice service-learning efforts blend various social justice concerns—Roots in the City in Overtown and the Breaking Ground Program farmers market held at TACOLCY Park. These two markets were closed down by the City (District 5), even though they played an instrumental role in the life of the community. Youth L.E.A.D. youth learn about democracy and local political process. *~ Our learning political process is Key!*

Service-learning occurs through a 12-week service-learning program that *is* explores how food, environment, health, and social justice intersect and utilizes multi-faceted methods, such as hands-on activities, guest speakers, healthy food demonstrations, and field trips to urban farms, farmers markets, and supermarkets. In addition, service-learning is accomplished through the initiation of a service-learning project involving partnerships with other local organizations for increasing access to healthy foods.

Youth L.E.A.D. partners with other local initiatives, such as the planning and building of community gardens. Support for youth with leadership potential are placed in paid positions of leaderships that allows them to mentor other youth and increase their competencies for food and environmental justice activism. The following are testimonials (Healy, 2011):

> Kevin Lemonier, an Edison High senior, started reading labels, reducing portion size, and replacing junk foods with salads and fruits. When asked if he felt a difference with his new regime, Kevin explained to the other youth, "I have more energy. I don't have to take a nap when I get home from school anymore, and I've lost weight." Judith Faucet, a ninth grader, stopped eating red meat based on what she learned about the dangers of hormones and chemicals found in much of factory-farmed beef as well as its contribution to global warming. Judith has also learned that she loves almond milk and wants to learn more healthy recipes.

Environmental literacy can easily translate into health literacy and empowering youth to exercise judgement in eating foods that support their well-being rather than compromise it.

Youth internships provide opportunities for undertaking community outreach, learning job skills (including running a small business, math, and sales calculations), public speaking, community organizing, and coordinating local food systems.

Youth L.E.A.D. argues that youth can be an "Everyday Activist": "1. Be a smart consumer. Eat local foods, read labels, and buy foods with little to no packaging. 2. Use reusable bags and reduce use or plastic. Never use Styrofoam, which never biodegrades. 3. Get active in your community or school. Join or form a group that seeks to make your school or community healthier and more environmentally sustainable."

The case example of REEP, Roxbury Environmental Empowerment Project, shows how a community-based organization can undertake a variety of environmental justice campaigns that can also be the bases for the initiation of school-based environmental justice service-learning. The Boston organization was founded in 1995 with a specific focus to engage public school children and families. "REEP is a youth-led community organizing program. We build youth power for environmental justice in Roxbury, Dorchester and across the City of Boston."

REEP (http://www.ace-ej.org/reep) uses a collaborative model for involving other organizations in youth-led environmental justice campaigns that often bring food justice to the fore:

> REEP staff and alums work with classroom teachers in Boston Public Schools to conduct our environmental justice curriculum and support students to lead action projects for environmental justice. We have recently worked with Social Justice Academy, Dorchester Academy, Phillips Brooks House Association, Odyssey High School, and El Centro de Cardinal. Our student-led projects have included supporting local organizing efforts for food justice, creating school raised-bed gardens and a garden club, filming municipal vehicles breaking the anti-idling law, getting pollution filters installed on construction vehicles and garbage trucks, supporting the campaign for youth jobs, and supporting local campaigns for immigrant rights.

Collaboration effectively expands options for service-learning and the initiation of change efforts.

Videos were developed documenting their campaigns and served to educate the public but also introduced instrumental goals. Schools can contact REEP to establish a "Classroom Action Project." REEP holds an annual summit, which has been done over a 17-year period, providing Boston youth and interested adults with an opportunity to come together to hear success stories and lessons-learned presentations.

The following three environmental justice campaigns bring in other forms of social injustices: (1) Youth Way on the MBTA: This campaign represents a fight to make this system more respectful and responsive to youth; (2) Grow or Die (access to healthy and affordable foods); and (3) DERO (Diesel Emissions Reduction Ordinance).

Toxic Tours are offered and represent an effort to inform youth of community environmental justice issues. Tours focus on highlighting issues such as brownfields, air quality and asthma, population displacements, and governmental under-budgeting. REEP, in addition, host youth-led community events and political forums and undertake youth-led research on environmental justice.

Community Practice/Civic Engagement Case Illustrations

Case Selection Rationales

There certainly are numerous methods that can be used to create civic engagement and environmental justice. Community practitioners, for example, can develop workshops, conferences, forums, public television series, and other education experiences. Community-based organizations instituting summer programs focused on environmental health issues is one way that service-learning can be an effective way of engaging youth in school to engage in social action (Pate, Guerrero & Dobie, 2015), as the reader will see in the following case illustrations.

Two cases were selected to illustrate the power and potential reach of environmental justice and urban youth and the use of varied and combination of instructional methods. Pittsburgh's Youth Policy Institute initiative highlights how information technology can be an attractive method for engaging youth and educating the community.

The second case illustration is totally different from any of the case illustrations used in this book. In fact, it is not even a case. It is, however, a book that provides youth and adults with detailed instructions on how to conduct environmental social activism. The book, authored by Alan Dearling and Howie Armstrong, *Youth Action and the Environment* (1997), almost twenty years old but still highly relevant today, shows in a highly detailed manner how to undertake a wide variety of activist projects, and is an excellent resource for youth activist and adult allies.

Case Illustrations

Pittsburgh's Youth Policy Institute is a program of the Pittsburgh Transportation Equity Project. The Equity Project's mission is to "engage, educate, and empower African American residents, groups, community and faith-based leaders to become advocates for transportation policy, equity issues, and regional planning."

The Youth Policy Institute (http://reimaginerpe.org/node/329?qt-5_d_more_urban_justice_resources=1) developed a music CD that both educated the community but did so in an entertaining manner at their educational festival:

> In order to pass our newfound information along to the community, we made a CD mix of popular dance music. We printed facts about diesel exhaust in the CD liner and distributed it out for free at "Just Jam 4 Justice" festival, the other half of this year's Youth Policy Institute project. More than 100 residents from the immediate and surrounding communities attended . . . To make it happen, we secured the use of a green city lot

on which to hold the festival, solicited food and prize donations, recruited local hiphop and spoken word artists, and lined up speakers from organizations that deal with environmental health issues . . . In addition to featuring music performers, and guest speakers from environmental health and justice organizations, we delivered presentations on the impact of global warming on low-income populations and communities of color throughout the world. We paid particular attention to the increasing frequency of severe storms and the disproportionate impact on those who cannot afford to escape their fury, from the South Pacific to New Orleans.

Attention to making information accessible and meaningful led to innovative methods for reaching the community and providing a forum for Youth Policy Institute youth activists.

The use of music, free CDs, and a festival shows how creativity and innovation can enhance environmental social justice when local context dictates the most appropriate way to reach a desired audience.

A book represents another example of making information meaningful and accessible for environmental justice. *Youth Action and the Environment* is a workbook based upon numerous worldwide, field-based examples of civic engagement with youth of all ages and demographic backgrounds.

Although examples of environmental projects are presented, the authors endeavored to provide a theoretical foundation, separating this book from publications focused on providing activities without the requisite foundation upon which youth can see the relationship between theory and activity, and books stressing an academic perspective without requisite examples of activities. Youth empowerment is central to environmental social justice, and this requires efforts at introducing theories and concepts but not without examples to help translate theory and concepts into action and activities.

The authors take a novel approach to environmental social justice by viewing environmental justice as a children's rights issue (Dearling & Armstrong, 1997, p. 211):

> There was much debate, as we carried out the planning for *Youth Action and the Environment*, about whether this was an issue that should be considered "environmental" . . . The more we thought about it, it did seem to us that children's rights were a fundamental environmental issue. Simply because so many children die because their right to a clean, disease-free environment is not respected. Even if we look closer to home, we can find many examples where the rights of children are subjugated to the primacy of the industrial culture, with its attendant pollution.

Environmental justice is only limited by our imagination and one can be hard-pressed to exclude an urban justice issue that cannot be viewed from this viewpoint.

Youth rights are a theme that has appeared in various portions of this book. These rights are developed by youth and bring clarity, purpose, and focus to social justice activism. A rights dimension permeates social justice either implicitly or explicitly.

Determining what gets included or excluded in environmental justice campaigns because of how the environment touches so many aspects of a community's life, and no more so than when the community has been marginalized by the broader society, is a challenge. A children/youth rights perspective, as addressed in other case examples in this book, sets a fundamental foundation from which to emphasize environment over food and immigrant rights, for example, even though they and other social justice issues come together in the daily life of urban youth in this country.

Conclusion

Environmental social justice has taken on special significance for urban youth, and this issue holds tremendous potential for future social justice campaigns, particularly as environmental justice broadens its definition and focuses more on racial dimensions of the environment, including newcomers. Further, there are a wide variety of ways that environmental justice can be conceptualized by urban youth, with a comparable number of ways to engage in activism. Opportunities for urban youth to learn about environmental justice are plentiful, including the number of school and community-based settings offering options to engage in learning and address this social issue.

Chapter 8 highlights a close relationship between food justice and environmental justice and brings immigrant rights to the forefront. It also draws upon a different set of case illustrations that highlight other dimensions related to social justice service-learning and civic engagement.

8

YOUTH AND FOOD JUSTICE

Introduction

There is no segment of society that can exist without food. Youth are not a special group in this regard, and the need to eat is not restricted to any particular geographical area, so cities are no different than rural areas. However, youth are a special target for certain sectors of the food industry, as evidenced by the amount of advertising dollars that have been devoted to reaching them (Barr-Anderson et al., 2015; Chou, Rashad, & Grossman, 2008; Delgado, 2013; Herman et al., 2014; Parker, Olson, & Breiner, 2013), and cities have high concentrations of youth, making these places particularly attractive for targeting advertisements. Youth of color, not surprisingly, are the population segment hardest hit by the obesity crisis and face the greatest challenges in seeking justice (Kramer et al., 2013).

Bringing together youth, food justice, and inner cities makes for exciting and highly energized forces that can be concentrated for achieving significant social changes (Anguelovski, 2015; Cadieux & Slocum, 2015; Kwan, 2013). Thinking of urban youth as possessing assets further enhances their potential to achieve significant social change involving food justice (Ober et al., 2008) and offers endless possibilities for introducing innovative methods. Building on youth strengths is significantly different from building on their weaknesses and needs (Oman, Vesely, Aspy, & Tolma, 2015). The former necessitates a shift in paradigms and language.

Food security is considered a human right (Libal & Harding, 2015a) and it finds its way into discussions of food justice in a wide variety of socio-cultural contexts (Naylor, 2014). The concept of food democracy, too, is finding greater usage to capture the multifaceted aspects of food injustices and how different groups experience it (Carlson & Chappell, 2015).

Food justice as a salient issue for youth, as a result, must be viewed from a nuanced and cultural perspective because social justice in this arena can manifest itself in a multitude of obvious and subtle ways, and lends itself to being localized to urban communities (Grills et al., 2014). For example, there is a close relationship between being overweight or obese and of low socio-economic status, making this subject of particular relevance to urban youth of color of low income and wealth (Delgado, 2013; Vasquez et al., 2007).

Food justice, in similar fashion to the other two social justice issues that were covered in the preceding chapters, enjoys tremendous popularity among youth because it introduces physical space as an influential dimension; it is rare to be youth-focused and youth-friendly (space) when it comes to transforming physical space into food producing space.

It is a cause that significantly touches upon immigrant rights and environmental justice in the case of youth of color with newcomer parents and urban living in communities with sizeable numbers of newcomers (Crosley, 2014). Youth food action has the potential for helping youth realize individual and community goals in the process of achieving various forms of social justice (Schusler et al., 2009), with these gains far exceeding adult expectations.

Environmentally food-focused activism can transpire within academic settings, with potential benefits spreading beyond schools into communities. Kerckhoff and Reis (2014), for example, discuss the rewards of youth and teachers coming together in an Ontario Canadian high school environmental club and the potential for encouraging environmental activism. Adults, in turn, can play an influential role in helping to create a cadre of youth environmental-food activists within and outside of the academy (Mueller & Tippins, 2014).

As the reader will see, the case examples presented in this chapter highlight for the reader how adult allies and community-based organizations can foster youth environmental justice efforts. In urban communities with sizeable numbers of undocumented residents, immigrant rights can easily be combined with food and environmental justice, with each justice issue increasing in importance as a result.

Evolution of Food Justice

Social justice movements have origins, although almost always debated, and they evolve and grow when they resonate with the populace or sub-groups; food justice is no exception. Its evolution has broadened this social justice issue and movement into new and exciting areas, further attesting to its importance in this nation's marginalized urban areas. An intersectional view has opened up the potential for disparate groups to come together in search of similar social justice goals and outcomes.

Some scholars trace the origins of food justice to the 1960s and 1970s and the Civil Rights Movement and efforts to address hunger and adequate nutrition for children and youth (Gottlieb & Fisher, 1996). Others argue that the food justice movement evolved out of a growing concern that the global food system is unsustainable and unjust (Levkoe, 2006), resulting in an awareness and action to alter systems; we are entering an era in which our agricultural system relies on capitalistic principles, causing a tendency to create standardized and unhealthy food through industrialization (Hinrichs & Allen, 2008). This trend has stripped food of its most basic value, which is to nurture both body and soul, with consequences for the health of this country and its youth (Alkon, 2013; Pratt, Stevens, & Daniels, 2008).

However, the consequences have been most severely felt in marginalized communities, primarily among those that are urban-based and of color, which can ill afford poor nutrition, further making them dependent upon food from an insecure source. Youth, in turn, have suffered from targeted marketing of unhealthy food, the overabundance of fast food establishments within their neighborhoods, and limited access to fresh fruits and vegetables (Treuhaft & Karpyn, 2011). Adding limited options for physical exercise in safe and conducive settings further compromises their health. Further, if undocumented, fears of deportation essentially force these youth into an underground existence.

The conceptualizing of the city or community as a public dining room helps to concretize food justice by highlighting the kinds of food available and within reach of residents (Abedania, 2014). Lack of access to fresh and healthy food, when combined with lack of access to safe places for exercise, has been responsible largely for the epidemic of obesity in these communities (Delgado, 2013).

Cadieux and Slocum (2015) propose that efforts to undertake food justice can be conceptualized as falling into four arenas: (1) trauma/inequity; (2) exchange; (3) land; and (4) labor arrangements that enable people to deal with power relations across relevant scales aiming to effect systemic changes. This conceptualization illustrates the broad reach of this form of social justice, although these categories are not mutually exclusive of each other but provide a focus for practitioners and academics. Introducing a spatial dimension again, as in the case of cities, further facilitates each of these dimensions being operationalized separately or in various combinations in food justice campaigns.

The evolution of food justice has continued to increase its reach into new arenas and groups. Prisons are one of the latest systems that have been the focus of food justice (Watkins, 2013). Absence of healthy and diet-related food for those inmates with severe health conditions, for example, is compounded by the racial composition of this nation's prison system, introducing racial and socioeconomic class (racial and class justice) dimensions. The introduction of spatial aspects, limiting physical exercise, brings in an environmental justice dimension to the discussion on food justice. Homelessness, too, brings food justice into any discussion of the environment (Tarasuk et al., 2009).

The subject of food is important in everyone's life and is certainly the case when discussing youth, and no more so when discussing those who are low-income/low-wealth and urban residents and the role of food literacy in their lives (Vidgen & Gallegos, 2014). Nutrition, particularly healthy nutrition, is critical in the lives of youth because of how they are growing and how it influences school performance (Larson & Story, 2015). There are cultural dimensions to food that often get overlooked in discussions pertaining to health, performance, and social interventions (Delgado, 2015a).

Slocum and Cadieux (2015, p. 27) introduce an important and often overlooked dimension in discussion of food justice:

> Over those twenty years, practitioners and scholars have argued that the food movement was in danger of creating an "alternative" food system for the white middle class. Alternative food networks drew on white imaginaries of an idyllic communal past, promoted consumer-oriented, market-driven change, and left yawning silences in the areas of gendered work, migrant labor, and racial inequality. Justice was often beside the point. Now, among practitioners and scholars we see an enthusiastic surge in the use of the term food justice but vagueness on the particulars.

A two-tiered system of food, one healthy and available (price and accessibility) to a select consumer and another cheap (price and accessibility) and unhealthy, further accentuated justice issues related to food.

Healthy nutrition becomes a social justice issue because of how certain segments of the youth population do not have access to healthy nutrition (Smith et al., 2013). Youth of color living in low-income and low-wealth urban communities can be considered as living in a food desert, where it is almost impossible to find fresh fruits and vegetables, for example, just like it is almost impossible to find water in a desert. Obesity and health are profoundly related, with wide consequences for youth, their families, and communities.

Democratic principles can be learned and practiced through the food justice movement (Levkoe, 2006). Anyone interested in the flexibility of applying food justice to a localized environment will have no difficulty in finding examples of why these social justice issues have relevance to urban youth, as evidenced in the service-learning and civic engagement case illustrations that follow later on in this chapter.

Food Deserts and Social Justice

The concept of food desert takes on added significance when applied to urban centers. The image of a desert is one closely associated with non-urban areas of the country. However, when this concept is applied to an inner city, it focuses on the absence of fresh fruits and vegetables that are both available and at a fair market price (Hendrickson, Smith, & Eikenberry, 2006; Mead, 2008; Walker, Keane, & Burke, 2010). Poor quality food at high costs and easy availability of low-nutrition food (Borradaile et al., 2009) are the norm in these urban communities. Prevalence and use of sodas with high sugar content and poor nutritional value becomes a social justice issue for urban youth, for example (Hoffman, 2013; Noonan, 2015).

Cummins (2014) traces the origins and early evolution of this concept:

> The term "food desert" was reputedly first used by a resident of a public sector housing scheme in the west of Scotland in the early 1990s to capture the experience of living in a deprived neighborhood where food was expensive and relatively unobtainable. The phrase first appeared in an "official" publication in 1995, as part of a report from a policy working group investigating grocery distribution and food retailing on behalf of the Low Income Project Team of the UK government's Nutrition Task Force. Since then the term has been increasingly used by academics, policymakers, and community groups as shorthand to describe populated urban areas where residents do not have access to an affordable and healthy diet. Government reports in the United Kingdom and elsewhere have since suggested that food deserts may damage public health by restricting the availability and affordability of foods that form the components of a healthy diet. These reports have resulted in several health and social policy initiatives designed to promote adequate retail provision of food for those on low incomes, or who live in the poorest neighborhoods.

Creating a social justice issue into an image helps popularize this injustice in a manner that can appeal to a wide range of audiences with a variety of formal educational backgrounds, helping to create coalitions to seek justice.

The graphic and highly descriptive nature of *food desert* needs to be contextualized as occurring in communities that are low-income and highly stressed (Larsen & Gilliland, 2008). Movements of supermarkets away from inner cities, for example, severely restricts access to nutritious foods at an affordable price, setting into motion ecological conditions that result in food deserts (Ghosh-Dastidar et al., 2014).

The Many Faces of Food Justice

Food injustice is a subject that can have many different manifestations in marginalized urban communities (Hilmers, Hilmers, & Dave, 2012; Meals, 2012). The lack of access to quality food, as noted in discussion on food deserts, is a popular way of thinking about the subject. However, there are numerous other ways that food injustice can alter youth lives and that of their communities. These other manifestations can find their way into employment practices, ill health due to poor nutrition intake (Cannuscio, Weiss, & Asch, 2010), compromising educational attainment (Bodor et al., 2010; Sealy, 2010), and poor self-esteem (Cardinal et al., 2014; Russell-Mayhew et al., 2012), for example.

The relationship between overweight and obesity stands out for how it impacts key aspects related to health (Smalls, 2013). Finally, the social stigma of obesity has financial, social, and emotional consequences (Browne, 2012; Delgado, 2013). These consequences are further exacerbated when race/ethnicity (racism) is taken into account (Greenhalgh & Carney, 2014; He et al., 2013; Rivera, 2014) and contextually grounded within an environmentally compromised urban setting (Sbicca, 2012).

The many faces of food justice must be viewed from a positive rather than challenging perspective because it allows local circumstances to dictate how to frame food justice campaigns in a manner that resonates for communities. It also facilitates bridging immigrant rights and environmental justice, which, again, lends itself to local grounding, as evident in the case illustrations that will follow.

Food Justice and Youth Researchers

The role and importance of research in food justice campaigns is well recognized, as it is in other forms of social injustices like environmental and immigrant rights. Introducing youth as primary researchers, as in earlier portions of this book, or co-researchers (McLaughlin, 2006; Soohoo, 1993) adds an often-missing nuance to the findings (Gilbert, 2011; Kellett, 2005; Noonan, 2015; Seymour, 2013) and increases their competencies in the process (Delgado, 2006; Ozer & Douglas, 2013; Sato, 2013). Salvio (2013) argues that youth have a fundamental right to undertake research on issues of significance in their lives. Food justice clearly qualifies.

Youth can play a critical role in providing insights into how food justice influences their framing food justice issues at the community level and thereby shaping how a food justice campaign takes hold at the local level (Mansfield, 2014). Not only can they conduct research, they can also be part of an advisory committee informing the research process (Lund, 2014). The use of qualitative methods offers great potential for engaging youth in participatory social-justice–inspired community research (Ozer et al., 2013; Vasquez et al., 2007). Participatory qualitative research facilitates praxis, a critical aspect of social justice (Alvesson & Sköldberg, 2009).

Photovoice is an example of a visual qualitative method with great appeal for youth, and its potential regarding food justice is starting to receive the attention it deserves. Harper et al. (2014, p. 1), for example, describe the use of a youth participatory photovoice project in a western Massachusetts city with a high concentration of Latino youth. The authors found that participatory visual research "afforded opportunities for young people to develop sensory awareness, to critique stereotypes applied to them, and to gain insights on policy processes and social change in the food justice policy arena."

Leung (2014), too, used photovoice with primarily Latino middle-school youth in New York City and found that "photovoice enables youth to express their health perceptions and could be an effective tool for youth to reflect on their food environment and identify opportunities to promote positive change at the individual-level and within their communities." Other qualitative methods can be combined with photovoice to provide a nuanced and culturally grounded picture of food justice and its interrelationship with other forms of injustices (Delgado, 2015a).

Community Practice/Service-Learning Case Illustrations

To what extent do youth engaging in food justice service-learning influence the curriculum and project selection? The answer to this question on participation and decision-making will dictate whether the service-learning experience is typical, which is adult-determined, or empowering and youth-centered, which is what this book is advocating. Having adults dictate the service-learning experience is counter to the values and principles at the center of youth social activism, and critical service-learning and civic engagement.

This does not mean, however, that the curriculum on social justice and activism is totally developed by youth or that adults simply get out of the way. Collaborative partnerships or co-learning relationships are very much in order in the selection of the social justice issue to be addressed, particularly since service-learning projects are often initiated in schools or institutions of higher learning where adults are in positions of authority and power. Even the most progressive of these institutions will have adults dictating the nature of service-learning experiences. Youth-adult decision-making on food social issues and eventual service-learning projects is essential if the learning experience for youth is to be meaningful and facilitate their engagement process.

Case Selection Rationales

The following case examples address the role that youth must play in shaping food-focused service-learning when social justice values are incorporated into the learning and service. Two west coast cases were selected to illustrate community examples. The first case originates in Washington State and involves a youth ministry and a limited time period. The second example uses a youth adult-allies conference (East Side Stories: Youth Transformation Across Los Angeles) to introduce an innovative approach to service-learning and food justice, and a strategy for broadening the social network of youth activists.

Case Illustrations

The case illustration of the Youth Ministries for Peace and Social Justice Center for Community Justice illustrates civic engagement during a short but intensive period of time. School spring breaks bring a window for intensive civic engagement over a short time period of one to two weeks, offering educational institutions an opportunity to initiate social justice volunteer projects. The University of Puget Sound (Washington State) offers students an alternative break program that focuses on social justice civic engagement addressing power and oppression and its various manifestations. In 2015, the service-learning focus was on disability justice. Previous themes addressed Sustainable Food Justice, Justice and Service in Tacoma, Immigration and Citizenship, and Service in Seattle. The program is structured in a unique manner (http://www.ympi.org):

> Our conference-style break program will incorporate volunteering, larger group sessions and two distinct tracks for smaller group engagement. These two tracks will participate in concurrent sessions, one focusing on ableism and one on mental health. We will be working with L'Arche Tahoma Hope Farms and TACID, partnering with faculty from the Occupational Therapy School, and taking a critical look at ourselves, the university, and our society through the lens of disability rights.

This form of collaboration involving helping professions not "normally" associated with social justice highlights the appeal and potential of service-learning across a broad audience.

This final case illustration of food justice and service-learning takes a very different approach when compared to other case examples used in this book (Gonzales, 2012). In similar fashion to other case illustrations, this case combined food justice, immigration politics, but also sexual identity, which has only been touched upon in the previous examples and in this book. Further, this case highlights the use of a conference format that brought together adult allies and youth from throughout Los Angeles. The East Side Stories: Youth Transformation Across Los Angeles conference sought to foster youth empowerment and community activism. The use of a conference as a service-learning method is unique when it is focused on youth and their adult allies. A number of community organizations were part of this effort, demonstrating the broad reach of this social justice issue: Youth Justice Coalition, the Coalition for Educational Justice, the Rosemead High School Gay Straight Alliance, the Dream Resource Center, the Labor/Community Strategy Center, Watts Youth Collective, the Black Male Youth Academy and the UCLA IDEA Council of Youth Research. Collaboration, although it can be labor intensive, opens up the possibility of combining resources to undertake more ambitious projects and to expand the social network of youth activists and their allies. Putting together a city-wide conference is an example of what can be accomplished when there is a conscious effort to share and learn from others' efforts at achieving social justice.

Los Angeles high school students presented workshops highlighting their food activism and research undertaken as part of their school clubs and organizations, and sought to expand our understanding that "educational spaces can be settings where critical pedagogy and political education can empower minds, which can inspire action and transformation for social justice" (https://www.facebook.com/events/375663045807104). Opportunity for youth activists to come together to share and learn from each other are rare, particularly in forums that place youth in positions of experts. These gatherings also serve to help youth activists to expand their citywide contacts, which can be tapped currently and in future endeavors as youth enter adulthood.

Community Practice/Civic Engagement Case Illustrations

Case Selection Rationales

Two cases again have been selected to provide the reader with examples of community practice, food justice, and civic engagement. The first case is based in New York City and shows the power of collaboration between different community-based organizations, including governmental agencies. The second case of The Philly Food Justice introduces the role of a Bill of Rights in shaping food justice social actions. Although on the surface it appears that these are two very different cases, the first case builds upon principles, values, and rights, while the second case relies on the importance of collaboration in bringing rights to fruition.

Case Illustrations

It is appropriate to start this section on food justice community practice and civic engagement with a case illustration (The Health Equity Project, New York City) that has multiple youth-focused food justice goals, which address youth capacity enhancement, learning, and service. Tsui and colleagues (2012) provide an excellent example of a collaborative effort at a food justice social action campaign in New York City.

Interestingly, at no time was there any mention of civic engagement or service-learning, although this case illustrates how youth social activism can bring together these two approaches. Thus, the reader must be prepared to abandon labels when promoting or describing their projects. This project focused on addressing six goals that combined youth, food justice, and social activism (Tsui et al., 2012, p. 811):

> 1. Introduce youth to social, economic, and political factors that shape food environments and to the influence of food on health outcomes; 2. Provide youth with community-based participatory research skills so that they can become advocates and inform city agencies and service providers of how to better serve their communities; 3. Engage youth in analyzing and then acting to change their neighborhood food environments; 4. Help build young activist community leaders who can address community food access

and other matters of community concern; 5. Provide DPHOs with a replicable process (i.e., curriculum) for engaging youth groups in studying and changing food environments that act as social determinants of health; and 6. Increase the capacity of DPHOs to address the social determinants of health by engaging community and youth organizations in an ongoing dialogue.

The Health Equity Project initiative involved collaborations between youth organizations, city government, a high school, and a university and covered a three-year period, showing the power of collaboration and its ability to sustain an intervention over an extended period of time.

The Philly Food Justice (2015) case example provides readers with a Bill of Rights (17) regarding youth food justice and sets a wonderful context for food justice learning and service. The following rights integrate many of the key elements addressed in this book and illustrate the close inter-relationship of food justice and other social justice issues for urban youth:

(1) We have the right to culturally affirming food; (2) We have the right to sustainable food; (3) We have the right to nutritional education; (4) We have the right to healthy food at school; (5) We have the right to genetic diversity and GMO- [Genetically Modified Seeds and Produce] Free Food; (6) We have the right to poison-free food; (7) We have the right to beverages and foods that don't harm us; (8) We have the right to local food; (9) We have the right to fair food; (10) We have the right to good food subsidies; (11) We have the right to organic food and organic farmers; (12) We have the right to cultivate unused land; (13) We have the right to save our seed; (14) We have the right to an ozone layer; (15) We have a right to support our farmers through direct market transactions; (16) We have the right to convenient food that is healthy; and (17) We have the right to leadership education.

These food rights were developed by youth embracing an explicit set of values that are based in social justice and reflect what urban youth believe this nation's food system should be like. Readers can certainly appreciate the power of these social-justice–inspired rights and the comprehensive foundation they set for service-learning projects that bring together various social injustices. The case illustrations used throughout this book could easily have several of these rights serve as a guide in service-learning project developments.

Conclusion

Youth food justice social action campaigns are viable and highly attractive, as evidenced in this chapter. The importance of food from nutritional and cultural perspectives is well understood. Food is also symbolic, and those who are marginalized can easily understand social justice issues related to its availability and sustenance. Urban youth are attracted to food justice when they are provided with the necessary supports and affirming adult allies and when they have the power to shape how food justice is conceptualized and addressed.

The three social movements focused on in this section and book were selected because of their currency, their attractiveness to youth, their help in illustrating youth agency/praxis, and the role they can play in youth-centered and intergenerational campaigns. Further, these movements bring the capacity to integrate a wide range of spatial social justice goals and social benefits, and have benefited from increasing academic attention, making them of great relevance to understanding how youth can assume prominent roles in society (Han, 2004).

This chapter highlights the close relationship food has with youth and urban communities with sizeable numbers of unauthorized residents, and why immigrant rights and environmental justice are so interrelated. The following chapter on cross-cutting themes brings injustice issues to the fore and introduces environmental and immigrant justice from a different vantage point.

9

CROSS-CUTTING THEMES

Introduction

There are a number of critical themes that cut across the literature on critical service-learning and civic engagement as well as all three youth social-justice–focused campaigns and movement case illustrations and the professional literature. These themes, as the reader will see, highlight interrelationships, intersectionality, commonalities, uniqueness, as well as differences. Social justice service-learning, civic engagement, and youth activism are evolving at a rapid pace, and this bodes well for those of us interested in these topics. Difficult conceptual, ethical, research, and practice issues will emerge as part of this evolution, however, but that does not mean that they are insurmountable.

A total of eight themes have been identified in this section because of their significance, although the reader can no doubt identify many others. These themes are not meant to be covered comprehensively. Rather, sufficient information will be provided to give the reader a sense of why the theme was important to be included in this chapter, but clearly justice will not be done due to limited space. Each theme can easily have a chapter or book devoted to it. These themes highlight the dynamic and exciting nature of the subject and its importance for marginalized youth, urban areas, and the nation as a whole.

The eight themes that follow are not in any order of importance.

1. Youth Research and Scholarly Capabilities

It stands to reason that we, as adults, take the position that youth possess knowledge that we, in turn, must seek to capture and disseminate to a broad audience of interested parties and stakeholders (White et al., 2012), which, incidentally, can also mean youth. However, some adults, particularly academics, would argue with this position and may not consider youth to be an audience, either. The follow-up question then becomes, what role will youth play in a knowledge creation and dissemination endeavor (Delgado, 2015a)?

Can and will we devise ways of obtaining this information, and will youth play the conventional role of research subject? In other words, adults remain experts of youth lives. Or will we help youth uncover and disseminate this information on their terms, making them the experts of their own lives? In fact, it can be argued that historians and social scientists are most interested in learning about youth in order to better understand adults. Further, will we facilitate the identification and use of this knowledge to create social justice changes in their lives? It simply is not possible for youth to be activists without being researchers because both roles are intertwined and reinforce each other (Choudry, 2014; Futch, 2013).

The answers to these questions have profound social and political implications for how the research process is conceptualized and carried out (Delgado, 2006, 2015a; Watson & Marciano, 2015). Community practitioners are in excellent positions to undertake research on environmental justice and training youth in participatory research methods (Quijada Cerecer et al., 2013). This training can also emphasize critical praxis, an essential element in any form of social-justice–directed activism related to the environment (Checkoway, 2013). Youth, as a result, will be equipped to undertake their own research, and when necessary, seek the alliances of adults (Driskell, Fox, & Kudva, 2008; Smith et al., 2014).

Engaging in research and evaluation has been proposed as an attractive way for urban community-based organizations to engage youth in environmental justice causes, for example. A five-part framework has been proposed (Riemer, Lynes, & Hickman, 2014) to facilitate this process of engagement: (1) the engagement activity; (2) the engagement process; (3) initiating and sustaining factors; (4) mediators and moderators; and (5) outcomes.

Knowledge gained through social activism participation must be codified and shared with others (Conway, 2013), including communities. Adults can broaden the reach of these youth insights and experiences because of our access to scholarly avenues and classrooms in the nation's institutions of higher learning. Collaborative understandings resulting in codifying this knowledge is one way that we as adults can help rectify historical oversights (Harris, Wyn, & Younes, 2010), bringing tremendous potential for addressing social justice and intersectionality (Brockenbrough, 2014; Taylor & Dwyer, 2014).

2. Adult Allies (Intergenerational Relations)

The subject of youth social activism will forever be tied to the question of where adults stand in relation to their participation and leadership in these undertakings (Nygreen, Kwon & Sanchez, 2006; Sacks, 2009) and how much we embrace social justice in the work that we undertake by making these efforts more inclusive.

Do we simply stand by and say that we have no role in youth-led social justice campaigns and movements? Do we take the position that youth can turn to adults if, and when, they need and ask for assistance? What happens in intergenerational campaigns and movements? In essence, the answers to these and other questions related to youth and adult allies need to be raised and answered in an affirmative manner.

Youth-adult partnerships in social action have started to get the attention they warrant in the professional literature, but we have a long way to go in increasing our knowledge base on the subject (Christens et al., 2014; Harter et al., 2011). Kirshner (2008), for example, identified three significant ways that adult allies can work with youth activists: (1) facilitation; (2) apprenticeship; and (3) joint work.

There is a fourth way, however, and it has youth leading with adults assisting or functioning as allies. This perspective is still in its infancy but has tremendous implications for youth community practice involving service-learning and civic engagement. Youth activism on sexual health in Ecuador and Peru is a fine example of how sexual health concerns can be addressed by involving adult allies through a variety of "interconnected strategies" that include state-directed protests, social advocacy, and organizational development (Coe et al., 2015).

Delgado and Staples (2007) as well as countless others in the field see adults playing critical roles as youth allies and doing so without being condescending and disempowering. Our ability and willingness to become more aware of adultism and its deleterious consequences on youth-adult partnerships will go a long way towards ensuring their success as social activists. Many in the field, and that includes the author of this book, view adultism as being the most significant barrier in youth activism, regardless of whether we use service-learning and civic engagement as the vehicles for achieving societal changes.

3. Typology of Youth Participation and Community Practice

Participation is a popular buzzword in contemporary urban studies and probably nowhere more so than when discussing youth-focused interventions (Delgado & Staples, 2007). Yet, participation's meaning does not enjoy a universal definition; it can imply a deepening of democratic deliberation for some, while others will take it to mean grassroots resistance to powerful elites and neoliberalism policies (Riemer, Lynes, & Hickman, 2014; Silver, Scott, & Kazepov, 2010). This wide political lacuna causes misunderstandings and tensions, if not outright conflict, in the field.

The concept of participation plays an influential role in service-learning and civic engagement. However, the degree to which youth participate in an active and meaningful manner is open to interpretation. In essence, the "devil is in the details" when discussing participation, necessitating conceptual clarity. Critical service-learning and civic engagement, too, would benefit from this clarity, and a participation typology can assist youth, adult-ally practitioners, and academics in the planning of social justice campaigns.

Ho, Clarke, and Dougherty (2015) provide a brief overview of the literature on youth participation and illustrate how this concept has evolved over the past decade, including how marginalized youth context has shaped this evolution, and concluded based upon their research that "youth are more impactful and aim for higher scales of impact than we give them credit for: Youth think big and are risk takers. Do not forget to celebrate and acknowledge youth-led successes and impact. Certain topics might be more accessible for youth to have impact on than might others: Young people tend to work much more frequently on topics categorized under equality, empowerment, and social justice."

The development of a typology for creating an understanding of youth participation has profound implications for the youth activism field (Voight & Torney-Purta, 2013; Wong, Zimmerman, & Parker, 2010). A user-friendly typology allows those engaged in social-justice–inspired service-learning and civic engagement to plan, implement, and evaluate initiatives in a thoughtful manner, with an ability to anticipate challenging stages.

A typology, in addition, lays out broad parameters of key categories and potential timelines, bringing the integration of key theoretical concepts and interactional (political) considerations attached to each stage, highlighting particular rewards and challenges along the way. There certainly is no magical number as to the stages or phases of a typology. Some practitioners/academics may prefer a low number while others have a propensity to embrace typologies consisting of a large number, allowing greater specificity.

The following three-part framework or typology, with analytical (theoretical) and interactional (political) dimensions, can appeal to both academics and practitioners, including urban youth, and represents a "basic" level that can be expanded upon:

> Level 1: Conventional/Charity Paradigm (youth provide a service that is not social justice-focused);
> Level 2: Leadership Development (a view that youth have potential and every effort must be made to development their competencies to lead but adults are still in charge); and
> Level 3: Youth-Led Service-Learning and Civic Engagement (this level epitomizes the central thrust of this book). Each of these levels, in turn, can be further sub-divided representing various gradations to take into account local circumstances and goals.

4. The Role of Information Technology and Social Media

Information dissemination is synonymous with social media, and it is impossible to develop a sound and deep understanding of youth activism and youth community practice without a corresponding attention to the role of information technology and social media and youth mastery/competencies (Costanza-Chock, 2008; Davidson, 2014; Wayne, 2007). Youth media on social activism brings a nuanced perspective that provides valuable insights that adults cannot have because of their age vantage point (Kulick, 2014).

There is a new form of literacy that youth possess and use in their quest to participate and shape public life (Soep, 2014). The role, function (texting, tweeting, tracking), and importance of the mobile phone during street protests is beyond dispute for its ability to connect protesters in real time, a critical element in social protests (Neumayer & Stald, 2014).

Lim (2012) analyzed the Egyptian uprisings of early 2011 and concluded that social media provided an instrumental vehicle for shaping issues, propagating unifying symbols, and transforming "online activism into offline protests." Sullivan and Xie (2009) found in a study in China the importance of "social linking patterns" between environmental activists, which can concomitantly facilitate activism on the ground and in cyberspace. Velasquez and LaRose (2014), in turn, found that online media increases youth collective efficacy in social activism campaigns.

Conner & Slattery (2014, p. 14) see tremendous potential in the use of new social media tools for empowering youth in their efforts to achieve social justice based on their study of the Philadelphia Student Union:

> As the gulfs between low-income and more affluent youth widen, researchers and practitioners continue to search for effective means of closing gaps in academic achievement, digital participation, and civic engagement . . . The Philadelphia Student Union integrated new media into its core functions and how the student members experience these tools. Drawing on extant research, we argue that when situated within an organizing framework, new media tools can help to promote the digital literacy, academic achievement, and civic engagement of low-income youth of color, who have otherwise limited opportunities to contribute to the civic life of their communities.

Youth possess media competencies that can be reinforced through school and after-school activities, and these competencies can aid them academically and in social justice campaigns.

Herrera (2014) reports in her book, *Wired Citizenship: Youth Learning and Activism in the Middle East*, how youth are innovative and challenging in their quest to seek social justice worldwide and how social media connect youth to make their campaigns successful. Hathcock and Dickerson (2015), in turn, describe the use of digital technologies as a promising vehicle for promoting youth activism in environmental science, and in this case, through a student-created documentary film.

These types of efforts tap into youth technological competencies and re-enforce their roles as experts. In addition, they expand the audience for lessons learned in carrying out social activism campaigns and serve as an historical record for future generations to learn from.

5. The Many Ways Service-Learning Can Transpire

Adult involvement in helping to prepare youth to engage in social activism and movements can occur within and outside of schools. Within schools and after-school programs, projects can be developed that provide youth with an opportunity to exercise their democratic rights. Outside of school, endless possibilities exist within community-based settings.

The worlds outside and inside of schools can be breached through projects originating in schools and transpiring out in communities, with a potential for other benefits to occur that break down barriers between communities and schools located within their geographic areas (Rondini, 2015). The possibilities for constructing service-learning and civic engagement opportunities are only limited by our imagination and willingness as adults to view youth as peers rather than as subordinates, and there is no subject area that cannot have a social justice focus to increase the relevance of the academic subject and activities (Carson & Raguse, 2014). The increased use of films, for example, brings a method that can be used in either school or community-based organizations, facilitating a dialogue between adults and youth (Lee & Priester, 2015).

6. The Potential of Collaboration and Partnerships

The reader has no doubt seen the role and importance of social justice service-learning and civic engagement drawing upon collaborative partners in staging initiatives (Bottrell, 2015; Wagner, & Mathison, 2015). The bringing together of resources, access, and determination improves the likelihood of initiatives achieving success (Berry & Russell, 2012; Lee, 2013), and ensures greater owner-ship on the part of the community and the institutions serving them.

Collaborations always look logical on paper yet are arduous to successfully accomplish. In fact, successful collaborations are often built upon failed attempts in which lessons are learned and addressed. Yet, the power of collaborations is more than the individual partners.

Successful collaborations help ensure that social justice issues have the requisite resources and commitment to make them successful (Chang, 2015; Peffer, 2014). In addition, collaborations provide youth with the experience and competencies they can continue using as they age out, which is extremely important in the field of human services; collaboration becomes an important tool in a youth social activist's toolbox (Neville, 2015; Olsen, 2015).

7. Youth Leadership Enhancement and Development

Social justice service-learning and civic engagement cannot afford to ignore the need for creating and supporting youth in leadership roles (Colby, Clark, & Bryant Jr, 2014; Priest & Clegorne, 2015). It may be tempting for adults to be satisfied in providing opportunities for youth to engage in social activism as important members of teams. However, embracing youth leadership potential brings a unique perspective and goal to service-learning and civic engagement with a social justice focus (Longo & Fleming, 2014; Mitchell, 2014). Further, leadership opportunities take on added significance in situations involving immigrant youth (Obenchain & Callahan, 2014). These youth are able to socially navigate a world far larger than that of their parents and adult family members, increasing their importance to this community.

An embrace of a co-learner role (Bottrell, 2015) provides adult allies with an approach that allows them to navigate institutional requirements with a set of principles guiding social justice service-learning and civic engagement in situations where the institutions cannot accept youth as leaders in their own right. Youth can assume leadership for various project stages in situations that are not conducive to having them assume overall leadership, opening up leadership possibilities (McLaughlin et al., 2009; Newman, Dantzler & Coleman, 2014).

8. Context and Even More Context

It is fitting to end this chapter on cross-cutting themes with attention to the role and importance of context in shaping how critical service-learning and civic engagement is influenced by where it is grounded or transpires (Bringle & Hatcher, 2009; Kahne & Sporte, 2008). In the case of this book, context involves a geographical area (urban), a specific age group (youth), and racial and ethnic background (African American, Asian, Latino, and Native American).

These three perspectives on context shape learning environments and how social justice is viewed and acted upon through service provision (Hurtado et al., 2012; Kinloch, Nemeth, & Patterson, 2014). This theme should not be of any surprise to readers because of the role context plays in community-focused social interventions of any kind. Grounding within a social context is key in shaping how social justice gets conceptualized and how communities respond to injustices (Mitchell, 2014; Warwick et al., 2012), and the strengths and assets that youth possess (Gosine & Islam, 2014).

Conclusion

Youth service-learning, civic engagement, and community practice are closely intertwined and offer the field a tremendous opportunity to make important contributions to social justice and democracy. The eight themes covered in this chapter reveal important philosophical and theoretical challenges for youth community practitioners. Yet, there is no denying that the field must acknowledge fault lines, particularly when community practice embraces a political foundation that rests on social justice.

The cross-cutting themes touch upon a whole host of factors covered throughout this book, and they find their way into the case illustrations in Chapters 6, 7, and 8. A social justice embrace narrows the divide between service-learning and civic engagement; the potential of these two approaches merging into one, with profound implications for community practice and education.

EPILOGUE

Epilogues provide authors with an opportunity to step back and highlight aspects of a book that require comment or observations because of their uniqueness or particular poignant relevance. The epilogue, in addition, can be written without the scholarly encumbrance usually associated with an academic book, such as citations to other scholarly articles, definition of key conceptual terms, and so on. Thus, this chapter is intended to be "reader-friendly."

A total of six themes are covered in this epilogue and reflect how this subject matter is evolving and bringing with it incredible rewards and challenges for youth, communities, adult practitioners, and academics.

1. It Certainly is a Fascinating Topic

I cannot help but marvel at the excitement associated with youth social justice campaigns and social movements, and those addressed in this book in particular, although countless others exist. All social action efforts bring excitement, urgency, and a sense of awe from bystanders as to the amount of work, sacrifice, and commitment they require and the meaningfulness of this experience for youth activists. The energy level and excitement experienced by participants is unmatched, too. Youth are often thought of as being hedonistic and living for the moment. Youth social activism counters this prevailing view. Witnessing youths' commitment to a social cause results in a need to better understand their motivation and willingness to openly defy adults, particularly those willing to be arrested for their cause (youth oppositional resistance). This enthusiasm is contagious. Youth lives will be positively changed forever as a result of these experiences, giving a profound meaning to what is often referred to as a "transformative" experience. Illeris (2014) discusses how transformative learning changes elements of identity. Those who are inspired by and led by youth find an added degree of wonder. We cannot help but be amazed by their energy and belief that the world can change and must do so for their and future generations. Having said this, there are many thorny scholarly questions that need to be posed and answered, which can be addressed when academics and youth come together.

2. The Role of the Academy

Those of us occupying academic positions are morally responsible for moving social justice agendas forward in our capacity to generate and disseminate knowledge to improve the lives of those facing social injustices. Mind you, it is not our position to lead, but to embrace and support. Such efforts make our work and lives that much more meaningful while serving to support the cause of social justice and urban youth, and they will help break down barriers between institutions of higher learning and communities.

Supporting social justice service-learning and civic engagement can unfold in a wide variety of ways. Those in the academy can engage in knowledge creation through research and scholarly writing, including generating funding for research and demonstration projects, and this circulates money within communities. Purchasing supplies, renting space, hiring local residents, and catering food are such examples. Every dollar spent in the community translates into $1.6 in circulation dollars (Delgado, 2011). More importantly, purchasing services and products within the community conveys to residents that we are there to support them in a wide variety of ways, not just through research or programming.

We can also make college/university space and resources available to youth groups for holding conferences, workshops, and guest lectures, for example. These resources can break down barriers between institutions and communities in a way that benefits all parties. Faculty, as opposed to administration, is probably in the best position to bring the community to the institution in a manner that is affirming and non-charity focused.

3. How Can Social Justice Be Integrated in Service-Learning and Civic Engagement?

The answer to this question is only limited by our imagination because there are countless numbers of ways; every day it seems like there are new ways of accomplishing this goal. Content related to social justice can be addressed through discussions, conferences, forums, internships, photovoice, photo-elicitation, field interviews, journals, exercises, guest lecturers, DVDs, field trips, book reports, and readings (academic and popular), for example.

The reader can no doubt discern that there is no one way of bringing to life social justice as it relates to immigrant rights, food, and environmental justice, particularly when taking a spatial justice perspective and a specific focus on urban youth. This flexibility in viewing social justice from a broad viewpoint, and no more so than when taking intersectionality into account, brings tremendous options to take into account local circumstances and context. Local context will determine what methods stand out for achieving success with youth. This same context must be taken into account for adults. A cookie-cutter approach does a disservice to critical service-learning and civic engagement. Social activism is one approach towards meeting local needs and issues. Other forms and methods, however, must be made available for youth not interested in social activism—in similar fashion to providing an extensive menu at a local restaurant, as noted in the next theme.

4. Is Flexibility a Blessing or a Curse in Discussing Methods?

The abundance of methods for combining learning and service provides organizations with a tremendous amount of flexibility to take into account budget, time, time frames, goals, interests, and opportunities that may present themselves. One size does not fit all when discussing social justice learning and service. This flexibility, unfortunately, can cause a great deal of confusion and tension because there is no set "ideal model" for how to operationalize social justice service-learning and civic engagement. Ambiguity can be a source of paralysis, but also an opportunity for creativity and innovation. Flexibility takes on added prominence when discussing newcomer communities and how best to engage, empower, and mobilize residents to address social injustices because this entails yet-to-be-developed approaches.

5. Interdisciplinary is the Way to Go

No one profession should be entrusted with "owning" social justice service-learning and civic engagement. In fact, if anyone is to "own" these approaches, it should be youth and their communities, since they play a central role in carrying social change. These social interventions have the potential to bring together educational and helping professions in ways that have generally not been explored.

This recommendation is not made without a profound understanding of the challenges of bringing about collaboration between professions. Collaborations are arduous to achieve under the best of circumstances. The challenges increase the moment we cross professions and organizations. Youth and their adult allies are in a propitious position to facilitate partnerships across professions and organizations because they are the focus of social interventions and not encumbered by academic/professional discipline history.

6. When Do Youth Stop Being Youth and Become Adults?

This question was initially raised earlier in this book because the answer has significant implications for how we view youth-inspired social action within service-learning/civic engagement community practice. The social construction of youth, however, makes it necessary to seek answers to this question for every generation because socio-cultural forces influence our definitions and perceptions of this life-stage. After all, the "luxury" of being a youth, as already noted earlier in this book, is not available to all youth.

Scholars must wrestle with this question and it requires active involvement of youth from varied backgrounds to arrive at a definition of meaning to them as well as practitioners and academics. In essence, this is not an intellectual exercise. Context meets chronology, and the answer will have significant implications for the field of social activism.

Conclusion

Critical service-learning and civic engagement is destined to reach new heights in the forthcoming decade. The "immigration" problem does not look like it will be "solved" anytime soon, as evidenced by political storms surrounding this social injustice. Urban environmental and food issues, too, unfortunately, will be with us for the foreseeable future. Yet, the hope or dream that youth activism brings must be recognized and fostered. Scholarship on this subject will only increase in significance, helping to fuel progress, but in all likelihood, it will flow from social actions as opposed to influencing social action. I believe that academics will be relegated to recording and interpreting history rather than making it.

REFERENCES

Aaltonen, S. (2013). 'Trying to push things through': Forms and bounds of agency in transitions of school-age young people. *Journal of Youth Studies*, 16 (3), 375–390.

Abbott, D., & Porter, S. (2013). Environmental hazard and disabled people: From vulnerable to expert to interconnected. *Disability & Society*, 28 (6), 839–852.

Abdelrahman, M. (2013). In praise of organization: Egypt between activism and revolution. *Development and Change*, 44 (3), 569–585.

Abedania, J. (2014). *Spatializing Commensality: The City as Public Dining Room* (Doctoral dissertation, University of Cincinnati).

Abrams, L. S., & Moio, J. A. (2009). Critical race theory and the cultural competence dilemma in social work education. *Journal of Social Work Education*, 45 (2), 245–261.

Abrego, L. J. (2006). "I can't go to college because I don't have papers": Incorporation patterns of Latino undocumented youth. *Latino Studies*, 4 (3), 212–232.

Adams, D., Nam, Y., Williams Shanks, T. R., Hicks, S., & Robinson, C. (2010). Research on assets for children and youth: Reflections on the past and prospects for the future. *Children and Youth Services Review*, 32 (11), 1617–1621.

Adams, M., Bell, L. A., & Griffin, P. (Eds.). (2007). *Teaching for diversity and social justice*. New York: Routledge.

Adams, R. (2008). *Empowerment, participation and social work*. Basingstoke: Palgrave Macmillan.

Adler, R. P., & Goggin, J. (2005). What do we mean by "civic engagement"?. *Journal of Transformative Education*, 3 (3), 236–253.

Aguirre, Jr., A., & Lio, S. (2008). Spaces of mobilization: The Asian American/Pacific Islander struggle for social justice. *Social Justice*, 35 (2), 1–17.

Aguirre, Jr, A., & Simmers, J. K. (2011). The DREAM Act and neoliberal practice: Retrofitting Hispanic immigrant youth in US society. *Social Justice*, 38 (3), 3.

Agyeman, J. (2005). *Sustainable communities and the challenge of environmental justice*. New York: New York University Press.

Agyeman, J., & Evans, T. (2003). Toward just sustainability in urban communities: Building equity rights with sustainable solutions. *The ANNALS of the American Academy of Political and Social Science*, 590 (1), 35–53.

Ainley, P., & Rainbird, H. (Eds.). (2014). *Apprenticeship: Towards a new paradigm of learning*. New York: Routledge.

Akom, A. A., Cammarota, J., & Ginwright, S. (2008). Youthtopias: Towards a new paradigm of critical youth studies. *Youth Media Reporter*, 2 (4), 1–30.

Aldana, A. (2015, January). "Checking a friend" vs "attended a protest": A youth-developed social action scale to measure anti-racist civic engagement. In *Society for Social Work and Research 19th Annual Conference: The Social and Behavioral Importance of Increased Longevity*. SSWR.

Aldana, R. E. (2008). Silent victims no more?: Moral indignation and the potential for Latino political mobilization in defense of immigrants. *Houston Law Review*, 4 (1), 73–97.

Alkon, A. (2008). Paradise or pavement: The social constructions of the environment in two urban farmers' markets and their implications for environmental justice and sustainability. *Local Environment*, 13 (3), 271–289.

Alkon, A. H. (2013). Historical background of food justice scholarship and major theoretical. In S. Zavestoski & J. Agyeman (Eds.), *Routledge international handbook of food studies* (pp. 295). New York.

Allen, K., Daro, V., & Holland, D. C. (2007). Becoming an environmental justice activist. In R. Sandler & P. C. Pezzullo (Eds.), *Environmental justice and environmentalism: The social justice challenge to the environmental movement* (pp. 105–134). Cambridge, MA: MIT Press.

Allen, P. (2014). Divergence and convergence in alternative agrifood movements: Seeking a path forward. Alternative Agrifood Movements: Patterns of Convergence and Divergence. *Rural Sociology and Development*, 21, 49–68.

Alvesson, M., & Sköldberg, K. (2009). *Reflexive methodology: New vistas for qualitative research*. London: Sage.

Ambrose, S. A., Bridges, M. W., DiPietro, M., Lovett, M. C., & Norman, M. K. (2010). *How learning works: Seven research-based principles for smart teaching*. New York: John Wiley & Sons.

Ameen, E. (2012). *On Becoming and Being a Homeless Youth Activist*. Open Access Dissertations. Paper 739. Retrieved from http://scholarlyrepository.miami.edu/oa_dissertations/739

Amenta, E., Caren, N., Chiarello, E., & Su, Y. (2010). The political consequences of social movements. *Annual Review of Sociology*, 36, 287–307.

American Youth Congress. (1936, July 4). *Declaration of the rights of American youth*. Retrieved from http://newdeal.feri.org/studnets/ayc.htm

Amnå, E. (2012). How is civic engagement developed over time? Emerging answers from a multidisciplinary field. *Journal of Adolescence*, 35 (3), 611–627.

Amodeo, M., & Collins, M. E. (2007). Using a positive youth development approach in addressing problem-oriented youth behavior. *Families in Society: The Journal of Contemporary Social Services*, 88 (1), 75–85.

Anderson, G. L., & Irvine, P. (1993). Informing critical literacy with ethnography. In *Critical literacy: Politics, praxis, and the postmodern* (pp. 81–104).

Anderson, K. S., & Sandmann, L. (2009). Toward a model of empowering practices in youth-adult partnerships. *Journal of Extension*, 47 (2), 1–8.

Andolina, M. W., Jenkins, K., Keeter, S., & Zukin, C. (2002). Searching for the meaning of youth civic engagement: Notes from the field. *Applied Developmental Science*, 6 (4), 189–195.

Andrzejewski, J., Baltodano, M., & Symcox, L. (Eds.). (2009). *Social justice, peace, and environmental education: Transformative standards*. New York: Routledge.

Anguelovski, I. (2013). New directions in urban environmental justice: Rebuilding community, addressing trauma, and remaking place. *Journal of Planning Education and Research*, doi:0739456X13478019

Anguelovski, I. (2015). Alternative food provision conflicts in cities: Contesting food privilege, injustice, and whiteness in Jamaica Plain, Boston. *Geoforum, 58*, 184–194.

Anitsal, M. M., Anitsal, I., Barger, B., & Fidan, I. (2014). Service learning across disciplines and countries. *Atlantic Marketing Journal*, 3 (2), 10.

Annamma, S. (2014). Undocumented and under surveillance. *Association of Mexican American Educators Journal*, 7 (3).

Apaliyah, G. T., Martin, K. E., Gasteyer, S. P., Keating, K., & Pigg, K. (2012). Community leadership development education: Promoting civic engagement through human and social capital. *Community Development*, 43 (1), 31–48.

Aparicio, A. (2008). Reconstructing political genealogies: Reflections on youth, racial justice, and the uses of history. *Souls*, 10 (4), 361–373.

Applebaum, B. (2014). Hold that thought! A response to "Respect Differences? Challenging the Common Guidelines in Social Justice Education". *Democracy and Education*, 22 (2), 5.

Arches, J. (2012). The role of groupwork in social action projects with youth. *Groupwork*, 22 (1), 59–77.

Arches, J. (2013). Social action, service learning, and youth development. *Journal of Community Engagement and Higher Education*, 5 (1).

Archibald, T. (2015). "They Just Know": The epistemological politics of "evidence-based" non-formal education. *Evaluation and program planning*, 48, 137–148.

Ardizzone, L. (2007). *Getting my word out: Voices of urban youth activists*. Albany, NY: State University of New York.

Ares, N. (2010). *Youth-full productions: Cultural practices and constructions of content and social spaces (Vol. 47)*. Peter Lang.

Armony, A. C. (2004). *The dubious link: Civic engagement and democratization*. Stanford University Press.

Armstrong, M. M. (2011). *Modeling the relationship between a social responsibility attitude and youth activism*. Atlanta, Georgia: Georgia State University.

Arnold, H. E., Cohen, F. G., & Warner, A. (2009). Youth and environmental action: Perspectives of young environmental leaders on their formative influences. *The Journal of Environmental Education*, 40 (3), 27–36.

Arnold, M. E., Dolenc, B., & Wells, E. E. (2008). Youth community engagement: A recipe for success. *Journal of Community Engagement and Scholarship*, 1 (1), 56–65.

Arnot, M., & Swartz, S. (2012). Youth citizenship and the politics of belonging: Introducing contexts, voices, imaginaries. *Comparative Education*, 48 (1), 1–10.

Aronowitz, S. (2013). *The death and rebirth of American radicalism*. New York: Routledge.

Associated Press. (2006, March 25). Immigration issues draws thousands in to the streets. *MSNBC*. Retrieved from http://www.msnbc.msn.com/id/11442705/ns/politics/t/immigration-issue-draws-thousands-streets/

Athanases, S. Z., & de Oliveira, L. C. (2014). Scaffolding versus routine support for Latina/o youth in an urban school: Tensions in building toward disciplinary literacy. *Journal of Literacy Research*, 46 (2), 263–299.

Aukerman, M. (2012). "Why do you say yes to Pedro, but no to me?" toward a critical literacy of dialogic engagement. *Theory into Practice*, 51 (1), 42–48.

Azzopardi, A. (2013). Youth activism. In Andrew Azzopardi (Ed.), *Youth: Responding to lives* (pp. 45–56). Dordrecht, Netherlands: SensePublishers.

Bacon, D. (2007, July 24). Time for a more radical immigrant-rights movement. *The American Prospect.* Retrieved from http://prospect.org/cs/articles?article=time_for_a_more_radical_immigrant rights_movement

Bajaj, M. (2011). Human rights education: Ideology, location, and approaches. *Human Rights Quarterly,* 33 (2), 481–508.

Bailey, A., & Russell, K. C. (2008). Psycho-social benefits of a service learning experience. *Journal of Unconventional Parks, Tourism & Recreation Research* (JUPTRR), 1 (1).

Baillie, C., Pawley, A., & Riley, D. M. (Eds.). (2012). *Engineering and social justice: In the university and beyond.* Lafayette, IN: Purdue University Press.

Baker, C. (2011). *Cultural studies: Theory and practice.* London: Sage.

Baker-Cristales, B. (2009). Mediated resistance: The construction of neoliberal citizenship in the immigrant rights movement. *Latino Studies,* 7 (1), 60–82.

Baldridge, B. J. (2014). Relocating the deficit: Reimagining Black youth in neoliberal times. *American Educational Research Journal,* doi:0002831214532514

Baldridge, B. J., Lamont Hill, M., & Davis, J. E. (2011). New possibilities: (re) engaging Black male youth within community-based educational spaces. *Race Ethnicity and Education,* 14 (1), 121–136.

Ballard, P. J. (2014). What motivates youth civic involvement?. *Journal of Adolescent Research,* doi:0743558413520224

Balsano, A. B. (2005). Youth civic engagement in the United States: Understanding and addressing the impact of social impediments on positive youth and community development. *Applied Developmental Science,* 9 (4), 188–201.

Bamber, P., & Hankin, L. (2011). Transformative learning through service-learning: No passport required. *Education + Training,* 53 (2/3), 190–206.

Banales, S. (2012). *Decolonizing being, knowledge, and power: Youth activism in California at the turn of the 21st century.* Berkeley, CA: University of California.

Banks, S., & Butcher, H. (2013). What is community practice? In S. Banks, H. L. Butcher, A. Orton, & J. Robertson (Eds.), *Managing community practice: Principles, policies and programmes* (p. 7). Bristol, England: Policy Press.

Banks, S., Butcher, H. L., Orton, A., & Robertson, J. (Eds.). (2013). *Managing community practice: Principles, Policies and Programmes.* Bristol, England: Policy Press.

Barnett, R. V., & Brennan, M. A. (2006). Integrating youth into community development: Implications for policy planning and program evaluation. *Journal of Youth Development,* 1 (2), 2–16.

Barr-Anderson, D. A. H. E. I. A. J., McCarthy, W. J., Yore, M., & Harris, K. A. (2015). Television viewing and food choice patterns in a sample of predominantly ethnic minority youth. In *The complexity of adolescent obesity: Causes, correlates, and consequences* (pp. 29–36).

Barrett, G., Wyman, M., & Coelho, V. S. P. (2012). Assessing the policy impacts of deliberative civic engagement. In *Democracy in motion: Evaluating the practice and impact of deliberative civic engagement* (pp. 181–206).

Barrett, M., & Brunton-Smith, I. (2014). Political and civic engagement and participation: Towards an integrative perspective. *Journal of Civil Society,* 10 (1), 5–28.

Barrett, M., & Zani, B. (Eds.). (2014). *Political and civic engagement: Multidisciplinary perspectives.* New York: Routledge.

Barry, M. (2014). Community engagement through service-learning. *Strategic Library* (4), 5.

Bartell, T. G. (2013). Learning to teach mathematics for social justice: Negotiating social justice and mathematical goals. *Journal for Research in Mathematics Education,* 44 (1), 129–163.

Bassey, M. O. (2010). Education for civic citizenship and social justice: A critical social foundations approach. *Education as Change*, 14 (2), 247–257.

Batsleer, J. (2013). Informal learning in youth work: Times, people and places. In *Working with young people* (pp. 99–108).

Batsleer, M. J. (2013). *Youth working with girls and women in community settings: A feminist perspective*. Ashgate Publishing, Ltd.

Battistoni, R. M. (2013). Civic learning through service learning. In P. H. Clayton, R. G. Bringle, & J. A. Hatcher (Eds.), *Research on service learning* (pp. 111–132). Sterling, VA: Stylus.

Beaumont, E. (2010). Political agency and empowerment: Pathways for developing a sense of political efficacy in young adults. In L. R. Sterrod, J. Tomey-Punta & C. A. Flanagan (Eds.), *Handbook of research on civic engagement in youth* (pp. 525–558). New York: John Wiley & Sons.

Becher, D. (2012). Political moments with long-term consequences. In M. P. Smith & M. MacQuarrie (Eds.), *Remaking urban citizenship: Organizations, institutions and the right to the city* (pp. 203–220). New Brunswick, NJ: Transaction Publishers.

Bednarz, S. W., Chalkley, B., Fletcher, S., Hay, I., Heron, E. L., Mohan, A., & Trafford, J. (2008). Community engagement for student learning in geography. *Journal of Geography in Higher Education*, 32 (1), 87–100.

Bedolla, L. G. (2012). Latino education, civic engagement, and the public good. *Review of Research in Education*, 36 (1), 23–42.

Bee, C., & Pachi, D. (2014). Active citizenship in the UK: Assessing institutional political strategies and mechanisms of civic engagement. *Journal of Civil Society*, 10 (1), 100–117.

Belfield, C. R., & Levin, H. R. (2012). *The economics of investing in opportunity youth*. Battlecreek, MI: W. K. Kellogg Foundation.

Bell, D. N., & Blanchflower, D. G. (2011). Young people and the Great Recession. *Oxford Review of Economic Policy*, 27 (2), 241–267.

Bell, L. A., & Desai, D. (2011). Imagining otherwise: Connecting the arts and social justice to envision and act for change: Special Issue Introduction. *Equity & Excellence in Education*, 44 (3), 287–295.

Bellino, M. J. (2014). Civic engagement in extreme times: The remaking of justice among Guatemala's "postwar" generation. *Education, Citizenship and Social Justice*. Advance online publication.

Ben-Arieh, A., & Kosher, H. (2014). Youth/adolescent rights. A. C. Michalos (Ed.), *Encyclopedia of quality of life and well-being research* (pp. 7303–7309). New York: Springer Publisher.

Bencze, L., Alsop, S., Ritchie, A., Bowen, M., & Chen, S. (2015). Pursuing youth-led socio-scientific activism: Conversations of participation, pedagogy and power. In M. P. Mueller & D. J. Tippins (Eds.), *EcoJustice, citizen science and youth activism* (pp. 333–347). New York: Springer International Publishing.

Bender, K., Thompson, S. J., McManus, H., Lantry, J., & Flynn, P. M. (2007). Capacity for survival: Exploring strengths of homeless street youth. *Child and Youth Care Forum*, 36 (1), 25–42.

Berg, M., Coman, E., & Schensul, J. J. (2009). Youth action research for prevention: A multi-level intervention designed to increase efficacy and empowerment among urban youth. *American Journal of Community Psychology*, 43 (3–4), 345–359.

Bergen, J. K., & McLean, L. R. (2015). Students as citizens: Conceptions of citizenship in a social studies curriculum. *TCI (Transnational Curriculum Inquiry)*, 11 (2), 1–24.

Berger, B. (2015). Experience and (civic) education. *PS: Political Science & Politics*, 48 (1), 61–64.

Berger, D. (2014). *Captive nation: Black prison organizing in the Civil Rights Era.* Chapel Hill, NC: UNC Press Books.

Berger, D., Boudin, C., & Farrow, K. (Eds.). (2005). *Letters from young activists: Today's rebels speak out.* New York: Nation Books.

Bernacki, M. L., & Jaeger, E. (2008). Exploring the impact of service-learning on moral development and moral orientation. *Michigan Journal of Community Service Learning,* 14 (2).

Bernier, A. (2011). Representations of youth in local media: Implications for library service. *Library & Information Science Research,* 33 (2), 158–167.

Berry, A., & Russell, T. (2012). Collaboration and community building in teacher educators' work. *Studying Teacher Education,* 8 (3), 205–207.

Bersaglio, B., Enns, C., & Kepe, T. (2015). Youth under construction: The United Nations' representations of youth in the global conversation on the post-2015 development agenda. *Canadian Journal of Development Studies/Revue canadienne d'études du développement* (ahead-of-print), 1–15.

Beyerlein, K., Trinitapoli, J., & Adler, G. (2011). The effect of religious short-term mission trips on youth civic engagement. *Journal for the Scientific Study of Religion,* 50 (4), 780–795.

Bhabha, J. (2013). *Adolescents: Current rights for future opportunities.* New York: UNICEF Regional Office for South Asia.

Bhattacharjya, M., Birchall, J., Caro, P., Kelleher, D., & Sahasranaman, V. (2013). Why gender matters in activism: Feminism and social justice movements. *Gender & Development,* 21 (2), 277–293.

Billett, P. (2012). Indicators of youth social capital: The case for not using adult indicators in the measurement of youth social capital. *Youth Studies Australia,* 31 (2), 9–18.

Billett, P. (2014). Dark cloud or silver lining? The value of bonding networks during youth. *Journal of Youth Studies* (ahead-of-print), 1–10.

Billett, S. (2008). Learning throughout working life: A relational interdependence between personal and social agency. *British Journal of Educational Studies,* 56 (1), 39–58.

Birdwell, J., Scott, R., & Horley, E. (2013). Active citizenship, education and service learning. *Education, Citizenship and Social Justice,* 8 (2), 185–199.

Bishop, E. C., & Willis, K. (2014). 'Without hope everything would be doom and gloom': Young people talk about the importance of hope in their lives. *Journal of Youth Studies* (ahead-of-print), 1–16.

Bishop, E. M. (2014). *Becoming Activist: Collaboratively Documenting the Critical Literacy Praxis of Urban Youth Organizers* (Doctoral dissertation, University of Pittsburgh).

Blanchet-Cohen, N., & Bedeaux, C. (2014). Towards a rights-based approach to youth programs: Duty-bearers' perspectives. *Children and Youth Services Review,* 38 (1), 75–81.

Blanchet-Cohen, N., & Brunson, L. (2014). Creating settings for youth empowerment and leadership: An ecological perspective. *Child & Youth Services,* 35 (3), 216–236.

Bloemraad, I., & Trost, C. (2008). It's a family affair: Intergenerational mobilization in the spring 2006 protests. *American Behavioral Scientist,* 52 (4), 507–532.

Bloom, A. (Ed.). (2001). *Long time gone: Sixties America then and now.* New York: Oxford University Press.

Blouin, D. D., & Perry, E. M. (2009). Whom does service learning really serve? Community-based organizations' perspectives on service learning. *Teaching Sociology,* 37 (2), 120–135.

Blow, C. M. (2014, December 8). A new age of activism. *The New York Times,* p. A25.

Blumberg, R. L. (2009). The Civil Rights Movement (from Civil Rights: The 1960s freedom struggle). In J. Goodwin & J. M. Jasper (Eds.), *The social movements reader: Cases and examples, 2nd ed.* (pp.15–23). New York: John-Wiley-Blackwell.

Blundo, R. (2010). Social justice becomes a living experience for students, faculty, and community. *Journal of Teaching in Social Work*, 30 (1), 90–100.

Blyth, D. A. (2006). Toward a new paradigm for youth development. *New Directions for Youth Development, 2006* (112), 25–43.

Bodor, J. N., Rice, J. C., Farley, T. A., Swalm, C. M., & Rose, D. (2010). The association between obesity and urban food environments. *Journal of Urban Health*, 87 (5), 771–781.

Boehm, A., & Cnaan, R. A. (2012). Towards a practice-based model for community practice: Linking theory and practice. *J. Soc. & Soc. Welfare*, 39, 141.

Boggs, G. L., & Kurashige, S. (2012). *The next American revolution: Sustainable activism for the twenty-first century.* Berkeley, CA: Univ of California Press.

Bogre, M. (2012). *Photography as activism: Images for social change.* New York: Taylor & Francis.

Bohnert, A., Fredricks, J., & Randall, E. (2010). Capturing unique dimensions of youth organized activity involvement theoretical and methodological considerations. *Review of Educational Research*, 80 (4), 576–610.

Boland, J. A. (2014). Orientations to civic engagement: Insights into the sustainability of a challenging pedagogy. *Studies in Higher Education*, 39 (1), 180–195.

Bolivar, W., Dorfman, A., Fundora, C., & Pean, G. (2002). Unleash the power of immigrants . . . organize! *Social Policy Magazine*. Retrieved from http://www.highbeam.com/doc/1G1–98124106.html

Bomer, R., Dworin, J., May, L., & Semingson, P. (2009). What's wrong with a deficit perspective?. *The Teachers College Record*. Retrieved from http://www.tcrecord.org

Bond, P. (2004). Climate governance according to the ideals of justice. Retrieved from http://146.230.128.54/ccs/files/Bond%20Climate%20governance%20a ccording%20 to%20ideals%20of%20justice.pdf

Boone-Heinonen, J., & Gordon-Larsen, P. (2012). Obesogenic environments in youth: Concepts and methods from a longitudinal national sample. *American Journal of Preventive Medicine*, 42 (5), e37–e46.

Borradaile, K. E., Sherman, S., Vander Veur, S. S., McCoy, T., Sandoval, B., Nachmani, J., . . . & Foster, G. D. (2009). Snacking in children: The role of urban corner stores. *Pediatrics*, 124 (5), 1293–1298.

Borrero, N. E., Yeh, C. J., Cruz, I., & Suda, J. (2012). School as a context for "othering" youth and promoting cultural assets. *Teachers College Record*, 114 (2), 1–37.

Bosco, F. J. (2010). Play, work or activism? Broadening the connections between political and children's geographies. *Children's Geographies*, 8 (4), 381–390.

Bottrell, D. (2009). Dealing with disadvantage resilience and the social capital of young people's networks. *Youth & Society*, 40 (4), 476–501.

Bottrell, D. (2015). Schools and communities fit for purpose. In H. Proctor, P. Brownlee, & P. Freebody (Eds.), *Controversies in Education* (pp. 27–38). New York: Springer International Publishing.

Boulianne, S., & Brailey, M. (2014). Attachment to community and civic and political engagement: A case study of students. *Canadian Review of Sociology/Revue canadienne de sociologie*, 51 (4), 375–388.

Bowen, G. A. (2014). Promoting social change through service-learning in the curriculum. *The Journal of Effective Teaching*, 51–62.

Bowen, W. M., Salling, M. J., Haynes, K. E., & Cyran, E. J. (1995). Toward environmental justice: Spatial equity in Ohio and Cleveland. *Annals of the Association of American Geographers*, 85 (4), 641–663.

Boykoff, J. (2013). *The suppression of dissent: How the state and mass media squelch US American social movements*. New York: Routledge.

Boyle, M. P., McLeod, D. M., & Armstrong, C. L. (2012). Adherence to the protest paradigm: The influence of protest goals and tactics on news coverage in US and international newspapers. *The International Journal of Press/Politics*, doi:1940161211433837

Boyle-Baise, M., & Langford, J. (2004). There are children here: Service learning for social justice. *Equity & Excellence in Education*, 37 (1), 55–66.

Brabant, M., & Braid, D. (2009). The devil is in the details: Defining civic engagement. *Journal of Higher Education Outreach and Engagement*, 13 (2), 59–88.

Brady, M. (2014). An appetite for justice. In R. Milkman & E. Ott (Eds.), *New labor in New York: Precarious workers and the future of the labor movement* (p. 229). Ithaca, NY: ILR Press.

Brake, M. (2013). *The sociology of youth culture and youth subcultures (Routledge Revivals): Sex and drugs and rock'n'roll?*. New York: Routledge.

Brant, C. A., & Tyson, C. A. (2014). Activism and the hip-hop generation. *Theory & Research in Social Education*, 42 (1), 141–146.

Branton, R., Martinez-Ebers, V., Carey, T. E., & Matsubayashi, T. (2015). Social protest and policy attitudes: The case of the 2006 immigrant rallies. *American Journal of Political Science*, 39 (2), 390–402.

Brennan, M. A., Barnett, R. V., & Lesmeister, M. K. (2007). Enhancing local capacity and youth involvement in the community development process. *Community Development*, 38 (4), 13–27.

Brenner, N., Marcuse, P., & Mayer, M. (Eds.). (2011). *Cities for people, not for profit: Critical urban theory and the right to the city*. New York: Routledge.

Bridgeland, J. M., DiIulio Jr, J. J., & Wulsin, S. C. (2008). *Engaged for success: Service-learning as a tool for high school dropout prevention*. Washington, D.C.: Civic Enterprises.

Bridgeland, J. M., & Milano, J. A. (2012). *Opportunity road: The promise and challenge of America's forgotten youth*. Washington, D.C.: Civic Enterprises.

Brill, C. L. (1994). The effects of participation in service-learning on adolescents with disabilities. *Journal of Adolescence*, 17 (4), 369–380.

Bringle, R. G., Clayton, P. H., & Price, M. (2009). Partnerships in service learning and civic engagement. *Partnerships: A Journal of Service Learning & Civic Engagement*, 1 (1), 1–20.

Bringle, R. G., & Hatcher, J. A. (2009, Fall). Innovative practices in service-learning and curricular engagement. *New directions for higher education* (147), 37–46.

Bringle, R. G., Hatcher, J. A., & McIntosh, R. E. (2006). Analyzing Morton's typology of service paradigms and integrity. *Michigan Journal of Community Service Learning*, 13 (1), 5–15.

Britt, L. L. (2012). Why we use service-learning: A report outlining a typology of three approaches to this form of communication pedagogy. *Communication Education*, 61 (1), 80–88.

Britton, S. A., & Tippins, D. J. (2015). Teaching with citizen science—It's more than just putting out fires!. In M. Mueller & D. J. Tippins (Eds.), *EcoJustice, citizen science and youth activism* (pp. 207–222). New York: Springer International Publishing.

Brockenbrough, E. (2014). Becoming queerly responsive: Culturally responsive pedagogy for Black and Latino urban queer youth. *Urban Education*, doi:0042085914549261

Brodhead, F., & Hood, R. J. (2006). *Youth in community economic development: Final report.* Canadian CED Network.

Brodkin, K. (2009). *Power politics: Environmental activism in south Los Angeles.* Rutgers University Press.

Brotherton, D.C. (2008). Beyond social reproduction: Bringing resistance back in gang theory. *Theoretical Criminology,* 12 (1), 55–77.

Brown, G., & Pickerill, J. (2009). Space for emotion in the spaces of activism. *Emotion, Space and Society,* 2 (1), 24–35.

Brown, N., Griffis, R., Hamilton, K., Irish, S., & Kanouse, S. (2007). What makes justice spatial? What makes spaces just? Three interviews on the concept of spatial justice. *Critical Planning,* 14, 6.

Browne, N. T. (2012). Weight bias, stigmatization, and bullying of obese youth. *Bariatric Nursing and Surgical Patient Care,* 7 (3), 107–115.

Brueggemann, W. (2013). *The practice of macro social work.* Independence, KY: Cengage Learning.

Buchanan, S. (1977). *The portable Plato.* Penguin e-book.

Bucholtz, M. (2002). Youth and cultural practice. *Annual Review of Anthropology,* 31, 525–552.

Buckingham, D. (2014). Selling youth: The paradoxical empowerment of the young consumer. *Youth Cultures in the Age of Global Media,* 202–223.

Bulanda, J. J., Bruhn, C., Byro-Johnson, T., & Zentmyer, M. (2014). Addressing mental health stigma among young adolescents: Evaluation of a youth-led approach. *Health & Social Work,* 39 (2), 73–80.

Bulanda, J. J., Szarzynski, K., Siler, D., & McCrea, K. T. (2013). "Keeping It Real": An evaluation audit of five years of youth-led program evaluation. *Smith College Studies in Social Work,* 83 (2–3), 279–302.

Bullard, R. D., Johnson, G. S., & Torres, A. O. (2011). *Environmental health and racial equity in the United States: Building environmentally just, sustainable, and livable communities.* Washington, D.C.: American Public Health Association.

Bullard, R. D., & Lewis, J. (1996). *Environmental justice and communities of color.* San Francisco, CA: Sierra Club Books.

Burawoy, M. (2015). Facing an unequal world. *Current Sociology,* 63 (1), 5–34.

Burd-Sharps, S., & Lewis, K. (2013). *One in seven: Ranking youth disconnection in the 25 largest metro areas.* Retrieved from www.measureofamerica.org

Burek, K., & Zeidler, D. L. (2015). Seeing the forest for the trees! Conservation and activism through socioscientific issues. In M. Mueller & D. J. Tippins (Eds.), *EcoJustice, citizen science and youth activism* (pp. 425–441). New York: Springer International Publishing.

Burke, K. J., Greene, S., & McKenna, M. K. (2014). A critical geographic approach to youth civic engagement: Reframing educational opportunity zones and the use of public spaces. *Urban Education,* doi:0042085914543670

Burkemper, E., Hutchison, W. J., Wilson, J., & Stretch, J. J. (2013). *Practicing social justice.* New York: Routledge.

Burridge, A. (2010). Youth on the line and the No Borders movement. *Children's Geographies,* 8 (4), 401–411.

Bushouse, B. K. (2005). Community nonprofit organizations and service-learning: Resource constraints to building partnerships with universities. *Michigan Journal of Community Service Learning,* 12 (1), 32–40.

Butcher, H. (2013). Organisational management for community practice: A framework. *Managing Community Practice: Principles, Policies and Programmes,* 47.

Butin, D. W. (Ed.). (2005). *Service-learning in higher education: Critical issues and directions.* London, England: Palgrave Macmillan.

Butin, D. W. (2007). Justice-learning: Service-learning as justice-oriented education. *Equity & Excellence in Education*, 40 (2), 177–183.

Butin, D. W. (2010). *Service-learning in theory and practice: The future of community engagement in higher education.* London, England: Palgrave Macmillan.

Butin, D. (2015). Dreaming of justice: Critical service learning and the need to wake up. *Theory Into Practice*, 54 (1), 5–10.

Buxton, C. A. (2010). Social problem solving through science: An approach to critical, place-based, science teaching and learning. *Equity & Excellence in Education*, 43 (1), 120–135.

Bryant, A., & Payne, Y. (2013). Evaluating the impact of community-based learning: Participatory action research as a model for inside-out. In S. W. Davis & B. S. Roswell (Eds.), *Turning teaching inside out: A pedagogy of transformation for community-based education* (pp. 227–242). London, England: Palgrave Macmillan.

Cadieux, K. V., & Slocum, R. (2015). What does it mean to do food justice. *Journal of Political Ecology*, 22, 1–26.

Cahill, C. (2010). 'Why do they hate us?' Reframing immigration through participatory action research. *Area*, 42 (2), 152–161.

Cahir, J., & Werner, A. (2013). Escaping the everyday: Young people's use of text messages and songs. *Youth Studies Australia* [online], 32 (2), 59.

Calvert, M., Emery, M., & Kinsey, S. (Eds.). (2013). *Youth programs as builders of social capital: New directions for youth development, Number 138.* New York: John Wiley & Sons.

Camangian, P. R. (2013). Teach like lives depend on it: Agitate, arouse, and inspire. *Urban Education*, doi:0042085913514591

Camino, L. A. (2000). Youth-adult partnerships: Entering new territory in community work and research. *Applied Developmental Science*, 4 (S1), 11–20.

Camino, L. (2005). Pitfalls and promising practices of youth–adult partnerships: An evaluator's reflections. *Journal of Community Psychology*, 33 (1), 75–85.

Camino, L., & Zeldin, S. (2002). From periphery to center: Pathways for youth civic engagement in the day-to-day life of communities. *Applied Developmental Science*, 6 (4), 213–220.

Cammarota, J. (2008). The cultural organizing of youth ethnographers: Formalizing a praxis-based pedagogy. *Anthropology and Education Quarterly*, 39 (1), 45–58.

Cammarota, J. (2011). From hopelessness to hope: Social justice pedagogy in urban education and youth development. *Urban Education*, 46 (4), 828–844.

Cammarota, J. (2014). The social justice education project. In J. Cammarota & A. Tomero (Eds.), *Raza studies: The public option for educational revolution* (pp. 107–121). Tucson, AZ: University of Arizona Press.

Cammarota, J., & Romero, A. F. (2009). A social justice epistemology and pedagogy for Latina/o students: Transforming public education with participatory action research. *New Directions for Youth Development, 2009* (123), 53–65.

Campbell, D., & Erbstein, N. (2012). Engaging youth in community change: Three key implementation principles. *Community Development*, 43 (1), 63–79.

Campbell, G. (2014). *Mapping community with African-Canadian youth newcomers: Settlement narratives and welcoming communities.* Waterloo, Ontario, Canada: University of Waterloo.

Campbell, J., & Oliver, M. (2013). *Disability politics: Understanding our past, changing our future.* New York: Routledge.

Cannuscio, C., Bugos, E., Hersh, S., Asch, D. A., & Weiss, E. E. (2012). Using art to amplify youth voices on housing insecurity. *American Journal of Public Health*, 102 (1), 10–12.

Cannuscio, C. C., Weiss, E. E., & Asch, D. A. (2010). The contribution of urban food-ways to health disparities. *Journal of Urban Health*, 87 (3), 381–393.

Canton, R. (2014). Human rights and youth justice in Europe. In W. Taylor & R. Earle (Eds.), *Youth justice handbook: Theory, policy and practice* (p. 211–220). New York: Routledge.

Cardinal, B. J., Whitney, A. R., Narimatsu, M., Hubert, N., & Souza, B. J. (2014). Obesity bias in the gym: An under-recognized social justice, diversity, and inclusivity issue. *Journal of Physical Education, Recreation and Dance*, 85 (6), 3–6.

Carlson, J., & Chappell, M. J. (2015). *Deepening food democracy*. Minneapolis, Minnesota: Institute for Agriculture and Trade Policy.

Carlton-Laney, I., & Burwell, N. Y. (2014). *African American community practice models: Historical and contemporary responses*. New York: Routledge.

Carrasco, T. A. U., & Seif, H. (2014). Disrupting the dream: Undocumented youth reframe citizenship and deportability through anti-deportation activism. *Latino Studies*, 12 (2), 279–299.

Carruthers, D. V. (Ed.). (2008). *Environmental justice in Latin America: Problems, promise, and practice*. Cambridge: MIT Press.

Carson, R. L., & Raguse, A. L. (2014). Systematic review of service-learning in youth physical activity settings. *Quest*, 66 (1), 57–95.

Carter, E. W., Swedeen, B., & Moss, C. K. (2012). Engaging youth with and without significant disabilities in inclusive service learning. *Teaching Exceptional Children*, 44 (5), 46–54.

Carter, E. W., Swedeen, B., Moss, C. K., & Pesko, M. J. (2010). "What Are You Doing After School?" Promoting extracurricular involvement for transition-age youth with disabilities. *Intervention in School and Clinic*, 45 (5), 275–283.

Cartwright, A. (2010). Science service learning. *Journal of Chemical Education*, 87 (10), 1009–1010.

Case, A. D., & Hunter, C. D. (2012). Counterspaces: A unit of analysis for understanding the role of settings in marginalized individuals' adaptive responses to oppression. *American Journal of Community Psychology*, 50 (1–2), 257–270.

Castillo, A. (2014). Massacre of dreams: Essays on Xicanisma. In A. M. Garcia (Ed.). *Chicana feminist thought: The basic historical writings* (pp. 310–312). New York: Routledge.

Cauce, A. M., Cruz, R., Corona, M., & Conger, R. (2011). The face of the future: Risk and resilience in minority youth. In C. Gustovo, L. J. Crockett, & M. A. Carranza (Eds.), *Health disparities in youth and families* (pp. 13–32). New York: Springer.

Ceaser, D. (2014). Unlearning adultism at Green Shoots: A reflexive ethnographic analysis of age inequality within an environmental education programme. *Ethnography and Education*, 9 (2), 167–181.

Celio, C. I., Durlak, J., & Dymnicki, A. (2011). A meta-analysis of the impact of service-learning on students. *Journal of Experiential Education*, 34 (2), 164–181.

Cermak, M. J., Christiansen, J. A., Finnegan, A. C., Gleeson, A. P., White, S. K., & Leach, D. K. (2011). Displacing activism? The impact of international service trips on understandings of social change. *Education, Citizenship and Social Justice*, 6 (1), 5–19.

Chaaban, J., & Cunningham, W. (2011). *Measuring the economic gain of investing in girls: The girl effect dividend*. Washington, D.C.: The World Bank Group.

Chan, W. Y., Ou, S. R., & Reynolds, A. J. (2014). Adolescent civic engagement and adult outcomes: An examination among urban racial minorities. *Journal of Youth and Adolescence*, 43, 1829–1843.

Chanan, G., & Miller, C. (2013). *Rethinking community practice: Developing transformative neighbourhoods*. Bristol, England: Policy Press.

Chang, B. (2013). Voice of the voiceless? Multiethnic student voices in critical approaches to race, pedagogy, literacy and agency. *Linguistics and Education*, 24 (3), 348–360.

Chang, B. (2015). In the service of self-determination: Teacher education, service learning, and community re-organizing. *Theory into Practice* (just accepted).

Chapter, K. B. P., & Mustapha, N. (2010). Religion as a spring for activism: Muslim women youth in Canada. In Z. Kassam (Ed.), *Women and Islam* (pp. 325–342). Santa Barbara, CA: Praeger.

Charmaraman, L. (2013). Congregating to create for social change: Urban youth media production and sense of community. *Learning, Media and Technology*, 38 (1), 102–115.

Chaskin, R. J. (2009). Toward a theory of change in community-based practice with youth: A case-study exploration. *Children and Youth Services Review*, 31 (10), 1127–1134.

Chatterton, P. (2010). Seeking the urban common: Furthering the debate on spatial justice. *City*, 14 (6), 625–628.

Checkoway, B. (1996). *Adults as allies*. Ann Arbor, MI: University of Michigan School of Social Work.

Checkoway, B. (2003). Young people as competent citizens. *Community Development Journal*, 38 (4), 298–309.

Checkoway, B. (2005). Youth participation as social justice. *CYD Journal*, Fall (1), 15–17.

Checkoway, B. (2009). Youth civic engagement for dialogue and diversity at the metropolitan level. *The Foundation Review*, 1 (2), 5.

Checkoway, B. (2011). What is youth participation? *Children and Youth Services Review*, 33 (2), 340–345.

Checkoway, B. (2013). Education for democracy by young people in community-based organizations. *Youth & Society*, 45 (3), 389–403.

Checkoway, B., & Aldana, A. (2013). Four forms of youth civic engagement for diverse democracy. *Children and Youth Services Review*, 35 (11), 1894–1899.

Checkoway, B., & Gutierrez, L. M. (2006). Youth participation and community change: An introduction. In B. N. Checkoway & L. Gutierrez (Eds.), *Youth participation and community change* (pp. 1–9). New York: Haworth Press.

Checkoway, B., & Richards-Schuster, K. (2004). Youth participation in evaluation and research as a way of lifting new voices. *Children, Youth and Environments*, 14 (2), 84–98.

Cheezum, R. R. (2012). *Inter-Organizational Collaborations Working to Change Policies that Affect Adolescents: A Qualitative Study of Three Youth-Serving Inter-organizational Collaborations* (Doctoral dissertation, The University of Iowa).

Chen, W. Y., Propp, J., & Lee, Y. (2014). Connection between adolescent's exposure to community violence and future civic engagement behaviors during their young adulthood. *Child and Adolescent Social Work Journal*, 27, 1–11.

Cho, S., Crenshaw, K. W., & McCall, L. (2013). Toward a field of intersectionality studies: Theory, applications, and praxis. *Signs*, 38 (4), 785–810.

Chonody, J., Martin, T., & Welsh, J. A. (2014). Looking through the lens of urban teenagers: Reflections on participatory photography in an alternative high school. *Reflections: Narratives of Professional Helping*, 18 (4), 35–44.

Chou, S. Y., Rashad, I., & Grossman, M. (2008). Fast-food restaurant advertising on television and its influence on childhood obesity. *Journal of Law and Economics*, 51 (4), 599–618.

Choudry, A. (2014). Activist research and organizing: Blurring the boundaries, challenging the binaries. *International Journal of Lifelong Education*, 33 (4), 472–487.

Christens, B. D. (2012). Toward relational empowerment. *American Journal of Community Psychology*, 50 (1–2), 114–128.

Christens, B. D., Collura, J. J., Kopish, M., & Varvodic, M. (2014). Youth organizing for school and neighborhood improvement. In K. L. Patterson & R. M. Silverman (Eds.), *Schools and urban revitalization: Rethinking institutions and community development* (pp. 151–166). New York: Routledge.

Christens, B. D., & Dolan, T. (2011). Interweaving youth development, community development, and social change through youth organizing. *Youth & Society*, 43 (2), 528–548.

Christens, B. D., & Kirshner, B. (2011). Taking stock of youth organizing: An interdisciplinary perspective. *New Directions for Child and Adolescent Development* (134), 27–41.

Christens, B. D., & Speer, P. W. (2011). Contextual influences on participation in community organizing: A multilevel longitudinal study. *American Journal of Community Psychology*, 47 (3–4), 253–263.

Christens, B. D., & Speer, P. W. (2015). Community organizing: Practice, research, and policy implications. *Social Issues and Policy Review*, 9 (1), 193–222.

Chung, H. L., & Probert, S. (2011). Civic engagement in relation to outcome expectations among African American young adults. *Journal of Applied Developmental Psychology*, 32 (4), 227–234.

Chupp, M. G., & Joseph, M. L. (2010). Getting the most out of service learning: Maximizing student, university and community impact. *Journal of Community Practice*, 18 (2/3), 190–212.

Cincotta, R. P. (2013). Half a chance: Youth bulges and transitions to liberal democracy. *Environmental Change and Security Program Report*, 13, 10–18.

Cintron-Moscoso, F. (2010). Cultivating youth proenvironmental development: A ecological approach. *Ecopsychology*, 2 (1), 33–40.

Cipolle, S. B. (2010). *Service-learning and social justice: Engaging students in social change.* Lanham, MD: Rowman & Littlefield Publishers.

Clark, G. (2006, April 4). If you walk out, know why. *San Antonio Express-News*, p. CI.

Clay, A. (2006). "All I need is one mic": Mobilizing youth for social change in the post-Civil Rights Era. *Social Justice*, 33 (2), 105–121.

Clay, A. (2012). *The hip-hop generation fights back: Youth, activism and post-Civil Rights politics.* New York: NYU Press.

Clevenger, C., & Cadge, W. (2014). Engaging emerging adults. In *Changing spirituality of emerging adults* (pp. 1–17). Washington, D.C.: Catholic University of America.

Clifford, D., & Burke, B. (2009). *Anti-oppressive ethics and values in social work.* Basingstoke, UK: Palgrave Macmilliam.

Coe, A. B. (2014, July). Constructing gender within youth activism. In *XVIII ISA World Congress of Sociology* (July 13–19, 2014). Isaconf.

Coe, A. B., Goicolea, I., Hurtig, A. K., & San Sebastian, M. (2015). Understanding how young people do activism: Youth strategies on sexual health in Ecuador and Peru. *Youth & Society*, 47(1), 3–28.

Coffey, J., & Farrugia, D. (2014). Unpacking the black box: The problem of agency in the sociology of youth. *Journal of Youth Studies*, 17 (4), 461–474.

Cohen, C. J. (2010). *Democracy remixed: Black youth and the future of American politics.* New York: Oxford University Press.

Cohen, E. E. (1945, January 7). A teen-age bill of rights. *The New York Times Magazine*, p. 16–17.

Cohen, S. (2014). *The gay liberation youth movement in New York: 'An army of lovers cannot fail'.* New York: Routledge.

Colby, S., Bercaw, L., Clark, A. M., & Galiardi, S. (2009). From community service to service-learning leadership: A program perspective. *New Horizons in Education*, 57 (3), 20–31.

Colby, S. A., Clark, A. M., & Bryant Jr, J. A. (2014). Developing service-learners into service-leaders. *International Journal of Research on Service-Learning in Teacher Education*, 2, 1–30.

Cole, A. G. (2007). Expanding the field: Revisiting environmental education principles through multidisciplinary frameworks. *The Journal of Environmental Education*, 38 (2), 35–45.

Cole, L. W., & Foster, S. R. (2001). *From the ground up: Environmental racism and the rise of the environmental justice movement.* New York: NYU Press.

Coleman, E. (2014). *Science youth action research: Promoting critical science literacy through relevance and agency.* Chicago, IL: Loyola University.

Coleman, R., & McCombs, M. (2007). The young and agenda-less? Exploring age-related differences in agenda setting on the youngest generation, baby boomers, and the civic generation. *Journalism & Mass Communication Quarterly*, 84 (3), 495–508.

Coleman, S., & Gotze, J. (2001). *Bowling together: Online public engagement in policy deliberation.* London: Hansard Society.

Collins, C. R., Neal, J. W., & Neal, Z. P. (2014). Transforming individual civic engagement into community collective efficacy: The role of bonding social capital. *American Journal of Community Psychology*, 54 (3–4), 328–336.

Collins, R., Esson, J., O'Neill Gutierrez, C., & Adekunle, A. (2013). Youth in motion: Spatialising youth movement(s) in the social sciences. *Children's Geographies*, 11 (3), 369–376.

Cone, R. (2003). Service-learning and civic education: Challenging assumptions. *Peer Review*, 5 (3), 12–15.

Conner, J. O. (2011). Youth organizers as young adults: Their commitments and contributions. *Journal of Research on Adolescence*, 21 (4), 923–942.

Conner, J. (2012). The value of youth organizing. *Berkman Center Research Publication* (2013–12). Cambridge, MA: Harvard University.

Conner, J. (2014). Lessons that last: Former youth organizers' reflections on what and how they learned. *Journal of the Learning Sciences*, 23 (3), 447–484.

Conner, J., & Slattery, A. (2014). New media and the power of youth organizing: Minding the gaps. *Equity & Excellence in Education*, 47 (1), 14–30.

Conner, J., & Zaino, K. (2014). Orchestrating effective change: How youth organizing influences education policy. *American Journal of Education*, 120 (2), 173–203.

Conner, J., Zaino, K., & Scarola, E. (2013). "Very powerful voices": The influence of youth organizing on educational policy in Philadelphia. *Educational Policy*, 27 (3), 560–588.

Conway, J. M. (2013). *Praxis and politics: Knowledge production in social movements.* New York: Routledge.

Cooper, S. B., Cripps, J. H., & Reisman, J. I. (2013). Service-learning in deaf studies: Impact on the development of altruistic behaviors and social justice concern. *American Annals of the Deaf*, 157 (5), 413–427.

Corb, A., & Grozelle, R. (2014). A new kind of terror: Radicalizing youth in Canada. *Journal Exit-Deutschland. Zeitschrift für Deradikalisierung und demokratische Kultur*, 1, 32–58.

Corcoran, T. (2011). Lost generation? New strategies for youth and education. *London Review of Education*, 9 (1), 129–130.

Corrunker, L. (2012). "Coming Out of the Shadows": DREAM Act activism in the context of global anti-deportation activism. *Indiana Journal of Global Legal Studies*, 19 (1), 143–168.

Costanza-Chock, S. (2008). The immigrant rights movement on the Net: Between "Web 2.0" and comunicacion popular. *American Quarterly*, 60 (3), 851–864.

Costanza-Chock, S. (2012). *Youth and social movements: Key lessons for allies.* Retrieved from http://cyber.law.harvard.edu/sites/cyber.law.harvard.edu/files/KBWYouthandSocialMovements2012_0.pdf

Costanza-Chock, S. (2012). *Youth and social movements: Key lessons for allies.* The Kinder and Braver World Project: Research Series.

Côté, J. E. (2014). Towards a new political economy of youth. *Journal of Youth Studies*, 17 (4), 527–543.

Côté, J. E., & Levine, C. G. (2014). *Identity, formation, agency, and culture: A social psychological synthesis.* Florence, KY: Psychology Press.

Cox, L. (2011). *Building counter culture: The radical praxis of social movement milieux.* Helsinki, Finland: Into-ebooks.

Creswell, J. W. (2013). *Qualitative inquiry and research design: Choosing among five approaches, 3rd edition.* Thousand Oaks, CA: Sage Publication.

Crocetti, E., Jahromi, P., & Meeus, W. (2012). Identity and civic engagement in adolescence. *Journal of Adolescence*, 35 (3), 521–532.

Crosley, K. L. (2014). Advancing the boundaries of urban environmental education through the food justice movement. *Canadian Journal of Environmental Education (CJEE)*, 18, 46–58.

Cruikshank, M. (1992). *The gay and lesbian liberation movement.* New York: Routledge.

Cruz, N. I., & Giles, D. E. (2000). Where's the community in service-learning research. *Michigan Journal of Community Service Learning*, 7 (1), 28–34.

Cummins, S. (2014). Food deserts. In W. C. Cockerham, R. Dingwall & S. R. Quah (Eds.), *The Wiley Blackwell encyclopedia of health, illness, behavior, and society.* New York: John Wiley Online.

Cutts, B. B., Darby, K. J., Boone, C. G., & Brewis, A. (2009). City structure, obesity, and environmental justice: An integrated analysis of physical and social barriers to walkable streets and park access. *Social Science & Medicine*, 69 (9), 1314–1322.

Dakin, E. K., Parker, S. N., Amell, J. W., & Rogers, B. S. (2014). Seeing with our own eyes: Youth in Mathare, Kenya use photovoice to examine individual and community strengths. *Qualitative Social Work*, doi:1473325014526085

Daley, A., Solomon, S., Newman, P. A., & Mishna, F. (2008). Traversing the margins: Intersectionalities in the bullying of lesbian, gay, bisexual and transgender youth. *Journal of Gay & Lesbian Social Services*, 19 (3–4), 9–29.

D'Ambrosi, L., & Massoli, L. (2012). Bridging and bonding connections beyond the web: Youth movements and civic engagement. *International Review of Sociology*, 22 (3), 530–551.

Daniels, E. A. (2012). Critical classroom praxis and conclusion. In *Fighting, loving, teaching* (pp. 65–73). Rotterdam, Netherlands: SensePublishers.

Daniels, E., Harnischfeger, A., Hos, R., & Akom, A. (2010). Youth as active agents: Counter-narrating the source of reform. *Youth-full productions: Cultural practices and constructions of content and social spaces.* New York: Peter Lang.

Dantley, M., Beachum, F., & McCray, C. (2009). Exploring the intersectionality of multiple centers within notions of social justice. *Journal of School Leadership*, 18 (2), 124–133.

Dar, A. (2014). *"I like going places": The Everyday and Political Geographies of South Asian Immigrant Youth in New York City* (Doctoral dissertation, Rutgers University-Camden Graduate School).

d'Arlach, L., Sánchez, B., & Feuer, R. (2009). Voices from the community: A case for reciprocity in service-learning. *Michigan Journal of Community Service Learning*, 16 (1), 5–16.

Daud, R., & Carruthers, C. (2008). Outcome study of an after-school program for youth in a high-risk environment. *Journal of Park and Recreation Administration*, 26 (2).

David, J. L. (2009). Service learning and civic participation. *Educational Leadership*, 66 (8), 83–84.

Davidson, J. (2014). Youth community inquiry: New media for community and personal growth. Edited by Bertram C. Bruce, Ann Peterson Bishop, & Nama R. Budhathoki. *QRE-Qualitative Research in Education*, 3 (3), 364–368.

Dawes, N. P., & Larson, R. (2011). How youth get engaged: Grounded-theory research on motivational development in organized youth programs. *Developmental Psychology*, 47 (1), 259.

Day, J. K. (2014). *Disengaged and untrusting? Young adults' feelings of social integration and trust during the Great Recession*. Corvallis, OR: Oregon State University.

Day, K. (2006). Active living and social justice: Planning for physical activity in low-income, black, and Latino communities. *Journal of the American Planning Association*, 72 (1), 88–99.

Deans, T. (1999). Service-learning in two keys: Paulo Freire's critical pedagogy in relation to John Dewey's pragmatism. *Michigan Journal of Community Service Learning*, 5 (1), 15–29.

Deardorff, M. D. (2015). Black political thought. In M. Gibbons, D. Coole, E. Ellis, & K. Ferguson (Eds.), *The encyclopedia of political thought*. New Ork: John Wiley Online.

Dearling, A., & Armstrong, H. (1997). *Youth activism and the environment*. Dorset, England: Russell House Publishing Limited.

Debies-Carl, J. S. (2013). Are the kids alright? A critique and agenda for taking youth cultures seriously. *Social Science Information*, 52 (1), 110–133.

Deeley, S. J. (2010). Service-learning: Thinking outside the box. *Active Learning in Higher Education*, 11 (1), 43–53.

DeFilippis, J., & Faust, B. (2014). Immigration and community development in New York City. *Urban Geography* (ahead-of-print), 1–19.

DeFilippis, J., Fisher, R., & Shragge, E. (2010). *Contesting community: The limits and potential of local organizing*. New Brunswick, NJ: Rutgers University Press.

Delgado, M. (1999). *Social work practice in nontraditional urban settings*. New York: Oxford University Press.

Delgado, M. (2000). *New arenas for community social work practice with urban youth: The use of the arts, humanities, and sports*. New York: Columbia University Press.

Delgado, M. (2002). *New frontiers for youth development in the twenty-first century: Revitalizing and broadening youth development*. New York: Columbia University Press.

Delgado, M. (2006). *Designs and methods for youth-led research*. Thousand Oaks, CA: Sage Publications.

Delgado, M. (2007). *Social work practice with Latinos: Use of a cultural assets paradigm*. New York: Oxford University Press.

Delgado, M. (2009). *Older adult-led health promotion in urban communities: Models and interventions*. Lanham, MD: Rowman & Littlefield.

Delgado, M. (2011). *Latinos small businesses and the American dream: Community social work and economic and social development*. New York: Columbia University Press.

Delgado, M. (2013). *Social justice and the urban obesity crisis: The potential for the social work profession.* New York: Columbia University Press.

Delgado, M. (2015a). *Urban youth and photovoice: Visual ethnography in action.* New York: Oxford University Press.

Delgado, M. (2015b). *Baby boomers of color: Social work policy and practice.* New York: Columbia University.

Delgado, M. (in press). *Celebrating urban life: Fairs, festivals and parades.* Toronto, Canada: University of Toronto Press.

Delgado, M., & Humm-Delgado, D. (2013). *Asset assessments and community social work practice.* New York: Oxford University Press.

Delgado, M., Jones, L. K., & Rohani, M. (2005). *Social work practice with immigrant and refugee youth in the United States.* Boston: Allyn & Bacon.

Delgado, M., & Staples, L. (2007). *Youth-led community organizing: Theory and action.* New York: Oxford University Press.

Delgado, M., & Staples, L. (2012). Youth-led organizing: Community engagement and opportunity creation. In M. Weil (Ed.), *Handbook of community practice, second edition* (pp. 547–566). Thousand Oaks, CA: Sage Publications.

Delgado, M., & Zhou, M. (2008). *Youth-led health promotion in urban communities: A capacity enhancement perspective.* Lanham, MD: Rowman & Littlefield Publishers.

de los Angeles Torres, M. (2013). Chicago youth activists home matters in their search for democracy. In I. R. Torres & N. Del Rio (Eds.), *Citizens in the present: Youth civic engagement in the Americas* (pp. 29–59). Urbana, IL: University of Illinois Press.

Delp, L., Brown, M., & Domenzain, A. (2005). Fostering youth leadership to address workplace and community environmental health issues: A university-school community partnership. *Health Promotion Practice,* 6 (3), 270–285.

D'Emilio, J. (2009). The gay liberation movement. In J. Goodwin & J. M. Jasper (Eds.), *The social movements reader: Cases and examples, 2nd ed.* (pp. 36–41). New York: John-Wiley-Blackwell.

Derr, V., Chawla, L., Mintzer, M., Cushing, D. F., & Van Vliet, W. (2013). A city for all citizens: Integrating children and youth from marginalized populations into city planning. *Buildings,* 3 (3), 482–505.

Desmond, K. J., Stahl, S. A., & Graham, M. A. (2011). Combining service learning and diversity education. *Making Connections: Interdisciplinary Approaches to Cultural Diversity,* 13 (1), 24–30.

de Vreede, C., Warner, A., & Pitter, R. (2014). Facilitating youth to take sustainability actions: The potential of peer education. *The Journal of Environmental Education,* 45 (1), 37–56.

Dias, M., & Callahan, B. (2015). Youth activism: Considering higher ground. In *EcoJustice, citizen science and youth activism* (pp. 313–322). New York: Springer International Publishing.

Di Chiro, G. (2008). Living environmentalisms: Coalition politics, social reproduction, and environmental justice. *Environmental Politics,* 17 (2), 276–298.

Dichtl, J., & Sacco, N. (2014). *Putting history to work in the world.* The National Council on Public History.

Dick, K. J., Carter, J., & Ingram, S. (2014). A service learning project in Honduras as an enhancement to the undergraduate engineering design experience. *Global Journal of Engineering Education,* 16 (2), 65–72.

Dikec, M. (2001). Justice and the spatial imagination. *Environment and Planning A,* 33 (10), 1785–1806.

Dimitriadis, G. (2011). Studying resistance: Some cautionary notes. *International Journal of Qualitative Studies in Education*, 24 (5), 649–654.

Doetsch-Kidder, S. (2012). *Social change and intersectional activism: The spirit of social movement*. London, England: Palgrave Macmillan.

Dohrn, B. (2005). Preface. In D. Berger, C. Boudin & K. Farrow (Eds.), *Letters from young activists: Today's rebels speak out* (pp. xiiii–xxiii). New York: Nation Books.

Dolan, P. (2012). Travelling through social support and youth civic action on a journey towards resilience. In M. Ungar (Ed.), *The social ecology of resilience* (pp. 357–366). New York: Springer.

Donaldson, L. P., & Daughtery, L. C. (2011). Introducing asset-based models of social justice into service learning: A social work approach. *Journal of Community Practice*, 19 (1), 80–99.

Dooley, J. C. (2007). *The impact of service-learning on student attitudes toward race and social justice*. Milwaukee, WI: Marquette University.

Dorado, S., & Giles Jr, D. E. (2004). Service-learning partnerships: Paths of engagement. *Michigan Journal of Community Service Learning*, 11 (1), 25–37.

Dover, A. G. (2013). Teaching for social justice: From conceptual frameworks to classroom practices. *Multicultural Perspectives*, 15 (1), 3–11.

Drake, D. H., Fergusson, R., & Briggs, D. B. (2014). Hearing new voices: Re-viewing youth justice policy through practitioners' relationships with young people. *Youth Justice*, 14 (1), 22–39.

Driskell, D., Fox, C., & Kudva, N. (2008). Growing up in new New York: Youth space, citizenship, and community change in a hyperglobal city. *Environment and Planning*, 40 (XX), 2831–2844.

DuBois, D. L., Portillo, N., Rhodes, J. E., Silverthorn, N., & Valentine, J. C. (2011). How effective are mentoring programs for youth? A systematic assessment of the evidence. *Psychological Science in the Public Interest*, 12 (2), 57–91.

Duke, N. N., Skay, C. L., Pettingell, S. L., & Borowsky, I. W. (2009). From adolescent connections to social capital: Predictors of civic engagement in young adulthood. *Journal of Adolescent Health*, 44 (2), 161–168.

Duncan-Andrade, J. (2006). Urban youth, media literacy, and increased critical civic participation. S. Ginwright, P. Noguera, & J. Cammarota (Eds.), *Beyond resistance* (pp. 149–170). Routledge: New York.

Dunham, C. C. (1998). Generation units and the life course: A sociological perspective on youth and the anti-war movement. *Journal of Political and Military Sociology*, 26 (2), 137–155.

Dymond, S. K., Renzaglia, A., & Chun, E. J. (2008). Elements of high school service learning programs. *Career Development for Exceptional Individuals*, 31 (1), 37–47.

Egger, J. B. (2008). No service to learning: "Service-learning" reappraised. *Academic Questions*, 21 (2), 183–194.

Ehresman, T. G., & Okereke, C. (2014). Environmental justice and conceptions of the green economy. *International Environmental Agreements: Politics, Law and Economics*, 15 (1), 13–27.

Ehrlich, T. (Ed.). (2000). *Civic responsibility and higher education*. Santa Barbara, CA: Greenwood Publishing Group.

Eidson, K. W., Nickson, L., & Hughes, T. (2014). Service learning and social action: Feeding preservice teachers' souls. *Kappa Delta Pi Record*, 50 (2), 70–75.

Einfeld, A., & Collins, D. (2008). The relationships between service-learning, social justice, multicultural competence, and civic engagement. *Journal of College Student Development*, 49 (2), 95–109.

Ekman, J., & Amnå, E. (2012). Political participation and civic engagement: Towards a new typology. *Human Affairs*, 22 (3), 283–300.

Elliott, D. S., Menard, S., Rankin, B., Elliott, A., Wilson, W. J., & Huizinga, D. (2006). *Good kids from bad neighborhoods: Successful development in social context*. New York: Cambridge University Press.

Ellis, C. (2002). Being real: Moving inward toward social change. *International Journal of Qualitative Studies in Education*, 15 (4), 399–406.

Ellis-Williams, A. (2007). Discovering the possibilities: A study of African American youth resistance and activism. *Educational Foundation*, 21 (1–2), 107–118.

Endres, D., & Gould, M. (2009). "I am also in the position to use my whiteness to help them out": The communication of whiteness in service learning. *Western Journal of Communication*, 73 (4), 418–436.

Ennis, G., & West, D. (2013). Using social network analysis in community development practice and research: A case study. *Community Development Journal*, 48 (1), 40–57.

Epstein, S. E. (2010). Activists and writers: Student expression in a social action literacy project. *Language Arts*, 363–372.

Epstein, S. E. (2013). What is my role? Establishing teacher and youth worker responsibilities in social action projects. *Teachers and Teaching*, 19 (5), 492–506.

Erbstein, N. (2013). Engaging underrepresented youth populations in community youth development: Tapping social capital as a critical resource. *New Directions for Youth Development* (138), 109–124.

Erstad, O. (2012). The learning lives of digital youth—beyond the formal and informal. *Oxford Review of Education*, 38 (1), 25–43.

Eskridge, Jr, W. N., & Eskridge, W. N. (2013). *Equality practice: Civil unions and the future of gay rights*. New York: Routledge.

Espino, M. M., & Lee, J. J. (2011). Understanding resistance: Reflections on race and privilege through service-learning. *Equity & Excellence in Education*, 44 (2), 136–152.

Eva, N., & Sendjaya, S. (2013). Creating future leaders: An examination of youth leadership development in Australia. *Education + Training*, 55 (6), 584–598.

Evans, A. (2014). On the origins of hip hop. D. Maudlin & M. Vellinga (Eds.), *Consuming architecture: On the occupation, appropriation and interpretation of buildings* (pp. 185–202). New York: Routledge.

Evans, D. M., Fox, M., & Fine, M. (2010). Producing selves and knowledges: Reflections on participatory youth inquiry. In N. Ares (Ed.), *Youth full-productions: Cultural practices and constructions of content and social spaces* (p. 97–124). New York: Peter Lang.

Evans, S. D. (2007). Youth sense of community: Voice and power in community contexts. *Journal of Community Psychology*, 35 (6), 693–709.

Evans, S. D., & Prilleltensjy, I. (2007). Youth and democracy: Participation for personal, relational, and collective well-being. *Journal of Community Psychology*, 35 (4), 681–692.

Evans, S. M. (2001). Sources of the second wave: The rebirth of feminism. In A. Bloom (Ed.), *Long time gone: Sixties America then and now* (pp. 119–208). New York: Oxford University Press.

Eyler, J. (2009). The power of experiential education. *Liberal Education*, 95 (4), 24–31.

Eyler, J. S., & Giles, D. E. (1999). *Where's the learning in service-learning?* San Francisco, CA: Jossey-Bass Inc.

Ezbawy, Y. A. (2012). The role of the youth's new protest movements in the January 25th Revolution. *IDS Bulletin*, 43 (1), 26–36.

Faber, D. (1998). The struggle for ecological democracy and environmental justice. In D. Faber (Ed.), *The struggle for ecological democracy: Environmental justice movements in the United States* (pp. 1–26). New York: The Guilford Press.

Faber, D. (2007). A more "productive" environmental justice politics: Movement alliances in Massachusetts for clean production and regional equity. In R. Sandler & P. C. Pezzullo (Eds.), *Environmental justice and environmentalism: The social justice challenge to the environmental movement* (pp. 135–164). Cambridge, MA: MIT Press.

Factor, R., Kawachi, I., & Williams, D. R. (2011). Understanding high-risk behavior among non-dominant minorities: A social resistance framework. *Social Science & Medicine*, 73 (9), 1292–1301.

Fainstein, S. S. (2010). *The just city*. Ithaca, NY: Cornell University Press.

Farnham, S., Keyes, D., Yuki, V., & Tugwell, C. (2012, February). Puget sound off: Fostering youth civic engagement through citizen journalism. In *Proceedings of the ACM 2012 conference on Computer Supported Cooperative Work* (pp. 285–294). ACM.

Farnsworth, V. (2010). Conceptualizing identity, learning and social justice in community-based learning. *Teaching and Teacher Education*, 26 (7), 1481–1489.

Farthing, R. (2010). The politics of youthful antipolitics: Representing the 'issue' of youth participation in politics. *Journal of Youth Studies*, 13 (2), 181–195.

Feenstra, G. (2002). Creating space for sustainable food systems: Lessons from the field. *Agriculture and Human Values*, 19 (1), 99–106.

Fehrman, D., & Schutz, A. (2011). Beyond the catch-22 of school-based social action programs: Toward a more pragmatic approach for dealing with power. *Democracy and Education*, 19 (1), 3.

Fernández, J. S., & Langhout, R. D. (2014). "A community with diversity of culture, wealth, resources, and living experiences": Defining neighborhood in an unincorporated community. *American Journal of Community Psychology*, 53 (1–2), 122–133.

Ferrari, J. R., & Chapman, J. G. (2014). *Educating students to make a difference: Community-based service learning*. New York: Routledge.

Ferrera, M. J., Sacks, T. K., Perez, M., Nixon, J. P., Asis, D., & Coleman, R. W. L. (2015). Empowering immigrant youth in Chicago: Utilizing CBPR to document the impact of a youth health service corps program. *Family & Community Health*, 38 (1), 12–21.

Fields, A., Snapp, S., Russell, S. T., Licona, A. C., & Tilley, E. H. (2014). Youth voices and knowledges: Slam poetry speaks to social policies. *Sexuality Research and Social Policy*, 1–12.

Filbert, K. M., & Flynn, R. J. (2010). Developmental and cultural assets and resilient outcomes in First Nations young people in care: An initial test of an explanatory model. *Children and Youth Services Review*, 32 (4), 560–564.

Fincher, R., & Iveson, K. (2012). Justice and injustice in the city. *Geographical Research*, 50 (3), 231–241.

Fine, M. (2006). Bearing witness: Methods for researching oppression and resistance—A textbook for critical research. *Social Justice Research*, 19 (1), 83–108.

Fine, M. (2009). Postcards from metro America: Reflections on youth participatory action research for urban justice. *The Urban Review*, 41 (1), 1–6.

Fine, M. (2012). Troubling calls for evidence: A critical race, class and gender analysis of whose evidence counts. *Feminism & Psychology*, 22 (1), 3–19.

Fine, M., Freudenberg, N., Payne, Y., Perkins, T., Smith, K., & Wanzer, K. (2003). "Anything can happen with police around": Urban youth evaluate strategies of surveillance in public places. *Journal of Social Issues*, 59 (1), 141–158.

Fine, M., Jaffe-Walter, R., Pedraza, P., Futch, V., & Stoudt, B. (2008). Swimming: On oxygen, resistance, and possibility for immigrant youth under siege. *Anthropology and Education Quarterly*, 38 (1), 76–96.

Fine, M., & Ruglis, J. (2009). Circuits and consequences of dispossession: The racialized realignment of the public sphere for US youth. *Transforming Anthropology*, 17 (1), 20–33.

Finn, S. (2013). *Writing for social action: Affect, activism, and the composition classroom*. Amherst, MA: University of Massachusetts.

Fiorina, M. P. (1999). Extreme voices: A dark side of civic engagement. *Civic Engagement in American Democracy, 395*, 405–413.

Fisher, C. B., Busch-Rossnagel, N. A., Jopp, D. S., & Brown, J. L. (2012). Applied developmental science, social justice, and socio-political well- being. *Applied Developmental Science*, 16 (1), 54–64.

Fisher, R., & Corciullo, D. (2011). Rebuilding community organizing education in social work. *Journal of Community Practice*, 19 (4), 355–368.

Fitch, P., Steinke, P., & Hudson, T. (2013). Research and theoretical perspectives on cognitive outcomes of service learning. In P. H. Clayton, R. G. Bringle, & J. A. Hatcher (Eds.), *Research on service learning: Conceptual frameworks and assessment, Vol. 2A: Students and faculty* (pp. 57–83). Sterling, VA: Stylus.

Fitzgerald, H. E., & Primavera, J. (2013). *Going public: Civic and community engagement*. East Lansing: Michigan State University Press.

Flam, H., & King, D. (2007). *Emotions and social movements*. New York: Routledge.

Flanagan, C. (2009). Young people's civic engagement and political development. In A. Furlong (Ed.), *Handbook of youth and young adulthood* (pp. 293–300). New York: Routledge.

Flanagan, C. A., Kim, T., Collura, J., & Kopish, M. A. (2015). Community service and adolescents' social capital. *Journal of Research on Adolescence*, 25 (2), 295–309.

Flanagan, C., & Levine, P. (2010). Civic engagement and the transition to adulthood. *The Future of Children*, 20 (1), 159–179.

Flanagan, C., Swetsen, A. K., Gill, S., Gallay, L. S., & Curnsille, P. (2009). Ethnic awareness, prejudice, and civic commitments in four ethnic groups of American adolescents. *Journal of Youth and Adolescence*, 38 (4), 500–518.

Flanagan, C., Syvertsen, A., & Wray-Lake, L. (2007). Youth political activism: Sources of public hope in the context of globalization. *Approaches to Positive Youth Development*, 243–256.

Flasher, J. (1978). Adultism. *Adolescence*, 13 (51), 517–523.

Fletcher, A. (2012). *Meaningful student involvement*. Retrieved from http://adamfletcher.net/tag/meaningful-student-involvement/

Fletcher, A., & Vavros, J. (2006). *The guide to social change by and for youth*. Olympia, WA: CommonAction.

Flores, E. (2012). Latinos and faith-based recovery from gangs. In C. Chen & R. Jeung (Eds.), *Sustaining faith traditions: Race, ethnicity, and religion among the Latino and Asian American second generation* (pp. 113–132). New York: New York University Press.

Flores, M. P., De La Rue, L., Neville, H. A., Santiago, S., ben Rakemayahu, K., Garite, R., . . . & Ginsburg, R. (2014). Developing social justice competencies: A consultation training approach. *The Counseling Psychologist*, 42 (7), 998–1020.

Flores, W. V. (2003). New citizens, new rights: Undocumented immigrants and Latino cultural citizenship. *Latin American Perspectives*, 30 (2), 87–100.

Foley, M. S. (2013). *Front porch politics: The forgotten heyday of American activism in the 1970s and 1980s.* New York: Macmillan.

Forest, D. E., Kimmel, S. C., & Garrison, K. L. (2013). Launching youth activism with award-winning international literature. *Journal of Language and Literacy Education,* 9 (1), 136–160.

Forman, Jr, J. (2004). Community policing and youth as assets. *Journal of Criminal Law and Criminology,* 95 (1), 1–48.

Forman, M. (2013). 'Hood work: Hip-hop, youth advocacy, and model citizenry. *Communication, Culture & Critique,* 6 (2), 244–257.

Fortin, R., Jackson, S. F., Maher, J., & Moravac, C. (2014). I WAS HERE: Young mothers who have experienced homelessness use Photovoice and participatory qualitative analysis to demonstrate strengths and assets. *Global health promotion,* doi:1757975914528960

Fox, J. A., & Bada, X. (2009). *Migrant civic engagement.* Center for Global, International and Regional Studies.

Fox, M., Mediratta, K., Ruglis, J., Stoudt, B., Shah, S., & Fine, M. (2010). Critical youth engagement: Participatory action research and organizing. In L. R. Sterrod, J. Tomey-Punta & C. A. Flanagen (Eds.), *Handbook of research on civic engagement in youth* (pp. 621–649). New York: John Wiley & Sons.

France, A., & Roberts, S. (2014). The problem of social generations: A critique of the new emerging orthodoxy in youth studies. *Journal of Youth Studies* (ahead-of-print), 1–16.

Francis, D., & Le Roux, A. (2012). Using life history to understand the interplay between identity, critical agency and social justice education. *Journal for New Generation Sciences,* 10 (2), 14–29.

Franklin, S. (2014a). Race, class, and community organizing in support of economic justice initiatives in the twenty-first century. *Community Development Journal,* 49 (2), 181–197.

Franklin, S. M. (2014b). *After the rebellion: Black youth, social movement activism, and the Post-Civil Rights generation.* New York: New York University Press.

Frederick, R., Cave, A., & Perencevich, K. C. (2010). Teacher candidates' transformative thinking on issues of social justice. *Teaching and Teacher Education,* 26 (2), 315–322.

Fregoso, R. L. (2014). For a pluriversal declaration of human rights. *American Quarterly,* 66 (3), 583–608.

Frei, R. (2014, July). Social memories In South America: Generational narratives in times of political youth activism. In *XVIII ISA World Congress of Sociology* (July 13–19, 2014). Isaconf.

Friesem, E. (2014). A story of conflict and collaboration: Media literacy, video production and disadvantaged youth. *Journal of Media Literacy Education,* 6 (1), 4.

Frink, J., Ares, N., Mukhopadhyay, K., & Tsoumani, E. (2010). Hybridity and transformation: Social spaces and youth cultural practices. In N. Ares (Ed.), *Youth-full productions: Cultural practices and constructions of content and social spaces* (p. 65). New York: Peter Lang.

Frost, R. A., Strom, S. L., Downey, J., Schultz, D. D., & Holland, T. A. (2010). Enhancing student learning with academic and student affairs collaboration. *The Community College Enterprise,* 16 (1), 37–51.

Fuller, D., & Kitchin, R. (Eds.). (2004). *Radical theory/critical praxis: Academic geography beyond the academy?.* Victoria, BC, Canada: Praxis Press.

Furco, A., & Billig, S. (Eds.). (2002). *Service-learning: The essence of the pedagogy (Vol. 1).* IAP.

Furco, A., & Root, S. (2010). Research demonstrates the value of service learning. *Phi Delta Kappan,* 91 (5), 16–20.

Furlong, A. (Ed.). (2009). *Handbook of youth and young adulthood: New perspectives and agendas*. New York: Routledge.

Furman, G. (2012). Social justice leadership as Praxis developing capacities through preparation programs. *Educational Administration Quarterly*, 48 (2), 191–229.

Futch, V. A. (2011). (Re) presenting spaces of/for "at-opportunity" urban youth. *Curriculum Inquiry*, 41 (1), 98–109.

Futch, V. A. (2013). Utilizing the theoretical framework of collective identity to understand processes in youth programs. *Youth & Society*, doi:0044118X13509288

Gaby, S., & Caren, N. (2012). Occupy online: How cute old men and Malcolm X recruited 400,000 US users to OWS on Facebook. *Social Movement Studies*, 11 (3–4), 367–374.

Gallardo, M. E. (Ed.). (2013). *Developing cultural humility: Embracing race, privilege and power*. SAGE Publications.

Gallhofer, S., & Haslam, J. (2004). Accounting and liberation theology: Some insights for the project of emancipatory accounting. *Accounting, Auditing & Accountability Journal*, 17 (3), 382–407.

Gallo, R. G., Townshend, T. G., & Lake, A. A. (2014). Exploring urban parks and their peripheral food environments using a case study approach: Young people and obesogenic environments. *Urban Design International*, 20 (1), 28–43.

Galston, W. A. (2007). Civic knowledge, civic education, and civic engagement: A summary of recent research. *International Journal of Public Administration*, 30 (6–7), 623–642.

Gamble, D. N., & Weil, M. (2010). *Community practice skills: Local to global perspectives*. New York: Columbia University Press.

Gambone, M. A., Yu, H. C., Lewis-Charp, H., Sipe, C. L., & Lacoe, J. (2006). Youth organizing, identity-support, and youth development agencies as avenues for involvement. *Journal of Community Practice*, 14 (1–2), 235–253.

Garcia, E. (2013). *Children of the sleeping giant: Social activism among Latino Youth in the United States* (Masters Thesis, Texas A.M. University).

Garcia, M. L., Mizrahi, T., & Bayne-Smith, M. (2010). Education for interdisciplinary community collaboration and development: The components of a core curriculum by community practitioners. *Journal of Teaching in Social Work*, 30 (2), 175–194.

Gardner, J. (2011). Placed blame: Narratives of youth culpability. *Urban Education*, doi:0042085911399792

Gardner, M. (2013). *Linking activism: Ecology, social justice, and education for social change*. New York: Routledge.

Gastic, B., & Johnson, D. (2009). Teacher-mentors and the educational resilience of sexual minority youth. *Journal of Gay & Lesbian Social Services*, 21 (2–3), 219–231.

Geller, J. D., Zuckerman, N., & Seidel, A. (2014). Service-learning as a catalyst for community development: How do community partners benefit from service-learning?. *Education and Urban Society*, doi:0013124513514773

Getrich, C. M. (2008). Negotiating boundaries of social belonging: Second-generation Mexican youth and the Immigrant Rights Protests of 2006. *American Behavioral Scientist*, 52 (4), 533–556.

Ghai, D., & Vivian, J. M. (2014). *Grassroots environmental action: people's participation in sustainable development*. New York: Routledge.

Ghosh-Dastidar, B., Cohen, D., Hunter, G., Zenk, S. N., Huang, C., Beckman, R., & Dubowitz, T. (2014). Distance to store, food prices, and obesity in urban food deserts. *American Journal of Preventive Medicine*, 47(5), 587–595.

Gibson, M., Hauf, P., Long, B. S., & Sampson, G. (2011). Reflective practice in service learning: Possibilities and limitations. *Education + Training*, 53 (4), 284–296.

Gilbert, K. M. (2011). *Youth Voices of Bounty and Opportunity: High School Students' Experiences With Food and Community* (Masters Thesis, Portland State University).

Gilbride-Brown, J. K. (2008). *(E) Racing Service-Learning as Critical Pedagogy: Race Matters* (Doctoral dissertation, The Ohio State University).

Gilchrist, R., Hodgson, T., Jeffs, T., Spence, J., Stanton, N., & Walker, J. (2010). *Reflecting the past: Essays in the history of youth and community work*. London: Russell House Publish. Ltd.

Gillis, A., & Mac Lellan, M. (2010). Service learning with vulnerable populations: Review of the literature. *International Journal of Nursing Education Scholarship*, 7 (1).

Ginwright, S. A. (2003). Youth organizing: Expanding possibilities for youth development. *Occasional Papers Series on Youth Organizing*, 1.

Ginwright, S. A. (2007). Black youth activism and the role of critical social capital in Black community organizations. *American Behavioral Scientist*, 51 (3), 403–418.

Ginwright, S. A. (2010). Building a pipeline for justice: Understanding youth organizing and the leadership pipeline. *Occasional Paper Series*, 10.

Ginwright, S., & Cammarota, J. (2006). Introduction. In S. Ginwright, P. Noguera & J. Cammarota (Eds.), *Beyond resistance: Youth activism and community change* (pp. xiii–xxii). New York: Routledge.

Ginwright, S., & Cammarota, J. (2007). Youth activism in the urban community: Learning critical civic praxis within community organizations. *International Journal of Qualitative Studies in Education*, 20 (6), 693–710.

Ginwright, S., & Cammarota, J. (2009). Youth activism in the urban community: Learning critical civic praxis within community organizations. *International Journal of Qualitative Studies in Education*, 20 (6), 693–710.

Ginwright, S., Noguera, P., & Cammarota, J. (Eds.). (2006). *Beyond resistance: Youth activism and community change*. New York: Routledge.

Giroux, H. A. (2011). Fighting for the future: American youth and the global struggle for democracy. *Cultural Studies, Critical Methodologies*, 11 (4), 328–340.

Giroux, H. A. (2012). *Disposable youth, racialized memories, and the culture of cruelty*. New York: Routledge.

Giroux, H. (2014). Class casualties: Disappearing youth in the age of George W. Bush. *Workplace: A Journal for Academic Labor*, 11, 20–34.

Gleeson, S. (2008). Organizing for immigrant labor rights: Latino immigrants in San Jose and Houston. *Civic Hopes and Political Realities: Immigrants, Community Organizations, and Political Engagement*, 107, 119.

Goddard, T., & Myers, R. R. (2013). Youth injustice innovation on the West Coast: Examining community-based social justice organizations through a left realist lens. *W. Criminology Rev.*, 14, 51.

Goethem, A., Hoof, A., Orobio de Castro, B., Van Aken, M., & Hart, D. (2014). The role of reflection in the effects of community service on adolescent development: A meta-analysis. *Child Development*, 85 (6), 2114–2130.

Goffman, E. (2009). *Stigma: Notes on the management of spoiled identity*. New York: Simon and Schuster.

Gold, S. (2006, March 31). Student protests echo the '60s, but with a high-tech buzz; youths used a popular website to organize their walkouts. And some did know what a 'sit-in' was. *Los Angeles Times*, p. A1.

Golombek, S. B. (2006). Children as citizens. *Journal of Community Practice*, 14 (1/2), 11–30.

Gonzales, A. (2013). *Pessimism of the mind and optimism of the spirit: Latino youth activism, democracy and the politics of immigration reform after 2012*. Henasres Instituto Franklin-UAH, 5 (8), 57–79.

Gonzales, C. (2012, June 7). High school students from the Los Angeles area present conference at Roosevelt High. *Boyle Heights Beat*.

Gonzales, R. G. (2008). Left out but not shut down: Political activism and the undocumented student movement. *Northwestern Journal of Law and Social Policy*, 3 (2), 219–239.

Gonzalez, D. A. (2014). *Cultivating Civic Engagement Through Organizational Relationships at Grassroots Levels* (Doctoral dissertation, The University of Texas at San Antonio).

Gonzalez, H. (2006, April 16). Marching to honor our parents. *The Denver Post*, p. E6.

Goode, E., & Ben-Yehuda, N. (2010). *Moral panics: The social construction of deviance*. John Wiley & Sons.

Goodman, R. D., Williams, J. M., Chung, R. C. Y., Talleyrand, R. M., Douglass, A. M., McMahon, H. G., & Bemak, F. (2015). Decolonizing traditional pedagogies and practices in counseling and psychology education: A move towards social justice and action. In R. Goodman & P. C. Gorski (Eds.), *Decolonizing "multicultural" counseling through social justice* (pp. 147–164). New York: Springer.

Goodman, S. (2003). *Teaching youth media: A critical guide to literacy, video production & social change* (Vol. 36). New York: Teachers College Press.

Goodnough, K. (2014). Examining the potential of youth-led community of practice: Experience and insights. *Educational Action Research* (ahead-of-print), 1–17.

Goodwin, J., & Jasper, J. M. (2009a). Editors' introduction. In J. Goodwin & J. M. Jasper (Eds.), *The social movements readers: Cases and concepts*, 2nd ed. (pp. 3–7). New York: Wiley-Blackwell.

Goodwin, J., & Jasper, J. M. (2009b). Introduction. In J. Goodwin & J. M. Jasper (Eds.), *The social movements readers: Cases and concepts*, 2nd ed. (pp. 411–413). New York: Wiley-Blackwell.

Goodwin, J., Jasper, J. M., & Polletta, F. (Eds.). (2009). *Passionate politics: Emotions and social movements*. Chicago: University of Chicago Press.

Goodwin-De Faria, C., & Marinos, V. (2012). Youth understanding assertion of legal rights: Examining the roles of age and power. *The International Journal of Children's Rights*, 20 (3), 343–364.

Gordon, H. R. (2007). Allies within and without: How adolescent activists conceptualize ageism and navigate adult power in youth social movements. *Journal of Contemporary Ethnography*, 36 (6), 631–668.

Gordon, H. R. (2008). Gendered paths to teenage political participation parental power, civic mobility, and youth activism. *Gender & Society*, 22 (1), 31–55.

Gordon, H. R. (2010). *We fight to win: Inequality and the politics of youth activism*. New Brunswick, NJ: Rutgers University Press.

Gordon, H. R., & Taft, J. K. (2011). Rethinking young political socialization: Teenage activists talk back. *Youth & Society*, 43 (4), 1499–1527.

Gormally, S., & Coburn, A. (2013). Finding Nexus: Connecting youth work and research practices. *British Educational Research Journal*, 40 (5), 869–885.

Gosine, K., & Islam, F. (2014). "It's like we're one big family": Marginalized young people, community, and the implications for urban schooling. *School Community*, 24 (2), 33.

Gottlieb, R. (2009). Environmental justice: Where we live, work, play . . . and eat: Expanding the environmental justice agenda. *Environmental Justice*, 2 (1), 7–8.

Gottlieb, R., & Fisher, A. (1996). "First feed the face": Environmental justice and community food security. *Antipode*, 28 (2), 193–203.

Gould, L., Mogford, E., & DeVoght, A. (2010). Successes and challenges of teaching the social determinants of health in secondary schools: Case examples in Seattle, Washington. *Health Promotion Practice*, 11 (3), Suppl., 26S–33S.

Grady, J., Marquez, R., & Mclaren, P. (2012). A critique of neoliberalism with fierceness: Queer youth of color creating dialogues of resistance. *Journal of Homosexuality*, 59 (7), 982–1004.

Graff, J. M. (2013). Children's literature as tools of and for activism: Reflections of JoLLE's inaugural Activist Literacies Conference. *Journal of Language and Literacy Education*, 9 (1), 136–143.

Graham, A., & Fitzgerald, R. (2010). Progressing children's participation: Exploring the potential of a dialogical turn. *Childhood*, 17 (3), 343–359.

Graham, M. (2011). Changing paradigms and conditions of childhood: Implications for the social professions and social work. *British Journal of Social Work*, 41 (8), 1532–1547.

Gray, M., Coates, J., & Hetherington, T. (Eds.). (2012). *Environmental social work*. New York: Routledge.

Greenhalgh, S., & Carney, M. A. (2014). Bad biocitizens?: Latinos and the US "Obesity Epidemic". *Human Organization*, 73 (3), 267–276.

Griffin, P., & Ouellett, M. L. (2007). Facilitating social justice education courses. In M. Adams & L. A. Bell (Eds.), *Teaching for diversity and social justice* (pp. 89–113). New York: Routledge.

Grills, C., Villanueva, S., Subica, A. M., & Douglas, J. A. (2014). Communities creating healthy environments: Improving access to healthy foods and safe places to play in communities of color. *Preventive Medicine*, 69, S117–S119.

Gruenewald, D. A. (2008). The best of both worlds: A critical pedagogy of place. *Environmental Education Research*, 14 (3), 308–324.

Guion-Utsler, J. E. (2013). *"A Certain Kind of Person": The Development of Social Justice Allies Through Critical Service-Learning* (Doctoral dissertation, The Ohio State University).

Guo, C., Webb, N. J., Abzug, R., & Peck, L. R. (2013). Religious affiliation, religious attendance, and participation in social change organizations. *Nonprofit and Voluntary Sector Quarterly*, 42 (1), 34–58.

Guthrie, K. L., & McCracken, H. (2010). Teaching and learning social justice through online service-learning courses. *The International Review of Research in Open and Distance Learning*, 11 (3), 78–94.

Gutierrez, L. (2014). Youth social justice engagement in the face of anti-Latina/o immigrant illegitimacy. *The Urban Affairs*, 46 (2), 307–323.

Gutierrez, L., Gant, L. M., & Richards-Schuster, K. (2014). Community organization in the twenty-first century: Scholarship and practice directions for the future. *Journal of Community Practice*, 22 (1–2), 1–9.

Gutstein, E. (2003). Teaching and learning mathematics for social justice in an urban, Latino school. *Journal for Research in Mathematics Education*, 34 (1), 37–73.

Gutstein, E. (2012). Connecting community, critical, and classical knowledge in teaching mathematics for social justice. In S. Mukhopadhyay and W.-M. Roth (Eds.), *Alternative forms of knowing (in) mathematics* (pp. 300–311). Dordrecht, Netherlands: Sense Publishers.

Hacker, K. (2013). *Community-based participatory research.* Thousand Oaks, CA: Sage Publications.

Hamdy, N., & Gomaa, E. H. (2012). Framing the Egyptian uprising in Arabic language newspapers and social media. *Journal of Communication,* 62 (2), 195–211.

Hammock, A. C. (2011). Identity construction through theatrical community practice. *Qualitative Social Work,* 10 (3), 364–380.

Hale, A. (2008). Service learning with Latino communities effects on preservice teachers. *Journal of Hispanic Higher Education,* 7 (1), 54–69.

Hale, S., & Kadoda, G. (2014). The changing nature of political activism in Sudan: Women and youth 'activists' as catalysts in civil society. In Elke Grawert (Ed.), *Forging two nations: Insights on Sudan and South Sudan* (pp. 65–79). Addis Ababa, Ethiopia: Organization for Social Science Research in Eastern and Southern Africa.

Haluza-DeLay, R. (2013). Educating for environmental justice. In *International handbook of research on environmental education* (pp. 394–403).

Han, S.-K. (2004). Ashore on the land of joiners: Intergenerational social incorporation of immigrants. *International Migration Review,* 38 (2), 732–746.

Hardcastle, D. A., Powers, P. R., & Wenocur, S. (2011). *Community practice: Theories and skills for social workers.* New York: Oxford University Press.

Hardina, D. (2013). *Analytical skills for community organization practice.* New York: Columbia University Press.

Harkavy, I., & Benson, L. (1997). *De-platonization and democratization of education as the basis of service learning.* Philadelphia, PA: University of Pennsylvania.

Harkavy, I., & Hartley, M. (2010). Pursuing Franklin's dream: Philosophical and historical roots of service-learning. *American Journal of Community Psychology,* 46 (3–4), 418–427.

Harper, K., Sands, C., Angarita, D., & Totman, M. (2014). *Youth participation in changing food systems: Toward food justice youth development.*

Harre, K. (2007). Community service or activism as an identity project for youth. *Journal of Community Practice,* 35 (6), 711–724.

Harries, B. (2012). *Talking Race in Everyday Spaces of the City* (Doctoral dissertation, University of Manchester).

Harris, A., Wyn, J., & Younes, S. (2010). Beyond apathetic or activist youth: 'Ordinary'young people and contemporary forms of participation. *Young,* 18 (1), 9–32.

Harris, M. B. (2013). *School experiences of gay and lesbian youth: The invisible minority.* New York: Routledge.

Harrison, J. (2008). Lessons learned from pesticide drift: A call to bring production agriculture, farm labor, and social justice back into agrifood research and activism. *Agriculture & Human Values,* 25 (2), 163–167.

Hart, D., & Gullan, R. L. (2010). The sources of adolescent activism: Historical and contemporary findings. In L. R. Sterrod, J. Tomey-Punta & C. A. Flanagan (Eds.), *Handbook of research on civic engagement in youth* (pp. 67–90). New York: John Wiley & Sons.

Hart, D., Matsuba, M. K., & Atkins, R. (2008). The moral and civic effects of learning to serve. In L. Nucci, T. Krettenauer, & D. Narvaez (Eds.), *Handbook of moral and character education* (pp. 484–499). New York: Routledge.

Hart, D., Matsuba, K., & Atkins, R. (2014). Civic engagement and child and adolescent well-being. In A. A. Ben-Arieh, F. Casas, I. Frønes, & J. E. Korbin (Eds.), *Handbook of child well-being* (pp. 957–975). Netherlands: Springer.

Hart, R. A. (2013). *Children's participation: The theory and practice of involving young citizens in community development and environmental care.* New York: Routledge.

Hart, S. (2006). Breaking literacy boundaries through critical service-learning: education for the silenced and marginalized. *Mentoring & Tutoring*, 14 (1), 17–32.

Harter, L. M., Hamel-Lambert, J., & Millesen, J. (Eds.). (2011). *Participatory partnerships for social action and research*. Dubuque, IA: Kendall Hunt.

Hartley, M. (2009). Reclaiming the democratic purposes of American higher education: Tracing the trajectory of the civic engagement movement. *Learning and Teaching*, 2 (3), 11–30.

Harvey, D. (2010). *Social justice and the city (Vol. 1)*. Athens, Georgia: University of Georgia Press.

Hasday, J. (2014). *Women in the Civil Rights Movement*. Broomall, PA: Mason Crest.

Haski-Leventhal, D., Ronel, N., York, A. S., & Ben-David, B. M. (2008). Youth volunteering for youth: Who are they serving? How are they being served?. *Children and Youth Services Review*, 30 (7), 834–846.

Hathcock, S. J., & Dickerson, D. L. (2015). Hitting the big screen–Urban youth activism through documentary film. In M. P. Mueller & D. J. Tippins (Eds.), *EcoJustice, citizen science and youth activism* (pp. 385–396). New York: Springer International Publishing.

Hattam, R., Brennan, M., Zipin, L., & Comber, B. (2009). Researching for social justice: Contextual, conceptual and methodological challenges. *Discourse: Studies in the Cultural Politics of Education*, 30 (3), 303–316.

Hauge, C. (2014). Youth media and agency. *Discourse: Studies in the Cultural Politics of Education* (ahead-of-print), 1–14.

Haverkos, K. (2015). Living history—Challenging citizen science and youth activism through historical re-enacting. In M. P. Mueller & D. J. Tippins (Eds.), *EcoJustice, citizen science and youth activism* (pp. 193–206). New York: Springer International Publishing.

Hawken, P. (2007). *Blessed unrest: How the largest movement in the world came into being and why no one saw it coming*. New York: Viking Press.

Haydon, D. (2012). The effective implementation of rights-based standards. *Vulnerable Children and the Law: International Evidence for Improving Child Welfare, Child Protection and Children's Rights*, 23.

Hayduk, R. (2012). Global justice and OWS: Movement connections. *Socialism and Democracy*, 26 (2), 43–50.

He, M., Wilmoth, S., Bustos, D., Jones, T., Leeds, J., & Yin, Z. (2013). Latino church leaders' perspectives on childhood obesity prevention. *American Journal of Preventive Medicine*, 44 (3), S232–S239.

Head, B. W. (2011). Why not ask them? Mapping and promoting youth participation. *Children and Youth Services Review*, 33 (4), 541–547.

Healy, E. (2011, May 16). Youth LEAD takes on food justice in Miami. *Food Freedom*. Retrieved from https://foodfreedom.wordpress.com/2011/05/16/youth-lead-takes-on-food-justice-in-miami/

Heineman, K. J. (1994). *Campus wars: The peace movement at American state universities in the Vietnam era*. New York: NYU Press.

Helfenbein, R. J., & Huddleston, G. (2013). Youth, space, cities: Toward the concrete. *Taboo*, 13 (1), 5.

Hemming, P. J., & Madge, N. (2012). Researching children, youth and religion: Identity, complexity and agency. *Childhood*, 19 (1), 38–51.

Henderson, P., & Thomas, D. N. (2013). *Skills in neighbourhood work*. New York: Routledge.

Hendrickson, D., Smith, C., & Eikenberry, N. (2006). Fruit and vegetable access in four low-income food deserts communities in Minnesota. *Agriculture and Human Values*, 23 (3), 371–383.

Henry, M. E. (2011). Reflection matters: Connecting theory to practice in service learning courses. *Kappa Omicron Nu Forum*, 15 (2), 15–22.

Hensby, A., Sibthorpe, J., & Driver, S. (2012). Resisting the 'protest business': Bureaucracy, post-bureaucracy and active membership in social movement organizations. *Organization*, 19 (6), 809–823.

Herd, D., & Berman, J. (2014). Mobilizing for change: Activism and alcohol policy issues in inner city communities. *Social Movement Studies* (ahead-of-print), 1–21.

Herman, D. R., Baer, M. T., Adams, E., Cunningham-Sabo, L., Duran, N., Johnson, D. B., & Yakes, E. (2014). Life course perspective: Evidence for the role of nutrition. *Maternal and Child Health Journal*, 18 (2), 450–461.

Hernandez, M., Collins, T. W., & Grineski, S. E. (2015). Immigration, mobility, and environmental injustice: A comparative study of Hispanic people's residential decision-making and exposure to hazardous air pollutants in Greater Houston, Texas. *Geoforum*, 60, 83–94.

Herrera, L. (Ed.). (2014). *Wired citizenship: Youth learning and activism in the Middle East.* New York: Routledge.

Hess, D. J. (2009). *Localist movements in a global economy: Sustainability, justice, and urban development in the United States.* Cambridge, MA: MIT Press.

Hildreth, R. W. (2012). John Dewey on experience: A critical resource for the theory and practice of youth civic engagement. *Citizenship Studies*, 16 (7), 919–935.

Hill, L. R. (2014). *Youth speak out: Facilitating youth-led action research projects in DC.* Washington, D.C.: Capstone Collection.

Hilmers, A., Hilmers, D. C., & Dave, J. (2012). Neighborhood disparities in access to healthy foods and their effects on environmental justice. *American Journal of Public Health*, 102 (9), 1644–1654.

Hinds, J., & Sparks, P. (2009). Investigating identity, well-being, and meaning. *Ecopsychology*, 1 (4), 181–186.

Hine, T. (2000). *The rise and fall of the American teenager: A new history of the American adolescent experience.* New York: Perennial.

Hinrichs, C. C., & Allen, P. (2008). Selective patronage and social justice: Local Food consumer campaigns in historical context. *Journal of Agricultural and Environmental Ethics*, 21 (4), 329–352.

Hirsch, B. J. (2011). Learning and development in after-school programs. *Phi Delta Kappan*, 92 (5), 66–69.

Ho, E., Clarke, A., & Dougherty, I. (2015). Youth-led social change: Topics, engagement types, organizational types, strategies, and impacts. *Futures*, 67 (1), 52–62.

Hodson, D. (2014). Becoming part of the solution: Learning about activism, learning through activism, learning from activism. In J. L. Bencze & S. Alsop (Eds.), *Activist science and technology education* (pp. 67–98). New York: Springer Publisher.

Hoffman, B. (2013). *Behind the brands: Food justice and the 'Big 10' food and beverage companies.* Oxfam.

Hoffman-Kipp, P. (2008). Actualizing democracy: The praxis of teacher identity construction. *Teacher Education Quarterly*, 35 (3), 151–164.

Holland, J. (2012). Fragmented youth: Social capital in biographical context in young people's lives. *Assessing Social Capital: Concept, Policy and Practice*, 163 (177), 163–177. Cambridge Scholars Publishing in association with GSE Research.

Hollingsworth, K. (2012). Youth justice reform in the 'big society'. *Journal of Social Welfare and Family Law,* 34 (2), 245–259.

Holtgrave, P. L., Norrick, C., Teufel, J., & Gilbert, P. (2014). Building community and social capital by engaging capacity-building volunteers in intergenerational programs. *Journal of Intergenerational Relationships,* 12 (2), 192–196.

Hondagneu-Sotelo, P. (2008). *God's heart has no borders: How religious activists are working for immigrant rights.* Berkeley, CA: University of California Press.

Hope, E. C., & Jagers, R. J. (2014). The role of sociopolitical attitudes and civic education in the civic engagement of black youth. *Journal of Research on Adolescence,* 24 (3), 460–470.

Horn, B. R. (2014). "This is just like those projects from last semester!": Student empowerment and praxis at an urban Title I middle school. *Multicultural Perspectives,* 16 (3), 154–159.

Horn, D. (1973). Youth resistance in the Third Reich: A social portrait. *Journal of Social History,* 7 (1), 26–50.

Hörschelmann, K., & El Refaie, E. (2014). Youth citizenship beyond consensus: Examining the role of satire and humour for critical engagements in citizenship education. *Youth Cultures in the Age of Global Media,* 225.

Hosang, D. E. (2006). Family and community as the cornerstone of civic engagement: Immigrant and youth organizing in the South West. *National Civic Review,* 95 (4), 58–61.

Houwer, R. (2013). *Changing leaders, leading change: A leadership development model for marginalized youth in urban communities.* York, England: University of York.

Hoyt, B. R. (2008). A research study investigating the impact of service-learning on ethical decision making. *Scholarship for sustaining service-learning and civic engagement* (pp. 185–205).

Huey, R. (2012). *Protest in practice: The University of California Irvine's place in the Anti-Vietnam War Movement from 1965–1970.* Irvine, CA: University of Irvine.

Hugman, R., & Bartolomei, L. (2013). The ethics of participation in community work practice. In A. K. Larsen, V. Sewpaul & G. Oline Hole (Eds.), *Participation in community work: International perspectives* (pp. 19–29). New York: Routledge.

Hung, D., Lim, K. Y., & Jamaludin, A. (2014). An epistemic shift: A literacy of adaptivity as critical for twenty-first century learning. In D.W.L. Hung, K.Y.T. Lim, & S. S. Lee (Eds.), *Adaptivity as a transformative disposition* (pp. 3–14). New York: Springer Singapore.

Hurtado, S., Alvarez, C. L., Guillermo-Wann, C., Cuellar, M., & Arellano, L. (2012). A model for diverse learning environments. In *Higher education: Handbook of theory and research* (pp. 41–122). Springer Netherlands.

Hyde, C. (2015). Experiences of women activists: Implications for community organizing theory and practice. *The Journal of Sociology & Social Welfare,* 13 (3), 9.

Hytten, K., & Bettez, S. C. (2011). Understanding education for social justice. *Educational Foundations,* 25, 7–24.

Ife, J. (2012). *Human rights and social work: Towards rights-based practice.* Cambridge University Press.

Igietseme, N. (2014). *A Blueprint for Building a Multi-Generational Movement for Social Transformation in Boston* (Doctoral dissertation, Massachusetts Institute of Technology).

Illeris, K. (2014). Transformative learning re-defined as changes in elements of the identity. *International Journal of Lifelong Education* (ahead-of- print), 1–14.

Immigration Laws. (2006, May 1). Thousands march for immigrant rights. *CNN U.S.* Retrieved from http://articles.cnn.com/2006-05-01/us/immigrant.day_1_thousands-march-largest-protests-immigration-laws?_s=PM:US

Invernizzi, A., & Williams, J. (Eds.). (2013). *The human rights of children: From visions to implementation.* London, England: Ashgate Publishing.

Irby, D. J. (2015). Urban is floating face down in the mainstream using hip-hop-based education research to resurrect "the urban" in urban education. *Urban Education, 50* (1), 7–30.

Irwin, K., Edwards, K., & Tamburello, J. A. (2015). Gender, trust and cooperation in environmental social dilemmas. *Social Science Research, 50,* 328–342.

Irwin, S. (2013). *Rights of passage: social change and the transition from youth to adulthood (Vol. 4).* New York: Routledge.

Ito, M., Soep, E., Kligler-Vilenchik, N., Shreshtova, S., Gamber-Thompson, L., & Zimmerman, A. (2015). Learning connected civics: Narratives, practices, infrastructures. *Curriculum Inquiry, 45* (1), 10–29.

Iverson, S. V., & James, J. H. (2013). Self-authoring a civic identity: A qualitative analysis of change-oriented service learning. *Journal of Student Affairs Research and Practice, 50* (1), 88–105.

Iveson, K. (2011). Social or spatial justice? Marcuse and Soja on the right to the city. *City, 15* (2), 250–259.

Jack, G. (2004). On speech, critique and protection. *Ephemera, 4* (2), 121–134.

Jackson-Elmoore, C., Hula, R. C., & Reese, L. A. (2011). *Reinventing civil society: The emerging role of faith-based organizations.* Armonk, NY: ME Sharpe.

Jacobson, M., & Rugeley, C. (2007). Community-based participatory research: Group work for social justice and community change. *Social Work with Groups, 30* (4), 21–39.

Jacoby, B. (Ed.). (2003). *Building partnerships for service-learning.* New York: John Wiley & Sons.

Jacoby, B. (2015). *Service-learning essentials: Questions, answers, and lessons learned.* New York: John Wiley & Sons.

James, J. H., & Iverson, S. V. D. (2014). Conclusions: Re-visioning community engagement as feminist praxis. In S. Van Deventer Iverson & J. Hauver James (Eds.), *Feminist Community Engagement: Achieving Praxis* (pp. 193–222). New York: Palgrave Books.

Janes, J. E., Ibhawoh, B., Razack, N., & Gilbert, N. (2014). The trouble with triumph: Discourses of governmentality in mainstream media representations of urban youth. *Journal of Progressive Human Services, 25* (1), 50–69.

Janks, H. (2014). Critical literacy's ongoing importance for education. *Journal of Adolescent & Adult Literacy, 57* (5), 349–356.

Jarrett, R. L., Sullivan, P. J., & Watkins, N. D. (2005). Developing social capital through participation in organized youth programs: Qualitative insights from three programs. *Journal of Community Psychology, 33* (1), 41–55.

Jasper, J. M. (2011). Emotions and social movements: Twenty years of theory and research. *Annual Review of Sociology, 37,* 285–303.

Jasper, J. M. (2014). Constructing indignation: Anger dynamics in protest movements. *Emotion Review, 6* (3), 208–213.

Jay, G. (2008). Service learning, multiculturalism, and the pedagogies of difference. *Pedagogy, 8* (2), 255–281.

Jennings, L. B., Parra-Medina, D. M., Hilfinger-Messias, D. K., & McLoughlin, K. (2006). Toward a critical social theory of youth empowerment. *Journal of Community Practice, 14* (1–2), 31–55.

Jennings, M. K., & Stoker, L. (2004). Social trust and civic engagement across time and generations. *Acta politica*, 39 (4), 342–379.

Jensen, L. A. (2008). Immigrants' cultural identities as sources of civic engagement. *Applied Development Science*, 12 (2), 74–83.

Jensen, L. A., & Flanagan, C. A. (2008). Immigrant civic engagement: New translations. *Applied Development Science*, 12 (2), 55–56.

Johansson, A. W., & Lindhult, E. (2008). Emancipation or workability? Critical versus pragmatic scientific orientation in action research. *Action Research*, 6 (1), 95–115.

Johnson, E. (2014). Reconceptualizing Vulnerability in Personal Narrative Writing With Youths. *Journal of Adolescent & Adult Literacy*, 57 (7), 575–583.

Johnson, E., & Vasudevan, L. (2012). Seeing and hearing students' lived and embodied critical literacy practices. *Theory into Practice*, 51 (1), 34–41.

Johnson, K. R., & Hing, B. O. (2007). The immigrant rights marches of 2006 and the prospects of a New Civil Rights Movement. Harvard *Civil Rights-Civil Liberties Law Review*, 42., 99–138.

Johnson, L. P. (2014). The writing on the wall: enacting place pedagogies in order to reimagine schooling for Black male youth. *Discourse: Studies in the Cultural Politics of Education* (ahead-of-print), 1–12.

Johnson, T. (2011). All children are created equal too: The disparate treatment of youth rights in America. In B. Entzminger (Ed.), *Human rights at home and abroad: Past, present, and future* (pp. 70–76). Bloomburg, PA: Bloomburg University.

Johnston-Goodstar, K., Richards-Schuster, K., & Sethi, J. K. (2014). Exploring critical youth media practice: Connections and contributions for social work. *Social Work*, swu041.

Jones, B., & O'Donnell, M. (Eds.). (2012). *Sixties radicalism and social movement activism: retreat or resurgence? (Vol. 1)*. Anthem Press.

Jones, G. (2009). *Youth (key concepts)*. Cambridge, England: Polity Press.

Jones, G. (2012). Dynamic and socially embedded: Biographies of participation in youth. In P. Loncle, M. Cuconato, V. Muniglia, & A. Walther (Eds.), *Youth participation in Europe: Beyond discourses, practices and realities* (pp. 245–254). Bristol, England: Policy Press.

Jones, J. N., Bench, J. H., Warnaar, B. L., & Stroup, J. T. (2013). Participation as relational process: Unpacking involvement in social action and community service. *Afterschool Matters*, 18 (1), 9–16.

Jones, J. N., Warnaar, B. L., Bench, J. H., & Stroup, J. (2014). Promoting the development of moral identity, behavior, and commitment in a social action program. *Journal of Peace Education* (ahead-of-print), 1–21.

Jones, K. R., & Perkins, D. F. (2005). Determining the quality of youth-adult relationships within community-based youth programs. *Journal of Extension*, 43 (5), 1–10.

Jones, S. (2006). Reflections on the great immigration battle of 2006 and the future of the Americas. *Social Justice*, 33 (1), 6–20.

Jones, S. G., & Steinberg, K. S. (2012). Research on service learning suffers from a lack of clarity in defining service learning as an independent variable. *International Service Learning: Conceptual Frameworks and Research*, 89.

Joseph, M. C. (2012). Social agency of low-income young women in Gaborone City, Botswana. *Stud Changing Soc: Spec Iss on Youth Under Global Persp*, 1 (5), 37–62.

Juris, J.-S., & Pleyers, G. H. (2009). Alter-action: Emerging cultures of participation among youth global justice activists. *Journal of Youth Studies*, 12 (1), 57–75.

Kafai, Y. B., Desai, S., Peppler, K. A., Chiu, G. M., & Moya, J. (2008). Mentoring partnerships in a community technology centre: A constructionist approach for fostering equitable service learning. *Mentoring & Tutoring: Partnership in Learning*, 16 (2), 191–205.

Kafer, A. (2013). *Feminist, queer, crip.* Bloomington, IN: Indiana University Press.

Kahne, J., Chi, B., & Middaugh, E. (2006). Building social capital for civic and political engagement: The potential of high-school civics courses. *Canadian Journal of Education/ Revue canadienne de l'éducation*, 387–409.

Kahne, J. E., & Sporte, S. E. (2008). Developing citizens: The impact of civic learning opportunities on students' commitment to civic participation. *American Educational Research Journal*, 45 (3), 738–766.

Kajner, T., Chovanec, D., Underwood, M., & Mian, A. (2013). Critical community service learning: Combining critical classroom pedagogy with activist community placements. *Michigan Journal of Community Service Learning*, 19 (2), 36–48.

Kamete, A. Y. (2013). Defending illicit livelihoods: Youth resistance in Harare's contested spaces. In M. Hibbard, R. R. Freestone, & T. Ø. Sager (Eds.), *Dialogues in urban and regional planning* (pp. 43–69). Abingdon, UK: Routledge.

Kaplan, I. (2008). Being 'seen' and being 'heard': Engaging with students on the margins of education through participatory photography In *Doing research with children and young people* (175). New York: Routledge.

Karasik, R. J., & Wallingford, M. S. (2007). Finding community: Developing and maintaining effective intergenerational service-learning partnerships. *Educational Gerontology*, 33 (9), 775–793.

Katsiaficas, D., Futch, V. A., Fine, M., & Sirin, S. R. (2011). Everyday hyphens: Exploring youth identities with methodological and analytic pluralism. *Qualitative Research in Psychology*, 8 (2), 120–139.

Kawashima-Ginsberg, K., Marcelo, K. B., & Kirby, E. H. (2009). *Youth volunteering in the States: 2002 to 2007.* Center for Information & Research on Civic Learning & Engagement. Medford, MA: Tufts University.

Kegler, M. C., Rigler, J., & Honeycutt, S. (2010). How does community context influence coalitions in the formation stage? A multiple case study based on the Community Coalition Action Theory. *BMC Public Health*, 10 (1), 90.

Kehily, M. J. (2014). Sex'n'drugs'n'rock'n'roll: Young people as consumers. *Youth Justice Handbook: Theory, Policy and Practice*, 41.

Keil, R. (2009). The urban politics of roll-with-it neoliberalization. *City*, 13 (2–3), 230–245.

Kellett, M. (2005). *How to develop children as researchers: A step by step guide to teaching the research process.* Thousand Oaks, CA: Sage.

Kellner, D., & Share, J. (2005). Toward critical media literacy: Core concepts, debates, organizations, and policy. *Discourse: Studies in the Cultural Politics of Education*, 26 (3), 369–386.

Kelshaw, T., Lazarus, F., & Minier, J. (2009). *Partnerships for service- learning: Impacts on communities and students.* New York: John Wiley & Sons.

Kendall, J. (1990). Principles of good practice in combining service and learning. In *Combining service and learning: A resource book for community and public service* (37). Raleigh, NC: National Society for Internships and Experiential Education.

Keniston, K. (1962). Social change and youth in America. *Daedalus*, 91, 145–171.

Kennelly, J. J. (2008). *Citizen youth: Culture, activism, and agency in an era of globalization.*

Kennelly, J. (2009). Good citizen/bad activist: The cultural role of the state in youth activism. *The Review of Education, Pedagogy, and Cultural Studies*, 31 (2–3), 127–149.

Kennelly, J. (2011). *Citizen youth: Culture, activism, and agency in a neoliberal era.* Palgrave New York: Macmillan.

Kerckhoff, A. S., & Reis, G. (2014). Responsible stewards of the earth: Narratives of youth activism in high school (science). In *Activist science and technology education* (pp. 465–476). Dordrect, Netherlands: Springer Netherlands.

Kielsmeier, J. C. (2010). Build a bridge between service and learning. *Phi Delta Kappan*, 91 (5), 8–15.

Kientz, S. C. (2013). *POVERTY SLAM! How slam poetry transforms the lives of impoverished youth.* Lexington, VA: Washington & Lee University Library.

Kieslmier, J. C. (2000). *Service-learning.* Washington, D.C.: National Youth Leadership Council.

Kim, H. (2014). Understanding civic engagement in Asia: The role of social capital. In *XVIII ISA World Congress of Sociology* (July 13–19, 2014). Isaconf.

Kim, J., & Sherman, R. F. (2006). Youth as important civic actors: From the margins to the center. *National Civic Review*, 95 (1), 3–6.

Kim, R. H. (2013). "Never knew literacy could get at my soul": On how words matter for youth, or notes toward decolonizing literacy. *Review of Education, Pedagogy, and Cultural Studies*, 35 (5), 392–407.

Kimbler, K. J., & Ehman, A. C. (2014). Gerontology and youth focused service learning: The relation between service recipient age and student responses. *Gerontology & Geriatrics Education* (just accepted).

Kincheloe, J. L., McLaren, P., & Steinberg, S. R. (2011). Critical pedagogy and qualitative research. In N. Denzin & Y. Lincoln (Eds.), *The SAGE handbook of qualitative methods in health research*, 4th ed. (pp. 163–178). Thousand Oaks, CA: Sage.

King, W. (2011). *Stolen childhood: Slave youth in nineteenth-century America.* Indiana University Press.

Kinloch, V. (2012). *Crossing boundaries-teaching and learning with urban youth.* New York: Teachers College Press.

Kinloch, V. (2014). This issue: Critical service-learning initiatives. *Theory Into Practice* (just accepted).

Kinloch, V., Nemeth, E., & Patterson, A. (2014). Reframing service-learning as learning and participation with urban youth. *Theory into Practice* (just accepted).

Kirshner, B. (2006). Apprenticeship learning and youth activism. In S. Ginwright & P. Noguera (Eds.), *Beyond resistance: Youth activism and community change* (pp. 37–58). New York: Routledge.

Kirshner, B. (2007). Introduction youth activism as a context for learning and development. *American Behavioral Scientist*, 51 (3), 367–379.

Kirshner, B. (2008). Guided participation in three youth activism organizations: Facilitation, apprenticeship, and joint work. *The Journal of the Learning Sciences*, 17 (1), 60–101.

Kirshner, B. (2009). "Power in numbers": Youth organizing as a context for exploring civic identity. *Journal of Research on Adolescence*, 19 (3), 414–440.

Krishner, B. (2014). Activism. R. J. Levesque (Ed.), *Encyclopedia of Adolescence* (pp. 49–56). New York: Springer.

Kirshner, B., & Geil, K. (2010). "I'm about to really bring it!" Access points between youth activities and adult community leaders. *Children, Youth and Environments*. Retrieved from http://www.ucdenver.edu/academics/colleges/ArchitecturePlanning/discover/centers/CYE/Publications/Documents/CYE-WP3-2010%20website%20version.pdf

Klodawsky, F., Aubry, T., & Farrell, S. (2006). Care and the lives of homeless youth in neoliberal times in Canada. *Gender, Place and Culture*, 13 (4), 419–436.

Knaus, C. B. (2014). What if we all wore Hoodies?. In *(Re)Teaching Trayvon* (pp. 163–185). Rotterdam, Netherlands: SensePublishers.

Koch, J. M., Ross, J. B., Wendell, J., & Aleksandrova-Howell, M. (2014). Results of immersion service learning activism with peers anticipated and surprising. *The Counseling Psychologist*, 42 (8), 1215–1246.

Koffel, C. (2003). Globalisation of youth activism and human rights. *Global Youth Action Network and Peace Child International*, 117–127. Retrieved from http://www.uscrossier. org/pullias/wp-content/uploads/2012/06/koffel.pdf

Kramer, K., Schwarte, L., Lafleur, M., & Williams, J. D. (2013). Targeted marketing of junk food to ethnic minority youth: Fighting back with legal advocacy and community engagement. In J. D. Williams, K. E. Pasch, & C. A. Collins (Eds.), *Advances in communication research to reduce childhood obesity* (pp. 389–405). Springer New York.

Krasny, M. E., Kalbacker, L., Stedman, R. C., & Russ, A. (2015). Measuring social capital among youth: Applications in environmental education. *Environmental Education Research*, 21 (1), 1–23.

Krauss, S. E., Collura, J., Zeldin, S., Ortega, A., Abdullah, H., & Sulaiman, A. H. (2013). Youth–adult partnership: Exploring contributions to empowerment, agency and community connections in Malaysian youth programs. *Journal of Youth and Adolescence*, 43 (9), 1550–1562.

Kudryavtsev, A., Krasny, M. E., & Stedman, R. C. (2012). The impact of environmental education on sense of place among urban youth. *Ecosphere*, 3 (4), art29.

Kulick, R. (2014). What do you see that I cannot? Peer facilitations of difference and conflict in the collective production of independent youth media. *Interface: A Journal on Social Movements*, 6 (2), 301–327.

Kumashiro, K. K. (2009). *Against common sense: Teaching and learning toward social justice, revised edition*. New York: Taylor & Francis.

Kurien, P. (2013). Religion, social incorporation, and civic engagement: Second-generation Indian American Christians. *Review of religious research*, 55 (1), 81–104.

Kwan, A. (2013). Youth food activism. In P. B. Thompson & D. M. Kaplan (Eds.), *Encyclopedia of food and agricultural ethics* (pp. 431–437). New York: Springer International.

Kwon, S. A. (2006). Youth of color organizing for juvenile justice. In S. Ginwright, P. Noguera, & J. Cammarota (Eds.), *Beyond resistance* (pp. 215–228). New York: Routledge.

Kwon, S. A. (2008). Moving from complaints to action: Oppositional consciousness and collective action in a political community. *Anthropology & Education Quarterly*, 39 (1), 59–76.

Ladson Billings, G. (2011). Boyz to men? Teaching to restore Black boys' childhood. *Race Ethnicity and Education*, 14 (1), 7–15.

Lakin, R., & Mahoney, A. (2006). Empowering youth to change their world: Identifying key components of a community service program to promote positive development. *Journal of School Psychology*, 44 (6), 513–531.

Lamotte, M. (2014). Rebels without a pause: Hip-hop and resistance in the city. *International Journal of Urban and Regional Research*, 38 (2), 686–694.

Langman, L. (2005). From virtual public spheres to global justice: A critical theory of internetworked social movements. *Sociological Theory*, 23 (1), 42–74.

Langseth, M., & Plater, W. M. (Eds.). (2004). *Public work and the academy: An academic administrator's guide to civic engagement and service-learning*. Bolton, MA: Anker Publishing Co., Inc.

Lankshear, C., & Knobel, M. (2011). *New literacies: Everyday practices and social learning.* New York: McGraw-Hill International.

Larsen, K., & Gilliland, J. (2008). Mapping the evolution of 'food deserts' in a Canadian city: Supermarket accessibility in London, Ontario, 1961–2005. *International Journal of Health Geographics*, 7 (1), 16.

Larson, N., & Story, M. (2015). Barriers to equity in nutritional health for US children and adolescents: A review of the literature. *Current Nutrition Reports*, 1–9.

Larson, R. W., & Angus, R. M. (2011). Adolescents' development of skills for agency in youth programs: Learning to think strategically. *Child Development*, 82 (1), 277–294.

Larson, R. W., & Tran, S. P. (2014). Invited commentary: Positive youth development and human complexity. *Journal of Youth and Adolescence*, 43 (6), 1012–1017.

Larson, R., Walker, K., & Pearce, N. (2005). A comparison of youth-driven and adult-driven youth programs: Balancing inputs from youth and adults. *Journal of Community Psychology*, 33 (1), 57–74.

Laursen, E. K. (2014). Respectful youth cultures. *Reclaiming Children and Youth*, 22 (4), 48–52.

Lavie-Ajayi, M., & Krumer-Nevo, M. (2013). In a different mindset: Critical youth work with marginalized youth. *Children and Youth Services Review*, 35 (10), 1698–1704.

Law, M. (2002). Participation in the occupations of everyday life. *American Journal of Occupational Therapy*, 56 (6), 640–649.

Lawler, J., Joseph, A., & Narula, S. (2014). Engaging college students on a community engagement with high school students with disabilities. *Contemporary Issues in Education Research (CIER)*, 7 (3), 195–204.

Ledwith, M. (2011). *Community development: A critical approach.* Bristol, England: Policy Press.

Lee, C. (2002). Environmental justice: Building a unified vision of health and the environment. *Environmental Health Perspectives*, 110 (2), 141–144.

Lee, C. D. (2010). Forward. In N. Aries (Ed.), *Youth-full productions* (pp. ix–xii). New York: Peter Lang.

Lee, D. K. (2013). *Teacher education for democracy and social justice.* New York: Routledge.

Lee, J. A. (2013). *The empowerment approach to social work practice.* New York: Columbia University Press.

Lee, J. B. (2009, August 25). A Latino legacy endures. *The New York Times*, p. 16.

Lee, N., & Motzkau, J. (2011). Navigating the bio-politics of childhood. *Childhood*, doi:0907568210371526

Lee, O. E. K., & Priester, M. A. (2015). Increasing awareness of diversity through community engagement and films. *Journal of Social Work Education*, 51 (1), 35–46.

LeFrançois, B. A. (2014). Adultism. *Encyclopedia of critical psychology*, 47–49.

Le Grange, L. (2007). The 'theoretical foundations' of community service-learning: From taproots to rhizomes. *Education as Change*, 11 (3), 3–13.

Lenoir, G. (2007). Blacks and immigrants: More allies than adversaries. *Race, Poverty & the Environment*, 14 (1), 28–29.

Lenzi, M., Vieno, A., Sharkey, J., Mayworm, A., Scacchi, L., Pastore, M., & Santinello, M. (2014). How school can teach civic engagement besides civic education: The role of democratic school climate. *American Journal of Community Psychology*, 54 (3–4), 251–261.

Leonard, J., Brooks, W., Barnes-Johnson, J., & Berry, R. Q. (2010). The nuances and complexities of teaching mathematics for cultural relevance and social justice. *Journal of Teacher Education*, 61 (3), 261–270.

Leonard, P., & McLaren, P. (Eds.). (2002). *Paulo Freire: A critical encounter.* New York: Routledge.

Leontidou, L. (2010). Urban social movements in 'weak'civil societies: The right to the city and cosmopolitan activism in Southern Europe. *Urban Studies,* 47 (6), 1179–1203.

Lesko, N., & Talburt, S. (Eds.). (2012). *Keywords in youth studies: Tracing affects, movements, knowledges.* New York: Routledge.

Lester, B. T., Ma, L., Lee, O., & Lambert, J. (2006). Social activism in elementary science education: A science, technology, and society approach to teach global warming. *International Journal of Science Education,* 28 (4), 315–339.

Lester, J. P., Allen, D. W., & Hill, K. M. (2001). *Environmental injustice in the United States: Myths and realities.* Boulder, CO: Westview Press.

Leung, M. M. (2014, November). Utilizing photovoice to understand youth perspectives of their food environment in low-income New York City neighborhoods. In *142nd APHA Annual Meeting and Exposition* (November 15–November 19, 2014). APHA.

Levesque-Bristol, C., Knapp, T. D., & Fisher, B. J. (2010). The effectiveness of service-learning: It's not always what you think. *Journal of Experiential Education,* 33 (3), 208–224.

Levine, P. (2007). *The future of democracy: Developing the next generation of American citizens.* Medford, MA: Tufts University Press.

Levine, P. (2008). The civic engagement of young immigrants: Why does it matter?. *Applied Development Science,* 12 (2), 102–104.

Levine, D. P. (2011). *The capacity for civic engagement: Public and private worlds of the self.* London, England: Palgrave Macmillan.

Levine, P. (2011). What do we know about civic engagement. *Liberal Education,* 97 (2), 12–19.

Levinson, M. (2010). The civic empowerment gap: Defining the problem and locating solutions. In L. R. Sherrod, J. Torney-Purta, & C. A. Flanagan (Eds.), *Handbook of research on civic engagement in youth* (pp. 331–361). New York: John Wiley & Sons.

Levkoe, C. Z. (2006). Learning democracy through food justice movements. *Agriculture and Human Values,* 23 (1), 89–98.

Leydens, J. A., & Lucena, J. C. (2014). Social justice: A missing, unelaborated dimension in humanitarian engineering and learning through service. *International Journal for Service Learning in Engineering, Humanitarian Engineering and Social Entrepreneurship,* 9 (2), 1–28.

Lewi, H., & Nichols, D. (2014). "You never appreciate what you have until there is a chance you may lose it": Community activism and the conservation of public swimming pools. *Fabrications: The Journal of the Society of Architectural Historians, Australia and New Zealand,* 24 (1), 114–133.

Lewis, A. B. (2009). *The shadows of youth: The remarkable journey of the civil rights generation.* New York: Macmillan.

Lewis, A. E. (2013). The "nine lives" of oppositional culture?. *Du Bois Review: Social Science Research on Race,* 10 (01), 279–289.

Lewis, R. K. (2011). Promoting positive youth development by understanding social contexts. *Journal of Prevention & Intervention in the Community,* 39 (4), 273–276.

Lewis-Charp, H., Yu, H. C., & Soukamneuth, S. (2006). Civic activist approaches for engaging youth in social justice. In S. Ginwright, P. Noguera, & J. Cammarota (Eds.), *Beyond resistance: Youth activism and community change* (pp. 21–35). New York: Routledge.

Lewison, M., Flint, A. S., & Van Sluys, K. (2002). Taking on critical literacy: The journey of newcomers and novices. *Language Arts,* 79 (5), 382–392.

Liang, B., Spencer, R., West, J., & Rappaport, N. (2013). Expanding the reach of youth mentoring: Partnering with youth for personal growth and social change. *Journal of Adolescence*, 36 (2), 257–267.

Libal, K. R., & Harding, S. (2015a). Building a movement to recognize food security as a human right in the United States. In K. Libal & S. Harding (Eds.), *Human rights-based community practice in the United States* (pp. 61–77). New York: Springer International Publishing.

Libal, K. R., & Harding, S. (2015b). Human rights-based approaches to community practice in the United States: A call to action. In K. Libal & S. Harding (Eds.), *Human rights-based community practice in the United States* (pp. 1–17). New York: Springer International Publishing.

Libby, M., Sedonaen, M., & Bliss, S. (2006). The mystery of youth leadership development: The path to just communities. *New Directions for Youth Development* (109), 13–25.

Liebenberg, L., & Theron, L. C. (2015). Innovative qualitative explorations of culture and resilience. In L. C. Theron, L. Liebenberg, & M. Ungar (Eds.), *Youth resilience and culture* (pp. 203–215). New York: Springer International.

Lim, M. (2012). Clicks, cabs, and coffee houses: Social media and oppositional movements in Egypt 2004–2011. *Journal of Communication*, 62 (2), 231–248.

Lindsey, T. B. (2015). Let me blow your mind: Hip hop feminist futures in theory and praxis. *Urban Education*, 50 (1), 52–77.

Ling, P. J., & Monteith, S. (Eds.). (2014). *Gender in the Civil Rights Movement*. Routledge.

Link, H., McNally, T., Sayre, A., Schmidt, R., & Swap, R. J. (2012). The definition of community: A student perspective. *Partnerships: A Journal of Service-Learning and Civic Engagement*, 2 (2), 1–9.

Litvina, D., & Omelchenko, E. (2013). Rhetorical and everyday aspects of anarchist informal education. *Educational Studies* (2), 133–153.

Llera, D. J., & Katsirebas, E. (2010). Remapping the journey of lesbian youth through strength and "truth telling." *Journal of Lesbian Studies*, 14 (1), 26–35.

Loader, B. D., Vromen, A., & Xenos, M. A. (2014). The networked young citizen: Social media, political participation and civic engagement. *Information, Communication & Society*, 17 (2), 143–150.

Lombardo, C., Zakus, D., & Skinner, H. (2002). Youth social action: Building a global latticework through information and communication technologies. *Health Promotion International*, 17 (4), 363–371.

Longo, N. V., & Fleming, K. (2014). Civic learning and practiced wisdom: Intergenerational reflections on the work of democracy. *Michigan Journal of Community Service Learning*, 21 (1), 98.

Lopez, A. (2008). *Does Chicano rap empower the twenty-first century immigrants' rights movement in the United States?* New York: Pace University.

Lorenzo, T., Motau, J., van der Merwe, T., Janse van Rensburg, E., & Cramm, J. M. (2015). Community rehabilitation workers as catalysts for disability: Inclusive youth development through service learning. *Development in Practice*, 25 (1), 19–28.

Love, R. (2008). On linkages: Access to healthy food in a low-income urban community: A service-learning experience. *Public Health Reports*, 123 (2), 244.

Luke, A. (2012). Critical literacy: Foundational notes. *Theory into practice*, 51 (1), 4–11.

Lund, D. E. (2010). *Drawing insights from former youth leaders in social justice activism*. Working Paper Series WP10–06, Prairie Metropolis Centre, University of Alberta, Edmonton. Retrieved from http://pmc. metropolis. net/Workingpapers/index.htm

Lund, D. E. (2014). *Supporting youth social justice activism: Fostering a dialogical relationship.*

Lund, D. E., & Carr, P. R. (Eds.). (2008). *Doing democracy: Striving for political literacy and social justice (Vol. 322).* New York: Peter Lang.

Lundberg, M., & Wuermli, A. (Eds.). (2012). *Children and youth in crisis: Protecting and promoting human development in times of economic shocks.* Washington, D.C.: World Bank Publications.

Lykes, M. B. (2013). Participatory and action research as a transformative praxis: Responding to humanitarian crises from the margins. *American Psychologist*, 68 (8), 774.

Lyon, B. (2008). Changing tactics: Globalization and the U.S. immigrant worker rights movement. *UCLA Journal of International Law and Foreign Affairs*, 13, 161–196.

MacNair, R. H. (2014). *Research strategies for community practice.* New York: Routledge.

Macrine, S. L. (2011). *The War on Youth.* Educational Review, 14 (7), 1–18.

Maddison, S., & Scalmer, S. (2006). *Activist wisdom: practical knowledge and creative tension in social movements.* Kensington, NSW, Australia: UNSW Press.

Makhoul, J., Alameddine, M., & Afifi, R. A. (2012). 'I felt that I was benefiting someone': Youth as agents of change in a refugee community project. *Health Education Research*, 27 (5), 914–926.

Males, M. A. (1996). *Scapegoat generation: America's war on adolescents.* Monroe, ME: Common Courage Press.

Males, M. A. (1999). *Framing youth: 10 myths about the next generation.* Monroe, ME: Common Courage Press.

Malinick, T. E., Tindall, D. B., & Diani, M. (2013). Network centrality and social movement media coverage: A two-mode network analytic approach. *Social Networks*, 35 (2), 148–158.

Manganelli, S., Lucidi, F., & Alivernini, F. (2014). Adolescents' expected civic participation: The role of civic knowledge and efficacy beliefs. *Journal of Adolescence*, 37 (5), 632–641.

Mannino, C. A., Snyder, M., & Omoto, A. M. (2011). Why do people get involved? Motivations for volunteerism and other forms of social action. In D. Dunning (Ed.), *Social motivation* (pp. 127–146). Florence, KY: Psychology Press.

Mansfield, K. C. (2013). How listening to student voices informs and strengthens social justice research and practice. *Educational Administration Quarterly*, doi:0013161X13505288

Mansfield, K. C. (2014). How listening to student voices informs and strengthens social justice research and practice. *Educational Administration Quarterly*, 50 (3), 392–430.

Marbley, A. F., & Dawson, S. C. (2008). African American youth involvement in civic affairs: A social action framework for community and civic engagement. *Black History Bulletin*, 71 (2), 34–35.

Marcias, T. (2008). Working toward a just, equitable, and local food system: The social impact of community-based agriculture. *Social Science Quarterly*, 89 (5), 1086–1101.

Marcelli, E. A., Power, G., & Spalding, M. J. (2001). Unauthorized Mexican immigrants and business-generated environmental hazards in Southern California. *Critical Planning*, 8 (1), 23–40.

Marcus, B. J., Omoto, A. M., & Winter, P. L. (2011). Environmentalism and community: Connections and implications for social action. *Ecopsychology*, 3 (1), 11–24.

Mare, A. (2013). A complicated but symbiotic affair: The relationship between mainstream media and social media in the coverage of social protests in southern Africa. *Ecquid Novi: African Journalism Studies*, 34 (1), 83–98.

Marri, A. R., & Walker, E. N. (2008). "Our leaders are us": Youth activism in social movements project. *The Urban Review*, 40 (1), 5–20.

Marschall, M. J., & Stolle, D. (2004). Race and the city: Neighborhood context and the development of generalized trust. *Political Behavior*, 26 (2), 125–153.

Marshall, C., & Rossman, G. B. (2010). *Designing qualitative research.* Thousand Oaks, CA: Sage.

Martin, D. G., & Miller, B. (2003). Space and contentious politics. *Mobilization: An International Journal*, 8 (2), 143–156.

Martin, W. (2014). Community-based service learning: The platform for applied learning. *Journal of Human Resources Education*, 8 (1), 1–13.

Martinez, L. M. (2005). Yes we can: Latino participation in unconventional politics. *Social Forces*, 84 (1), 135–155.

Martinez, R. A. (2014). *Counter Culture Youth: Immigrant Rights Activism and the Undocumented Youth Vanguard* (Doctoral dissertation, University of New Mexico).

Mary, A. A. (2014). Re-evaluating the concept of adulthood and the framework of transition. *Journal of Youth Studies*, 17 (3), 415–429.

Mason, C. (2012). The civic engagement of young people living in areas of socio-economic disadvantage. *Debates in Citizenship Education*, 80.

Mason, J., & Hood, S. (2011). Exploring issues of children as actors in social research. *Children and Youth Services Review*, 33 (4), 490–495.

Masten, A. S., Liebkind, K., & Hernandez, D. J. (Eds.). (2012). *Realizing the potential of immigrant youth.* New York: Cambridge University Press.

Masuda, J. R., Poland, B., & Baxter, J. (2010). Reaching for environmental health justice: Canadian experiences for a comprehensive research, policy and advocacy agenda in health promotion. *Health promotion international*, daq041.

Maton, K. I. (2008). Empowering community settings: Agents of individual development, community betterment, and positive social change. *American Journal of Community Psychology*, 41 (1–2), 4–21.

Matsuoka, A., & Sorenson, J. (2014). Social justice beyond human beings: Trans-species social justice. *Animals in Social Work: Why and How They Matter*, 64.

Maulucci, M. S. R. (2012). Social justice research in science education: Methodologies, positioning, and implications for future research. In B. J. Fraser, K. Tobin & C. J. McRobbie (Eds.), *Second international handbook of science education* (pp. 583–594). Amsterdam, Netherlands: Springer Netherlands.

Mayer, M. (2012). The "right to the city" in urban social movements. In N. Brenner, P. Marcuse, & M. Mayer (Eds.), *Cities for people, not for profit: Critical urban theory and the right to the city* (pp. 63–85). New York: Routledge.

Mayer, M. (2013). First world urban activism: Beyond austerity urbanism and creative city politics. *City*, 17 (1), 5–19.

Mayhew, M. J., & Fernández, S. D. (2007). Pedagogical practices that contribute to social justice outcomes. *The Review of Higher Education*, 31 (1), 55–80.

Mayo, P. (2004). *Liberating praxis: Paulo Freire's legacy for radical education and politics.* London, ON, Canada: Cente for Digital Philosophy, University of Western Ontario.

McAdams, D. P. (2013). Life authorship: A psychological challenge for emerging adulthood, as illustrated in two notable case studies. *Emerging Adulthood*, doi:2167696813481774

McBride, A. M. (2006). Civic engagement, older adults, and inclusion. *Generations*, 30 (4), 66–71.

McClay, W., & McAllister, T. (Eds.). (2014). *Why place matters: Geography, identity, and civic life in modern America.* New York: Encounter Books.

McCormack, B., & Titchen, A. (2006). Critical creativity: Melding, exploding, blending. *Educational Action Research*, 14 (2), 239–266.

McCurdy, P. (2012). Social movements, protest and mainstream media. *Sociology compass*, 6 (3), 244–255.

McGarvey, C. (2005). Immigrants and civic engagement. *National Civic Review*, 94 (3), 35–41.

McInerney, P. (2009). Toward a critical pedagogy of engagement for alienated youth: Insights from Freire and school-based research. *Critical Studies in Education*, 50 (1), 23–35.

McInerney, P., & Smyth, J. (2014). 'I want to get a piece of paper that says I can do stuff': Youth narratives of educational opportunities and constraints in low socio-economic neighbourhoods. *Ethnography and Education* (ahead-of-print), 1–14.

McIntyre-Mills, J. J. (2003). *Critical system praxis for social and economic justice: Participatory policy design and governance for a global age*. New York: Kluwer.

McKay, C. (2010). Critical service learning: A school social work intervention. *Children & Schools*, 32 (1), 5–13.

McKenzie, K. B., Christman, D. E., Hernandez, F., Fierro, E., Capper, C. A., Dantley, M., . . . & Scheurich, J. J. (2008). From the field: A proposal for educating leaders for social justice. *Educational Administration Quarterly*, 44 (1), 111–138.

McLaren, P. (2003). Critical pedagogy: A look at the major concepts. In A. Darder, M. P. Baltodano & R. D. Torres (Eds.), *The critical pedagogy reader* (pp. 69–96). New York: Routledge.

McLaughlin, H. (2006). Involving young service users as co-researchers: Possibilities, benefits and costs. *British Journal of Social Work*, 36 (8), 1395–1410.

McLaughlin, M., Scott, W. R., Deschenes, S., Hopkins, K., & Newman, A. (2009). *Between movement and establishment: Organizations advocating for youth*. Palo Alto, CA: Stanford University Press.

McNeese, T. (2013). *Disability rights movement*. Edina, MN: ABDO Publishing Company.

McQuade, S. (2014). Creating "open space" to promote social justice. In R. Milkman & E. Ott (Eds.), *New labor in New York: Precarious workers and the future of the labor movement* (p. 208). Ithaca, NY: Cornell University Press.

McReynolds, J. (2014). Service learning from the perspective of community partner organizations. *Journal of Undergraduate Research*, XVII.

Mead, M. N. (2008). Urban issues: The sprawl of food deserts. *Environmental Health Perspectives*, 116 (8), A335–A336.

Meals, K. (2012). Nurturing the seeds of food justice: Unearthing the impact of institutionalized racism on access to healthy food in urban African-American communities. *Scholar*, 15, 97–138.

Menjívar, C., & Kanstroom, D. (Eds.). (2013). *Constructing immigrant 'illegality': Critiques, experiences, and responses*. New York: Cambridge University Press.

Merves, M. L., Rodgers, C. R., Silver, E. J., Sclafane, J. H., & Bauman, L. J. (2015). Engaging and sustaining adolescents in community-based participatory research: Structuring a youth-friendly community-based participatory research environment. *Family & Community Health*, 38 (1), 22–32.

Metz, E. (2014). State of the field: Youth community service in the USA. In *Handbook of Child Well-Being* (pp. 977–997). Springer Netherlands.

Meyer, D. S. (2009). How social movements matter. In J. Goodwin & J. M. Jasper (Eds.), *The social movements reader: Cases and examples*, 2nd ed. (pp. 417–422). New York: John-Wiley-Blackwell.

Meyer, J. W., & Jepperson, R. L. (2000). The 'actors' of modern society: The cultural construction of social agency. *Sociological Theory*, 18 (1), 100–120.

Meyers, S. A. (2009). Service learning as an opportunity for personal and social transformation. *International Journal of Teaching and Learning in Higher Education*, 21 (3), 373–381.

Mike, H. M. L., Kelleher, J., & Kaestner, K. (2014). *The experiences of volunteering and service learning: A case study of a service learning project at "Crossroads Foundation."*

Miller, A. (2014). The politics of radical pedagogy. In M. Bose, P. Horrigan, C. Doble, & S. C. Shipp (Eds.), *Community matters: Service-learning in engaged design and planning* (pp. 151–166). New York: Routledge.

Miller, B., & Nicholls, W. (2013). Social movements in urban society: The city as a space of politicization. *Urban Geography*, 34 (4), 452–473.

Miller, J., & Garran, A. M. (2008). *Racism in the United States: Implications for the helping professions*. Independence, KY: Wadsworth.

Miller, L., Hess, K., & Orthmann, C. (2013). *Community policing: Partnerships for problem solving*. Independence, KY: Cengage Learning.

Miller, P. M., & Engel, M. T. (2011). Forging vertical linkages on the public sphere: School-church engagement. *Educational Foundation*, 25 (1–2), 25–42.

Miller, R. L., Kobes, S. K., & Forney, J. C. (2008). Building the capacity of small community-based organizations to better serve youth. In M. Shinn & H. Yoshikawa (Eds.), *Toward positive youth development: Transforming schools and community programs* (pp. 173–192). New York: Oxford University Press.

Minkler, M. (2012). Introduction to community organizing and community building. In M. Minkler (Ed.), *Community organizing and community building for health and welfare* (pp. 5–26). New Brunswick, NJ: Rutgers University Press.

Mironesco, M. (2014). Using service learning to enhance a hybrid course curriculum in the "politics of food". *MERLOT Journal of Online Learning and Teaching*, 10 (3), 524–534.

Mitchell, D. (2003). *The right to the city: Social justice and the fight for public space*. New York: Guilford Press.

Mitchell, T. D. (2008). Traditional vs. critical service-learning: Engaging the literature to differentiate two models. *Michigan Journal of Community Service Learning*, 14 (2).

Mitchell, T. D. (2013). Deepening community engagement speaks to our commitment to develop innovations in community-based learning and service that. In A. Hoy & M. Johnson (Eds.), *Deepening community engagement in higher education: Forging new pathways* (p. 263). London, England: Palgrave Macmillan.

Mitchell, T. D. (2014). Using a Critical Service-Learning Approach to Facilitate Civic Identity Development. *Theory Into Practice* (just-accepted).

Mitra, D. (2006). Increasing student voice and moving toward youth leadership. *The Prevention Researcher*, 13 (1), 7–10.

Mitra, D. L. (2009). Collaborating with students: Building youth-adult partnerships in schools. *American Journal of Education*, 115 (3), 407–436.

Mitra, D. L., Frick, W. C., & Crawford, E. R. (2011). The ethical dimensions of student voice activities in the United States. In G. Czerniawski & W. Kidd (Eds.), *The student voice handbook: Bridging the academic/practitioner divide* (pp. 367–378). Bingley BD United Kingdom: Emerald Group Publishing.

Mitra, D., Serriere, S., & Kirshner, B. (2013). Youth participation in US contexts: Student voice without a national mandate. *Children & Society*, 28 (4), 292–304.

Mix, T. L. (2011). Rally the people: Building local-environmental justice grassroots coalitions and enhancing social capital. *Sociological Inquiry*, 81 (2), 174–194.

Mockler, N., & Groundwater-Smith, S. (2015). *Engaging with student voice in research, education and community* (pp. 109–125). New York: Springer International Publishing.

Moely, B. E., Furco, A., & Reed, J. (2008). Charity and social change: The impact of individual preferences on service-learning outcomes. *Michigan Journal of Community Service Learning*, 15 (1), 37–48.

Molee, L. M., Henry, M. E., Sessa, V. I., & McKinney-Prupis, E. R. (2010). Assessing learning in service-learning courses through critical reflection. *Journal of Experiential Education*, 33 (3), 239–257.

Moll, A., & Renault, L. (2014). Rebirth, empowerment, and youth leading social change: Non-formal education in Honduras. *Gender & Development*, 22 (1), 31–47.

Montgomery, S. E. (2014). Critical democracy through digital media production in a third-grade classroom. *Theory & Research in Social Education*, 42 (2), 197–227.

Moore, S. A. (2011). Preface: Social justice in child, youth and family studies. *International Journal of Child, Youth and Family Studies*, 2 (3/4), 353–360.

Moran-Ellis, J., Bandt, A., & Sünker, H. (2014). Children's well-being and politics. In A. Ben-Arieh, F. Casas, I. Frønes & J. E. Korbin (Eds), *Handbook of child well-being* (pp. 415–435). Amsterdam, Netherlands: Springer Netherlands.

Morgan, M. L., Vera, E. M., Gonzales, R. R., Conner, W., Vacek, K. B., & Coyle, L. D. (2009). Subjective well-being in urban adolescents: Interpersonal, individual, and community influences. *Youth & Society*, 44 (3), 331–347.

Morimoto, S. A. (2010). Networked democracy: School-based volunteerism and youth civic engagement. *Research in Political Sociology*, 18, 129–149.

Morimoto, S. A. (2013). Civic engagement and the emergence of race: American youth negotiate citizenship. *Sociological Studies of Children and Youth*, 16, 153–175.

Morimoto, S. A., & Friedland, L. A. (2013). Cultivating success: Youth achievement, capital and civic engagement in the contemporary United States. *Sociological Perspectives*, 56 (4), 523–546.

Morland, K., Diez Roux, A. V., & Wing, S. (2006). Supermarkets, other food stores, and obesity. The Atherosclerosis risk in communities study. *American Journal of Preventive Medicine*, 30 (4), 333–339.

Morrel-Samuels, S., Hutchison, P., Perkinson, L., Bostic, B., & Zimmerman, M. (2015). *Selecting, implementing and adapting youth empowerment solutions.*

Morrell, E. (2004). *Becoming critical researchers: Literacy and empowerment for urban youth (Vol. 227)*. New York: Peter Lang.

Morrell, E. (2008). *Critical literacy and urban youth: Pedagogies of access, dissent, and liberation*. New York: Routledge.

Morrell, E., & Duncan-Andrade, J. M. (2002). Promoting academic literacy with urban youth through engaging hip-hop culture. *English Journal*, 88–92.

Morris, A. (2014). The groundbreaking Wichita sit-in movement: What has this got to do with the liberation of Black people? R. C. Smith, C. Johnson & R. G. Newby (Eds.), *The impact of Ronald W. Walters on African American thought and leadership* (pp. 57–84). Albany, NY: State of New York University Press.

Morsillo, J., & Prilleltensky, I. (2007). Social action with youth: Interventions, evaluation, and psychopolitical validity. *Journal of Community Psychology*, 35 (6), 725–740.

Mosedale, S. (2014). Women's empowerment as a development goal: Taking a feminist standpoint. *Journal of International Development*, 26 (8), 1115–1125.

Mosley, J. (2013). Recognizing new opportunities: Reconceptualizing policy advocacy in everyday organizational practice. *Social Work*, 58 (3), 231–239.

Muhlke, C. (2008, October 12). Food fighters. *The New York Times*, p. 78.

Mueller, M. P., & Tippins, D. J. (Eds.). (2014). *EcoJustice, citizen science and youth activism: Situated tensions for science education* (Vol. 1). New York: Springer.

Mueller, S. (2014). *"People are people": Benefits of inclusive service.*

Mumm, J. (1997). Democracy needs direct participation. *The Good Society*, 7 (3), 32–34.

Musgrove, F. (2013). *Youth & Social Order Ils 149*. New York: Routledge.

Musil, C. M. (2009). Educating students for personal and social responsibility. In B. Jacoby & Associates (Eds.), *Civic engagement in higher education* (pp. 49–68).

Nabatchi, T., Gastil, J., Weiksner, G. M., & Leighninger, M. (Eds.). (2012). *Democracy in motion: Evaluating the practice and impact of deliberative civic engagement*. New York: Oxford University Press.

Nash, G. B. (2006). *The unknown American Revolution: The unruly birth of democracy and the struggle to create America*. New York: Penguin.

Navarro, A. (2014). *Mexican American youth organization: Avant-garde of the Chicano movement in Texas*. Austin, TX: University of Texas Press.

Naylor, R. L. (Ed.). (2014). *The evolving sphere of food security*. New York: Oxford University Press.

Negrón-Gonzales, G. (2009). Hegemony, ideology & oppositional consciousness: Undocumented youth and the personal-political struggle for educational justice. *Institute for the Study of Social Change Fellows Working Papers*. Berkeley, CA: University of California.

Negrón-Gonzales, G. (2013). Navigating "illegality": Undocumented youth & oppositional consciousness. *Children and Youth Services Review*, 35 (8), 1284–1290.

Nelson, B. (2013). The legacy of Ludlow: Exploring labor dynamics with urban youth. *Youth Theatre Journal*, 27 (1), 74–86.

Nenga, S. K., & Taft, J. K. (2013). Introduction: Conceptualizing youth engagement. *Sociological Studies of Children and Youth*, 16, xvii–xxiii.

Neumayer, C., & Stald, G. (2014). The mobile phone in street protest: Texting, tweeting, tracking, and tracing. *Mobile Media & Communication*, 2 (2), 117–133.

Neville, H. A. (2015). Social justice mentoring supporting the development of future leaders for struggle, resistance, and transformation. *The Counseling Psychologist*, 43 (1), 157–169.

Newman, J. L., Dantzler, J., & Coleman, A. N. (2014). Science in action: How middle school students are changing their world through STEM service-learning projects. *Theory Into Practice* (just accepted).

Newman, M. (2006, May 1). Immigrants stage protests across U.S. *The New York Times*. Retrieved from http://www.nytimes.com/2006/05/01/us/01cnd-immig.html?sq=immigrant%20protests%20may%202006&st=cse&scp=4& pagewanted=all Retrieved 8–3–11

Niblet, B. (2015). *Narrating Activist Education: Teachers' Stories of Affecting Social and Political Change* (Master's Thesis, Lakehead University). Retrieved from http://thesis.lakeheadu.ca:8080/handle/2453/604

Nicholls, W. (2013a). *The DREAMers: How the undocumented youth movement transformed the immigrant rights debate*. Palo Alto, CA: Stanford University Press.

Nicholls, W. (2013b). Voice and power in the immigrant rights movement. In C. Menjívar & D. Kanstroom (Eds.), *Constructing immigrant 'illegality': Critiques, experiences, and responses* (pp. 225–245). New York: Cambridge University Press.

Nieto, S., & McDonough, K. (2011). "Placing equity front and center" revisited. In *Studying diversity in teacher education* (pp. 363–384).

Nissen, L. B. (2011). Community-directed engagement and positive youth development: Developing positive and progressive pathways between youth and their communities in Reclaiming Futures. *Children and Youth Services Review*, 33, S23–S28.

Nixon, J. T. (2014). *Speaking out for change: Using a dialogic approach and diverse, multimodal texts to enhance critical literacy* (Doctoral dissertation, University of Victoria).

Noguera, P., & Cannella, C. M. (2006). Youth agency, resistance, and civic activism: The public commitment to social justice. In S. Ginwright, P. Noguera, & J. Cammarota (Eds.), *Beyond resistance* (pp. 333–347). New York: Routledge.

Nolan, K. M. (2011). Oppositional behavior in urban schooling: Toward a theory of resistance for new times. *International Journal of Qualitative Studies in Education*, 24 (5), 559–572.

Nolas, S. M. (2014). Exploring young people's and youth workers' experiences of spaces for 'youth development': creating cultures of participation. *Journal of Youth Studies*, 17 (1), 26–41.

Noonan, J. (2015). When soda is a social justice issue: Design and documentation of a participatory action research project with youth. *Educational Action Research* (ahead-of-print), 1–13.

Nordås, R., & Davenport, C. (2013). Fight the youth: Youth bulges and state repression. *American Journal of Political Science*, 57 (4), 926–940.

North, C. (2008). What is all this talk about "social justice"? Mapping the terrain of education's latest catchphrase. *The Teachers College Record*, 110 (6), 1182–1206.

Norvell, K. H., & Gelmon, S. B. (2011). Assessing civic engagement. In R. L. Miller, E. Amsel, B. M. Kowalewski, B. C. Beins, K. D. Keith, & B. F. Peden (Eds.), *Promoting student engagement* (Vol. 1; pp. 265–270). Retrieved from http://stp.wildapricot.org/Resources/Documents/ebooks/pse2011vol1.pdf#page=270

Nygreen, K., Kwon, S. A., & Sanchez, P. (2006). Urban youth building community. *Journal of Community Practice*, 14 (1–2), 107–123.

Obenchain, K. M., & Callahan, R. M. (2014). Building the civic potential of immigrant youth. *Social Education*, 78 (4), 179–182.

Ober Allen, J., Alaimo, K., Elam, D., & Perry, E. (2008). Growing vegetables and values: Benefits of neighborhood-based community gardens for youth development and nutrition. *Journal of Hunger & Environmental Nutrition*, 3 (4), 418–439.

Ochoa, G. L., & Ochoa, E. C. (2007). Framing Latina/o immigration, education, and activism. *Sociology Compass*, 1 (2), 701–719.

O'Donoghue, J. L., & Strobel, K. R. (2007). Directivity and freedom: Adult support of activism among urban youth. *American Behavioral Scientist*, 51 (3), 465–485.

Ohmer, M. L. (2007). Citizen participation in neighborhood organizations and its relationship to volunteers' self-and collective efficacy and sense of community. *Social Work Research*, 31 (2), 109–120.

Ohmer, M. L., & Korr, W. S. (2006). The effectiveness of community practice interventions: A review of the literature. *Research on Social Work Practice*, 16 (2), 132–145.

Olemdo, I. M. (2007). *Addressing controversy in the classroom: Teaching about immigrant rights in Chicago schools*. Great Institute Publication No. GCP-07–07. Chicago, IL: College of Urban Planning and Public Affairs, University of Illinois at Chicago.

Olsen, M. M. (2015). Somewhere between the ideal and the real, the civic engagement "expert" learns and lets go. In A. E. Lesen (Ed.), *Scientists, experts, and civic engagement: Walking a fine line* (pp. 27–42). London, England: Ashgate.

Ollis, T. (2011). Learning in social action: The informal and social learning dimensions of circumstantial and lifelong activists. *Australian Journal of Adult Learning*, 51 (2), 248.

Oman, R. F., Vesely, S. K., Aspy, C. B., & Tolma, E. L. (2015). Prospective associations among assets and successful transition to early adulthood. *American Journal of Public Health*, 105 (1), e51–e56.

O'Meara, K. (2008). Motivation for faculty community engagement: Learning from exemplars. *Journal of Higher Education Outreach and Engagement*, 12 (1), 7–30.

O'Meara, K., & Niehaus, E. (2009). Service-learning is . . . How faculty explain their practice. *Michigan Journal of Community Service Learning*, 16 (1), 17–32.

Omoto, A. M. (Ed.). (2014). *Processes of community change and social action.* Florence, KY: Psychology Press.

Opotow, S. (2011). Social injustice. In D. J. Christie (Ed.), *The encyclopedia of peace psychology.* Malden, MA: Blackwell Publisher.

Orsini, M. (2010). From "community run" to "community based"? Exploring the dynamics of civil society-state transformation in urban Montreal. *défavorisées: La mondialisation et la santé des Canadiens*, 172.

Orton, A. (2013). Conclusion: Sustaining community practice for the future. In S. Banks, H. Butcher, A. Orton, & J. Robertson (Eds.), *Managing community practice: Principles, policies and programmes* (pp. 191–204). Bristol, England: Policy Press.

O'Shea, E. (2013). First steps to developing service learning initiatives using emancipatory action research. *Australasian Journal of University-Community Engagement*, 8 (1), 25–50.

Otis, M. D. (2006). Youth as engaged citizens and community change advocates through the Lexington Youth Leadership Academy. *Journal of Community Practice*, 14 (1/2), 71–88.

Ottaway, M., & Hamzawy, M. (2011). *Protest movements and political change in the Arab world.* New York. NY: Carnegie Endowment for International Peace.

Ozer, E. J., & Douglas, L. (2013). The impact of participatory research on urban teens: An experimental evaluation. *American Journal of community psychology*, 51 (1–2), 66–75.

Ozer, E. J., Newlan, S., Douglas, L., & Hubbard, E. (2013). "Bounded" empowerment: Analyzing tensions in the practice of youth-led participatory research in urban public schools. *American Journal of Community Psychology*, 52 (1–2), 13–26.

Pachi, D., & Barrett, M. (2014). Civic and political engagement among ethnic minority and immigrant youth. In R. Dimitrova, M. Bender, & F. van de Vijver (Eds.), *Global perspectives on well-being in immigrant families* (pp. 189–211). New York: Springer.

Pallares, A., & Flores-Gonzalez, N. (Eds.). (2010). *Marcha: Latino Chicago and the immigrant rights movement.* Urbana, IL: University of Illinois Press.

Parker, L., Olson, S., & Breiner, H. (Eds.). (2013). *Challenges and opportunities for change in food marketing to children and youth: Workshop summary.* Washington, D.C.: National Academies Press.

Pasek, J., Kenski, K., Romer, D., & Jamieson, K. H. (2006). America's youth and community engagement: How use of mass media is related to civic activity and political awareness in 14- to 22-year-olds. *Communication Research*, 33 (3), 115–135.

Pasque, P. A., & Harris, B. (2013). Moving from social justice to social agency: Keeping it messy. In K. A. Kline (Ed.), *Reflection in action: A guidebook for student affairs professionals and teaching faculty.* Sterling, VA: Stylus Press.

Pate, P. E., Guerrero, A., & Dobie, D. F. (2015). Carrizo Springs, Texas—The story of the Systems Academy of Young Scientists (SAYS). In M. P. Mueller & D. J. Tippins (Eds.), *EcoJustice, citizen science and youth activism* (pp. 223–245). New York: Springer International Publishing.

Pauliina Kallio, K., & Häkli, J. (2011). Are there politics in childhood?. *Space and Polity*, 15 (1), 21–34.

Pearce, K. E., Freelon, D., & Kendzior, S. (2014). The effect of the Internet on civic engagement under authoritarianism: The case of Azerbaijan. *First Monday*, 19 (6). Retrieved from http://firstmonday.org/ojs/index.php/fm/article/view/5000/4092

Pearce, N. J., & Larson, R. W. (2006). How teens become engaged in youth development programs: The process of motivational change in a civic activism organization. *Applied Developmental Science*, 10 (3), 121–131.

Pearrow, M. M. (2008). A critical examination of an urban-based youth empowerment strategy: The teen empowerment program. *Journal of Community Practice*, 16 (4), 509–525.

Peffer, R. G. (2014). *Marxism, morality, and social justice*. Princeton, NJ: Princeton University Press.

Pellow, D. N. (2004). *Garbage wars: The struggle for environmental justice in Chicago*. Cambridge, MA: MIT Press.

Pellow, D. N., & Brehm, H. N. (2015). From the new ecological paradigm to total liberation: The emergence of a social movement frame. *The Sociological Quarterly*, 56 (1), 185–212.

Percy-Smith, B., & Thomas, N. (Eds.). (2010). *A handbook of children and young people's participation: Perspectives from theory and practice*. New York: Routledge.

Perkins, D. D., Bess, K. D., Cooper, D. G., Jones, D. L., Armstead, T., & Speer, P. W. (2007). Community organizational learning: Case studies illustrating a three-dimensional model of levels and orders of change. *Journal of Community Psychology*, 35 (3), 303–328.

Peréa, F. C., Groman, D., Lozano, A. M. T., Koomas, A., & Martinez, L. S. S. (2014). Urban parks and community development needs: Stories through images captured by youth. *Children Youth and Environments*, 24 (1), 158–172.

Perri, M. (2007). Vaughan youth cabinet: Youth participation in community planning and design. *Children Youth and Environments*, 17 (2), 581–593.

Peterson, T. H., Dolan, T., & Hanft, S. (2010). Partnering with youth organizers to prevent violence: An analysis of relationships, power, and change. *Progress in Community Health Partnerships: Research, Education, and Action*, 4 (3), 235–242.

Petrucka, P., Brooks, S., Smadu, G., McBeth, B., Bassendowski, S., Mackay, A., . . . & Fudger, S. (2014). At street level: Learnings, voices, experiences, and lifestyles of street involved youth. *Nursing and Health*, 2 (2), 48–56.

Pezzullo, P. C., & Sandler, R. (2007). Introduction: Revisiting the environmental justice challenge to environmentalism. In R. Sandler & P. C. Pezzullo (Eds.), *Environmental justice and environmentalism: The social justice challenge to the environmental movement* (pp. 1–24). Cambridge, MA: MIT Press.

Phillips, A. (2011). Service-learning and social work competency-based education: A "goodness of fit"?. *Advances in Social Work*, 12 (1), 1–20.

Philly Food Justice. (2015). *The Youth Food Bill of Rights*. Retrieved from http://www.youthfoodbillofrights.com/

Piotrowski, G. (2014, July). Youth social movements and democratization. In *XVIII ISA World Congress of Sociology* Isaconf. Retrieved from https://isaconf.confex.com/isaconf/wc2014/webprogram/Paper48680.html

Pipes, P. F., & Ebaugh, H. R. (2002). Faith-based coalitions, social services, and government funding. *Sociology of Religion*, 63 (1), 49–68.

Pittman, K., Ferber, T., & Irby, M. (2000). *Youth as effective citizens.* Takoma Park, MD: International Youth Foundation.

Pittman, K., Martin, S., & Williams, A. (2007, July). Core principles for engaging young people in community change. In *Forum for youth investment.* Forum for Youth Investment. The Cady-Lee House, 7064 Eastern Avenue NW, Washington, D.C. 20012–2031.

Polletta, F. (2012). *Freedom is an endless meeting: Democracy in American social movements.* Chicago, IL: University of Chicago Press.

Pompa, L. (2002). Service-learning as crucible: Reflections on immersion, context, power, and transformation. *Michigan Journal of Community Service Learning*, 9 (1), 67–76

Poncelet, J. A. P. (2014). *A Community-Based Grassroots Organization in the South Bronx as a Catalyst for Youth Organizing and Activism: Analyzing the Dynamics of a Transformative Youth Program* (Doctoral dissertation, University of Washington).

Pope, I. V. (2014). Critical civic consciousness: Exploring the US civic opportunity gap with Giroux and Freire. *Citizenship Teaching & Learning*, 9 (3), 241–256.

Popple, K. (2012). Community practice. In M. Gray, J. Midgley, S. A. Webb (Eds.), *The SAGE handbook of social work* (pp. 279–294). Thousand Oaks, CA: Sage.

Porfilio, B. J., & Gorlewski, J. A. (2012). Promoting active citizenship through the arts and youth: Canadian youth-led organizations as beacons of hope and transformation. *International Journal of Progressive Education*, 8 (3), 48–61.

Porta, D. D. (2013). *Can democracy be saved: Participation, deliberation and social movements.* New York: John Wiley & Sons.

Porta, D. D., & Diani, M. (2006). *Social movements: An introduction.* New York: Wiley & Sons.

Powell, L. A., Williamson, J. B., & Branco, K. J. (1996). *The senior rights movement: Framing the policy debate in America.* New York: Twayne Publishers.

Powers, M., & Faden, R. (2006). *Social justice: The moral foundations of public health and health policy.* New York: Oxford University Press.

Pratt, C. A., Stevens, J., & Daniels, S. (2008). Childhood obesity prevention and treatment: Recommendations for future research. *American Journal of Preventive Medicine*, 35 (3), 249–252.

Preiss, B., & Brunner, C. (Eds.). (2013). *Democracy in crisis: The dynamics of civil protest and civil resistance (Vol. 64).* Berlin, Germany: LIT Verlag Münster.

Prentice, M. (2007). Service learning and civic engagement. *Academic Questions*, 20 (2), 135–145.

Price, P. L., Lukinbeal, C., Gioioso, R. N., Arreola, D. D., Fernández, D. J., Ready, T., & de los Angeles Torres, M. (2011). Placing Latino civic engagement. *Urban Geography*, 32 (2), 179–207.

Priest, K. L., & Clegorne, N. A. (2015). Connecting to experience: High-impact practices for leadership development. *New Directions for Student Leadership*, 2015 (145), 71–83.

Prince, D. (2014). What about place? Considering the role of physical environment on youth imagining of future possible selves. *Journal of Youth Studies*, 17 (6), 697–715.

Prior, R. W. (2013). Knowing what is known: The subjective objective partnership. In S. McNiff (Ed.), *Art as research: Opportunities and challenges* (pp. 161–169). Bristol, UK: Intellect.

Pritzker, S., LaChapelle, A., & Tatum, J. (2012). "We need their help": Encouraging and discouraging adolescent civic engagement through Photovoice. *Children and Youth Services Review*, 34 (11), 2247–2254.

Proehl, K. (2012). Politicizing youth: Childhood studies on social change. *American Quarterly*, 64 (1), 171–180.

Pryor, B. N. K., & Outley, C. W. (2014). Just spaces: Urban recreation centers as sites for social justice youth development. *Journal of Leisure Research*, 46 (3), 272–290.

Pulido, L. (2007). A day without immigrants: The racial and class politics of immigrant exclusion. *Antipode*, 39 (1), 1–7.

Purcell, R., & Beck, D. (2010*). Popular education practice for youth and community development work*. Thousand Oaks, CA: SAGE.

Pyles, L. (2013). *Progressive community organizing: A critical approach for a globalizing world.* New York: Routledge.

Quane, J. M., & Rankin, B. H. (2006). Does it pay to participate? Neighborhood- based organizations and the social development of urban adolescents. *Children and Youth Services Review*, 28 (10), 1229–1250.

Quick, K. S., & Feldman, M. S. (2011). Distinguishing participation and inclusion. *Journal of Planning Education and Research*, 31 (3), 272–290.

Quijada, D. (2008). Reconciling research, rallies, and citizenship: Reflections on youth-led diversity workshops and inter-cultural alliances. *Social Justice*, 35 (1), 76–90.

Quijada Cerecer, D. A., Cahill, C., & Bradley, M. (2013). Toward a critical youth policy praxis: Critical youth studies and participatory action research. *Theory Into Practice*, 52 (3), 216–223.

Quinn, B. (2014). Other-oriented purpose: The potential roles of beliefs about the world and other people. *Youth & Society*, 46 (6), 779–800.

Quintelier, E. (2008). Who is politically active: The athlete, the scout member or the environmental activist? Young people, voluntary engagement and political. *Acta Sociologica*, 51 (4), 355–370.

Quiroz-Martinez, J., Wu, D. P., & Zimmerman, K. (2005). *ReGeneration: Young people shaping environmental justice.* Oakland, CA: Movement Strategy Center.

Qvortrup, J. (2014). Sociology: Societal structure, development of childhood, and the well-being of children. In *Handbook of child well-being* (pp. 663–707). Rotterdam, Netherlands: Springer Netherlands.

Raby, R. (2005). What is resistance?. *Journal of Youth Studies*, 8 (2), 151–171.

Racher, F. E., & Annis, R. C. (2007). Respecting culture and honoring diversity in community practice. *Research and Theory for Nursing Practice*, 21 (4), 270.

Rachieff, P. (2008, August 21). Immigrant rights are labor rights. *ZNET: A community of people committed to social change.*

Radcliffe, J. (2006, April 11). "Children make up large part of rally; many parents say they pulled youngsters from school after being counted present." *Houston Chronicle*, p. B6.

Ramey, H. L., & Rose-Krasnor, L. (2012). Contexts of structured youth activities and positive youth development. *Child Development Perspectives*, 6 (1), 85–91.

Ranieri, M., & Bruni, I. (2013). Mobile storytelling and informal education in a suburban area: A qualitative study on the potential of digital narratives for young second-generation immigrants. *Learning, Media and Technology*, 38 (2), 217–235.

Ransom, L. S. (2009). Sowing the seeds of citizenship and social justice service-learning in a public speaking course. *Education, Citizenship and Social Justice*, 4 (3), 211–224.

Read, S., & Overfelt, D. (2014). *Civic engagement: 10 questions to shape an effective plan.* Washington, D.C.: ICMA Publishing.

Reason, R. D., & Hemer, K. (2014). *Civic learning and engagement: A review of the literature on civic learning, assessment, and instruments.* Retrieved from http://www.aacu.org/sites/default/files/files/qc/CivicLearningLiteratureReviewRev1-26-15.pdf

Redmond, S., & Dolan, P. (2014). Towards a conceptual model of youth leadership development. *Child & Family Social Work.*

Reichert, E. (Ed.). (2013). *Challenges in human rights: A social work perspective.* New York: Columbia University Press.

Reiman, R. A. (2010). *The New Deal and American youth: Ideas and ideals in a Depression decade.* Athens, GA: University of Georgia Press.

Reimers, F. (2007). Civic education when democracy is in flux: The impact of empirical research on policy and practice in Latin America. *Citizenship Teaching and Learning,* 3 (2), 22–39.

Reis, G., Ng-A-Fook, N., & Glithero, L. (2015). Provoking EcoJustice—Taking citizen science and youth activism beyond the school curriculum. In M. P. Mueller & D. J. Tippins (Eds.), *EcoJustice, citizen science and youth activism* (pp. 39–61). London, England: Springer International Publishing.

Reisch, M. (2012). *The History of Community Practice in US Social Work: Interdisciplinary Scholarship for Community Practice in the 21st C.* Retrieved from http://archive.hshsl.umaryland.edu/handle/10713/2658

Reisch, M. (Ed.). (2014). *The Routledge international handbook of social justice.* New York: Routledge.

Reisch, M., Ife, J., & Weil, M. (2012). Social justice, human rights, values, and community practice. In M. O. Weil, M. S. Reisch, & M. L. Ohmer (Ed.), *Handbook of community practice* (pp. 73–103). Thousand Oaks, CA: Sage.

Reitan, R., & Gibson, S. (2012). Climate change or social change? Environmental and leftist praxis and participatory action research. *Globalizations,* 9 (3), 395–410.

Reiter, H. (2014). Youth research as transformative social critique. P. Kelly (Ed.), *A critical youth studies for the 21st century* (pp. 349–373). Leiden, Holland: Brill Academic Publishers:

Rendón, L. I. (2009). *Sentipensante (sensing/thinking) pedagogy: Educating for wholeness, social justice and liberation.* Sterling, VA: Stylus Publishing, LLC.

Reyes, M., Páez, A., & Morency, C. (2014). Walking accessibility to urban parks by children: A case study of Montreal. *Landscape and Urban Planning,* 125, 38–47.

Reynaert, D., & Roose, R. (2014). Children's rights and the capability approach: Discussing children's agency against the horizon of the institutionalised youth land. In *Children's rights and the capability approach* (pp. 175–193). Rotterdam, Netherlands: Springer Netherlands.

Reynolds, J. F., & Chun, E. W. (2013). Figuring youth citizenship: Communicative practices mediating the cultural politics of citizenship and age. *Language & Communication,* 33 (4), 473–480.

Reynolds, K. (2015). Disparity despite diversity: Social injustice in New York City's urban agriculture system. *Antipode,* 47 (1), 240–259.

Rheingans, R., & Hollands, R. (2013). 'There is no alternative?': Challenging dominant understandings of youth politics in late modernity through a case study of the 2010 UK student occupation movement. *Journal of Youth Studies,* 16 (4), 546–564.

Rheingold, H. (2008). Using participatory media and public voice to encourage civic engagement. In *Civic life online: Learning how digital media can engage youth* (pp. 97–118).

Rhoads, R. A. (2009). Learning from students as agents of social change: Toward an emancipatory vision of the university. *Journal of Change Management,* 9 (3), 309–322.

Rhodes, E. L. (2005). *Environmental justice in America: A new paradigm.* Bloomingdale, IN: Indiana University Press.

Richards-Schuster, K. (2015, January). Youth participatory methods for evaluating youth civic engagement: findings from a multi-year evaluation program. In *Society for*

Social Work and Research 19th Annual Conference: The Social and Behavioral Importance of Increased Longevity. SSWR.

Richards-Schuster, K., Juras, J., Young, S. R., & Timmermans, R. J. (2013). What constitutes youth organizing? Exploring the role of conservative contexts in understanding practice. *Children and Youth Services Review,* 35 (8), 1291–1296.

Richards-Schuster, R., & Dobbie, D. (2011). Tagging walls and planting seeds: Creating spaces for youth civic action. *Journal of Community Practice,* 19 (3), 234–251.

Richardson, C., & Reynolds, V. (2012). "Here we are, amazingly alive": Holding ourselves together with an ethic of social justice in community work. *International Journal of Child, Youth and Families,* 1 (1), 1–19.

Riemer, M., Lynes, J., & Hickman, G. (2014). A model for developing and assessing youth-based environmental engagement programmes. *Environmental Education Research,* 20 (4).

Rigolon, A., & Flohr, T. L. (2014). Access to parks for youth as an environmental justice issue: Access inequalities and possible solutions. *Buildings,* 4 (2), 69–94.

Rivera, L. M. (2014). Ethnic-racial stigma and health disparities: From psychological theory and evidence to public policy solutions. *Journal of Social Issues,* 70 (2), 198–205.

Roach, C. M. (2009). *Community collaboratives: Building civic capacity for youth development.* Palo Alto, CA: Stanford University.

Robbins, C. G. (2012). Disposable youth/damaged democracy: Youth, neoliberalism, and the promise of pedagogy in the work of Henry Giroux. *Policy Futures in Education,* 10 (6), 627–641.

Roberts, J. (2008). From experience to neo-experiential education: Variations on a theme. *Journal of Experiential Education,* 31 (1), 19–35.

Roberts, R. A., Bell, L. A., & Murphy, B. (2008). Flipping the script: Analyzing youth talk about race and racism. *Anthropology & Education Quarterly,* 39 (3), 334–354.

Robinson, T. (2000). Service learning as justice advocacy: Can political scientists do politics? *PS: Political Science and Politics,* 33 (3), 605–612.

Rockwell, L. (2006, April 14). Students help push debate on illegals; young immigrants seek path to college. *The Atlanta Journal-Constitution,* p. A4.

Rodríguez, L. F., & Brown, T. M. (2009). From voice to agency: Guiding principles for participatory action research with youth. *New Directions for Youth Development,* 2009 (123), 19–34.

Rodríguez, L. F., & Oseguera, L. (2015). Our deliberate success: Recognizing what works for Latina/o Students across the educational pipeline. *Journal of Hispanic Higher Education,* doi:1538192715570637

Roehlkepartain, E. C. (2009). *Service-Learning in Community-Based Organizations: A Practical Guide to Starting and Sustaining High-Quality Programs.* National Service-Learning Clearinghouse. Retrieved from http://www.communityservicelearning.ca/en/documents/Service-LearninginCommunity-BasedOrganizationsToolkit2009.pdf

Rogaly, B. (2012). *Class, spatial justice and the production of not-quite citizens.* Retrieved from http://placesforall.co.uk/wp-content/uploads/pdfs/Citizenship-Symposium-PDF-moocow-12–3–13.pdf

Rogers, J., Mediratta, K., & Shah, S. (2012). Building power, learning democracy: Youth organizing as a site of civic development. *Review of Research in Education,* 36 (1), 43–66.

Rogers, J., Morrell, E., & Enyedy, N. (2007). Studying the struggle: Contexts for learning and identity development for urban youth. *American Behavioral Scientist,* 51 (3), 419–443.

Rogers, R., & Schaenen, I. (2014). Critical discourse analysis in literacy education: A review of the literature. *Reading Research Quarterly*, 49 (1), 121–143.

Rogers, T., Schroeter, S., Wager, A., & Hague, C. (2014). Public pedagogies of street-entrenched youth: New literacies, identity and social critique. In K. Sanford, T. Rogers, & M. Kendrick (Eds.), *Everyday youth literacies* (pp. 47–61). Sinapore: Springer Singapore.

Rogers, T., Winters, K. L., Perry, M., & LaMonde, A. M. (2014). *Youth, critical literacies, and civic engagement: Arts, media, and literacy in the lives of adolescents*. New York: Routledge.

Rohe, J. F. (2006). *Ethics of immigration policy: A collection of essays*. Petoskey, MI: Social Contract Press.

Rohlinger, D. A., Kail, B., Taylor, M., & Conn, S. (2012). Outside the mainstream: Social movement organization media coverage in mainstream and partisan news outlets. *Research in Social Movements, Conflicts and Change*, 33 (1), 51–80.

Roholt, R. V., Baizerman, M., & Hildreth, R. W. (2014). *Becoming citizens: Deepening the craft of youth civic engagement*. New York: Routledge.

Romley, J. A., Cohen, D., Ringel, J., & Sturm, R. (2007). Alcohol and environmental justice: The density of liquor stores and bars in urban neighborhoods in the United States. *Journal of Studies on Alcohol and Drugs*, 68 (1), 48.

Rondini, A. C. (2015). Observations of critical consciousness development in the context of service learning. *Teaching Sociology*, doi:0092055X15573028

Ross, K. (2014). Quality as critique: Promoting critical reflection among youth in structured encounter programs. *Journal of Peace Education* (ahead-of- print), 1–21.

Ross, L. (2010). Sustaining youth participation in a long-term tobacco control initiative: Considerations of a social justice perspective. *Youth & Society*, 43 (2), 681–704.

Rothman, J. (2007). Multi modes of intervention at the macro level. *Journal of Community Practice*, 15 (4), 11–40.

Rubin, B. (2007). "There's still not justice": Youth civic identity development amid district school and community contexts. *Teachers College Record*, 109 (2), 449–481.

Ruck, M., Harris, A., Fine, M., & Freudenberg, N. (2008). Youth experiences of surveillance. In M. Flynn & D. C. Brotherton (Ed.). *Globalizing the streets: Cross-cultural perspectives on youth, social control, and empowerment* (pp. 15–32). New York: Columbia University Press.

Ruglis, J. (2011). Mapping the biopolitics of school dropout and youth resistance. *International Journal of Qualitative Studies in Education*, 24 (5), 627–637.

Rury, J. L., & Hill, S. (2013). An end of innocence: African-American high school protest in the 1960s and 1970s. *History of Education*, 42 (4), 486–508.

Russell, S. T., Muraco, A., Subramaniam, A., & Laub, C. (2009). Youth empowerment and high school gay-straight alliances. *Journal of Youth and Adolescence*, 38 (7), 891–903.

Russell-Mayhew, S., McVey, G., Bardick, A., & Ireland, A. (2012). Mental health, wellness, and childhood overweight/obesity. *Journal of Obesity*.

Ryan, B. (2013). *Feminism and the women's movement: Dynamics of change in social movement ideology and activism*. New York: Routledge.

Sachau, D., Courtney, C. L., Olson, D., Nolan, J., & Fee, S. (2014). Service learning in developing nations. In W. Reichman (Ed.), *Industrial and organizational psychology help the vulnerable: Serving the underserved* (pp. 227–245). New York: Palgrave Macmillan.

Sacks, R. E. (2009). *Natural Born Leaders: An Exploration of Leadership Development in Children and Adolescents* (Doctoral dissertation, University of Toronto).

Sadowski, M., Chow, S., & Scanlon, C. P. (2009). Meeting the needs of LGBTQ youth: A "relational assets" approach. *Journal of LGBT Youth, 6* (2–3), 174–198.

Saha, R. K. (2013). *ENST 489S. 01: Environmental Justice Issues and Solutions: Service Learning.* Retrieved from http://scholarworks.umt.edu/cgi/viewcontent.cgi?article=1024&context=syllabi

Saltmarsh, J. (2005). The civic promise of service learning. *Liberal Education, 91* (2), 50.

Sanchez, L. (2006, March 26). Instead of pickets, students grab their pencils. *San Diego Union Tribune,* p. B1.

Sandmann, L. R., Kiely, R. C., & Grenier, R. S. (2009). Program planning: The neglected dimension of service-learning. *Michigan Journal of Community Service Learning, 15* (2), 17–33.

Sanjek, R. (2009). *Gray panthers.* Philadelphia, PA: University of Pennsylvania Press.

Santiago, A. M., Soska, T., & Gutierrez, L. (2014). Responding to community crises: The emerging role of community practice. *Journal of Community Practice, 22* (3), 275–280.

Santos, R. M., Ruppar, A. L., & Jeans, L. M. (2011). Immersing students in the culture of disability through service learning. *Teacher Education and Special Education: The Journal of the Teacher Education Division of the Council for Exceptional Children, 35* (1), 49–63.

Sarkissian, W., & Bunjamin-Mau, W. (2012). *SpeakOut: The step-by-step guide to Speak-Outs and community workshops.* New York: Routledge.

Sasser, J. (2011). Justice for all? Youth environmental activism and the new framings of social justice. *Differentakes: A Publication of the Population and Development Program, 72.* Retrieved from http://popdev.hampshire.edu/sites/default/files/uploads/u4763/DT%2072%20Sasser.pdf

Sasser, J. S. (2014). The wave of the future? Youth advocacy at the nexus of population and climate change. *The Geographical Journal, 180* (2), 102–110.

Sato, T. C. (2013). *Examining how youth of color engage youth participatory action research to interrogate racism in their science experiences.* Retrieved from http://adsabs.harvard.edu/abs/2013PhDT.......329S

Sbicca, J. (2012). Growing food justice by planting an anti-oppression foundation: Opportunities and obstacles for a budding social movement. *Agriculture and Human Values, 29* (4), 455–466.

Schamber, J. F., & Mahoney, S. L. (2008). The development of political awareness and social justice citizenship through community-based learning in a first-year general education seminar. *The Journal of General Education, 57* (2), 75–99.

Schlosberg, D. (2007). *Defining environmental justice: Theories, movements, and nature.* New York: Oxford University Press.

Schlosberg, D. (2013). Theorising environmental justice: the expanding sphere of a discourse. *Environmental Politics, 22* (1), 37–55.

Schulz, D. (2007). Stimulating social justice theory for service-learning practice. In J. Z. Calderón, G. Eisman & R. A. Corrigan (Eds.), *Race, poverty, and social justice: Multidisciplinary perspectives through service learning* (pp. 13–30). Sterling, VA: Stylus.

Schusler, T. M. (2013). Environmental action and positive youth development. *Across the Spectrum* (pp. 93–115). In M. C. Monroe & M. E. Krasny (Eds.), *Across the spectrum: Resources for environmental educators.* North American Association of Environmental Education, Washington, D.C. [online].

Schusler, T. M., & Krasny, M. E. (2008). *Youth participation in local environmental action: An avenue for science and civic learning?* (pp. 268–284). Rotterdam, Netherlands: Springer Netherlands.

Schusler, T. M., & Krasny, M. E. (2015). Science and democracy in youth environmental action–Learning "good" thinking. In M. P. Mueller & D. J. Tippins (Eds.), *EcoJustice, citizen science and youth activism* (pp. 363–384). Switzerland: Springer International Publishing.

Schusler, T. M., Krasny, M. E., Peters, S. J., & Decker, D. J. (2009). Developing citizens and communities through youth environmental action. *Environmental Education Research*, 15 (1), 111–127.

Schutz, A., & Sandy, M. G. (2011). *Collective action for social change: An introduction to community organizing*. New York: Palgrave Macmillan.

Schwartz, N. A., von Glascoe, C. A., Torres, V., Ramos, L., & Soria-Delgado, C. (2015). "Where they (live, work and) spray": Pesticide exposure, childhood asthma and environmental justice among Mexican-American farmworkers. *Health & Place*, 32, 83–92.

Schwartz, S. E., Rhodes, J. E., Spencer, R., & Grossman, J. B. (2013). Youth initiated mentoring: Investigating a new approach to working with vulnerable adolescents. *American Journal of Community Psychology*, 52 (1–2), 155–169.

Scott, D. L. (2008). Service learning: The road from the classroom to community-based macro intervention. *Journal of Policy Practice*, 7 (2–3), 214–225.

Scott, M. (2014). Rethinking community practice. *Community Development Journal*, 49 (2), 346–349.

Scott, W. R., Deschenes, S., Hopkins, K., Newman, A., & McLaughlin, M. (2006). Advocacy organizations and the field of youth services: Ongoing efforts to restructure a field. *Nonprofit and Voluntary Sector Quarterly*, 35 (4), 691–714.

Sealey-Ruiz, Y., & Greene, P. (2011). Embracing urban youth culture in the context of education. *The Urban Review*, 43 (3), 339–357.

Sealy, Y. M. (2010). Parents' food choices: Obesity among minority parents and children. *Journal of Community Health Nursing*, 27 (1), 1–11.

Seif, H. (2010). The civic life of Latina/o immigrant youth: Challenging boundaries and creating safe spaces. In L. R. Sherrod, J. Torney-Porta & C. A. Flanagan (Eds.), *Handbook of research on civic engagement in youth* (pp. 445–470). New York: John Wiley & Sons.

Seif, H. (2011). "Unapologetic and unafraid": Immigrant youth come out from the shadows. *New Directions for Child and Adolescent Development* (134), 59–75.

Selner-O'Hagan, M. B., Kindlon, D. J., Buka, S. L., Raudenbush, S. W., & Earls, F. J. (1998). Assessing exposure to violence in urban youth. *Journal of Child Psychology and Psychiatry*, 39 (2), 215–224.

Semple, K. (2011, May 21). Illegal immigrants' children face hardships, study says. *The New York Times*, p. A15.

Serido, J., Borden, L. M., & Perkins, D. F. (2011). Moving beyond youth voice. *Youth & Society*, 43 (1), 44–63.

Seymour, K. (2013). Using incentives: Encouraging and recognising participation in youth research. *Youth Studies Australia*, 31(3), 51–59.

Shah, B. (2007). Being young, female and Laotian: Ethnicity as social capital at the intersection of gender, generation, 'race' and age. *Ethnic and Racial Studies*, 30 (1), 28–50.

Shah, S. (2011). *Building transformative youth leadership: Data on the impacts of youth organizing*. New York: Funders' Collaborative on Youth Organizing.

Shapiro, V. B., Oesterle, S., Abbott, R. D., Arthur, M. W., & Hawkins, J. D. (2013). Measuring dimensions of coalition functioning for effective and participatory community practice. *Social Work Research*, 37 (4), 349–359.

Shaw, A., Brady, B., McGrath, B., Brennan, M. A., & Dolan, P. (2014). Understanding youth civic engagement: Debates, discourses, and lessons from practice. *Community Development*, 45 (4), 300–316.

Shaw, R. (2008). Beyond the fields. *Cesar Chavez, The UFW, and the struggle for justice in the 21st century*. Berkeley, CA: University of California Press.

Shaw, S., & Roberson, L. (2009). Service-learning: Recentering the Deaf community in interpreter education. *American Annals of the Deaf*, 154 (3), 277–283.

Shaw-Raudoy, K., & McGregor, C. (2013). Co-learning in youth-adult emancipatory partnerships: The way forward?. *International Journal of Child, Youth and Family Studies*, 4 (3.1), 391–408.

Sheffield, E. C. (2011). *Strong community service learning: Philosophical perspectives. Adolescent cultures, school, and society* (Vol. 53). New York: Peter Lang.

Sheffield, E. C. (2015). Toward radicalizing community service learning. *Educational Studies*, 51 (1), 45–56.

Shehata, D. (2008). Youth activism in Egypt. *Arab Reform Brief*, 23.

Sherrod, L. R. (2006). Promoting citizenship and activism in today's youth. *Beyond resistance*, 287–299.

Sherrod, L. R., Flanagan, C. A., Kassimir, R., & Syvertsen, A. K. (Eds.). (2005). *Youth activism: An international encyclopedia, Vol. II*. Westport, CT: Greenwood Publisher.

Sherrod, L. R., Torney-Porta, J., & Flanagan, C. A. (Eds.). (2010). *Handbook of research on civic engagement in youth*. New York: John Wiley & Sons.

Shier, M. L., McDougle, L., & Handy, F. (2014). Nonprofits and the promotion of civic engagement: A conceptual framework for understanding the "civic footprint" of nonprofits within local communities. *Canadian Journal of Nonprofit and Social Economy Research*, 5 (1).

Shiller, J. T. (2013). Preparing for democracy: How community-based organizations build civic engagement among urban youth. *Urban Education*, 48 (1), 69–91.

Shor, I. (1999). What is critical literacy. *Journal for Pedagogy, Pluralism & Practice*, 4 (1), 1–26.

Shor, I. (2012). *Empowering education: Critical teaching for social change*. Chicago, IL: University of Chicago Press.

Shragge, E. (2013). *Activism and social change: Lessons for community organizing*. Toronto, Canada: University of Toronto Press.

Silver, H., Scott, A., & Kazepov, Y. (2010). Participation in urban contention and deliberation. *International Journal of Urban and Regional Research*, 34 (3), 453–477.

Simmons, L., & Harding, S. (2011). Engaging youth in community practice—An imperative for the future. *Journal of Community Practice*, 19 (3), 229–233.

Simonet, D. (2008). Service-learning and academic success: The links to retention research. *Minnesota Campus Compact*, 1–13.

Simons, L., Fehr, L., Hogerwerff, F., Blank, N., Georganas, D., & Russell, B. (2011). The application of racial identity development in academic-based service learning. *International Journal of Teaching and Learning in Higher Education*, 23 (1), 72–83.

Sipos, Y., Battisti, B., & Grimm, K. (2008). Achieving transformative sustainability learning: Engaging head, hands and heart. *International Journal of Sustainability in Higher Education*, 9 (1), 68–86.

Siqueira, C. E., Gaydos, M., Monforton, C., Slatin, C., Borkowski, L., Dooley, P., . . . & Keifer, M. (2014). Effects of social, economic, and labor policies on occupational health disparities. *American Journal of Industrial Medicine*, 57 (5), 557–572.

Sister, C., Wolch, J., & Wilson, J. (2010). Got green? Addressing environmental justice in park provision. *GeoJournal*, 75 (3), 229–248.

Skrbis, Z., Woodward, I., & Bean, C. (2014). Seeds of cosmopolitan future? Young people and their aspirations for future mobility. *Journal of Youth Studies*, 17 (5), 614–625.

Slocum. R. (2006). Anti-racist practice and the work of community food organizations. *Antipode*, 38 (2), 327–349.

Slocum, R., & Cadieux, K. V. (2015). Notes on the practice of food justice in the US: Understanding and confronting trauma and inequity. *Journal of Political Ecology*, 22, 27–52.

Salvio, P. M. (2013). Exercising 'the right to research': Youth-based community media production as transformative action. *English in Education*, 47 (2), 163–180.

Smalls, M. N. B. (2013). *A Synthesis of the Literature on the Relationship Between Food Access and Overweight and Obesity in African American Adolescents* (Doctoral dissertation, University of Pittsburgh).

Smith, D., Miles-Richardson, S., Dill, L., & Archie-Booker, E. (2013). Interventions to improve access to fresh food in vulnerable communities: A review of the literature. *International Journal on Disability and Human Development*, 12 (4), 409–417.

Smith, J., McCarthy, J. D., McPhail, C., & Augustyn, B. (2001). From protest to agenda building: Description bias in media coverage of protest events in Washington, DC. *Social Forces*, 79 (4), 1397–1423.

Smith, L., Beck, K., Bernstein, E., & Dashtguard, P. (2014). Youth participatory action research and school counseling practice: A school-wide framework for student well-being. *Journal of School Counseling*, 12 (21).

Smith, R. (2010). Children's rights and youth justice: 20 years of no progress. *Child Care in Practice*, 16 (1), 3–17.

Smyth, J., Down, B., & McInerney, P. (2014). *Socially critical youth voice in the socially just school* (pp. 21–41). Springer Netherlands.

Snellman, K., Silva, J. M., Frederick, C. B., & Putnam, R. D. (2015). The engagement gap: Social mobility and extracurricular participation among American youth. *The ANNALS of the American Academy of Political and Social Science*, 657 (1), 194–207.

Soohoo, S. (1993, December). Students as partners in research and restructuring schools. *The Educational Forum*, 57 (4), 386–393.

Spencer, M. B., & Spencer, T. R. (2014). Invited commentary: Exploring the promises, intricacies, and challenges to Positive Youth Development. *Journal of Youth and Adolescence*, 43 (6), 1027–1035.

Spencer, R., Tugenberg, T., Ocean, M., Schwartz, S. E., & Rhodes, J. E. (2013). "Somebody who was on my side": A qualitative examination of youth initiated mentoring. *Youth & Society*, doi:0044118X13495053

Soep, E. (2014). *Participatory politics: Next-generation tactics to remake public spheres*. Cambridge, MA: MIT Press.

Soifer, S. D., McNeely, J. B., Costa, C. L., & Pickering-Bernheim, N. (2014). *Community economic development in social work*. New York: Columbia University Press.

Soja, E. (2009). The city and spatial justice. *Justice Spatiale/Spatial Justice*. Retrieved from http://www.jssj.org/wp-content/uploads/2012/12/JSSJ1-1en4.pdf

Soler-i-Martí, R. (2014). Youth political involvement update: Measuring the role of cause-oriented political interest in young people's activism. *Journal of Youth Studies* (ahead-of-print), 1–21.

Solís, J., Fernández, J. S., & Alcalá, L. (2013). Mexican immigrant children and youth's contributions to a community centro: Exploring civic engagement and citizen constructions. *Sociological Studies of Children and Youth*, 16, 177–200.

Solorzano, D., & Delgado Barnal, D. (2001). Examining trans-formational resistance through a critical race and Laterit theory framework: Chicana and Chicano students in an urban context. *Urban Education*, 36 (3), 308–342.

Somma, N. M. (2010). How do voluntary organizations foster protest? The role of organizational involvement on individual protest participation. *The Sociological Quarterly*, 51 (3), 384–407.

Song, L. K. (2014). Race, transformative planning, and the just city. *Planning Theory*, doi:1473095213517883

Soska, T., & Butterfield, A. K. J. (2013). *University-community partnerships: Universities in civic engagement*. New York: Routledge.

Soto, H. (2006, March 30). Students protests continue: Young activists are learning a "Big lesson" in bid to effect change. *The San Diego Tribune*, p. B1.

Spencer, M. B., & Spencer, T. R. (2014). Invited commentary: Exploring the promises, intricacies, and challenges to positive youth development. *Journal of Youth and Adolescence*, 43 (6), 1027–1035.

Staeheli, L., & Nagel, C. R. (2013). Whose awakening is it? Youth and the geopolitics of civic engagement in the 'Arab Awakening'. *European Urban and Regional Studies*, 20 (1), 115–119.

Stanley, A. (2009). Just space or spatial justice? Difference, discourse, and environmental justice. *Local Environment*, 14 (10), 999–1014.

Stanton-Salazar, R. D. (2011). A social capital framework for the study of institutional agents and their role in the empowerment of low-status students and youth. *Youth & Society*, 43 (3), 1066–1109.

Staples, L. (2012). Community organizing for social justice: Grassroots groups for power. *Social Work with Groups*, 35 (3), 287–296.

Stepick, A., & Stepick, C. D. (2002). Becoming American, constructing ethnicity: Immigrant youth and civic engagement. *Applied Developmental Science*, 6 (4), 246–257.

Stepick, A., Stepick, C. D., & Labissiere, Y. (2008). South Florida's immigrant youth and civic engagement: Major engagement: Minor differences. *Applied Development Science*, 12 (2), 57–65.

Stewart, C. J., Smith, C. A., & Denton Jr, R. E. (2012). *Persuasion and social movements*. Long Grove, IL: Waveland Press.

Stewart, T. (2012). Adultism: Discrimination by another name. In *The 21st century Black Librarian in America: Issues and challenges* (pp. 75–78).

Stoecker, R. (2013). *Research methods for community change: A project-based approach*. Thousand Oaks, CA: Sage.

Stoecker, R., Loving, K., Reddy, M., & Bollig, N. (2010). Can community-based research guide service learning? *Journal of Community Practice*, 18 (2–3), 280–296.

Stoecker, R., Tryon, E. A., & Hilgendorf, A. (Eds.). (2009). *The unheard voices: Community organizations and service learning*. Philadelphia, PA: Temple University Press.

Stoecklin, D., & Bonvin, J. M. (2014). The capability approach and children's rights. *Agency and Participation in Childhood and Youth: International Applications of the Capability Approach in Schools and Beyond*, 63.

Stolberg, S. G. (2015, April 28). Violent clashes rock Baltimore after funeral. *The New York Times*, A1, A15.

Stovell, D. (2005). From hunger strike to high school: Youth development, social justice, and school formation. In S. Ginwright, P. Noguera, & J. Cammarota (Eds.), *Beyond resistance: Youth activism and community change* (pp. 97–109). New York: Routledge.

Stover, L. T., & Bach, J. (2012). Young adult literature as a call to social activism. In J. A. Hayn & J. S. Kaplan (Eds.), *Teaching young adult literature today: Insights, considerations, and perspectives for the classroom teacher* (pp. 203–223). Plymouth, England, Rowman & Littlefield.

Street, B. (2003). What's "new" in New Literacy Studies? Critical approaches to literacy in theory and practice. *Current Issues in Comparative Education*, 5 (2), 77–91.

Street, B. V. (2014). *Social literacies: Critical approaches to literacy in development, ethnography and education*. New York: Routledge.

Suárez-Orozco, C., Pimentel, A., & Martin, M. (2009). The significance of relationships: Academic engagement and achievement among newcomer immigrant youth. *The Teachers College Record*, 111 (3), 712–749.

Suárez-Orozco, C., Rhodes, J., & Milburn, M. (2009). Unraveling the immigrant paradox academic engagement and disengagement among recently arrived immigrant youth. *Youth & Society*, 41 (2), 151–185.

Sue, J. L., & Craig, W. M. (2014). *Connecting Research and Practice in Youth Mentoring. Do Relationships Matter? An Examination of a School-Based Intergenerational Mentoring Program* (Master's Thesis, Kingston, ON, Canada, Queens University).

Suffla, S., Seedat, M., & Bawa, U. (2015). Reflexivity as enactment of critical community psychologies: Dilemmas of voice and positionality in a multi-country photovoice study. *Journal of Community Psychology*, 43 (1), 9–21.

Suhonen, R. (2014). *Youth civic engagement in Bhutan: Obedient citizens or social activists?*. Retrieved from https://dspace.mah.se/bitstream/handle/2043/17547/DP_2014_Suhonen_FINAL.pdf?sequence=2

Sukarieh, M., & Tannock, S. (2011). The positivity imperative: A critical look at the 'new'youth development movement. *Journal of Youth Studies*, 14 (6), 675–691.

Sullivan, J., & Xie, L. (2009). Environmental activism, social networks and the internet. *The China Quarterly*, 198, 422–432.

Sullivan, P. J., & Larson, R. W. (2009). Connecting youth to high-resource adults: Lessons from effective youth programs. *Journal of Adolescent Research*, 25 (1), 99–123.

Sundstrom, R. R. (2008). *The browning of America and the evasion of social justice*. New York: SUNY Press.

Suro, R., & Escobar, G. (2006). *2006 National survey of Latinos: The immigrant debate*. Washington, D.C.: Hispanic Pew Center.

Suyemoto, K. L., Day, S. C., & Schwartz, S. (2014). *Exploring effects of social justice youth programming on racial and ethnic identities and activism for Asian American youth*. Retrieved from http://psycnet.apa.org/journals/aap/6/2/125

Suzuki, D., & Mayorga, E. (2014). Scholar-activism: A twice told tale. *Multicultural Perspectives*, 16 (1), 16–20.

Swarts, H. (2011). Drawing new symbolic boundaries over old social boundaries: Forging social movement unity in congregation-based community organizing. *Sociological Perspectives*, 54 (3), 453–477.

Switzer, J. V. (2003). *Disabled rights: American disability policy and the fight for equity*. Washington, D.C.: Georgetown University Press.

Sylvester, D. E. (2010). Service learning as a vehicle for promoting student political efficacy. *Journal for Civic Commitment*, 14.

Sze, J., & London, J. K. (2008). Environmental justice at the crossroads. *Sociological Compass*, 2 (4), 1331–1354.

Sze, J. (2007). *Noxious New York: The racial politics of urban health and environmental justice*. Cambridge: MIT Press.

Sziarto, K. M., & Leitner, H. (2010). Immigrants riding for justice: Space-time and emotions in the construction of a counterpublic. *Political Geography*, 29 (7), 381–391.

Taft, J. K. (2010). *Rebel girls: Youth activism and social change across the Americas*. New York: NYU Press.

Taft, J. K., & Gordon, H. R. (2013). Youth activists, youth councils, and constrained democracy. *Education, Citizenship and Social Justice*, 5 (4), 21–41.

Taines, C. (2012). Intervening in alimentation: The outcomes for urban youth of participating in school activism. *American Educational Research Journal*, 49 (1), 53–86.

Tarasuk, V., Dachner, N., Poland, B., & Gaetz, S. (2009). Food deprivation is integral to the 'hand to mouth' existence of homeless youths in Toronto. *Public Health Nutrition*, 12 (09), 1437–1442.

Tarulli, D., & Skott-Myhre, H. (2006). The immanent rights of the multitude: An ontological framework for conceptualizing the issue of child and youth rights. *International Journal of Childrens Rights*, 14 (2), 187.

Tavener-Smith, K. (2014). Contemporary youth resistance culture: Viability, relevancy and pragmatism. *Critical Arts*, 28 (1), 51–56.

Taylor, D. E. (2000). The rise of the environmental justice paradigm injustice framing and the social construction of environmental discourses. *American Behavioral Scientist*, 43 (4), 508–580.

Taylor, D. E. (2011). Introduction: The evolution of environmental justice activism, research, and scholarship. *Environmental Practice*, 13 (04), 280–301.

Taylor, J., & Dwyer, A. (2014). Queer youth research/ers. In P. Kelly (Ed.), *A critical youth studies for the 21st century* (p. 251). Leiden, Holland: Brill Academic Publisher.

Taylor, W. C., Poston, W. S. C., Jones, L., & Kraft, M. K. (2006). Environmental justice: Obesity, physical activity, and healthy eating. *Journal of Physical Activity and Health*, 3 (Suppl. 1), S30–S54.

Taylor, Z., & Józefowicz, I. (2012). Intra-urban daily mobility of disabled people for recreational and leisure purposes. *Journal of Transport Geography*, 24, 155–172.

Teelucksingh, C., & Masuda, J. R. (2014). Urban environmental justice through the camera: Understanding the politics of space and the right to the city. *Local Environment*, 19 (3), 300–317.

Teixeira, S. (2015). "It seems like no one cares": Participatory photo mapping to understand youth perspectives on property vacancy. *Journal of Adolescent Research*, 30 (3), 390–414.

Terry, G. (2009). No climate justice without gender justice: An overview of the issues. *Gender & Development*, 17 (1), 5–18.

Teruelle, R. (2011). Social media and youth activism. *Social Media: Usage and Impact*, 201–217.

Theiss-Morse, E., & Hibbing, J. R. (2005). Citizenship and civic engagement. *Annu. Rev. Polit. Sci.*, 8, 227–249.

Theron, L. C., & Malindi, M. J. (2010). Resilient street youth: A qualitative South African study. *Journal of Youth Studies*, 13 (6), 717–736.

Thinking, U. D. (2015). Queering service learning. In J. C. Hawley (Ed.), *Expanding the circle: Creating an inclusive environment in higher education for LGBTQ students and studies* (pp. 209–224). Albany, NY: State University of New York Press.

Thomas, A. J., Barrie, R., Brunner, J., Clawson, A., Hewitt, A., Jeremie Brink, G., & Rowe-Johnson, M. (2014). Assessing critical consciousness in youth and young adults. *Journal of Research on Adolescence*, 24 (3), 485–496.

Thomas, M. L., O'Connor, M. K., & Netting, F. E. (2011). A framework for teaching community practice. *Journal of Social Work Education*, 47 (2), 337–355.

Thompson, R., Russell, L., & Simmons, R. (2014). Space, place and social exclusion: An ethnographic study of young people outside education and employment. *Journal of Youth Studies*, 17 (1), 63–78.

Thomson, A. M., Smith-Tolken, A., Naidoo, T., & Bringle, R. (2008). Service learning and community engagement: A cross cultural perspective. In meeting of the *International Society for Third Sector Research*, Barcelona, Spain.

Thomson, P. (2009). Involving children and young people in educational change: Possibilities and challenges. In *Second international handbook of educational change* (pp. 809–824). Springer Netherlands.

Tidball, K. G., & Krasny, M. E. (2011). Urban environmental education from a social-ecological perspective: Conceptual framework for civic ecology education. *Cities and the Environment (CATE)*, 3 (1), 11.

Tilley-Lubbs, G. A. (2009). Good intentions pave the way to hierarchy: A retrospective autoethnographic approach. *Michigan Journal of Community Service Learning*, 16 (1), 59–68.

Tilton, J. (2010). *Dangerous or endangered?: Race and the politics of youth in urban America*. New York: NYU Press.

Tilton, J. (2013). Rethinking youth voice and institutional power: Reflections from inside a service learning partnership in a California juvenile hall. *Children and Youth Services Review*, 35 (8), 1189–1196.

Tinkler, A., Tinkler, B., Gerstl-Pepin, C., & Mugisha, V. M. (2014). The promise of a community-based, participatory approach to service-learning in education. *Journal of Higher Education Outreach and Engagement*, 18 (2), 209–232.

Tinkler, A., Tinkler, B., Hausman, E., & Tufo-Strouse, G. (2014). Key elements of effective service-learning partnerships from the perspective of community partners. *Partnerships: A Journal of Service-Learning and Civic Engagement*, 5 (2), 137–152.

Tobey, A. E., & Jellinghaus, K. (2012). De (fencing) with youth: Moving from the margins to the center. *The Journal of Social Theory in Art Education*, 32, 128–144.

Toporek, R. L., & Worthington, R. L. (2014). Integrating service learning and difficult dialogues pedagogy to advance social justice training. *The Counseling Psychologist*, 42 (7), 919–945.

Torney-Purta, J., & Barber, C. (2011). Fostering young people's support for participatory human rights through their developmental niches. *American Journal of Orthopsychiatry*, 81 (4), 473.

Torre, M., & Fine, M. (2006). Researching and resisting: Democratic policy research by and for youth. In S. Ginwright, P. Noguera, & J. Cammarota (Eds.), *Beyond resistance* (pp. 269–285). New York: Routledge.

Torres, M. L. A. (2007). Youth activists in the age of postmodern globalization: Notes from an ongoing project. *Children, Youth and Environments*, 17 (2), 35–56.

Torres-Fleming, A., Valdes, P., & Pillai, S. (2011). *2010 Youth organizing field scan*. New York: Funders' Collaborative on Youth Organizing.

Torres-Harding, S. R., & Meyers, S. A. (2013). Teaching for social justice and social action. *Journal of Prevention & Intervention in the Community*, 41 (4), 213–219.

Torres-Harding, S. R., Steele, C., Schulz, E., Taha, F., & Pico, C. (2014). Student perceptions of social justice and social justice activities. *Education, Citizenship and Social Justice*, 9 (1), 55–66.

Travis, R., & Ausbrooks, A. (2012). EMPOWERMENTODAY: A model of positive youth development and academic persistence for male African Americans. *Children & Schools*, 34 (3), 186–189.

Travis, R., & Leech, T. G. (2014). Empowerment-based positive youth development: A new understanding of healthy development for African American youth. *Journal of Research on Adolescence*, 24 (1), 93–116.

Travis Jr., R., & Maston, A. (2014). Hip-Hop and pedagogy, more than meets the eye. In *See you at the crossroads: Hip hop scholarship at the intersections* (pp. 3–28). Dordrecht, Netherlands: SensePublishers.

Treuhaft, S., & Karpyn, A. (2011). *The grocery gap: Who has access to healthy food and why it matters.* Philadelphia, PA: The Food Trust.

Trickett, E. J., Beehler, S., Deutsch, C., Green, L. W., Hawe, P., McLeroy, K., . . . & Trimble, J. E. (2011). Advancing the science of community-level interventions. *Journal Information*, 101 (8).

Trudeau, D., & Kruse, T. P. (2014). Creating significant learning experiences through civic engagement: Practical strategies for community-engaged pedagogy. *Journal of Public Scholarship in Higher Education*, 4.

Tryon, E., Stoecker, R., Martin, A., Seblonka, K., Hilgendorf, A., & Nellis, M. (2008). The challenge of short-term service-learning. *Michigan Journal of Community Service Learning*, 14 (2), 16–26.

Tsui, E., Bylander, K., Cho, M., Maybank, A., & Freudenberg, N. (2012). Engaging youth in food activism in New York City: Lessons learned from a youth organization, health department, and university partnership. *Journal of Urban Health*, 89 (5), 809–827.

Tuck, E., & Yang, K. W. (Eds.). (2013). *Youth resistance research and theories of change.* New York: Routledge.

Tyner, K. (2014). *Literacy in a digital world: Teaching and learning in the age of information.* New York: Routledge.

Tyyskä, V. (2014). *Youth and society: The long and winding road.* Toronto, Canada: Canadian Scholars' Press.

Ugor, P. U. (2014). Introduction. Extenuating circumstances: African youth and social agency in a late-modern world. *Postcolonial Text*, 8 (3 & 4).

Ungar, M. (2013). The impact of youth-adult relationships on resilience. *International Journal of Child, Youth and Family Studies*, 4 (3), 328–336.

United States Agency of International Development (2014). *Youth in Development: Realizing the Demographic Opportunity.* Retrieved from http://www.usaid.gov/sites/default/files/documents/1870/Youth_in_Development_Policy_0.pdf

Urban, J. B., Lewin-Bizan, S., & Lerner, R. M. (2009). The role of neighborhood ecological assets and activity involvement in youth developmental outcomes: Differential impacts of asset poor and asset rich neighborhoods. *Journal of Applied Developmental Psychology*, 30 (5), 601–614.

U.S. Census Bureau. (2010a). Current Population Survey, Annual Social and Economic Supplement. Table 1: Population by sex and age, for Asian alone and White alone, not Hispanic: 2010 [Data file]. Retrieved from http://www.census.gov/population/www/socdemo/race/ppl-aa10.html

U.S. Census Bureau. (2010b). Current Population Survey, Annual Social and Economic Supplement. Table 1: Population by sex and age, for Black alone and White alone, not Hispanic [Data file]. Retrieved from http://www.census.gov/population/www/socdemo/race/ppl-ba10.html

U.S. Census Bureau. (2010c). Current Population Survey, Annual Social and Economic Supplement. Table 1: Population by sex, age, Hispanic origin, and race [Data file]. Retrieved from http://www.census.gov/population/www/socdemo/hispanic/cps2010.html

Valois, R. F. (2014). Life satisfaction and youth developmental assets. In A. C. Michalos (Ed.), *Encyclopedia of quality of life and well-being research* (pp. 3581–3589). New York: Springer.

Van Stekelenburg, J., & Klandermans, B. (2013). The social psychology of protest. *Current Sociology*, 61 (5–6), 886–905.

Vander Schee, C., & Kline, K. (2013). Neoliberal exploitation in reality television: Youth, health and the spectacle of celebrity 'concern'. *Journal of Youth Studies*, 16 (5), 565–578.

Vasquez, V. B., Lanza, D., Hennessey-Lavery, S., Facente, S., Halpin, H. A., & Minkler, M. (2007). Addressing food security through public policy action in a community-based participatory research partnership. *Health Promotion*, 8 (4), 342–349.

Vasquez, V. M. (2014). *Negotiating critical literacies with young children*. New York: Routledge.

Vaughan, C. (2014). Participatory research with youth: Idealising safe social spaces or building transformative links in difficult environments?. *Journal of Health Psychology*, 19 (1), 184–192.

Velasquez, A., & LaRose, R. (2014). Youth collective activism through social media: The role of collective efficacy. *New Media & Society*, doi:1461444813518391

Velez, V., Huber, L. P., Lopez, C. B., de la Luz, A., & Solorzano, D. G. (2008). Battling for human rights and social justice: A Latina/o critical race media analysis of Latina/o student youth activism in the wake of 2006 anti- immigrant sentiment. *Social Justice*, 35 (1), 7–27.

Venkatesh, S. (2008). *Gang leader for a day*. New York: Penguin Press.

Verjee, B. (2010). Service-learning: Charity-based or transformative. *Transformative Dialogues: Teaching & Learning Journal*, 4 (2), 1–13.

Vickery, J. (2014). Youths teaching youths. *Journal of Adolescent & Adult Literacy*, 57 (5), 361–365.

Vidgen, H. A., & Gallegos, D. (2014). Defining food literacy and its components. *Appetite*, 76, 50–59.

Vincent, C., Dill, D., Hernandez, D., & Hoyt, K. (2013). An aspect of assessment: Highlighting student voices on Transformative Learning. In *Conference Proceedings of the 2013 University of Central Oklahoma's Third Annual Transformative Learning Conference* (p. 105).

Vivoni, F. (2009). Spots of spatial desire: Skateparks, skateplazas, and urban politics. *Journal of Sport & Social Issues*, 33 (2), 130–149.

Voicu, M., & Rusu, I. A. (2012). Immigrants' membership in civic associations: Why are some immigrants more active than others?. *International Sociology*, 27 (6), 788–806.

Voight, A., & Torney-Purta, J. (2013). A typology of youth civic engagement in urban middle schools. *Applied Developmental Science*, 17 (4), 198–212.

Wade, R. C. (2007). Service-learning for social justice in the elementary classroom: Can we get there from here?. *Equity & Excellence in Education*, 40 (2), 156–165.

Wagner, W., & Mathison, P. (2015). Connecting to communities: Powerful pedagogies for leading for social change. *New Directions for Student Leadership*, 2015 (145), 85–96.

Waiton, S. (2013). Does youth have a future?. *Concept*, 18 (1). Retrieved from http://concept.lib.ed.ac.uk/index.php/Concept/article/viewFile/193/167

Wald, S. D. (2011). Visible farmers/invisible workers: locating immigrant labor in food studies. *Food, Culture and Society: An International Journal of Multidisciplinary Research*, 14 (4), 567–586.

Walker, A. (2014, November). Service provider's perspectives on barriers and facilitators to the school-community transition among youth with disabilities. In *142nd APHA Annual Meeting and Exposition* (November 15–November 19, 2014). APHA.

Walker, G. (2012). *Environmental justice: Cconcepts, evidence and politics*. London: Routledge.

Walker, J. A., Gambone, M. A., & Walker, K. C. (2011). Reflections on a century of youth development research and practice. *Journal of Youth Development*, 6 (3), 8–19.

Walker, K. C. (2011). The multiple roles that youth development program leaders adopt with youth. *Youth & Society*, 43 (2), 635–655.

Walker, K. C., & Saito, R. N. (2011). Youth Are Here: Promoting Youth Spaces through Community Mapping. *Afterschool Matters*, 14 (1), 30–39.

Walker, R. E., Keane, C. R., & Burke, J. G. (2010). Disparities and access to healthy food in the United States: A review of food deserts literature. *Health & Place*, 16 (5), 876–884.

Wallace, R. R. (2013). Service learning: Tutoring middle and high school struggling readers. In N. Zunker (Ed.), *Preparing effective leaders for tomorrow's schools* (pp. 257–281). College Station, TX: CEDER, Texas A&M University-Corpus Christi.

Walsh, F. (2012). Facilitating family resilience: Relational resources for positive youth development in conditions of adversity. In *The Social Ecology of Resilience* (pp. 173–185). Springer New York.

Walter, V. A. (2009). Sowing the seeds of praxis: Incorporating youth development principles in a library teen employment program. *Library Trends*, 58 (1), 63–81.

Wang, J. (2006, April 7). Auroa students rally for immigrants: More than 1,000 cut classes to march. *Chicago Sun Times*, p. 13.

Warren, J. L. (2012). Does service-learning increase student learning?: A meta-analysis. *Michigan Journal of Community Service Learning*, 18 (2), 56–61.

Warren, M. R., & Mapp, K. L. (2011). *A match on dry grass: Community organizing as a catalyst for school reform*. New York: Oxford University Press.

Warren, M. R., Mira, M., & Nikundiwe, T. (2008). Youth organizing: From youth development to school reform. *New directions for youth development* (117), 27–42.

Warwick, P., Cremin, H., Harrison, T., & Mason, C. (2012). The complex ecology of young people's community engagement and the call for civic pedagogues. *JSSE-Journal of Social Science Education*, 11 (3).

Wasserman, D., Asch, A., Blustein, J., & Putnam, D. (2013). *Disability and Justice*.

Waterman, A. S. (Ed.). (2014). *Service-learning: Applications from the research*. Routledge.

Watkins, C. M. (2013). *Cultivating resistance: Food justice in the criminal justice system*. Retrieved from http://scholarship.claremont.edu/cgi/viewcontent.cgi?article=1038&context=pitzer_theses

Watson, J., Washington, G., & Stepteau-Watson, D. (2015). Umoja: A culturally specific approach to mentoring young African American males. *Child and Adolescent Social Work Journal*, 1–10.

Watson, V. W., & Marciano, J. E. (2015). Examining a social-participatory youth co-researcher methodology: A cross-case analysis extending possibilities of literacy and research. *Literacy*, 49 (1), 37–44.

Watts, R. J., & Flanagan, C. (2007). Pushing the envelope on youth civic engagement: A developmental and liberation psychology perspective. *Journal of Community Psychology*, 35 (6), 779–792.

Wayne, Y. K. (2007). Organizing MySpace: Youth walkouts, pleasure, politics, and new media. *Educational Foundations*, 21 (1–2), 1–11.

Wearing, M. (2011). Strengthening youth citizenship and social inclusion practice—The Australian case: Towards rights based and inclusive practice in services for marginalized young people. *Children and Youth Services Review*, 33 (4), 534–540.

Weber, H. (2013). Demography and democracy: The impact of youth cohort size on democratic stability in the world. *Democratization*, 20 (2), 335–357.

Weil, F. (2011). Rise of community organizations, citizen engagement, and new institutions. In *Resilience and opportunity: Lessons from the US Gulf Coast after Katrina and Rita* (pp. 201–219). Baltimore, MD: Brookings Institution Press.

Weil, M. (Ed.). (2012). *Handbook of community practice, second edition*. Thousand Oaks, CA: Sage Publications.

Weil, M. (2014). *Community practice: Conceptual models*. New York: Routledge.

Weiner, L. (2006). Challenging deficit thinking. *Educational Leadership*, 64 (1), 42.

Weiss, J. (2011). Valuing youth resistance before and after public protest. *International Journal of Qualitative Studies in Education*, 24 (5), 595–599.

Weiss, M. (2003). Youth rising. *Applied Research Center*, 2003.

Weldon, L. (2011). *When protest makes policy: How social movements represent disadvantaged groups*. Ann Arbor, MI: University of Michigan Press.

Wells, C. (2014). Civic identity and the question of organization in contemporary civic engagement. *Policy & Internet*, 6 (2), 209–216.

Westheimer, J. (2011). No child left thinking: Democracy at-risk in American schools. *Colleagues*, 3 (2), 8.

Wheeler, J. (2014). *The effects of negative labeling on African American youth: A retrospective study* (Doctoral dissertation, California State University Long Beach).

White, D. J., Shoffner, A., Johnson, K., Knowles, N., & Mills, M. (2012). Advancing positive youth development: Perspectives of youth as researchers and evaluators. *Journal of Extension*, 50 (4), 1–10.

White, J. (2007, December). Knowing, doing and being in context: A praxis- oriented approach to child and youth care. *Child & Youth Care Forum* 36 (5–6), 225–244.

Williams, J. (2014). Being born sexed but not gendered: Challenging the constructed nature of gender with students. *Christian Teachers Journal*, 22 (1), 18.

Williams, J. L., Anderson, R. E., Francois, A. G., Hussain, S., & Tolan, P. H. (2014). Ethnic identity and positive youth development in adolescent males: A culturally integrated approach. *Applied Developmental Science*, 18 (2), 110–122.

Willis, C., & Stoecker, R. (2013). Grassroots organizations and leadership education. *Community Development*, 44 (4), 441–455.

Willis, V. (2013). 'let me in, i have the right to be here': Black youth struggle for equal education and full citizenship after the Brown decision, 1954–1969. *Citizenship Teaching & Learning*, 9 (1), 53–70.

Wilson, B. B. (2010). Social Movement Towards Spatial Justice: Crafting a Theory of Civic Urban Form. (Disseration, University of Texas, Austin, TX).

Wilson, J. R., & Schwier, R. A. (2009). Authenticity in the process of learning about instructional design. *Canadian Journal of Learning and Technology/La revue canadienne de l'apprentissage et de la technologie*, 35 (2). Retrieved from http://www.cjlt.ca/index.php/cjlt/article/view/520/253

Wilson, W. J. (2012). *The truly disadvantaged: The inner city, the underclass, and public policy*. Chicago, IL: University of Chicago Press.

Wittman, H., Desmarais, A., & Wiebe, N. (Eds.). (2010). *Food sovereignty: Reconnecting food, nature, and community*. Oakland, CA: Institute for Food & Development Policy.

Wolch, J., Wilson, J. P., & Fehrenbach, J. (2005). Parks and park funding in Los Angeles: An equity-mapping analysis. *Urban Geography*, 26 (1), 4–35.

Wolfe, M. (2013). Service Learning Partnerships Between High Schools and Community Agencies (Doctoral dissertation, Walden University).

Wong, N. T., Zimmerman, M. A., & Parker, E. A. (2010). A typology of youth participation and empowerment for children and adolescent health promotion. *American Journal of Community Psychology*, 46 (1–2), 100–114.

Woodman, D., & Wyn, J. (2013). Youth policy and generations: Why youth policy needs to 'rethink youth'. *Social Policy and Society*, 12 (2), 265–275.

Worrall, L. (2007). Asking the community: A case study of community partner perspectives. *Michigan Journal of Community Service Learning*, 14 (1), 5–17.

Wray-Lake, L., & Syvertsen, A. K. (2011). The developmental roots of social responsibility in childhood and adolescence. *New Directions for Child and Adolescent Development* (134), 11–25.

Wyness, M., Harrison, L., & Buchanan, I. (2004). Childhood, politics and ambiguity towards an agenda for children's political inclusion. *Sociology*, 38 (1), 81–99.

Xie, C. F., & Liao, Z. M. (2011). Protecting the legitimate rights and interests of young people: Some research of the working mechanism. *Journal of Guangxi Youth Leaders College*, 5, 009.

Yang, K. M., & Alpermann, B. (2014). Children and youth NGOs in China: Social activism between embeddedness and marginalization. *China Information*, 28 (3), 311–337.

Yates, L. (2015). Everyday politics, social practices and movement networks: Daily life in Barcelona's social centres. *The British Journal of Sociology*.

Yoder Clark, A. (2009). Power and service-learning: Implications in service-learning for social justice (Doctoral dissertation, The Claremont Graduate University and San Diego State University).

Young, M. R. (2010). The art and science of fostering engaged learning. *Academy of Educational Leadership Journal*, 14, 1–18.

Youniss, J., & Levine, P. (Eds.). (2009). *Engaging young people in civic life*. Nasville, TN: Nashville, TN: Vanderbilt University Press.

Youth Civic Leadership Academy. (2015). Retrieved from http//www.icirr.org/youthcivicleadershipacademy

Yowell, C. M. (2002). Dreams of the future: The pursuit of education and career possible selves among ninth grade Latino youth. *Applied Developmental Science*, 6 (2), 62–72.

Zaff, J. F., Ginsberg, K. K., Boyd, M. J., & Kakli, Z. (2014). Reconnecting disconnected youth: Examining the development of productive engagement. *Journal of Research on Adolescence*, 24 (3), 526–540.

Zaff, J. F., Hart, D., Flanagan, C. A., Youniss, J., & Levine, P. (2010). Developing civic engagement within a civic context. In R. M. Lerner & W. F. Overton (Eds.), *The handbook of life-span development*. New York: Wiley.

Zaff, J. F., Kawashima-Ginsberg, K., Lin, E. S., Lamb, M., Balsano, A., & Lerner, R. M. (2011). Developmental trajectories of civic engagement across adolescence: Disaggregation of an integrated construct. *Journal of Adolescence*, 34 (6), 1207–1220.

Zagofsky, T. M. (2013). Civic Engagement Unbound Social and Spatial Forms of Inclusion/Exclusion in Low-Income and Multiethnic Communities (Doctoral dissertation, University of California, Davis).

Zamora, S., & Osuji, C. (2014). Mobilizing African Americans for immigrant rights: Framing strategies in two multi-racial coalitions. *Latino Studies*, 12 (3), 424–448.

Zani, B., & Barrett, M. (2012). Engaged citizens? Political participation and social engagement among youth, women, minorities, and migrants. *Human Affairs*, 22 (3), 273–282.

Zeldin, S. (2004). Youth as agents of adult and community development: Mapping the processes and outcomes of youth engaged in organizational governance. *Applied Developmental Science*, 8 (2), 75–90.

Zeldin, S., Camino, L., & Calvert, M. (2007). Toward an understanding of youth in community governance: Policy priorities and research directions. *Análise Psicológica*, 25 (1), 77–95.

Zeldin, S., Camino, L., & Mook, C. (2005). The adoption of innovation in youth organizations: Creating the conditions for youth–adult partnerships. *Journal of Community Psychology*, 33 (1), 121–135.

Zeldin, S., Christens, B. D., & Powers, J. L. (2013). The psychology and practice of youth-adult partnership: Bridging generations for youth development and community change. *American Journal of Community Psychology*, 51 (3–4), 385–397.

Zeldin, S., & Leidheiser, D. (2014). *Youth-adult partnership: A priority for volunteer training and support.* Retrieved from http://fyi.uwex.edu/youthadultpartnership-training/files/2013/10/Youth-Adult-Parthership_A-Priority-for-Volunteer-Training-and-Support.pdf

Ziegert, A. L., & McGoldrick, K. (2008). When service is good for economics: Linking the classroom and community through service-learning. *International Review of Economics Education*, 7 (2), 39–56.

Zimmerman, A. M. (2011). *A dream detained: Undocumented Latino youth and the DREAM Movement.* Washington, D.C.: NACLA Report on the Americas, 67.

Zimmerman, A. M. (2012). *Documenting dreams: New media, undocumented youth and the immigrant rights movement.* University of Southern California Annenberg School for Communication and Journalism Civic Paths' Media, Activism, and Participatory Politics Project [Working paper, online], 6.

Zimpelman, M., & Stoddard, J. (2013). *Service-learning: Effective means to individual education.* Retrieved from http://mezimpelman.wmwikis.net/file/view/Megan+Zimpelman_Grad+Paper.pdf

Zins, J. E., & Elias, M. J. (2007). Social and emotional learning: Promoting the development of all students. *Journal of Educational and Psychological Consultation*, 17 (2–3), 233–255.

Zlolniski, C. (2008). Political mobilization and activism among Latinos/as in the United States. In H. Rodriguez, R. Saenz, & C. Menjivar (Eds.), *Latinas/os in the United States: Changing the face of America* (pp. 352–368). New York: Springer Publisher.

INDEX

66180123R00146

Made in the USA
San Bernardino, CA
09 January 2018